Beautiful, Bright, and Blinding

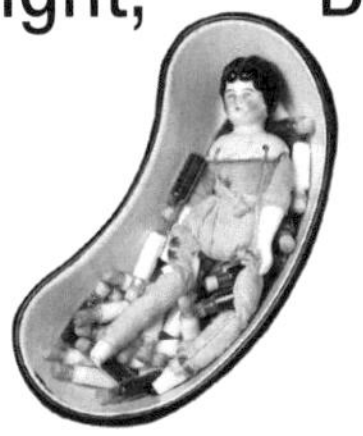

Beautiful, Bright, AND BLINDING

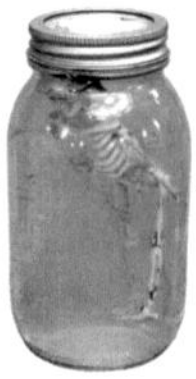

PHENOMENOLOGICAL AESTHETICS and THE LIFE OF ART

H. Peter Steeves

SUNY PRESS

Cover and page i illustrations: details from *The Human Genome Projection,* H. Peter Steeves, 2008.
Photos courtesy of John Sisson Photography, www.sissonphotography.com

Published by
State University of New York Press, Albany

Printed in the United States of America

For information, contact State University of New York Press, Albany, NY
www.sunypress.edu

Production, Laurie Searl
Marketing, Anne M. Valentine

Library of Congress Cataloging-in-Publication Data

Names: Steeves, H. Peter, author.
Title: Beautiful, bright, and blinding : phenomenological aesthetics and the life of art / H. Peter Steeves.
Description: Albany, NY : State University of New York, 2017. | Includes bibliographical references and index.
Identifiers: LCCN 2016047188 (print) | LCCN 2017033601 (ebook) | ISBN 9781438466552 (e-book) | ISBN 9781438466538 (hardcover : alk. paper) 9781438466545 (paperback : alk. paper)
Subjects: LCSH: Aesthetics, Modern. | Art—Philosophy. | Arts—History and criticism. | Phenomenology.
Classification: LCC BH151 (ebook) | LCC BH151 .S74 2017 (print) | DDC 111/.85—dc23
LC record available at https://lccn.loc.gov/2016047188

10 9 8 7 6 5 4 3 2 1

For *Ursa Minor*

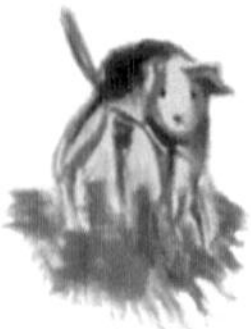

Contents

Section 3: Other Animal Others

Section 4: Laughing Beyond Modernity

Acknowledgments

Even the *Mona Lisa* was a team effort. As with any human undertaking, this book is not merely indebted to a community but could not exist in any way without that community. To my family, friends, and colleagues, I extend my most sincere gratitude.

Some chapters, and parts of some chapters, have appeared elsewhere, typically in a much-truncated or altered form. My thanks to Dawne McCance, editor of *Mosaic: A Journal for the Interdisciplinary Study of Literature,* who published versions of chapters 1 and 8 in her journal as, respectively, "Gone, Missing," v. 46, n. 3 (Sept. 2013): 1–26; and "Rachel Rosenthal Is an Animal," v. 39, n. 4 (Dec. 2006): 1–26. *Popular Culture Review* has published abridged versions of chapters 3 through 6 in the following forms: "The Concept of Conceptual Art: 'You Are Here' and Not Here," v. 24, n. 1 (Winter 2013): 5–24; "The Doubling of Death: Human, Animal, the Real, and the Irreal in the Films of Michael Haneke," v. 22, n. 2 (Summer 2011): 15–26; "Yep, Gaston's Gay: Disney and the Beauty of Beastly Love," v. 16, n. 1, (Winter 2005): 125–45; and "And Say the Zombie Responded? Or, How I Learned to Stop Living and Unlove the Undead," v. 23, n. 2 (Summer 2012): 5–26. Sections of chapter 7 appeared in a different form online in "The Man Who Mistook His Meal for a Hotdog," *Between the Species*, Issue IX, October 2009: http://digitalcommons.calpoly.edu/bts/vol13/iss9/5/. Various parts of chapter 9 have appeared in two places: "Postmodernity, Postmodernity, Does Whatever Postmodernity Does: A Post-Ironic Look at 'The Simpsons,'" *Television Quarterly: The Journal of the National Academy of Television Arts and Sciences*, v. XXXIX (Fall 2010): 12–18; and "'It's Just a Bunch of Stuff That Happened': The Simpsons and the Possibility of Postmodern Comedy," in *The Sitcom Reader: America Viewed and*

Skewed, edited by Mary M. Dalton and Laura R. Linder (Albany, NY: SUNY Press, 2005), 261–71. My thanks to Mary and Laura, whose sitcom reader opened up the field for many of us years ago. Finally, chapter 10, part of which was written for "Why So Serious? A Conference on Philosophy and Comedy" that Russell Ford and I organized at DePaul University in 2012, went on to be featured online in *Angelaki: Journal of the Theoretical Humanities* (v. 21, n. 3 [July 2016]). My thanks to Russ, the guest editor of *Angelaki*'s special issue that was our conference proceedings, as well as Helen Gough and the staff at Taylor and Francis.

My special thanks to Matthew Girson for allowing me not only to reprint images of so many of his oil paintings here, but for having created those paintings in the first place. I've been commenting on his work—riding the coattails of a real artist—for more than a dozen years now, and I look forward to decades more of the same garment travels. I am grateful, as well, to Felicia Campbell for many reasons, including being the model of a generous host and friend. Felicia created and has run the Far West Popular Culture Association conference for thirty years—a conference where brief, twenty-minute bits of some of these chapters were presented. She's amazing for a thousand reasons. I am grateful to Hazel Antaramian Hofman and the Fresno Armenian Art Museum for inviting me to present a lecture on the artwork of Arshile Gorky that became the skeleton of chapter 2, and to Dolores Wilbur and the Chicago Culture Center for inviting me to create an installation art exhibit at the Center as part of their "Site Unseen" exhibition, images of which appear in chapter 3 that were taken by Monika Lozinska and John Sisson—to whom I am also grateful for lending their artistic photographic talents. Jack Rutberg of Jack Rutberg Fine Arts, Inc., in Los Angeles was kind and generous with his time in locating the owners of the two Gorky images for me; I am very grateful for his help. Patrick Whistler and Bruce McDonald graciously provided the images from *Pontypool*; Jordan French and Jay Ives at BeeHex were so kind as to provide an image of their 3D pizza printing machine; and Claudia Pollak at WEGA-Filmproduktionsges.m.b.H was wonderful to work with in procuring the images from Michael Haneke's films. My thanks as well to DePaul University for providing me with a Faculty Research and Development Grant from the College of Liberal Arts and Social Sciences in summer 2014 to support work on this book. And very special thanks to DePaul's Father Edward Udovic (and the Vincentian Endowment Fund) for offering the financial support that made it possible to include the Arshile Gorky images in this book and to publish all of the book's images in color. It would be a gray world without Fr. Udovic's generosity.

At SUNY Press, my most sincere thanks to James Peltz, Andrew Kenyon, Daniel Otis, Anne Valentine, and Laurie Searl. I am truly grateful for their guidance and support seeing this book through to the end. It has been wonderful to work with Laurie once again on the production and design of a book, and I wish her the very best in her (semi-)retirement.

Rachel Rosenthal, the focus of chapter 8, entered my life in 2001 and was, until she passed away in 2015, my dear friend and the Platonic Ideal to me for what it means to be an artist, a human, and an animal. I miss her every day; the world is far less beautiful and bright without her. And though I never had the privilege of knowing Andy Kaufman personally, the same could be said of him. Chapter 10 is about, and is dedicated to, Andy. Today, I am lucky to call his sister, Carol Kaufman Kerman, my friend. My thanks to Carol, Michael, Pru, their entire family—and the spirit of Andy that is always, I hope, operative in my life.

To all of the people who have spoken with me over the years about this work and have provided inspiration of different sorts, my sincere thanks (and my apologies to all who are left off this list—a function of my slipping mind and not a lack of gratitude): Dennis Rohatyn, Bill Martin, Michael Naas, Anna Vaughn Clissold, David Wood, James Hart, Charles Klingler, Nicole Anderson, Bill and Charlotte Nickell, Robert Maldonado, Steve Ingeman, and especially Marinés Fornerino. Finally, my thanks to Maryse Meijer and Danielle Meijer, who helped coauthor a conference talk on Michael Haneke that led me to chapter 4. Maryse is one of the finest fiction writers of her generation: if you're looking for good art that will utterly blind you with truth and beauty (and maybe a dull butter knife when your back is turned), stop reading these acknowledgments and go buy her books immediately. And Danielle—she is my partner, sounding board, coconspirator, life coach, encourager, collaborator, wife, band mate, anarchic comrade in arms, fleshed-out horizon, love, and ultimate telos. Without her, I quite simply would not be here.

Introduction

The history of aesthetics is, for the most part, the history of metaphysics. From Plato on, if one wanted to know something about the nature of art, what constitutes beauty, or how a work of art "works," one turned to metaphysics. The questions have always been: *What, exactly, is beauty? What is an aesthetic object and how is it different from a regular object? What is art, what is its purpose, and how is art made and received?* All of these "is" questions mark the pursuit as one that has followed a well-worn path parallel to the path of metaphysics—with all of the assumptions and all of the problems that go along with that history. Modernity's move toward epistemology—toward asking how it is that we gain knowledge about a work of art, or how it is that we make judgments about art—was not really a radical break since it was always an epistemology founded on a metaphysical commitment, usually to an external world apart from the perceiver with things that could appear (where "appear" often implied some sort of distortion, a misrepresentation of what things really are—i.e., *mere* appearance). The Enlightenment faith that philosophy had in reason—as, for instance, Immanuel Kant's pondering whether or not judgment might be guided by a priori conditions—maintained this same orientation. Aesthetics, then, has always been a metaphysician's game, even though one might argue that it did not truly become a full-fledged subfield of philosophy until the early eighteenth century. We have always had art. Perhaps we have only recently had aesthetics. But the aesthetics we've had has almost always been a branch of philosophy not so subtly grafted to metaphysics and epistemology, growing from the same roots, rising in the same direction.

As part of what twentieth-century analytic philosophers came to call "value theory," there was an even greater challenge for aesthetics since it was typically taken to be founded on (what at least appear to be) subjective judgments about subjectively appearing things: you like Monet; I like Cézanne; who's to say who's "right"?[1] Unlike ethics, which has often seemed similarly challenged but where the stakes are more obviously high in the task of coming to some agreement because it might mean the difference between life and death, aesthetics has seldom been *the* pressing issue for philosophy. If we squabble over whether or not a flower arrangement is tacky, perhaps hurt feelings might hang in the balance but few murders or wars get started this way.

Yet just as ethics is not some compartmentalized aspect of life and philosophy—just as we can experience the goodness or badness of an action as such in the act itself, can investigate the ways in which the common Good can appear, and can discuss what it means to *live* ethically in every moment—so, too, is aesthetics not appropriately marginalized and not appropriately under the purview of metaphysics. We can experience the beauty of an object immediately, can investigate the ways in which a work of art can appear to consciousness, and can discuss what it means to *live* aesthetically in every moment. We can, that is, undertake a *phenomenology* of aesthetics, and in so doing come to discover that life and art are fundamentally intertwined—so much so that there is no room to separate them.

The project at hand, then, is an attempt to do just this—to practice a phenomenological aesthetics. We are asking about the being of art, it is true, but in so doing we are asking about how art appears, how consciousness is structured so that art appears, and what it means to live life such that the aesthetic is always already in play. It would be fundamentally misdirected to say that phenomenology supplants metaphysics in such a project, as even the notion of a "founding" is itself a conceit of a metaphysical worldview; but I do begin with the general assumption that part of what has held back aesthetics is the history of metaphysics, and that phenomenology, which approaches ontology in its own way, is useful for uncovering new possibilities. As we will discover, philosophical theories of language, space, time, seeing, representation, identity, morality, politics, life, and death play a role in the way we conceptualize the being of art. When these theories are informed by phenomenology, everything changes.

Phenomenology begins by looking at everyday experience and then analyzing the structures of that experience, the ways in which consciousness must be operating to make that experience possible, and, inevitably, the nature of the world. This "everydayness" is important here. Phenomenology might be capable of telling us how the experience of a complicated cultural artifact is different from the experience of a tree, but it importantly "works" on both. Rather than starting, as metaphysics might start, by analyzing what is Beauty, what is a perfect Triangle, or what is Justice, phenomenology asks you to sit in your room and look around, or walk through a forest and look around, or do whatever it is that you were doing before you picked up this book, and then start describing your experience of the mundane things that make up most of your daily life. We might be able to explain why, historically (and especially in a society with economic classes), the concepts of "high" and "low" culture developed, but phenomenology show us why this division is arbitrary in many ways, not the least of which is that phenomenology takes seriously the idea that philosophy begins with everyday experience. It is, in this way, a philosophy for the masses. For most people, Disney is more likely to appear in some form during some part of their day than is Duchamp; the potential hell of living after the zombie apocalypse is more likely to come up in conversation with a friend than is the hell carefully mapped out in Italian verse by Dante; and grabbing a hot dog at a baseball game is likely to be more recognizable as indicative of a great afternoon than is staying inside and researching the methodology for mapping out an anamorphic projection of a skull in a sixteenth-century painting by Hans Holbein. This is not to put down the latter, but it is to realize that the history of aesthetics has limited itself to a great extent to bourgeois practices, and this has, without a doubt, limited aesthetics itself. Disney, Duchamp, zombies, Dante, hot dogs, and Holbein skulls *all* appear in this book, each offering us something important to discuss and each offering some insight into what it means to be art, but none is taken to be more appropriate or a "higher" topic for aesthetic analysis than the next. I take it to be in the true spirit of phenomenology that we actually turn our attention to the everyday things themselves, and that is where we must begin when undertaking a phenomenological aesthetic.

If it is true that the history of aesthetics begins in parallel with metaphysics, and thus with such questions as what is Beauty and what is a perfect Triangle, we must also hear the unspoken word at the end of such queries—the word sadly, if silently, ringing across two-and-a-half millennia of philosophical analysis: "really." The metaphysician asks what is Beauty *really*, what is a perfect Triangle *really*. Though we are always after the truth of the matter in philosophy—always interested in what something *really* is—the meaning of the word "really" here is not marking a commitment to the search for truth. It is, instead, historically indicative of the ideology of metaphysics—an assumption that our experiences are generally wrong, our senses regularly lie to us, our perspective distorts, and our subjectivity gets in the way of discovering the truth about reality. Phenomenology does not assume that the world we experience is separate from truth and that to get to the truth we must get beyond our horrible subjectivity and our distorted perspective, though neither does it assume experience is always veridical. Both assumptions, instead, are "bracketed" and put aside (though it turns out that phenomenology has an answer that comes later, an answer that shows us how misdirected the question was from the start). The bracketing makes it possible for us to solve the problem of the history of metaphysical questions simply by ignoring such questions at the start. In keeping with Edmund Husserl, we thus begin not by asking, "What is a zombie *really*?" but instead by asking about our experience of zombies and then unpacking the ways in which consciousness takes up such an object.

As will become apparent to a reader who knows a bit about the history of philosophy, the phenomenological method that is worked out here chapter by chapter is indebted to Husserl, but it is not strictly Husserlian. I am not attempting to investigate what Husserl would have to say about zombies, for instance, but instead am using some of the tools of phenomenology—tools that I then typically pick up, alter, reshape, and redesign—in order to apply them toward the end of better understanding our experience of art and life in general. I believe that Husserl helps us get our bearings, but the phenomenological apparatus that informs the aesthetics project here is one that begins with Husserl and then attempts to move phenomenology in new directions, guided—for better or worse—by my own approach and techniques.

One of the many themes that runs throughout this book is the play of presence and absence. Husserl was the first to focus on and systematize this aspect of our conscious engagement with the world, and one could make a case that it became *the* major discovery to which those who write in Husserl's legacy are indebted—a list that includes Martin Heidegger, Maurice Merleau-Ponty, and Jacques Derrida, each of whom appears on the pages that follow, though always read through an historical lens that remembers this debt to Husserl yet also tries to push it forward in a new way. After performing the phenomenological reduction, looking at the way in which the world is given rather than looking at the world (e.g., paying attention to a painting *as it is experienced* rather than paying attention to a painting), we quickly discover that perspective affords us only one side of an object, yet it is a whole object of which we are typically conscious. The other sides are still there for us, still experienced, but they are present *as absent*. That absence can be an experience—and that presence and absence are not opposites but, through the play of the manifold by means of which they allow objects to be taken up by consciousness, make such conscious experience possible—is a major discovery. And presence and absence become important for our experience of aesthetic objects, especially.

In chapter 1, I discuss the oil paintings of Chicago-based contemporary artist Matthew Girson. We will see how his work is complex and beautiful, and how it challenges us to think about what it means to see art, to see history, and to see in general. Before that, though, and just to get our feet wet in the basics of phenomenology, let us consider a particularly striking 2016 diptych by Girson, starting by focusing on the camera at the very center of this work. (*See figure I.1.*)

As with any object of consciousness, when we see the camera that Girson has embedded between the painted canvas panels here, we immediately experience the back of the camera even though it is permanently against the wall

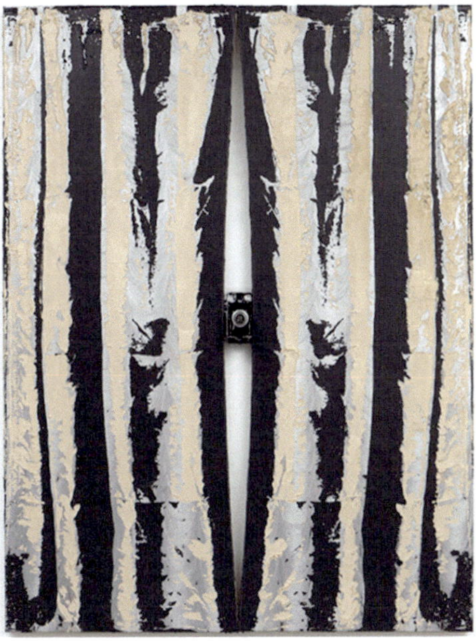

FIGURE I.1. Matthew Girson. *Sire, I'm Not A Fool Aloof A Ton, Mieris.* 2016. Oil on canvas with camera. 78 inches x 60 inches.

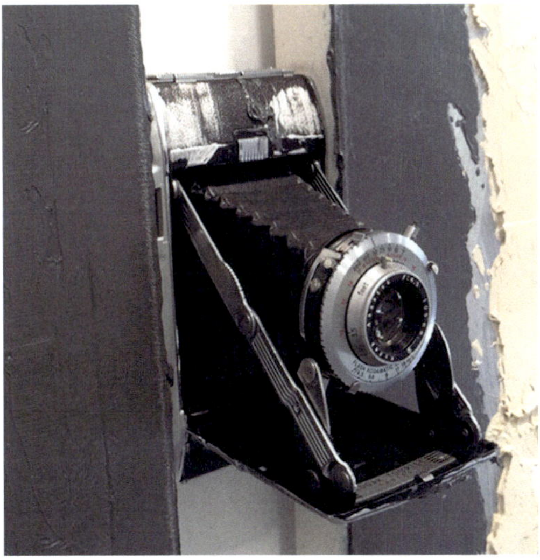

FIGURE I.2. Matthew Girson. *Sire, I'm Not A Fool Aloof A Ton, Mieris* (detail). 2016. Oil on canvas with camera. 78 inches x 60 inches.

and out of visual range. We experience the camera as a whole, with the back as presently-absent and the side we are currently seeing as presently-present. Part of what it means for a side to be presently-present is that it could be presently-absent if we were to walk around it to see the object from some other angle. (*See figure I.2, page 5.*) As we move around the camera in this work of art, it is given within a manifold with various parts of it moving from presence to absence, absence to presence. Indeed, the camera opens up to consciousness as an infinite manifold—appearing within an infinite horizon of possible appearings. This is because there is always some other angle from which to view the work. Husserl will say that we *perceive* the front and *apperceive* the back, where "apperceive" means the experience of the present-absence of that aspect of the object. The object is never fully captured, exhausted, or pinned down. It is never fully known. And yet there is a point at which, even though it is infinite, we feel confident in saying, "That is a camera." There is no perspective that is all-encompassing that will ground the eternal truth of such a claim. There is no view of the camera that does not involve perspective and thus, necessarily, a great deal of absence. The truth of the camera is not to be had in some abstract, unattainable, conceptually oxymoronic "view from nowhere" or "view from everywhere." What it means to experience the camera *objectively* is to experience it subjectively, but remembering that this subjective experience is a project, an ongoing process that is never complete. Objectivity is inherently a subjective enterprise.

It is not merely the case that my own possible perspectives and vantage points on the camera are infinite. It is also clear that you, and the community of other beings around me, are capable of seeing the same object from your own multiple perspectives. Part of the camera's immediate meaning for me is that it has the sense of a "public object"—the sense of being-in-the-world such that what I see from here and what you see from there are the same thing. I see as a body, as a physical, enfleshed consciousness that is always in the world as well, sharing space with things and thus always to the right, to the left, above, under, beside, etc., an object. To know the camera truly would require an infinite *inter*-subjective project. I have to find out how it appears to you, how you are taking it in and experiencing it from over *there*. My experience of the camera is thus not only subjective but intersubjective, and this entails that what it means to be that camera is not only something that rushes away from me just as I think I have it nailed down because I am limited in my own finite experiences, but because I would also have to exhaust every possible subjective experience by every other being to know the camera fully. The fact that I cannot even really have your experience, but can only have an experience that is mine in which I try to take up your experience, is yet another reason that the object is an inexhaustible reserve of perspectives. When I see the camera, I experience the back as presently absent, then, but I also experience the sense in which I am not experiencing your experience of the camera. The fact that this other experience (i.e., your experience) is *present* for me means that there is another kind of present-absence at work. Whenever I perceive anything, I am apperceiving the vantage points and the experiences of a community of Others. The back and other sides of the camera are given to me as presently-absent, and so, too, are the myriad experiences of the camera that other subjects could have. Seeing doesn't just have a bit of apperceiving that goes along with it. It is *mostly* apperceiving. Visually, then, this is what it means to say that objects are wholes and that when we experience things, we experience them in terms of presence and absence.

But it gets more complicated still. We have been paying attention to the way in which "perspective" is a term that relates to the visual experience of something, but there are also cultural, historical, and other sorts of perspectives that are informed by the past, by personal history, and by one's sedimented way of seeing the world. That is, because we are today used to cellphones doubling as readily-available cameras, and because we are familiar with the design aesthetic of our culture's current moment in time, we immediately see the camera that Girson has embedded between his canvases as "old." This is not an added judgment that is tacked on to the experience later when we reflect on it. The camera immediately appears as old, as out-of-date, because we carry with us—seen and unseen, actively and passively—our ways of looking at and interpreting things. Such cultural, historical, biographical filters are not getting in the way of what the camera really is, but instead are what make it possible to see the camera at all. In precisely the same way in which the physical angle of my eyes does not get in the way of me experiencing the camera as it really is but rather having such a subjective perspective is what makes it possible for the camera to appear in the first place (and makes it possible for me to ask questions about the camera's true nature as well), so my own cultural, historical, and biographical filters are not obscuring some truth—they are not really *filtering* anything—but are, instead, precisely that which makes it possible to experience the object. So the experience of the camera's datedness is part of the immediate experience of the camera. It calls up, as presently absent, all of the other cameras to which it is related and by means of which its datedness is established. It appears within an horizonal manifold of visual angles, cultural meanings, past experiences, and so on.

The particular personal perspective that I bring to the experience of Girson's diptych will determine how I experience the title he has given the work (e.g., am I aware of what a palindrome is?), how I experience the content of the painting on the canvas (e.g., am I aware of much of the history of oil painting and thus how this work might fit into that history? am I aware of what it means to choose to paint "nonfiguratively" in the twenty-first century?), and how I might think about the meaning of the work (e.g., have I read a lot of Freud and thus cannot help but see the center of the work as a vaginal opening? or have I read a lot of Walter Benjamin and thus focus on the juxtaposition of a camera's ability to create an infinitely iterable aesthetic object by mechanically reproducing prints of a photograph with the painter's inability to create anything but one original? or have I been listening to a lot of Billie Holiday [or Kanye West], thinking of race relations and the sad "strange fruit" hanging from poplar trees, and thus come to wonder about the relation between what could be a forest of foreboding poplars painted there on the canvas and an old camera trying to bear witness to unspeakable crimes in the night?). Or say I put all of this together in the particular combination that marks the particular way in which we have experienced the world that gives rise to the particular way in which I experience the world, and I come to think that knowing that Girson's past work has, for the last few years, focused on painting curtains (mostly in the dark); and knowing that the title is a sort of joke that references Frans van Mieris, the seventeenth-century Dutch painter who once painted a still life (*Trompe-l'Oeil Still Life with a Flower Garland and a Curtain*, 1658) with his friend Adriaen van der Spelt that also contained a joke (in that it was a painting [of a painting] of flowers by van der Spelt with a nearly photorealistic blue curtain painted over the right side of that still-still life by van Mieris [because it was the custom at the time to cover paintings with a real curtain, and the two were not only trying to fool their audience into thinking that the curtain was real but also were probably referencing the ancient painters Zeuxis and Parrhasius, who, we are told in Pliny the Elder's *Historia naturalis* (79 CE), once held a competition to see who was the better artist, and on the day of the unveiling, birds started pecking at the grapes Zeuxis had painted in his still life, with Zeuxis thus declaring himself the winner even before Parrhasius pulled back the curtain from his painting—only to find that there was no curtain to pull back because his competitor's painting was of a curtain, and thus Zeuxis himself had been bested by Parrhasius]); and imagining that Girson knows the history and the pitfalls of judging artwork based on its "proximity to nature"; and knowing that I know that "proximity to nature" is always a bogus measure because art is never referential or constructed by a set of signs that point at something other, but is, instead, always a way of making things present in their absence, reveling in a nature that is always present, everywhere; and knowing that Girson has started using stencils made from his own photographs of famous oil paintings with curtains depicted in them, the stencils capturing the play of light and dark, shadow and highlight on the folds of those old painted curtains, all made anew in Girson's appropriation and reuse; and recognizing that there is thus a sort of collaboration between Girson and van Mieris going on that is similar to the collaboration between van der Spelt and van Mieris in which the artists are not truly *aloof* and the viewer is not truly *a fool;* and noting that the curtain (created from stencils made with the help of a camera, though one might not take it immediately to be a curtain and one can only see the absent trace of that camera in its production) appears to be opening between the two canvases, exposing a "real" camera to document our reaction, such that the only thing on stage, the only true *subject* of the painting that is revealed by the opening of the curtain, is our reaction to the painting; and knowing that I must run all of this through the lenses of race, sex, class, and all of the rest, allowing all of the apperceived perspectives to have their say and help the canvas come to meaning—only then can I finally come to have a rich sense of the meaning of the painting that is not separate from its materiality and its historicity, a meaning that is definite and yet infinitely open to change. Indeed. A complicated process, and still we have only just begun to flesh it out. Yet if I know nothing of palindromes, encyclopedias of history written in Latin, the history of oil painting and the history of philosophy, the dark past (and present) of American racism, the way in which curtains have figured in paintings of the past, or even what a "still life" is, I will not have the same experience as someone familiar with these topics, but I will still have a meaningful experience—a different experience informed by a different perspective.

The object is also made to come to meaning by seeing the other objects around it (e.g., is it in a gallery or a museum?), the context in which it is experienced (e.g., am I seeing it online, in a book, in person? am I seeing it in conjunction with an author trying to make a point about how phenomenology works or because someone has told me it's beautiful and I should see it for myself?), the time in which the experience is taking place (e.g., am I seeing it close to the time it was painted or decades or centuries later?), and so on. All of these sorts of perspectives are also there, also apperceived, and also make it possible to experience the object.

What will become interesting for us is not only uncovering the ways in which we might be able to answer the question of an aesthetic object's meaning by means of understanding how presence and absence function in our experience of the object, but also coming to realize how presence and absence in general are made clearer by an analysis of an aesthetic object. Further, we will see that what it means to take something as a work of art is, on the one hand, far more complex than we might have previously imagined, yet on the other hand, far simpler. Aesthetics, it turns out, is not an area of experience meant only for the philosopher to elucidate, only for the specialist to understand, only for the academic, the intelligentsia, the privileged to live. What it means to be experiencing anything in general is to be experiencing the aesthetic as always already functioning, always already at work. The aesthetic experience is thus nothing extraordinary, yet if we truly wish to understand how it functions and what this means for life and consciousness in general, there is a great deal of nuanced work to be done.

The play of presence and absence is just one theme we can pick up from phenomenology that will guide us as we press forward. There will prove to be many more. What follows will not be as explicit about the nuts and bolts of the theory at work. Rather than approach the study of art and the life of art by means of abstract reasoning, the proof of phenomenology is always in the pudding. And so what follows is a systematic investigation of different sorts of works of art—from paintings to movies, from television to food, from installations to performance art—with the goal being that as we look at these concrete things, as we (re)turn to the things themselves, we will see the force of a phenomenological aesthetic at work. We will see, that is, the way in which the practice of phenomenology helps us open up the work of art, the life of art, and the art of life. We will, as Miles Davis might say, together enjoy some tasty pudding.[2]

In chapter 1 the investigation begins with an analysis of what it means to see, and thus what it means to see a painting. In order to look at the act of looking, we will not look at it directly but instead take up questions of blindness, scotomas, absences, and anamorphic hiddenness—approaching the question of seeing from its blind spot, all while establishing some basic tools and methodologies that will serve us throughout the rest of the project. The paintings of Matthew Girson play a central role here as we investigate the way in which history, ethics and politics, the intercorporeal-intersubjective body, language, and presence and absence function so as to make a work of art come to presence. Chapter 1 is all about how to see a work of art, and thus sets the stage for the viewings to come.

In chapter 2, a brief excursion into the paintings and drawings of Arshile Gorky continues the same themes, adding to the mix a phenomenology of lines and a theory of delineation that makes objects into objects both in life and on a canvas. The way in which Gorky, taking up the tradition from Cézanne, uses a nuanced understanding of seeing and space further clarifies what it means to say that we live in a work of art, and that the work of art opens a world to us—a world that turns out not to be separate from the everyday world we normally inhabit.

Although grounded by four specific works of installation art, chapter 3 is still one of the most abstract parts of our investigation as we begin to ask more complicated questions about whether or not a work of art means something other than itself, represents something other than what it is. By asking after the concept of conceptual art, the first section of the book ends by discovering three more central themes for the phenomenological aesthetic being constructed: the way in which art and ethics are tied together; the way in which expression is related to feeling (and emotions are constitutive of reason); and the way in which thinking and living are always already art.

Section 2, which focuses mainly on film, begins with a chapter asking a specific question concerning the films of Michael Haneke: what does it mean to have a conscious being die in a work of fiction? Here, in chapter 4, we thus continue pushing the question of the ethics of art, but also investigate the relation between fiction and nonfiction that seems so integral to making art "work." What takes place in art seems both real and not-real, but what does this mean? It becomes clear that there is a way in which cinema has a relation to identity and death, especially as we consider how nonhuman animals appear on film; but it becomes just as clear that art is not merely a way of working out these sorts of existential questions in a safe space, for the power of fiction is anything but fictional.

Chapter 5 appears, at first, to switch tone: from the bleak cinema of an Austrian filmmaker known for hyperrealistic violence and unresolved narratives to the colorful animated movie musicals of a popular American corporation constructing its product for the youth mass market. But the films of Walt Disney prove just as ripe for existential analysis, and *Beauty and the Beast*, I argue, is actually a tragedy of Hanekean proportions. As we reach the halfway mark of the project, we thus take a break from being explicit about the phenomenological apparatus at work and instead turn to do a focused, close reading of the text of one movie, discovering that the phenomenologically informed conceptions of identity, ethics, history, presence, absence, language, and all the rest that we have been building up so far in the previous chapters can serve us well in interpreting a piece of art that might have otherwise have seemed banal, maudlin, and straightforward. We discover, in fact, there is nothing straight or straightforward about *Beauty and the Beast*.

Chapter 6 returns to a more overt and wide-ranging phenomenological analysis of absence, ethics, and language as central notions for aesthetics, specifically by means of investigating our culture's obsession with zombies. Paying special attention to the zombie movies of George A. Romero and the Canadian independent film *Pontypool*, we find parallels among the ways in which mourning, communication, and art function, ultimately questioning whether or not being in possession of logos is even really a good thing.

Although the figure of the nonhuman animal has appeared throughout the work—especially in the chapters on Haneke and zombies—the two chapters in section 3 take up the question of the animal's special relation to art. In chapter 7 the aesthetics of eating is put into conversation with the ethics of eating by means of an autobiographically informed discussion of what it means to prepare and eat food that is meant to look and taste like other food, what it means to desire and eat vegetarian meat substitutes that are, ostensibly, meant to mimic meat. And chapter 8 investigates the performance art of Rachel Rosenthal and the larger question of what it means for a nonhuman animal to appear on stage, for a nonhuman animal to be an artist and to be art. In both chapters, the way in which art is not a re-presentation of something but is, instead, one way of that thing appearing is central. Also, the relationship between phenomenology and postmodernity becomes key at this point as the project takes up the way in which the postmodern condition is properly in dialogue with phenomenology.

The phenomenology-postmodernity nexus continues to play a central role in the concluding section on comedy. In chapter 9, the animated television show *The Simpsons* is considered as a phenomenological unpacking of the show discovers that the rules by which it is operating as a work of art are rules that call into question some of the major assumptions of modernity. It is thus that we come to a discussion of postirony, quotational discourse, and the possibility that a work of art might—like life—be without a metanarrative that promises some sort of objective meaning outside of its own text.

Andy Kaufman, whose work is the focus of chapter 10, concludes the project by continuing the same discussion of the relationships among phenomenology, postmodernity, comedy, art, and life. By looking at Andy as a visual artist, performance artist, and author whose work demands that we come to see the act of living as, itself, an artistic endeavor, and the nature of comedy as the nature of life itself, we thus find ourselves in a place where we might draw the conclusion that what it means to be conscious, what it means to be living a life *as* something or someone, is to be an artist as well as a work of art, and that aesthetics is not something we can turn off and on, consider abstractly now and set aside later, but is instead our way of being in the world—a world full of dappled things, joyful things, sad things, and challenging things, but always a world in which the life of art is paramount.

SECTION 1

Painting, Seeing, Concepts

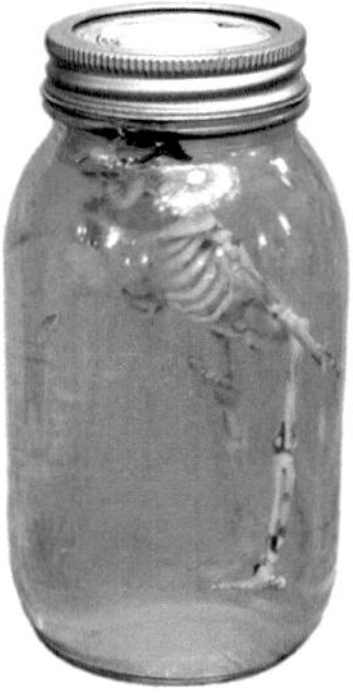

CHAPTER 1

Gone, Missing

> I am privileged, as it were, not only to dream about the specters of the night in all the helplessness and blind trust of sleep, but also at the same time to confront them in actuality with the calm judgment of the fully awake. . . . I long to say a last goodbye to everything up here, to go down into my burrow never to return again . . . [but] I find great difficulty in summoning the resolution to carry out the actual descent . . . without knowing what is happening behind my back and behind the door after it is fastened.[1]

In the late summer of 1911, Franz Kafka lines up with thousands to see a blank square of empty wall, a patch of vacant white marked only by four iron pegs. A few miles away, Pablo Picasso stares up—with unblinking, half-seeing eyes reaching out from the side of his face—at the police who have taken him into custody. Kafka leaves the Louvre with his friend Max Brod and the two men make their way to the theatre, settle down in the darkness, their vision adjusting as they prepare to watch the five-minute film *Nick Winter et le vol de la Joconde*. Thrown together just a few days after the theft itself, the film satirizes what all of Paris has been talking about: someone has stolen the *Mona Lisa*.

The absence of da Vinci's iconic work is news all across Europe. But not since Napoleon moved the painting into his private bedroom have the French, especially, pulled together to claim the woman with the strangely painted smile as legitimately their collective property. Now, though, the smile is like that of a Cheshire cat, faded from the wall, fading even from memory (*see figure 1.1*). They

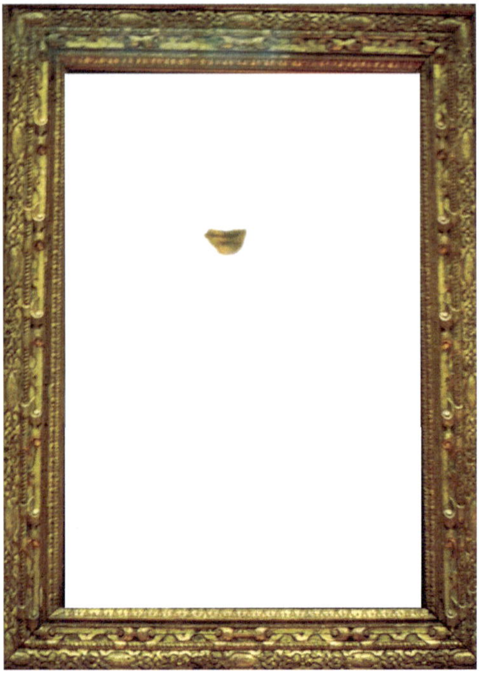

FIGURE 1.1. H. Peter Steeves. *The Missing Mona Lisa*. 2012. Photomontage.

must go to the museum to not-see it once more. The Louvre, having shut down for a week as the criminal investigation began, agrees to re-open. Picasso is soon exonerated. (It was his friend, poet Guillaume Apollinaire, who, it turns out, had implicated the painter while being held in jail on suspicion of the theft. Apollinaire, no lover of "high art," had recently called for the Louvre to be burned down. Only the police, it would seem, deem to take a poet at his word.) As the search continues for the true thief, attendance records at the Louvre are broken. Lines stretch out and around the museum with pilgrims coming to view the missing painting, shuffling past the empty spot on the wall in tears.

They come to see the *Mona Lisa* knowing they cannot see it. As historian and curator Helen Rees Leahy will later explain it, "[they showed up] to gaze, overcome with emotion, at the blank space. . . . According to one newspaper, the crowds 'contemplated at length the dusty space where the divine *Mona Lisa* had smiled. . . . It was even more interesting for them than if the Giaconda had been in its place.' This was an understatement: the blank wall was the sensation of Paris, [as patrons] . . . filed past . . . and paid their respects to the emptiness."[2]

The thief, it turns out, does not share the Parisians' sense of collective French ownership. But neither is he in it just for himself. Instead, Vincenzo

Peruggia, a low-level Louvre employee, has stolen the *Mona Lisa*—at first hiding it in a broom closet and then simply walking out of the museum with the painting under his top coat—in order to return it to Italy where he feels it truly collectively belongs. In two years, Peruggia will be caught in Florence. And the Italians will agree to return the masterpiece to Paris—after, of course, first taking several months to exhibit it throughout Italy. They will also refuse to extradite the thief, praising him for his patriotism and giving him a minor punishment in the name of good border relations. The *Mona Lisa* will thus eventually be restored to the wall of the Louvre in 1913; and, having repeatedly come en masse to celebrate and see its absence for two years, patrons, less interested, will begin cutting back their trips to the museum. The curators and the marketing department will learn an important lesson: presence is sometimes overrated.

But tonight, Kafka and Brod sit in the dark, unable to see how the future will unfold. The film unspools and, like most films, presents something like a truth (*see figure 1.2*).

Detective Nick Winter, stares at the blank spot on the wall where the painting used to hang, eventually turning around and noticing a shoe button on the

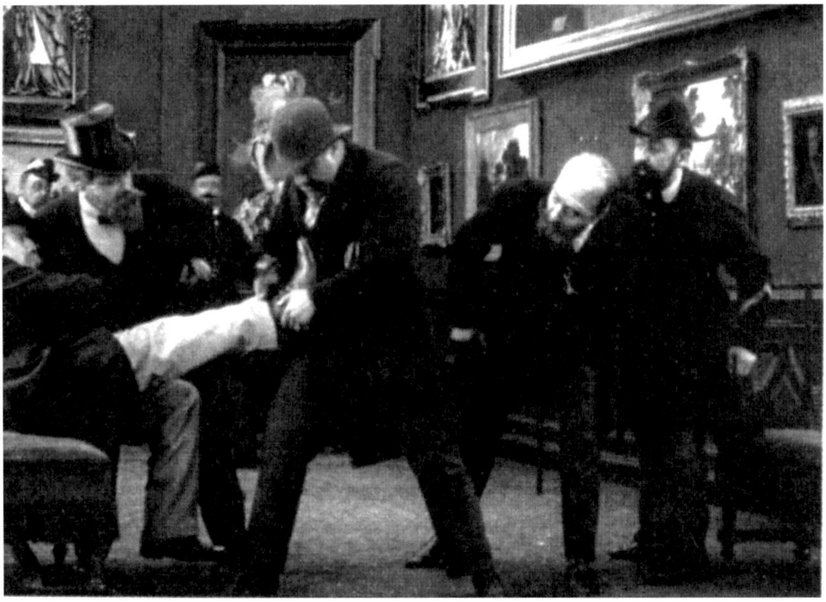

FIGURE 1.2. Still from the film *Nick Winter et le vol de la Joconde* [Nick Winter and the Theft of the Mona Lisa]. Dir. Paul Garbagni and Gérard Bourgeois. Pathé Frères, 1911. *Bulletin Hebdomadaire Pathé Frères* 34 (1911): N. pag.

ground. With this as his only clue, he disguises himself as a shoe-shiner, hoping no one will see his true identity. He begins stopping Parisians, forcing them to get their shoes shined in hopes of finding the thief—a man he imagines to be marked by the absence of a button. Unfortunately, the director of the Louvre, Monsieur Croumolle, is missing just such a button, and Winter mistakenly focuses all of his attention on the poor, innocent Croumolle. In the final moments of the film the museum is in turmoil; and though it is packed with people, no one notices—no one pays attention, no one sees—the thief sneak back in, replace the *Mona Lisa*, and steal away with Velazquez's *Princess* instead, taking time to drop off a note that reads, simply: "Forgive me. I am nearsighted. I actually meant to take the painting beside it."

This happened to me for the first time—unless I am blocking out all of the others, unless they are being blocked out, unless they have blocked themselves out—in the fall of 2000.

I had had a headache for three straight days. They were familiar to me at the time, nauseating and crippling, often moving me to tears and forcing me to retreat into a dark room. For as long as I can remember, I have preferred to be in dark spaces, even when my head was not hurting. I turn off as many lights as I can—always turning off all *fluorescent* lights—and work, see, and live with the dimmest of lamps after the sun goes down, which it always seems to have done no matter what time of day it is, since I refuse to open curtains and blinds at any hour, even covering most windows with dark, light-blocking fabric that gives the appearance of not so much stunting their ability to let in sun as obscuring the very fact of the windows, covering them over, pretending that they aren't even possibly there. Living with me is not easy, I know. One has to appreciate burrowlike conditions. And this night, more than a dozen years ago, seemed like any other night to be in pain. The only light in my office was from my computer screen, and I was wishing that I did not have to ride the train home because I knew that there would be noise, the smell of bodies, people, but mostly light—far too much light.

Caught up in such worries, I noticed in that moment that I suddenly could not make out the lower portion of what I had been typing. The screen, it seemed, had simply disappeared there—not gone black, really, but rather somehow strangely become invisible. Before I could even panic—and this was surely a cause to panic for me as I have loved darkness but ironically feared blindness my entire life—something in the empty space took shape and began to look like a fat caterpillar, an organic squiggle of bright neon light that was pulsing yellow, gold, green, orange, white, with spirals of bright color twisting up the body like the moving stripes on a barbershop pole. The vivid light grew in intensity; and my fear grew, too, as I turned to look in a different direction, horrified to find that the caterpillar followed me, always staying in the same field of vision. It was not a part of the computer screen; it was a part of my seeing. When I closed my eyes to escape the creature, it stayed with me, growing in magnitude again in the complete black of my inner eye, like some sort of afterimage from having stared for hours directly into the filament of a now unseen light bulb. It was a part of *me*.

I did not know at the time how literally this was the case, as a scotoma of this nature is actually a visual manifestation of the firing of neurons located in the back of the head within the occipital cortex. I was, reluctantly, "seeing" the activity of my forebrain. And, of course, this act of seeing was itself an instance of brain activity with its own neuronal structure. The caterpillar not only twisted and warped in on itself but was premetamorphosed: it was, in some real sense, the biophysical manifestation of the act of seeing that I was seeing—not so much a noumenal appearance of a Kantian moment of engaging with the world, but a sort of aberrant Husserlian *epoché*, a reduction where *noema* and *noesis* were truly two sides of the same coin, two aspects of the same moment of consciousness. This is what it looks like to look at something. Tellingly, as my brain struggled to put that experience itself into something visual, it necessarily also manifested as a sort of blindness: what it means *to see* is *to be blinded*.

But that night, sitting in the dark, I understood and saw very little. More lepidopterist than phenomenologist, I did not know then that it was my own brain that squirmed in front of me, pinned down yet never for a moment under control. At the realization that I might never escape seeing it, I felt terror. Not only was I unable to see what was there in the world behind this thing, unable to see whatever it would possibly obscure for the rest of my life, but I also might never be able simply not to see *it*. Closing my eyes had only made it worse. And the realization that it might now always be on, always be visible—that it might take from me the ability to see only darkness—was overwhelming and worse, even, than the thought of being blind.

Within fifteen minutes it began to dim. Half an hour after it had first appeared, it was gone. It would not return, missing, for another year.

This happened to Matthew Girson for the first time—unless I am misremembering the story he told me several months ago, unless he is misremembering the story his mother told him because he was too young to remember it himself, unless she was misremembering what took place years ago, unless we are all somehow blocking out something—in the summer of 1970.

As a toddler, Matthew Girson went missing. His parents searched for him everywhere. He had been seen just moments before on the kitchen floor behind his mother, plain as a button, but now he was gone. Everyone knew that he was too small to have stumbled or crawled very far in such a short amount of time. The fact that he was not to be found in the house, each room empty, must have meant that, in the back of their minds, everyone was thinking the worst. As the search progressed they ran through the permutations of "gone"—lost, abducted, missing—until his mother heard laughter coming from her bedroom. Underneath the bed, pressed up against the back wall in an impossible way in such a small space, Matthew Girson sat, covered in a blanket, laughing in his own dark world.

Within fifteen minutes he had been found. He would not go missing again for another year.

Memoirs of the Blind is one of Derrida's most personal works, though his person is always visible throughout all of his work, of course. Here he tells the story—or at least the narrator tells the story—of a youthful infatuation with drawing and the way in which his brother's talent, far greater and receiving more familial praise, drove Derrida to turn to words rather than lines in order to create. After recalling his failure to copy his brother's copies of family photographs—after admitting to something of a fratricidal desire—Derrida writes:

> I have never in my life drawn again, not even tried. Except once last winter—and I still keep the archive of this disaster—when the desire, and the temptation, came over me to sketch my mother's profile as I watched over her in her hospital bed. Bedridden for a year, surviving between life and death, almost walled up within the silence of this lethargy, she no longer recognizes me, her eyes veiled by cataracts. We can only hypothesize about the degree to which she sees, about what shadows pass before her, whether she sees herself dying or not.[3]

Derrida has been slipping in and out of tenses, seeing and not seeing, and speaking of childish things. Not only his own boyhood memories, memories that Freud will tell us are always on the verge of being unseen, but of being a child even when one is older. Always a child before one's mother's eyes, seeing or not. A child who asks philosophical questions about art: "The child within me wonders: how can one claim to look at both a model and the lines [*traits*] that one jealously dedicates with one's own hand to the thing itself? Doesn't one have to be blind to one or the other? Doesn't one always have to be content with the memory of the other? The experience of this shameful infirmity comes right out of a family romance."[4] This is where Derrida tells the story of his brother, a story I omit here only to point out that *jealousy* and *copying* are already at work in Derrida's text before he gets to thinking about the relationship between art and being seen by one's mother, between what is hidden in aesthetics and what is hidden in the family.

The child within Derrida is asking whether or not all drawing is founded on blindness, and thus if all seeing is as well. The worry is most clearly seen if we focus on the self-portrait, but it is there with all drawing and painting in general.

If I turn to look into a mirror in order to see myself in order to paint myself, I must study what I find in the mirror—an image of myself—but then I must turn my gaze to the canvas as I make the marks there that will represent what I see. To be more precise, though, we should not say "the marks that will represent what I see" but rather "the marks that will represent what I *have seen*" since at this particular moment of painting I am necessarily no longer seeing the image of myself in the mirror but I am, instead, now looking elsewhere. I am seeing the marks I am making on the canvas. As I make those marks, I am *seeing* the canvas and apparently just *remembering* the image I saw in the mirror. Thus, the act of painting is an act of blindness, an act of not-seeing what it is I am trying to paint. Similarly, when I turn back to the mirror in order to judge what I need to change, fix, add, work on next, etc.—when, that is, I turn back to the mirror to compare it to what I have put on the canvas—I am no longer looking at the canvas and thus am forced to *remember* the canvas image and compare it to what I am now directly perceiving. No matter which way I turn, I am apparently blind. No matter the direction toward which I instruct my gaze, I am forced to concentrate on what I *don't* see, on what I merely remember. Seeing, it would seem, is fundamentally a not-seeing. Or at least we could say that seeing X is fundamentally not being able to see X because Y is being seen instead.

Whether the subject of the painting is the artist him- or herself, a still life of apples, a land- or sky-scape, or anything at all, this same dynamic is supposedly always at work. If one paints from imagination, without a model present, the structure is even more apparent, though imagining takes the place of remembering. To *imagine* the temptation of St. Anthony is to have a mental image that is not an act of *seeing*. And to put such a scene down on canvas with paints is to go back and forth between the imagined and the seen, the scene imagined in one's head and the scene that is seen directly on the canvas. No matter where one is looking, it's what is *not seen* that is doing the most work.

All of this, however, while pointed in the right direction still basically misunderstands the structure of the aesthetic act. While it is true that the unseen is always making the seen possible, it is not the case that memory—or, for that matter, imagination—is a key ingredient for painting. Memory and imagination might very well be the first move, the initial acts of consciousness that spur one on to create, but when it comes time to put brush to canvas, they are used very little. Painting is all about seeing. It's just that seeing itself is always about presence and absence, what is seen and what is not-seen.

Say I wish to paint a portrait of a child. I sit her down in my studio, look at her carefully—which means looking at the way the light creates the color that creates her as-seen for my eyes—and then I turn to my canvas, brush full of paint, to put down a line, a mark. When I am putting that mark on the canvas

I am not phenomenologically engaged in an act of memory but rather in an act of direct perception, an act of seeing. The key is in correctly noting *what* it is that I am seeing in that moment. I am not, for instance, seeing a patch of color or a stroke of paint. I am, instead, seeing the whole of the child there before me on the blank canvas, though she is mostly apperceived, mostly present as absent, at the moment. Each bit of paint I put down brings her more fully into presence, but it is always an act of seeing in which I am engaged.[5] The child *is there on the canvas*—the same exact child that is also sitting as a model across the studio. This is because a painting is never a copy of something, an imitation. It is, rather, a literal re-presentation: a making present (again) of its subject. It is the subject that is thus present to consciousness on the canvas, not a copy of the subject. To think otherwise is to be caught up in a double-thing epistemology—as the history of metaphysics from Plato to Kant once forced us to be. Within this history, vision itself is seen as something of an artistic act since the mental representation, created through the subjective activity of the mind, is merely an imitation of whatever is "out there" in the world. We have spent 2,500 years trying to get things back together again, to cross the chasm, to undo the dreaded artistry of the eyes that gave us the representation rather than the object itself. But this cannot happen until we realize that appearance is not truly separate from being: appearance is never *mere* appearance. The object itself is precisely what is given to us through appearance, experience, consciousness, representation, subjectivity.

There are many ways for a child to be present. I can look directly at her, remember her, imagine her, say the world "child," look at a photo of her, paint a picture of her, etc. Each of these is a way of making the same thing—the same child—present, though each is marked differently by various structures of presence and absence. Language, for instance, does not denote. The word "child" is not a sign that stands in for a child, but is instead a way of making a child present. Language has a great deal of absence to it, but the object of consciousness is the same whether I say the word or look directly at the child in my studio. And the same is true in painting. In a way that is parallel to the manner in which language does not evoke a memory in order to call up a referent and come to sense, so, too, does the act of painting not rely on memory. What it means to be painting a portrait of a child is already to see the child on the canvas. When I say, "I am painting a portrait" I mean precisely this. That this seeing involves apperception as well as perception—absence as well as presence—should not be surprising. All seeing is thus.

Consequently, Derrida's specific childish worry is unwarranted, but it points to an even deeper truth about the relationship between seeing and blindness. One might come to this truth by means of phenomenological investigation, but one might also come to it through painting.[6] What it means to be looking at

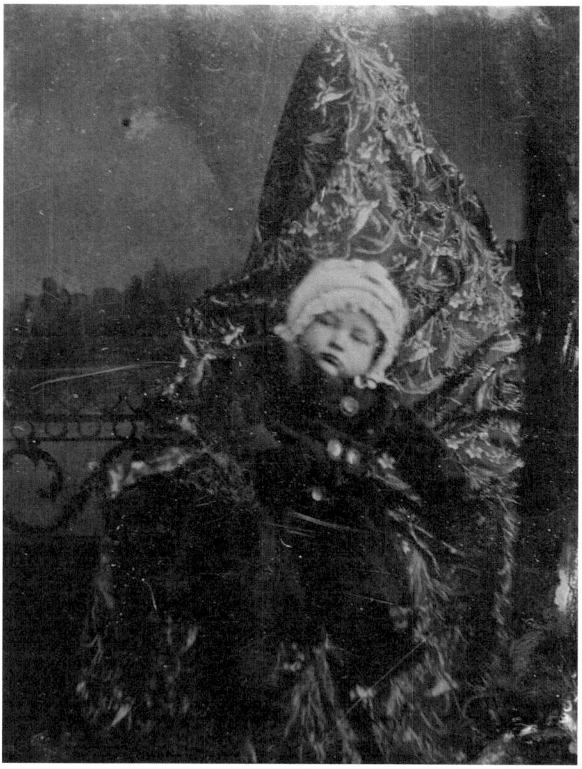

FIGURE 1.3. Victorian photograph. Unknown artist and subjects.

something is to be necessarily blinded—not because an act of memory or imagination gets in the way of the act of seeing, but because seeing itself is structured by what is not seen. And still the not-seen has its own kind of presence.

The Victorian camera lens, like the artist's eye, takes a while to see (*see figure 1.3*). In both cases, subjects need to be patient, to remain still in order to be seen. Children notoriously squirm and fuss, sometimes even running off, missing. And it was for this reason we imagine (because here we can only imagine, having nothing left to perceive) that the Victorians produced the tradition of "the hidden mother" photograph in which, to comfort the child whose portrait was being taken and to keep the child physically still, the photographer would have the mother sit in a chair holding her child, but since it was merely a portrait of the child that was wanted, the photographer would first cover the mother in a dark curtain, her body hidden from view in plain sight. Because once processed these photos would seem to depict a strange, ghostly figure holding a child, a further erasure would take place for the final presentation: a paper overlay would be placed on the finished photo with a central oval cut out—an oval just big enough to hide most of the covered mother and expose the child, who now seemed merely nestled in and surrounded by a strangely lumpy and crumpled bit of cloth.

It is often the case that the heavy curtains we place in our windows, that the darkness we seek, only amplifies the light. This is because it was always the case that the light was appearing all along by means of the darkness. If we say that capitalism is blind to the work that mothers have done precisely because it obscures this work by failing to call it "work," and if we say that men are blind to the oppression women have felt because what it has meant to be a woman is to have been seen by men, and if we say that missing children would usually not be found were it not for the unseen arms of mothers reaching under the bed, then we are saying the same thing about the doubly-hidden mother—the mother whose first hiding was not yet hidden enough, so it required a further hiding of the act of hiding—in the Victorian's photograph: what makes it possible for the child to appear is the present absence of the present steadying embrace of the mother behind the paper and behind the shroud. Our not-seeing her is what makes it possible to see that which is not-her. Let us be clear: there is always an ethic already at work in every act of seeing.

What remains in a sentence when □ is gone? How do □ make sense of it when that most prized of (non)things is obscured and does not appear? The subject, in all its dappled glory, hidden from view, forgotten and veiled. Why bother to speak: the subjectless sentence seems to be about nothing? Why bother to paint: the canvas with hidden subject seems empty of all meaning? Why bother to live: who, in the end, would be doing the living anyway?

What is consistently most startling in Matthew Girson's work is what appears as absent, what is so skillfully made present in its absence—a chance to speak, paint, and *be* without the need for a traditional subject. One cannot today take up oil painting and remain aloof from the history of oil painting, and yet one cannot—or should not—perpetuate the myth of the subject, the Cartesian thinking self that pulls at its own mental bootstraps, motherlessly slouching its way toward existence. With the (virgin) birth of the modern subject comes the birth of the object as well: objects to stand apart and at a distance from us; to be used and to delight us; to be owned and exchanged and valued by subjects; to be known through a vision that is thought to obscure—a *seeing* that, in relation to all of the other senses, most requires and celebrates distance from what is known. Girson's work demands that we stand back and read it through the context of history, and that we do so with an eye toward what is necessarily unspoken, our illusions of coherent subjectivity behind us. It demands, for instance, that we negotiate the obscuring shadows of German landscape painting, German Romantic images of the sublime, German horrors and holocausts.

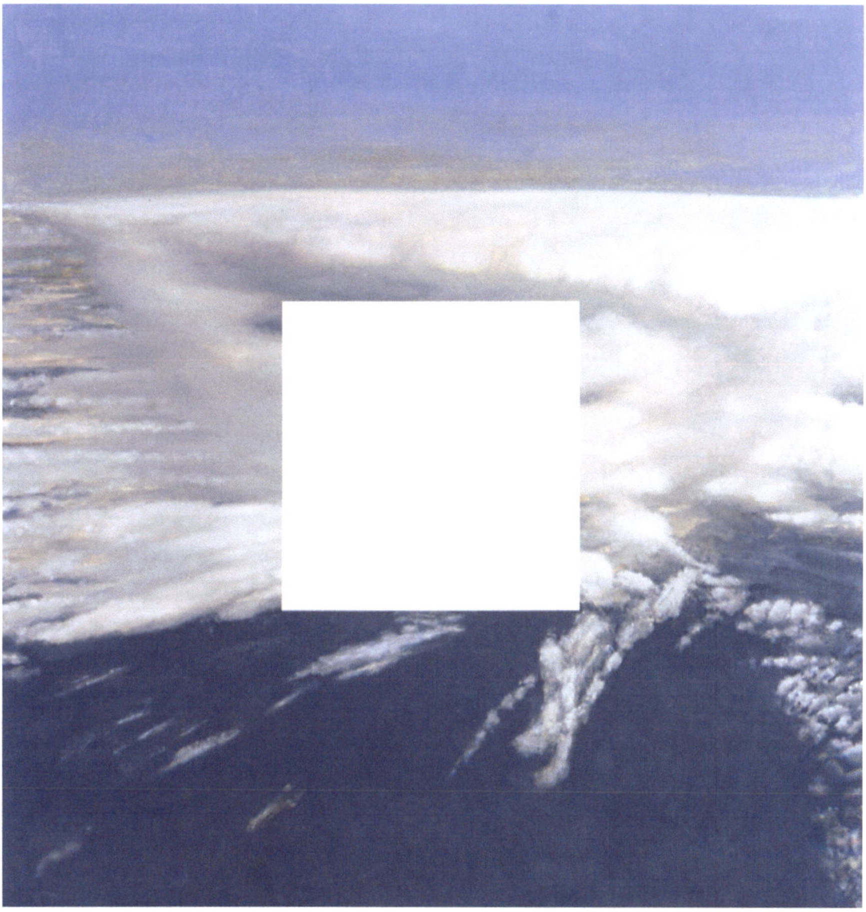

FIGURE 1.4. Matthew Girson. *Untitled (Scotoma) #6*. 2004. Oil on canvas. 63 inches x 63 inches.

I am recalling Girson's 2006 exhibition, *Satellites and Scotomas: After and Above*, in which the scotomas referred to large square canvases (63 x 63 inches) with cloudscapes blocked by a central square of white paint (*see figure 1.4*).[7] In each of these scotoma paintings, the square obscures the center of the canvas, the spot where we have come to expect the subject, blotting it out like an inverse eclipse of light. Elsewhere in the exhibition, Girson presented a series of *Satellite Views*, paintings of hurricanes as if seen from space, and a complete orbital map of his own head entitled *Dizzy Heights*. Here, there, and everywhere there is always something missing in Girson's work, something seen from above that is not quite fully seen because, perhaps, there is no longer truly any place that is above.

The central theme of how *presencing* simultaneously obscures is what concerns Girson and what is always at the heart of all seeing. It is, after all, the very act of looking that makes possible the blind spot, the act of painting that leaves parts of the world out-of-frame, the act of remembering that makes of forgetting a theme. What we forget is thus central to the question of what we presence, even if remembering is not the same as seeing. What constitutes the blockage is often thought to be the pathology, though without the pathological, too, there would be no norm.

The medical scotoma comes in many varieties. The *asthenopic scotoma* can make it appear as if parts of letters on a page have vanished.[8] The *negative relative scotoma* manifests itself as a partial blank or void. A *positive absolute scotoma* can appear as an hallucinatory pattern or a patch of white. Doctors struggle to find words for it all. The *positive scotoma*, they sometimes claim, is actually an "*enhancement* of vision."[9]

Psychoanalysis struggles as well, balanced precariously between modernity and postmodernity. An insistence that there is a self to be analyzed runs counter to Girson's desire to move painting in a different and self-less direction; a refusal to conflate the Ego and the self, a denial that conscious life is the whole story, propels him forward. After Freud, to be is to be hidden from one's self—motives, desires, and dreams stand back in the haze, with the mind, fractured, unable to theorize itself fully. How fitting, then, that so many of Girson's canvases are covered with clouds. One sees in clouds a Rorschachian harmony that uncovers those aspects of the psyche that typically remain unarticulated. One makes of the apparent cloudy chaos, order—the fluffy sheep, the little bunny, the happy squirrel, the foreboding vaginal chasm of the future opened wide to swallow one whole—and the order that is provided says something about the viewer, about those parts of the viewer that are hidden and obscured.

And yet it is not as if something is actively hiding from us in this work; it is not that Girson has obscured a secret that he means for only the most clever among us to uncover in full, in truth, in full disclosure of a hidden truth. Still, there is a certain anamorphic quality to his painting that helps us understand the necessary relationship between anamorphosis and all painting, between what is hidden and what is shown.

Let's back up for a moment and take the wider view.

Lacan's seventh lecture on the ethics of psychoanalysis argues that anamorphosis arose at a very particular point in the history of art, that it marks a very particular problem with perspective (both visual and conceptual). That is, at the moment when painters mastered the idea of the vanishing point as the way to manipulate perspective on a flat canvas, the problem of how *anything* shows itself was reframed. Suddenly, it became apparent that "the illusion of space is not the same as the creation of emptiness."[10] Vanishing-point perspective in painting is thought to give the illusion of space on a flat canvas. But the "space" in which a representation of something can first come to be—the pregnant emptiness of the blank canvas that is full of perspective (and truly full of the apperceived subject) yet demands no particular perspective immediately; the emptiness of thought itself that does not ask the question "is the image different from what is real?"—is theorized anew. Anamorphosis is thus a response to this. As such, it is always asking after the ontological status of the work of art, the object of consciousness, the act of seeing, knowing, and comprehending.

Again, and to be clear, it is not as if the anamorphic image seen from the side is getting us at what is *really* there. The hidden skull in Hans Holbein's *The Ambassadors* (1533), arguably the most famous anamorphic painting ever made, is not leading us to what is truer or closer to reality. Indeed, Lacan makes it clear that in order to see the anamorphic skull that is hidden in the painting (hidden, we might add, in the same blatantly unhidden way that the mothers are hidden in those eerie Victorian photographs: hidden conspicuously, hidden in plain sight, not hidden at all), the "main" image itself has to be obscured, blurred, and moved into non-sense. As one tilts the painting to make the skull come into focus, the rest of the painting becomes a blurry mess. What counts as "main" and "secondary" thus comes into question. What counts as original and representation thus also comes into question. Indeed, the point is that anamorphosis suggests that the very idea of *representation* is itself problematic when representation is thought to be still within the history of metaphysics. And thus *meaning*, too, is undermined by precisely those structures that we thought gave rise to meaning.[11]

The lesson, then, is that even when the hidden is finally exposed, we would be foolish to think that we now have uncovered the truth, the whole truth, and nothing but the truth. This is why Hagi Kenaan goes so far as to suggest that the hidden image is actually that which obscures the hidden image even in *The Ambassadors*. That is, the anamorphic skull in the famous painting is there to point to (while at the same time obscuring/hiding) what cannot be seen, what it is forbidden to see: the homosexual relationship between the two men in the painting. In other words, the somewhat obvious inclusion of the anamorphic image of the skull is a marker in the painting to get us to think about the manner in which it is a red herring, hiding what it is that the artist "truly" wishes to obscure. By means of a careful analysis of the curtain in the painting (again, these curtains) and the nature of wedding portraits of the same era, Kenaan thus argues that this go-to example for discussions of painted anamorphism is actually tied to queer theory from the start, and that the question, "What is it that is being obscured?" is always up for grabs because an answer to the question is itself a revealing, and revelation always carries with it an act of obscuring as well.

Squint from the side. Tilt these pages in your hand. Bring history through an awkward door to see it all, and fail to see it all, from an impossible angle. Look again at Girson's painting concerning what we cannot look at again.

In the *Scotoma* skyscape, one is intrigued by the *production* of the scotoma area as well as its effect. Girson obviously paints the white central square last. He paints, that is, the whole of the painting and then layers on the white square with a knife, thick and heavy, like mortar, like plaster, like all the technology of human building that obscures as it creates. Paint over paint over pain. The central scotoma area is tall. The paint is so thick that it literally stands above the clouds and casts a slight shadow on them. With a Marxist squint, we note how this marks the disappearance of labor. It is important, that is, that there is a central patch of clouds under that blockage, that the work of the artist disappears during—and due to—the production of the art. In capital's desire to reproduce, there is always more than what we see. One of the blind spots of capitalism, rising in tandem with the end of nature, is the exploitation that is fundamentally necessary to keep it going and keep us forgetting.

Writing in Germany—at about the same time and in the same place that Karl Marx is born—Carl Gustav Carus concludes that landscape painting in general cannot help but create a sense of the sublime, a sense that "*you are nothing; God is all.*"[12] Girson's work, however, comes in at an angle and provides us with alternative insights without making the modernist's mistake of inverting the claim by elevating us and denigrating God. Even the pure mathematics of Girson's canvases speaks in poetry. The "subject" of each painting is curved and soft—orbs, circles, balls, spirals, globes, clouds, heads. And yet the canvases themselves are rigidly square (not merely rectangular), and their order is square as well. The *Scotoma* paintings are divided into nine squares in a tic-tac-toe grid. It is the center square that is hidden, white, scotomized. It is as if there is a cross on the canvas, and the center of that cross is empty. No God, no salvation, no ethics after Auschwitz. The Cross is vacant, but not from something or someone ascending into the clouds. This triple trinity of threes leaves us only hollow, the Church as silent as a Heideggerian dormouse, and therefore just as complicit.

Everywhere there is the theme of what has gone missing in our ethics and our ontology. *Dizzy Heights* offers us eight views of the artist's head, turning, turning, turning—and where is the ninth (*see figure 1.5*)? Where is the center square, the conscience of the flesh, the subject—human or divine—to stand in the crosshairs? Where is the missing painting in an exhibition of paintings that keeps repeating the number nine? Is it hidden by its own production, like Girson himself decades earlier beneath the bed where his parents made him?

Stop. Squint. Pay attention to that which cannot be paid attention from another angle.

We are invited to see the *Scotoma* paintings as paintings of cloudscapes with a central image obscured. But what if nothing is being obscured? Or, more

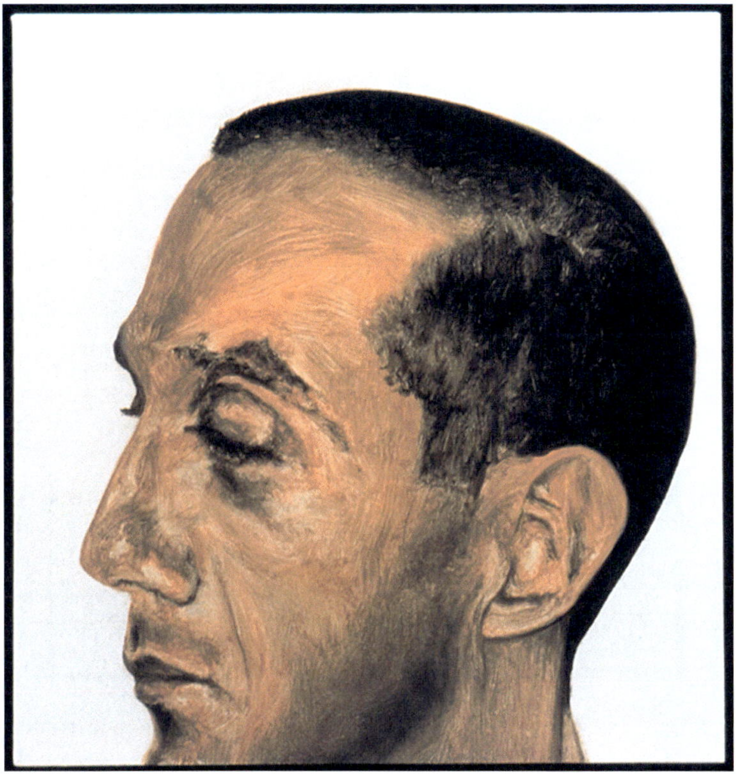

FIGURE 1.5. Matthew Girson. *Dizzy Heights VIII.* 2005. Oil on canvas. 20 inches x 20 inches.

properly, what if what we thought was being obscured is just obscuring something else, like Holbein's hidden, squishy skull hiding a forbidden relationship between the male subjects? What if the white square in the middle of Girson's *Scotoma* cloudscape is not covering over what is already there but rather is waiting for something new to fill its void? What if the *Scotoma* paintings are actually frames—if they themselves are not the subject, not the art, but are instead massive, decorative frames for a missing square of art meant to be hung at their centers? What if these are cloudy borders created to enframe, hold, point to, and present some other smaller painting—some smaller square painting—that will someday replace the central square of white? Such a painting would have to be just over 20 inches x 20 inches to fit in that middle square. And this is, in fact, the exact size of the eight self-portraits in *Dizzy Heights*. The artist's head is perfectly sized to fit at the center of his scotomized canvases, surrounded by a border of clouds.

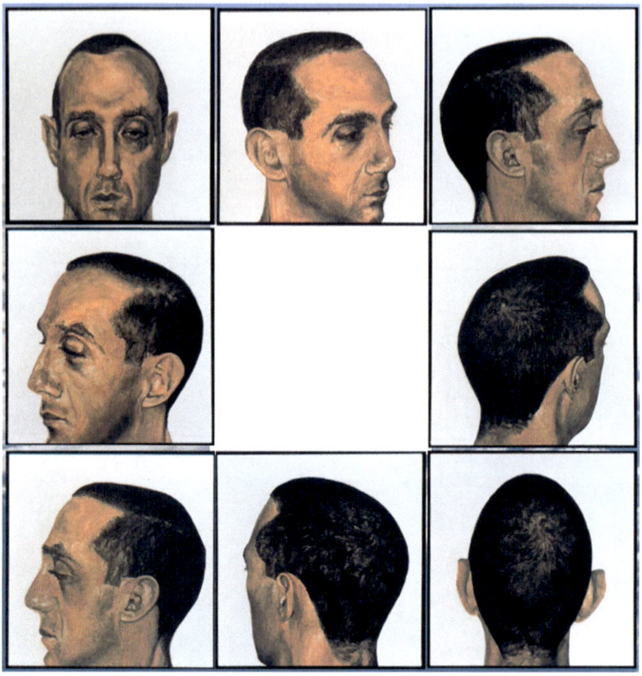

FIGURE 1.6. H. Peter Steeves. *The Dizzy Heights Frame.* Montage with eight paintings from Matthew Girson's *Dizzy Heights* series covering over Girson's *Untitled (Scotoma) #6. Dizzy Heights* paintings by Matthew Girson. 2005, oil on canvas, 20 inches x 20 inches.

The fact that there are only eight self-portraits and nine *Scotoma* cloudscapes, however, makes us pause. Even if we placed Girson's small rotating head at the center of each large *Scotoma* frame, there would still be one *Scotoma* cloud canvas without a subject. Is this what the work asks us to do? Do we rehang this exhibit in our mind, placing the eight small self-portraits in the center of eight (out of nine) of the large cloudscapes, leaving one cloudscape without a subject, empty, waiting, missing, hiding, vacant, like Elijah's chair in the clouds (*see figure 1.6*)?

No. These eight self-portraits, though perfectly proportioned to fill the void and stand in as *art*, will not take the place of the ninth white square. But, because they are perfectly proportioned, they could still be laid over the images of the clouds, mapping onto a single *Scotoma* canvas, tiled around the edge of the eight painted segments until the cloudscapes are obscured and only the center white scotoma is still visible. They could, that is, create a new frame—eight pieces of an enframing puzzle, now constituting a 360-degree trip around the author's globe. Yet to do this, to solve the hidden puzzle, would leave us with the central scotoma still remaining, now with a new blockage as well: the still-present scotoma square *and* the newly hidden cloudscapes.

We continue to await the coming of the subject. There is no possibility of completion here, no final uncovering, no hope to be done with history, interpretation, and duty. Man does not take the center square to block or to win. More truth only pushes something else into the shadows, out to the border.

One thinks of Caspar David Friedrich's early nineteenth-century canvases—the pinnacle, in many ways, of German Romantic landscapes—with their top-heavy skies, skies stretching past tomorrow and into heaven itself. For Friedrich, the horizon cannot be low enough, God's crosses cannot be old, rugged, full, and metaphorical enough.[13] Heinrich von Kleist, dramatist and contemporary to Friedrich, stands appropriately in awe. Writing on Friedrich's ability to "convey the sublime in nature," von Kleist remarks that the understanding is so clear and fully present in Friedrich's landscapes that it is "as if one's eyelids had been cut away."[14]

In a world without even the thoughtful respite of a nonseeing blink, one dreams of the scotoma, of the acknowledgement that no matter how the sublime is thought to appear, the cost is that which is ever-present and tragically obscured. It was, in fact, shortly after writing these loving words that von Kleist set most of his own work on fire, entered a Romantic's pact with a cancer-stricken woman, set out at the Christ-like age of thirty-three on a sunny, cloudless day to have tea on a sublime German hillside, and, having picnicked and chatted of art and talked up the sublime, shot the girl in the heart then himself in the head.

Let us think—using hearts and heads—about what is obscured, what goes unseen here. *Satellite View* is a series of paintings in which Girson presents the beauty of the hurricane without picturing its destruction (*see figure 1.7, page 32*). There is no white-square scotoma, yet our attention is always drawn to what is missing. In a hurricane itself, the eye *is* the scotoma rather than *has* a scotoma. The eye of the hurricane is, ironically, the one place it is hardest to see what surrounds us: the storm is not visible; the destruction is not visible; the peace and the beauty are there precisely as caused by the horror that is unseen. Is it because we have been thinking about Lacan and Freud that when we look at the still, calm center of the storm in Girson's painted hurricanes, the clouds seem to pucker and topologically turn in on themselves more like a scotomizing anus than an eye? There is a nineteenth-century argument that has, more recently, become more of joke that an invisible but thoughtful God is more rational to believe in than an invisible and thoughtless evolutionary process. "Take the cat," so goes the argument. "Can random, blind chance have made it such that the cat's fur just happens to have three holes in it perfectly lined up where the eyes and anus are?"

This is another way in which Girson's work is to be separated from the past even as it takes its place in line with all that has come before. The huge canvases on which Georgia O'Keeffe worked late in her life, filling them up with perfect

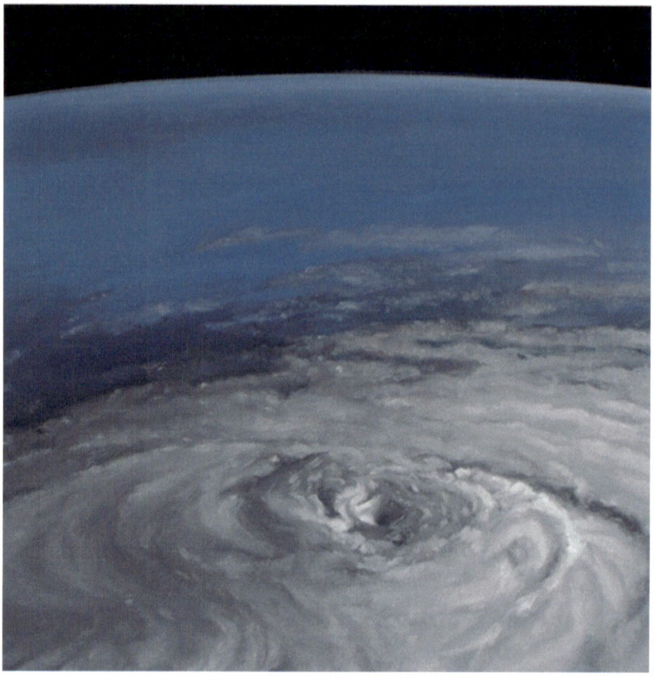

FIGURE 1.7. Matthew Girson. *Satellite View I.* 2006. Oil on canvas. 72 inches x 72 inches.

little ordered clouds, have all of the rationality and yet no hint of the horror.[15] They are cloudscapes on which the whole of heaven is seemingly visible, no apparent scotoma, no shying away from the pastel sunset, devoid, even, of the clinical sexuality at work in her paintings of flowers. For O'Keeffe at this point in her career, the close-up view of the earthly flower had been replaced by a far-away view of the cloudy sky, but it is as if the eye itself has ceased functioning in her work when she looks from above.

With most of Girson's canvases, the high horizon line continually places us below, down in the muck and the haze of existence. Even when we are caught in the clouds of the *Scotoma* paintings, the heavenly horizon is typically extraordinarily high, the heavens themselves out of reach. *Satellite View* keeps the Earth and its problems centered, the dark-cosmic-space-horizon again high on the canvas: we are stuck in orbit but will not rise further. And the self-portraits of *Dizzy Heights* refuse to center the head of the artist, instead offering us a cut-off chin and extra headspace; the horizon line always high, the effect again one of lowering us, grounding us, refusing us the chance to rise above even as we mistakenly think these paintings might be about rising above.

Margret Dreikausen's contemporary paintings of hurricanes seen from space are, like O'Keeffe's work, unhorrific.[16] Filled with angles and squares rather than orbs and spheres, there is beauty here, but the viewer is not caught up in the painting and made responsible. There is no hint of our complicity in the horror of the destruction that is taking place in the margins (which here means "in the center of the painting," for that is where the hurricane is doing its work), no sense in which the very means of production—as well as the technology being employed and the modernist ideology being accepted—mark our collusion with the violence.

It is the horror of memory that is always present—both present as present and present as absent—on Girson's canvases, hinting at the impossibility of the sublime. The portraits that comprise *Dizzy Heights*, for instance, stand like mug shots of the artist, testaments to some crime committed off canvas, the protean perpetrator of seven deadly sins plus one. Girson, standing in for us all, spins around like a hurricane caught in a strobe camera. The boy in the center of the painting, held aloft and static in each of the eight frames by an invisible mother's arms. Still he turns and spins and conducts his violence.

And yet, what does this miss? What, we must keep asking ourselves, is obscured by this act of whirling precession-presence?

Girson's work typically offers us a perspective that would be impossible without technology. He draws our attention to the mediated view, the construction of the sublime with the help of the subliminal, pointing to our complicity in allowing ourselves the distance of "objectivity" and selective memory.

The bombing of Dresden was said to be sublime from the sky; the perfect rationality of the Final Solution played out like a demonic mathematical proof full of Platonic Truth and Beauty. The illusion of detachment, the eye given to distant hazy unawareness mediated by the reason of machine and logic, made possible this collapse of horror into beauty, evil into good. Rationality will not save us. Reason—marched through history to its willful triumph—leads us to the techno-mechanization of Auschwitz, not away from it. And yet the Romantic, too, is on the same path, separating us from the world and reveling in detached awe at the spectacle of it all. This too, is the closeted legacy of the Holocaust: nature lovers, in techno-ecstatic delight, made mass murder into science . . . and called it art.

In *Dizzy Heights* we know that the artist, to make of himself an "object" for us, must employ technology to see—to separate himself from his self. Like any good magician, he uses mirrors. We are told that each of these self-portraits was done in one rushed sitting—the hurried and harried look of the artist legitimately captured as immediate and fresh. And we see him in these self-portraits looking down at the mirror, despondent, despairing, exhausted at the task. Thus he paints himself as given by the tool, as he appears in the technology. It is not a painting from memory, but a painting as he sees himself immediately as mediated by the mirror before him in the canvas. He rotates before us, seeming fully an orbiting orb, a cyclonic "subject," as well as a modern man in the throes of a computer scan in preparation for a 3D CGI technorgy that offers no chance for true ecstasy, no hope for living flesh as it is "perfected" in a binary world.

These paintings of the artist's head from eight different angles mark a fascination with the face. As part of the *Scotoma* exhibition, we struggle to take the *Dizzy Heights* paintings at face value. We see, or perhaps think we see, that Girson is giving us an overabundance of access to the apparent site of his subjectivity, that most celebrated seat of the Ego since Descartes: his head and his face. The Levinasian ethical demands seem overpowering: before ontology, before the subject and its concomitant object, comes the *Thou Shalt Not Kill.* Girson turns to and around us, and asks us to face up to our responsibilities. But more than this, we cannot help but read this series of paintings in conjunction with the history of art that scotomizes, and here we are drawn to Magritte's *The Son of Man* (1964).

Surely the most famous painting to deny us the traditional, centered subject, Magritte plays with the faux-scotoma in a way that is radically different from Girson: the businessman of Magritte's painting has his face obscured by an apple, not a square of white. Many have argued that this blocks out the most important part of a portrait, that Magritte's subject is thus no longer truly there. But of course, there is always a presence when such absence is created. There is, after all, an *apple* in the upper-middle part of Magritte's canvas, an apple that is a perfect subject for this painting. And it is thus that modernity's project is, in fact, unhinged: an artist is incapable of creating a truly subjectless painting. To admit this, even while trying to achieve it, is the (dizzy) height to which postmodernity takes us. As if to point to Magritte's limitations, Girson thus offers us not merely a series of scotoma paintings, but a full set of images to fill in the gap of Magritte's unpainted face. The head, and only the head, appears in *Dizzy Heights.* And it is thus as if we have *The (Other) Son of Man* before us as a confession of just what cannot be obscured in art.

Further, until we were asked to take up the perspective of the satellite—to embody a satellite view—few would have seen beauty in a hurricane. It is the technology that makes of nature a sublime object, as if "the big picture" is beautiful precisely for the way in which it diminishes my responsibility and obscures your suffering. In the *Scotoma* series, the skyscapes rather than landscapes also employ a point of view only attainable through technology—this time the airplane, the flying machine. The land no longer appears at all; those tied to it no longer matter. In these two series of paintings we see from the vantage point of the bomber and the fighter pilot, the robotic death drone and the Fox News Corporation broadcast satellite. The Other is in our sites, but our target is obscured. We stand aloft and find that the view from nowhere is actually only thought to be from nowhere because it masks its place and our accountability—it masks, or tries to mask, everything that has always mattered and will ever matter.

But if I try to reach out—to you, to a painted you, to you in all the ways that you can appear—with eyes and arms my own, is it not possible for me to uncover your suffering and even feel it? Doesn't art, especially, achieve just this?

Visitors to the Sistine Chapel have often felt the fear and pain in Michelangelo's Adam in *Expulsion from Paradise*, a fresco that depicts a serene angel striking out at the first man with a sword, the sword aimed squarely at Adam's neck as if to decapitate him. The angel seems fine with all of this, perhaps recognizing the sublime, but Adam recoils in terror and sadness. His body twists away; his hands are thrown up, wrists bent back, awkwardly. Something about the pose of the flesh, the comportment of his body, seems to resonate in the viewer and we immediately feel all of that guilt and horror and defensiveness tied up in the slant of a wrist.

This is not a surprise, argues David Freedberg, a professor of art history at Columbia University who was part of a 2012 research team that looked at the brain activity of people looking at art. Staring at the wrist detail from Michelangelo's painting, subjects were observed using transcranial magnetic stimulation, and it was discovered that "the image excited areas in the primary motor cortex that controlled the observers' own wrists."[17] Merely *seeing* Adam's bent-back wrists, that is, created the same brain activity in the viewers as if they, too, were bending back their own wrists to avoid the attack of angels. In terms of the neurophysiology, there is little difference between seeing a painted wrist turn and actually turning one's own wrist. That painted flesh is our flesh; that painted pain is communal; that expulsion is always our own.

If it is the case, then, that we feel, move, and live with the seen subjects of art, do we have *hidden* feelings about that which is always *obscured* in the work? Do our bodies blindly move in rhythm with the unseen as well, given that the unseen is always at work in the canvas?

Arlene Gordon, a social worker who lost her sight in her forties and is now in her seventies, reports: "If I move my arms back and forth in front of my eyes, I see them, even though I have been blind for more than thirty years." And Jacques Lusseyeran, a French Resistance fighter during World War II who was blinded many years earlier when he was only eight years old, had sensations of light well into his old age—"a formless, flooding, streaming radiance" caused by the firing of neurons in his visual cortex.[18] Is it too much to say that these are acts of seeing? Is it so hard to imagine a phantom limb appearing to the blind, a glowing scotoma taking shape before eyes that have been closed to the world since one was a child? The mind's eye sees (and doesn't see), too. People with blind spots, in fact, have the exact same blind spots—in the same place, of the same nature—in their mental imagery of things as well.[19] And so, if the blind can see an arm where there is an arm but there is not thought to be an act of looking, and if we can feel our wrist move when we see a painted wrist stand still, might it not be the case that our whole body is overcome with sensation each time we view a work of art, every inch of our flesh shimmering, quivering, responding, perceiving: *seeing*? Might it not be the case that everything that is hidden, missing, and absent in a painting might also be moving us—literally and otherwise?

To search for beauty in the sublime is to want to be inspired by awe. To yearn for awe is to desire not only wonder but dread, fear, and a false sense of being made nonresponsible in the face of that which overwhelms. The sublime is not worthy of celebration. It is also not worthy of anticelebration, itself a form of celebration, as the mere *abject*—a category and a concept too often held up by late-modernist hipsters and celebrated for its very horror, its nonbeauty, the dreck of Dasein. The technocrats and the romantics form a continuum within the liberal spectrum that happily welcomes National Socialism home at the end of a long day of finally solving perceived problems. It is one thing to have one's head in the clouds; it is another to think that such a perch—like a god's mythical view from nowhere—forgives us our sins merely because we can no longer see them. If it is the sublime, and the desire for the sublime, that has caused so much ethical trouble, then perhaps Girson's blinding us to the sublime makes us able to see what it has done and what we have become. And more than simple seeing—as seeing is always more than seeing—we feel, move, and live it as well. Like the mind moving our wrists all together when we encounter an angel who is just following orders, perhaps everything that is being scotomized, everything hidden in plain sight, everything under the curtain in every painting, everything clouded and unclouded, moves us as well.

Luke Howard, the nineteenth-century chemist who was the first to classify and systematize the various forms of clouds, turned for help in creating his schema to the accomplished botanist and mathematician, John Gough. Together, the two forged the framework for the visual recognition and scientific classification of clouds that is still used today, treating clouds as if they were living creatures, complete with genera and species names. *Stratus nebulosus* hangs low like fog, obscuring the path home. *Cumulus radiatus* spreads out in parallel lines that, like all parallel lines, converge at the horizon in order to seem as if they do not converge. *Cirrus vertabratus*, consisting of some of the highest and coldest collections of vapor, arches across the sky like a burrowing creature's skeleton. And *Stratus opacus* makes it impossible to see the sun or the moon or, some claim, the sky itself—if it is even possible to be unable to see the sky for the clouds. Everything ordered; everything there; everything making sense. Gough, the greatest seer of clouds, had, of course, been blind since the age of two.[20]

These paintings are so dark that it is sometimes difficult to see any image within them. After mortaring white squares across cloudysunny skies, Girson turned to

FIGURE I.8. Matthew Girson. *The Painter's Other Library Is the Poet's Other Night Sky, No. 15*. 2010. Oil on canvas. 20 inches x 15 inches.

painting everything so black that it is on the verge of not being seen at all. *The Painter's Other Library Is the Poet's Other Night Sky* (2010) is a series of barely visible canvases, each containing shelves of books depicted as if we have been locked in a library overnight and our eyes are just starting to make out our surroundings (*see figure 1.8*).[21] In the wrong light, one could pass by these canvases and think that they were empty expanses of black felt. In the right light, dark colors start to congeal and appear as books emerge a few feet in front of us. It helps to look away. And in a 2012 untitled series of fire paintings each image is created using only black paint—only one black pigment—flames leaping and crackling in the wind, in the night, in some distant land that is also nearby, turning unseen things to char. (*See figure 1.10.*)

In all of these black paintings our attention is drawn to absence and the limits of seeing. And these two series need to be seen together because they are about pushing looking to its dark limits—also, there is good reason to believe that those fires are actually bonfires: masses of burning books.

In a library it is becoming increasingly difficult to see the books. More contemporary technology crowds them out in every direction these days.[22] But if we squint—at least for an *Augenblick*—there they are. If we were to pick one up and open it, we would not see any words. It is difficult, as well, to see words in a book. Just as it is difficult to see letters in a word, or black lines on a white page such as the two black lines that just came together to form the letter "t" in the word "squint" a moment ago in the twenty-seventh word in this paragraph. Consciousness doesn't work this way. As you are reading this sentence, you are "seeing through" the words directly to their meaning—which is to say that you are presencing the things themselves in the peculiarly mostly-absent way that language typically makes things present. We might say that the words, letters, and lines on this page are hidden, obscured, or unseen. Or we might say that what it means truly to see a word on a page is to not-see the word. The sense data philosophers, of whom Bertrand Russell at a certain point in his life was an exemplar, went to great lengths to show how we actually see patches of color and then come to make inferences toward objects, eventually using memory to call up meanings we can then attach to those objects. But the point that Russell et al. missed is that they *had to go to great lengths* to show this. Seeing the word "book" as a bunch of black squiggles on a white surface—or even seeing it as four separate letters—takes a lot of work. We can do this if we try very hard, forcing the world toward nonsense. But this is not what it means to be conscious. This is not what it means to understand "book." In order to be in language we must not see language. In general, perhaps, in order to be we must not see.

When books on the shelves are barely there, we must not ask the artist, "Why can't we see them?" Instead, we should ask, "Why do we think we *can* see the two books—all of the books—in van Gogh's *Still Life with Bible* (1885)? Why do we believe that the old woman in Gerard Dou's *Portrait of an Old Woman Reading* (c. 1640) can see the book in front of her when she appears to have her eyes almost completely closed—or even possibly to be blind (*see figure 1.9*)? Why do we think we can see an unfractured book in Juan Gris's *Still Life with Book* (1913), a painting in which everything else is so cubistically cut up? What else is it that we really can't see when we *are* seeing books? And why do we think we deserve to see *anything* in the first place?"

I think I can see the night sky. But unlike the black-and-white night sky of normal human vision, I think I can see bright color in every star. The more we look at Girson's *The Painter's Other Library . . .* the more we realize that the tiny specs catching the light here and there are not bits of lint or fluff accidentally stuck to the canvas or the camera lens that reproduced the image for us. These tiny points are painted on. In fact, up close one can see that the dots of color that starrify the canvas were clearly the first things that were painted; the books came later. The black darkness of the books creeps up to the dots from every side and stops at a point, letting the dabs of color remain, erupting from underneath. For all we know, those tiny points are actually just the tip of massive Technicolor

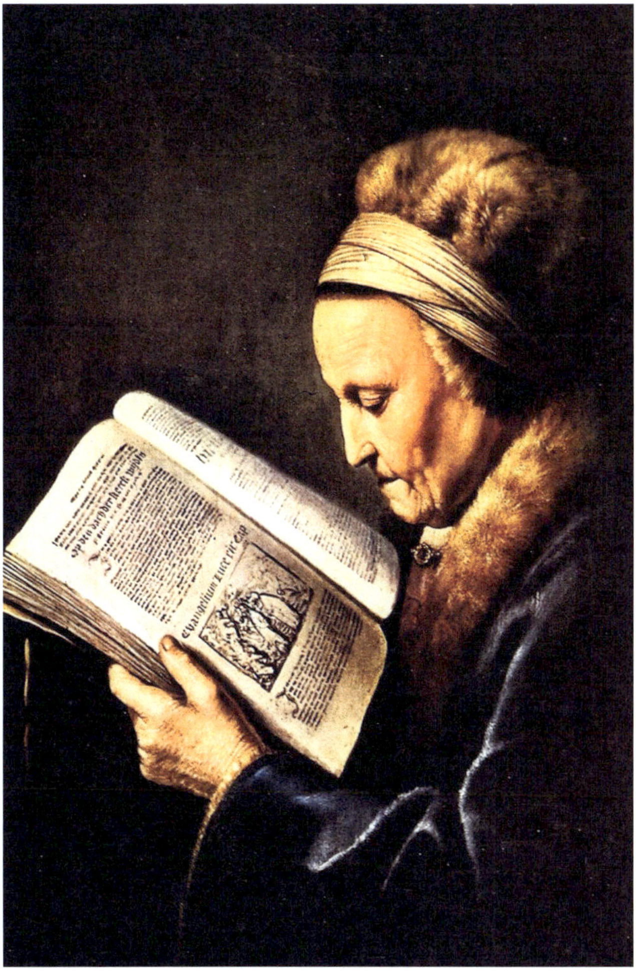

FIGURE 1.9. Gerard Dou. *Portrait of an Old Woman Reading*. c. 1640. Oil on panel. 28 inches x 21.9 inches.

icebergs just beneath the shadowy surface of the painting. It might very well be that the canvas has huge patches of bright color all over it, and the image of the books is covering this up, letting only tiny pinpoints peek out. That is, what we think is the central image might itself be the scotoma: what we take for the subject (books) is perhaps really that which is blocking the subject (bright patches of color). The true anamorphic vantage point might be accessible only from some impossible angle beneath, behind, under the rows of books. Coming to apperceive these possible huge swaths of color—color, we must remember, that is constituting the *night* sky—we start to appreciate the color in the dark books

FIGURE 1.10. Matthew Girson. *Untitled*. 2012. Oil on canvas. 11 inches x 14 inches.

all the more. We start to see how the blues settle, how the purples shimmer, how the reds emerge and undulate. So much seeing from an act of not-seeing. So much there by means of being not-there. It is so unclear what the central image is anymore, or even if there is such a thing as a center.

Sense data philosophy has difficulty with not-seeing. Radical empiricism, itself entangled in the history of metaphysics against which it squirms, will often go to extremes to make its case. In a precursor to this spirit, David Hume's *An Enquiry Concerning Human Understanding* (1748) ends with a famous paragraph that directs us to our local library: "When we run over libraries, persuaded of these claims, what havoc must we make? If we take in our hand any volume; of divinity or school metaphysics, for instance; let us ask, *Does it contain any abstract reasoning concerning quantity or number?* No. *Does it contain any experimental reasoning concerning matter of fact and existence?* No. Commit it then to the flames: for it can contain nothing but sophistry and illusion."[23] The etymology of "bonfire" dates back to the late fifteenth century, when it was clear that the word suggested a "bone fire" (*see figure 1.10*). Whether this was an actual fire of bones (something closer to a bone-pyre, perhaps) is unclear. There are some traditions, notably those of Northern Ireland, in which a bone-fire merely meant a sort of ceremonial public fire actually consisting of two separate fires between which the local cattle would be forced to walk in order to "cleanse" them.[24] Whatever was originally meant by the word, in the end there is probably little distinction. A civilization that cannot see the difference between a fellow creature and a meal is probably only cleansing eventually to cook. Bonfires are *always* about death. And though we might be tricked into thinking that there is a French history to the word when there is none, we might also note that a civilization that cannot see the difference between a celebrating public and a murderous public is likely to confuse every bonfire with a good (*bon*) fire.

On May 10, 1933, more than 25,000 books where happily consigned to the flames across Germany. Students, mostly, had been busy gathering "un-German" works for the last month since word had gone out that the bonfire celebrations would take place. And when the night finally came—a dark and star-filled night with little color to it—hundreds of thousands of citizens watched and took part. Music was played, food was eaten, and "fire oaths" were sworn. As midnight approached, the works of Kafka and Freud, along with dozens of other authors, were piled high, soaked with gasoline, and set on fire with torches in nearly every town with a university in Germany.[25] In a bonfire rally in Berlin, 40,000 people gathered to hear Goebbels declare the end of "Jewish intellectualism" and the birth of the new German—someone who will "not just be a man of books, but a man of character."[26] The newspapers reported that the speech and the spectacle were sublimely beautiful.

Not to be outdone, thirteen years later the allied forces occupying fallen Germany created a list of more than 30,000 "undemocratic, militaristic, and Nazi" books. Private residences, bookshops, and libraries across the country were searched (mostly by British and U.S. soldiers) using what *Time Magazine* then called "a typically Nazi device [for] . . . the suppression of ideas" as the texts from the list were systematically removed from the shelves on order of the four-power Coordinating Committee—the *bon* guys.[27] By the end of 1946, *millions* of copies of outlawed books were destroyed: shredded, gathered, and burned all across Germany—again.

One might wonder how a flame could be rendered in pure black when a fire is, after all, nothing but light. But when we realize that a fire is not really a thing but a process—an event, something that is done, something that we do—the point moves into focus. Girson allows the fire to appear on his canvas by letting light—full, glistening, white light—reflect and bounce off the mass of thick, black paint. We see the fire only by means of seeing how it interacts with other things, with its surroundings. This is, after all, what a fire is: something happening to other things. And as such, it is something happening to us.

The books that appear on every library shelf are made to appear there by means of taking the place of other books, and other things, that could be appearing. Perhaps no other institution carries the full weight of the Enlightenment as does the library. What began in Alexandria and continues today online in the last, gasping, dying breaths of the project was the idea that everything true, everything known, everything good, could be written down, collected, warehoused, and stored.[28] Everything in its right place (such that there are two colors in my head—black and white—and neither is truly a color). On, off. Included, excluded. Seen, unseen. To the Enlightenment mind, always obsessed with having the lights on, something is either known or unknown, and once it is known it can then be discarded because it is thought to be exhausted. Books become the trashcans of modernity; libraries, our landfill. This is why we can treat books as one treats refuse, why we imagine we can burn into charcoal the ideas they possess. Perhaps this was inevitable once thought became reified into a thing with pages, a thing that can be possessed, traded, and sold. Once books enter the scene, there are dangers. Being a "man of books" has its pitfalls, and *not* being a man of books is even more perilous. We might think that the two identities are opposites—one good and one bad—but they share the same value in the end: the value of the book. And the value of the fire. Ceaseless, horrific, unthinking, blind as justice, and never satiated.

Terrified by blindness though I might be, I have spent the majority of my life not seeing things. Not-seeing is the norm. I have not-seen the dark side of the moon; I have not-seen the Cézanne collection at the Musée d'Orsay. At this very moment, I am not-seeing nearly all of the universe—in fact, I am not-seeing most of the room in which I am sitting in my tiny corner of the universe: my book-filled, unlit, dark corner of the universe. All of this not-seeing makes it possible for me to see the work in front of me. So let us be clear: the scotoma and the darkness are not the pathologies. Seeing is the pathology. It always has been. Black is the new black.

> [Kafka] managed to represent so fully the everyday passage from hope to grief and from desperate wisdom to intentional blindness.[29]

The *positive scintillating scotoma* of the perpetual migraine sufferer flashes like a neon pulse of light across the visual field, hanging, floating, a digital ghost on a phosphorous screen strung up in an analog world. It appears in the field of vision like an escaped piece of technology, many patients claim. No, no. It is *natural*, like a glowing worm, claim others. Or a bolt, a flash from white cloud to black Earth.

An empty space on a wall smiles back in the void: what's gone missing is never fully gone. Girson's head in the clouds, feet on the ground. Every mother appearing, every burrow abandoned, the cinders of every fire still and unsmoldering. The painted message flashes, then holds still, now □. Beautiful, bright, and blinding.

CHAPTER 2 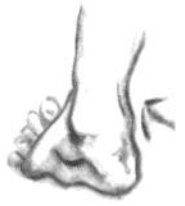

Arshile's Heel, Gorky's Line

> Generations of men are like the leaves.
> In winter, winds blow them down to earth,
> but then, when spring season comes again,
> budding wood grows more. And so with men—
> one generation grows, another dies away.
>
> —Homer's *Iliad,* 6.181–85

Beloveds, here we are. (We should address each other in this manner. The manner in which Gorky addressed those in his life to whom he was irrevocably tied.) Beloveds, here we are. (We should savor the word and taste it, keeping it close to us like we do the people it re-presents.) Beloveds, here we are, gathered to speak of the work of Gorky. (It was his favorite word, a trick and a trifle, an affectation of his command of English, this foreign tongue, caressed and pointed in the direction of those Others with whom the man's identity was tied: sister, children, family, friends, canvases. All were *beloveds*. Not simply loved, but beheld *as* loved. "Beloveds," writes Gorky to his sister Vartoosh, "the stuff of thought is the seed of the artist."[1] "Beloveds," writes Gorky to his sister and to Moorad and Karlen, "some people say that art is eternal. . . . Nonsense."[2] "Beloveds," writes Gorky on the wall of his studio before hanging himself: "Beloveds, goodbye.") No. Let us not speak this way just yet. Let us begin again.

Sing, Goddess, sing of the rage of Arshile. Sing of this man, split in two, thrown into a land across the sea, born anew in bitterness and his talent. "'Mother,' cried [Achilles], 'you bore me doomed to live but for a little season; surely Jove, who thunders from Olympus might have made that little glorious.'"[3] This man, then, who took the name of Achilles when he could have chosen any name, how do we reconcile the glory and the short life? How do we do more than merely nip at his heels when we speak of his body, his body of work, dragged before us?

Let us begin with the line.

"Drawing," writes Gorky, "is the basis of art. A bad painter cannot draw. But a good drawer can always paint. . . . Drawing gives the artist the ability to control his line and his hand."[4] And the line is what lives in the drawing. It is the line that animates all drawing.

Let us say that every brush stroke in a painting is a line. The fat head of the brush, even the long edge of the palette knife, make lines on the canvas with each application, each stroke. The painter stacks up these lines and points them all in the same direction to create his or her subject. But Gorky knows that there is more at stake. The true line is always an out-line. It creates a space of Here and There where before there was only one amorphous expanse. It divides inner and outer life, points to something existing, pulls objects into being.

Gorky's early model is Cézanne, and Cézanne knew this as well (*see figure 2.1*).[5] Consider Gorky's 1927 landscape *Staten Island* and his 1928 *Self Portrait*, which, in their final form, bear a striking resemblance to the work of Cézanne, though what should really inspire us is what inspired Gorky as well: Cézanne's *lines*. Gorky picks up the thread of them and does not let them go. He is not afraid to let the roof of a building be a roof by outlining it in black. He is not afraid to say "This is my nose" and "This is my shirt collar" by painting black lines to mark their point in space. It was Cézanne who taught Gorky to overcome the mistakes of the past and free his line, to free it, in part, by realizing that what it means to see something is to de*line*ate it. And though, as we have seen in the previous chapter, this means that something else is necessarily obscured—that blindness is necessary to seeing—the artist must embrace the line and allow it to delineate in order for there to be a world that is perceived. Unlike the Impressionists, whose canvases ran the risk of dissolving into an unmade gestalt, an out-of-focus world, a mass of spontaneous little brush strokes of light and color but no substance, Cézanne discovered the true nature of the creative line. And Gorky understood. He moved, then, from Cézanne to Picasso. He moved always in the direction of the line.

When we look at *The Artist and His Mother* (c. 1926), perhaps Gorky's most famous work, we note how lines construct the painting. We look at the photograph on which the painting was based. We study the graphite-on-squared-paper study that Gorky did to prepare his space, carving it up like a chess game. We see, for instance, in the graphite drawing, lines that will not be there in the final painting: lines that make up cuffs on the boys pants, fingers on his hands, buttons

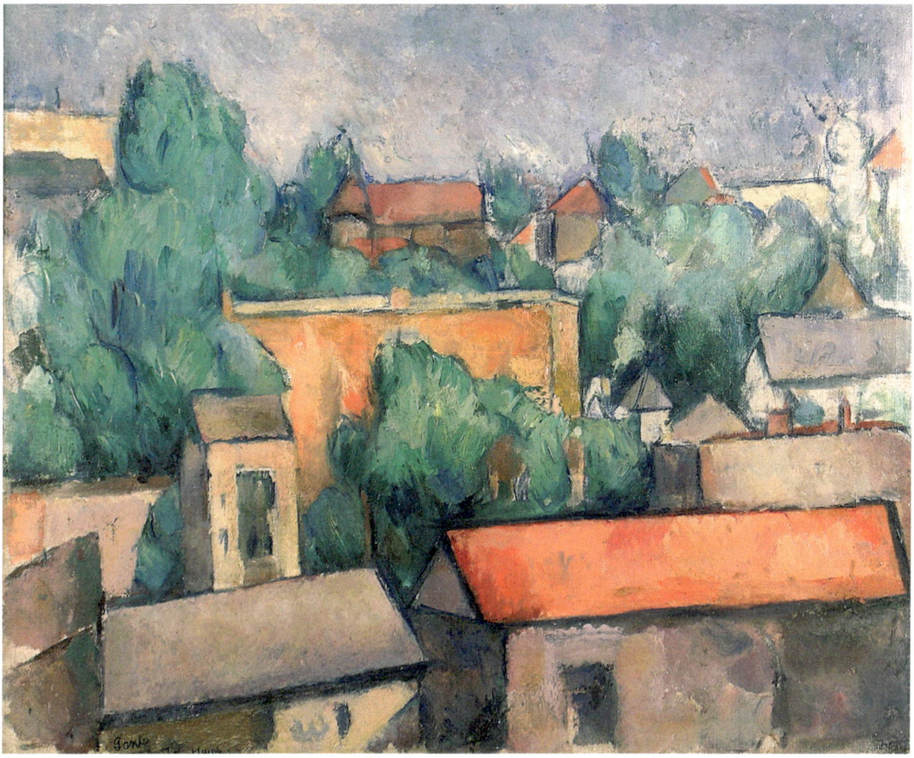

FIGURE 2.1. Arshile Gorky. *Staten Island*. 1927. Oil on Canvas. 16 inches x 20 inches; © 2016 The Arshile Gorky Foundation/Artists Rights Society (ARS), New York; private collection, courtesy Jack Rutberg Fine Arts, Los Angeles.

on his coat, and wrinkles in his mother's sleeves. Later, Gorky will not delineate such things, they will not become things in the painting because the line is taken away from them and turned elsewhere. *This is not what this moment is about*, he seems to be saying. We note, instead, the lines that make up the paint on the walls, the lines that bring each feature of the face into perfect being. And we see how lines are allowed to run free so as to make the depth of space and the lingering of time apparent in the painting.

How, for instance, does Gorky's line make depth and time possible? Pay close attention to the back wall behind the mother and child. Note the ledge behind his mother's left shoulder. As we follow this ledge across the wall—across the painting—we see it disappear behind the mother and then reappear over her right shoulder, but now it sits lower on the wall. The line is not straight, we might think. Gorky has made some mistake in painting it this way. But what is happening in reality is that there is motion within the painting.

All seeing takes place from a perspective. It is the nature of the world always to be given in perspective: we cannot escape it and we should not want to. If there is a low line on a wall—a line that marks a ledge or some sort of similar structure along the wall—when we see it from a distance, the line will be high up in our field of vision. As we walk toward the wall, however, the line will be lower for us. And so, in Gorky's painting, we see the ledge on the wall high above the mother's left shoulder and lower near her right shoulder. We are thus moving as we look at her. We approach her, and as we do, we see her grow closer, we see her before us, closer with every step we take. And all of this takes place within the painting and without our bodies ever having to move. Only our eyes move as we stand before Gorky's canvas. Our eyes take in the ledge to the right, then the mother, then the ledge to the left, and we have somehow traveled closer to the woman while standing still. But because we *are* our eyes, because there is no mind-body dualism, we—in whole—have truly moved. The space through which we have moved is the diagetic space of the painting, but this is no less real than the spacetime through which our bodies move during a typical day. The painting is part of our world, and we are part of its world as well. This is yet another false dualism. The world of the aesthetic object and the everyday world are the same. Gorky's mastery of the line is what makes this movement, and this realization, possible. And we know, as well, that since the line does not appear to continue lowering on the other side of the boy, our approach stops here. It is thus the mother we are approaching, not the boy. It is the mother to whom we are drawn near—the mother who once again calls to us, searching, when we have gone missing.

There is much more to be said here: we must wonder why Gorky chose to destroy the presence of flowers in the photograph, refusing to paint the little bouquet in his own hand and the floral print on his mother's apron; we must ask about the artist's relationship to his mirror-self in this painting, for the young Gorky here is strikingly not very young-looking in certain ways, the shadow of a beard on his face, the hint of a receding hairline, the scene staged just a bit as if he is a nervous suitor as much as a doting son to his mother; we must ask about the racialization of the skin tones in the work, the white ghost-face of the mother, the iconic arrangement of the figures, and so on. But what moves us—literally moves us—is Gorky's line.

We see this as well in some of the pencil drawings from the mid-1930s (*see figure 2.2*). These still lifes—tables with fruit and lamps and bowls and vases—have adopted the cubist's line and Cézanne's conception of multiple perspectives. Each part of a table, for instance, is seen from a different perspective. When we look at each different part of the table, we see it, and the things on it, as if from a particular perspective, but as our eyes move to another part of the table, the

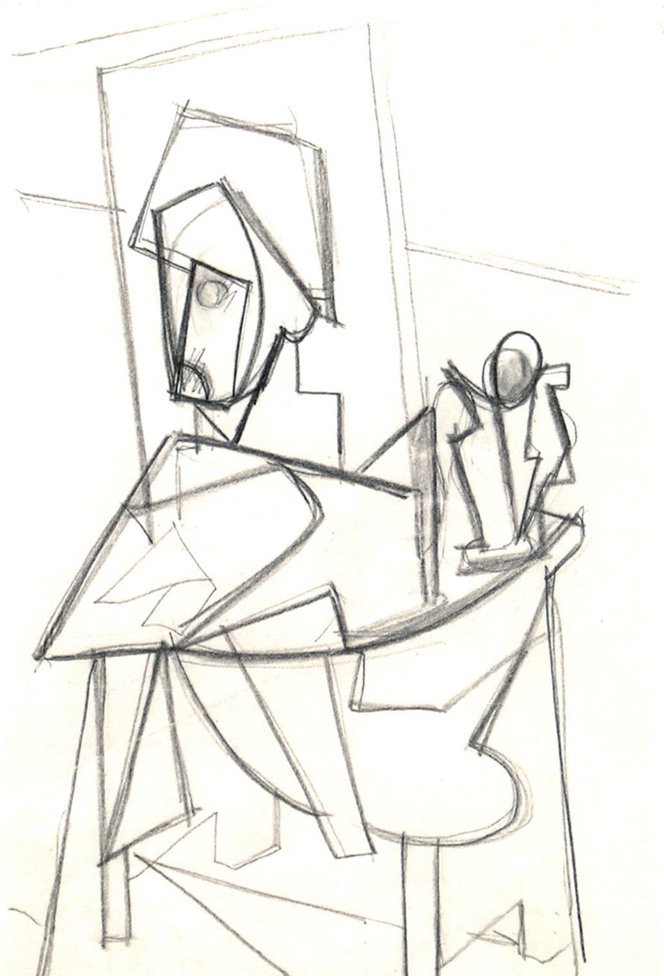

FIGURE 2.2. Arshile Gorky. *Untitled*. c. 1935. Graphite on Paper. 11.25 inches x 7.5 inches; © 2016 The Arshile Gorky Foundation/Artists Rights Society (ARS), New York; Private Collection, courtesy Jack Rutberg Fine Arts, Los Angeles.

perspective shifts. It is as if we have walked around the entire table without ever moving our feet while viewing the drawing. In these drawings, Gorky is a phenomenologist, studying and learning about the way in which the world presents itself to consciousness. He is becoming a master of his art.

When we first see an object, to say that we see it is to say that we see the line around it. Objects stand out from the flux for us in this way: we see lines. But because the shape of a thing is always changing depending on how we see it and what our perspective is, lines cannot fully contain the being of an object. This is why a line must be fluid and free if it is to be helpful and truthful. It must hold the object together but be willing to let it spill out. This is why Gorky's lines are allowed to run like mad, showing us the true fluidity of the world.

In the 1940s, Gorky began, or perhaps returned, to drawing lines with crayons. If we look at these little drawings—often smaller than a sheet of typing paper—we will see such fluid lines. Lines drawn in black, a mixture of all possible colors. We will note the way in which the objects are formed by these lines, yet when they are filled in with color, the color spills out and takes space beyond the outline: Gorky with his box of crayons, unwilling to stay within the lines when he starts coloring. It is, to be sure, a childish creative act, but only in all the best senses of the term. Gorky has drawn on one of them a cat and the sun and a person and a house. He draws them all in lines and then lets their color seep and run. Because one color next to another really does change the way we see each distinct object. In Gorky's sun, complete with a childish face and sun-rays all around, the yellow is both inside and outside of the sun, nearly touching the orange of the cat and the red of that cat's nose. And of course it is sunlight that makes the seeing of this orange cat with the red nose possible: the yellow of the sun does not belong to the sun but rather is part of all the colors that we see. We need lines to make objects out of an ever-malleable world, but they must be transitory and free lines.

One imagines that this is another reason that Gorky loved using crayon on such paper. The black crayon used to make the lines does not leave a solid trail of black, but rather the wax from the crayon sticks only to the upper parts of the paper's grain. The lines left behind thus show this grain and are filled with little holes; often they seem to be composed of little lines themselves. They are solid and yet not solid, and as such, these black wax crayon lines act like the walls of the cells in our body. They must be firm and sturdy to keep the integrity of the cell, but they must be permeable and open to bring nutrients in and waste out. They must individuate, that is, but also point to how everything is really connected. In a letter to his sister shortly before he died, Gorky suggested that he had discovered a truth: "[I] think of nature as a finite object and all of the plants, animals, rocks, waters, etc. as the cells . . . which give it its form and substance."[6] The black lines in these drawings show us these solid yet permeable cell walls.

Elsewhere, Gorky has pressed the colored crayon hard into the paper, making sure there is no grain, pushing and spreading the wax to cover the surface completely. These lines tell us: this is a cat, this is the sun, this is the world. They are each here yet they are all together. To those who fear the childish allusions, we need only remember that Gorky himself smartly admired children with their crayons. "When you watch children," he remarked, "they talk to themselves as they draw, indicating continuous inner associations, saying this is a house, this is a dog, and so on."[7] And so do these drawings speak to us: this is you and this is me and this is the world and these are all the cells that make us whole.

Gorky's most mature work is always childish in this wonderful way. By 1945, de Kooning had introduced Gorky to the liner brush—a brush composed of just a few hairs such that when dipped in a thinned paint would produce a fine and fluid line much like that of a pencil. But it was the pencil that continued to fascinate Gorky. It was the pencil that provided the most versatile lines—lines that could be dotted and dashed, broken and solid, here and there; lines that could become shading, could become outlines, could become things. In his final days, these were the inhabitants of Gorky's world. And since every work of art asks us to inhabit it, take up residence within it, and become it, these things, too, comprise the furniture of our world today. We see in these works from the last three years of his life bits and pieces of everything that had come before, yet we see something more. There is a sexuality that is more obvious, a freedom that is more fully realized. A table not only tilts and lets us move around it, but it turns into a plant, a tree, a bird, a flower, a person as the one continuous line moves through it and around it and into something else, bringing order to chaos and hope to the world.

Achilles, lining up his men for battle in Troy, repeatedly acknowledges that he knows that he will never return home. This soil will be his final home, this war his proof of greatness. Just as his mother knew from the beginning, there were two distinct paths for the young boy: home and happiness, or war and misery. The harder path, perhaps, is the one that asks the most of the man yet offers the world the greater reward. It is hard to say which path this is. Achilles, in his pain and his grief, will come to torture the corpse of his fallen enemy, Hektor. Losing honor, losing his contact with all that ties us together, Achilles's talents mark his demise as well as his heroic place in history. This is the fate of the greatest creators and the greatest destroyers. Consider, beloveds, the path of Paris's arrow that slew Achilles in distant Troy, the straight line it made for that one part of his body still vulnerable, the straight line that it makes for us all.

CHAPTER 3

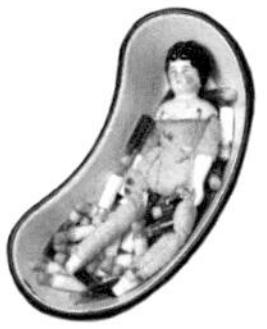

"You Are Here" and Not Here

The Concept of Conceptual Art

FIRST INSTALLATION

You Are Here: An Olfactory Map of Life, 2008 (Chicago)[1]

Description: Six antique wooden boxes sit on top of six old, rusted, metal stools in the middle of a large hall. Rope is tied between the stools, connecting them. Wooden boards with arrows painted on them are tied to the rope every five feet, indicating direction and flow to the "map." Each of the six boxes is labeled: Birth, Home, School, War, Truth, and Death. Birth is the starting point on the map and it leads directly to Home. Home then branches off in two directions: one path leads from Home to School, another leads from Home to War. Both School and War eventually lead to Truth; and Truth finally leads to Death. Each of the six boxes has a toe-tag indicating the (fictional) contents as well as a tube coming out of the side of the box to which an antique funnel is attached. The visitor takes up the tube and smells what is inside the box, with each smell representing what it is to occupy that different station in life. The smells are created through a variety of hidden contents not listed in the exhibit description (for instance, the Death box contains a rotting durian fruit, the School box contains old library books that were left in a damp basement for several months before the installation opened, etc.). Small, battery-operated fans inside the boxes blow the smells into the tubing and toward the external funnel to keep the air, and thus the smells, flowing. The visitor navigates through the map and through life by means of smell—but also, of course, by means of touch and vision. The tags read as follows:

Birth Contents: "gauze, blood, bleach, hope, afterbirth"

Home (that never was) Contents: "cookies, soap, apple pie, nurturing, freshly mown grass"

School Contents: "pencil shavings, textbooks, chalk, conformity, Tater Tots"

War Contents: "shell casings, oil, medals, honor, rotting flesh"

Truth Contents: "truth"

Death Contents: "ashes, soil, pine, regret, formaldehyde"

Materials used: Funnels, oxygen concentrator tubing from a nursing-home auction, antique hemp rope, antique metal stools, Canadian 120-year-old red barn wood, rusted wire, paper toe-tags, U.S. Army ammunition box, 150-year-old pine box, primitive golden oak glove box, antique W & J LANG Cake Biscuit Bakers box, lead school delivery box from the early 1900s, antique embalming fluid box, small fans, latex paint, unnamed contents of boxes.

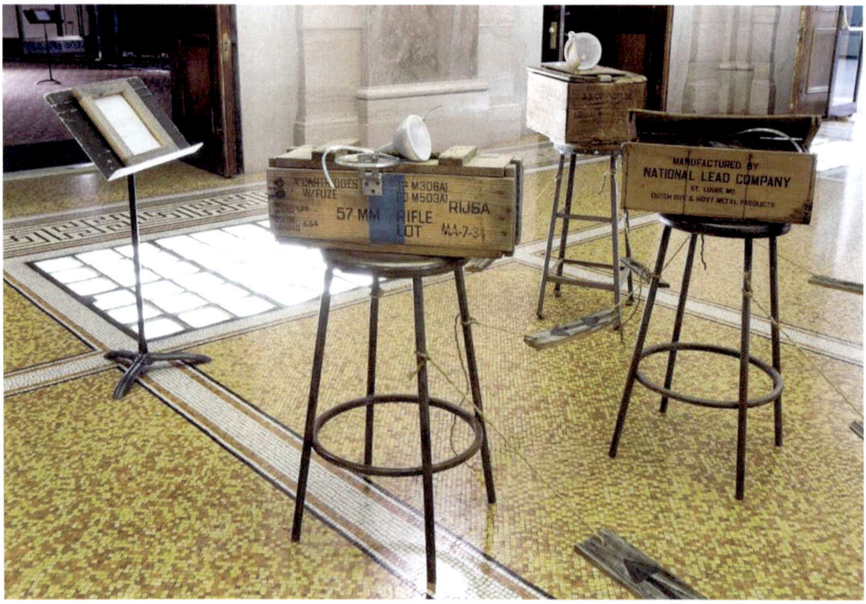

FIGURE 3.1. H. Peter Steeves. Detail of *An Olfactory Map of Life*. 2008. Photograph by Monika Lozinska.

In conceptual art, the idea driving the art is usually taken to be more important than the work of art itself. One might even say that the idea *is* the work of art itself, and thus any physical object becomes superfluous. That is, someone could have the idea of constructing a map that could be navigated by means of smell, and though the particular sensory way of interacting with such a work of art might seem to be central to the art itself, it is truly more about the *idea* of an olfactory map than about actually smelling anything. One could read the description of such an installation and legitimately ask, "How much have I missed by not actually, physically interacting with the objects as they have been described?"

The idea behind conceptual art is thus not only central to the art but seems to have become the aesthetic object itself. As a one-sentence definition of the movement, this does about as good a job as any of defining what is meant by "conceptual art"; yet it also leaves far too much unsaid. Ideas are always important in art. And is it truly the case that art can consist of merely ideas?

It is unclear when conceptual art per se began. Most art historians argue that the work of Marcel Duchamp, close to a century ago, marked its birth. The idea, that is, behind placing a urinal in a museum and calling it a "Fountain" seems to be more important than the actual fountain itself. As an audience, we do not miss much by not getting to see the urinal. Hearing or reading about it seems almost sufficient in and of itself; in other words, the work itself is the *idea* of putting the urinal on the wall. Once you are familiar with the idea, you are in the presence of the art.

There are art critics who argue that all art after Duchamp has been necessarily conceptual because he forced us to reconsider the nature of the aesthetic experience at an ontological level. Phenomenologically, at least we can say that it is certainly the case that a urinal on a museum wall is experienced differently than a urinal in a restroom. The latter seems to have little sense of the aesthetic to it.

Perhaps. But one of the most important things we can learn from conceptual art is that aesthetics is always a mode of appearing, not merely a category for understanding the being of traditional works of art displayed and presented in traditional spaces and manners. That is, when a urinal is placed in a museum, one of the things we are forced to contemplate is the beauty of the urinal—the smooth flow and curve of the lines, the sheen of the porcelain, the careful choices that went into the design, etc. The fact that the artist himself did little to create this object—all he did, really, was sign it and ask us to consider it as a work of art—means that we are then retroactively forced to think about the way in which such qualities were already there in the *everyday* urinals we have been seeing all our lives and taking for granted. The aesthetic, that is, is always already operational in our lives, though we have, perhaps, been taking it for granted and not giving it our full attention. In the same way that Gorky's paintings and drawings in the previous chapter showed us that the aesthetic space of the canvas and the space of our everyday world are really the same, so we are now coming to the same point from a different perspective: aesthetics itself is not anything other than living.

What constitutes art is, at least in part, a function of how we experience that thing. Context and setting can turn something into a full-blown aesthetic object even as it hints that all objects are aesthetic objects in reality. When we take something *as* art rather than *as* some other sort of thing, it is not as if a new object appears in the world. Rather, one way in which an object can appear is as an aesthetic object. Taken to the extreme, this becomes the claim that anything at all can be anything at all if we simply say it is and take it to be such. "Ceci n'est pas une pipe"? Well, it is and it isn't. And this is not *just* a urinal? It is and it isn't. In 1961, Robert Rauschenberg was asked to participate in an exhibition of portraits at "Galerie Iris Clert," and rather than painting something, he sent a telegram reading: "This is a portrait of Iris Clert if I say so." And it was—and it wasn't. What Rauschenberg was exhibiting was an idea. And the idea itself was the object of art, supposedly making the telegram into a portrait and the entire concept of doing so into the aesthetic experience for the audience.

The year 1961 was a good one for art. Apart from Rauschenberg's telegram, there was M. C. Escher's *Waterfall*, David Hockney's *We Two Boys Together Clinging*, Jasper Johns's *Maps*, and several performances by Rachel Rosenthal, whose work we will take up in chapter 8.[2] It is also the year that Yves Klein Blue was given a patent. The synthetic ultramarine pigment had been developed by Klein and a team of chemists, and once the patent was given, so that Klein essentially owned that particular hue of blue (and thus, in some sense, all works of art anyone else might ever create using that pigment), the artist moved toward even further distancing himself from the physical aesthetic object by having naked women covered in the pigment roll around on blank canvases as per his directions—directions he had given remotely, hundreds of miles away—thus making, in a somewhat lascivious and undoubtedly misogynistic assembly-line fashion, "paintings by Yves Klein."

It was in the early '60s, too, that Christo's work began gaining popularity. His *Iron Curtain* was a mass of oil barrels piled onto a Paris street in order to create a traffic jam, and the viewer was asked to consider the traffic jam and the idea of oil barrels creating a traffic jam itself as the work of art. By 1972, Fred Forrest had done something ostensibly nicer for the citizens of Paris by spending money to buy a blank page in *Le Monde* on which readers were encouraged to construct their own works of art. The work of art, he claimed, was the idea that there were so many different works of art to come out of the project and the idea that everyone had the freedom to make his or her own contribution in secret. Those blank pages, scotoma-like in their emptiness, today sell for a great deal of money. In the later '70s, Walter De Maria ordered a one-kilometer-long brass rod to be constructed in Germany and buried it vertically in the ground so that only a few centimeters were sticking out. Essentially, like Forrest's private newspaper drawings, this *Vertical Earth Kilometer* work could not be seen by anyone for what it was, but the *idea* that there was a kilometer of brass buried beneath the viewer and the *idea* that the object of art was essentially hidden from experience was the real work of art—a work of art, unlike the rod itself, that was thought to be accessible to everyone.

Certainly, the 1960s and '70s in general marked the ascendance of conceptual art as a full-fledged cultural movement, though this time period did not invent the idea of conceptual art. Duchamp's *Fountain* had come five or six decades earlier, and surely there are instances of conceptual art that can be traced back to the earliest aesthetic acts of humans. Diogenes, a contemporary and frenemy of Plato, was doing conceptual performance art in the guise of stand-up philosophy two-and-a-half millennia ago. This is, after all, the genius who refuted Zeno's argument that motion is not possible by standing up at the lecture, saying "I refute you," and then walking out. The same man who carried around a lantern in broad daylight and told the citizens of Athens, holding it up to their faces, that he needed it to help him see if he could find a true human because so far, no luck. The same artist who was called a dog by his detractors, so he urinated on them and bit them when they came too close. Diogenes lived his life as "Diogenes," as a true '70s *happening* (i.e., the 370s BCE), as the socially conscious and philosophically complicated Ziggy Stardust of Ancient Greece. And in making the concepts of philosophy into a work of art, he simultaneously made his life into a work of art, thereby showing us that life is, for all of us, already art. Living, Diogenes knew, is about ideas and about how we embody and enact them.[3]

The first thing that conceptual art does, then, is open a space that allows us to think of all objects—of the world and even ourselves—as art. But there are still more specific questions that can be raised precisely concerning the way in which we wonder about the relationship between *ideas* and *objects*.

SECOND INSTALLATION

You Are Here: The Human Genome Projection, 2008 (Chicago)

Description: Several structures in a large room masquerade as the centerpieces of a late-nineteenth-century traveling carnival/sideshow of medical oddities. In the middle stands a kiosk constructed from old barn wood, including a long table with an antique mannequin on it. The mannequin's brain has been mapped, with tags nailed to its head to indicate what that area of the brain is dedicated to processing/knowing (e.g., "flight or fight," "fear of death," "the name

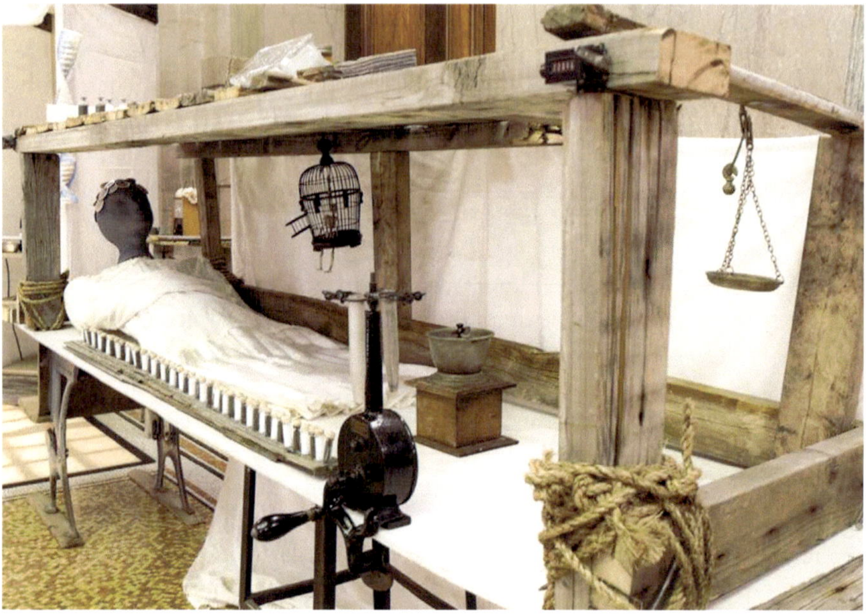

FIGURE 3.2. H. Peter Steeves. Detail of *The Human Genome Projection*. 2008. Photograph by Monika Lozinska.

of that guy who was in that thing," "*Dónde está la biblioteca,*" etc.). On the table there is a test-tube centrifuge with test tubes filled with ashes, an X-ray viewer with X-rays of broken bones from abused children, a small video screen (hidden inside a wooden box) scrolling through old-time photos of medical curiosities interspersed with modern images of DNA, a meat grinder into which the mannequin's hospital gown/wedding dress is being fed, vials of black and white powders, and Mason jars with embalmed "fetal skeletons." Nearby, there is a booth with a curtain. When one opens the curtain and enters the booth, a sensor is tripped so that Gregorian chants begin to play through hidden speakers. A light turns on inside an antique lighted microscope that sits on a metal hospital table with a sign inviting viewers to look into the microscope to see an actual sample of human DNA that has been fully mapped. The viewer can operate the microscope, focusing the image and changing the intensity of the bulb. Once the image comes into view, it is found to be a microdot that reads "You Are Not Here." Directly outside the booth are several tables constructed from old barn wood. One table has a test-tube mixer running on it, with several antique glass marbles in a pan that are labeled A, T, G, and C. The marbles clank around in the metal pan and hit each other in a constant series of new combinations. This percussive sound echoes throughout the hall in which the installation has been placed (the only sound apart from the chants, which are audible only to someone inside the microscope booth). Another table has an antique doll nailed to a metronome. The metronome clicks and flashes a light, increasing in tempo whenever anyone approaches the table. There is also a 5' x 5' x 5' box encased in glass inside of which there are spinning knives attached to fan (that seems to be short-circuiting), an oscilloscope, and a strobe light. An attendant dressed in a white lab coat and Butoh-style makeup carries a dirty wooden clipboard in one hand and an assortment of antique medical and pseudomedical devices in a Victorian walrus-skin doctor bag in the other hand. He walks slowly and deliberately through the exhibit, sizing up the visitors. He is always silent, but is constantly changing out the X-rays near the mannequin and, from time to time, stopping a spectator to measure and "test" him or her, recording his data on the clipboard with a stubby, dirty pencil.

Materials used: Antique toy child's metal tin cup, 1940s Sleep-Time doll, Seth Thomas vintage metronome used by a child who excelled at playing the violin by six years old and lost all knowledge of music due to traumatic brain injury at the age of twenty, antique Oxford Cutlery butter knives, 120-year-old barn wood and nails, black light, UV ink, UV paint, antique hemp rope, wood and leather bellows from early 1900s, tile, Telequipment S61 oscilloscope used by a General Electric scientist during the Korean War, vintage wooden pulley with hooks, Eimer & Amend antique hand-crank test tube centrifuge with test tubes, analog crank counters, antique coffee grinder, speakers, two antique school desks (c. 1910) taken from a school that a Nobel Prize winning scientist attended fifty years before winning that prize, round metal rim tags, vintage glass marbles recovered from a Chicago home that burned down in the mid-1960s, wooden case, rusted razor blades, blue lights, 1940s German nautical map mileage gauge with compass, recently recovered one-inch flechette darts dropped from U.S. helicopters during the Vietnam war to kill Viet Cong hiding in the jungle, antique scale, shadow box, photo of the artist's mother and uncle as children (c. 1951), 1950s enamelware medical tray, wooden birdcage, mason jars, Jell-o, miniature skeletons, Styrofoam head, female torso display mannequin, glass bottle and vials, human genome project Venter Collins card, X-ray light box, paper, multiple X-rays of children all under the age of seven thought to have been potential victims of child abuse, Graf-Apsco vintage 900 series lighted microscope, metal wheeled cart, MP3 player programmed with Gregorian chants, 1950s stainless steel medical tray and mirrored instrument, salt, soot taken from the ground of a metal blasting workshop, fabric, antique maps, carpet tacks, plywood, Victorian genuine walrus-hide doctor's bag, antique lab coat, assortment of antique medical and pseudoscientific medical devices, pencil.

Ideas are thus key to conceptual art. It is the concept that one is supposed to encounter, that one is meant to take up as the point of the work. In some cases,

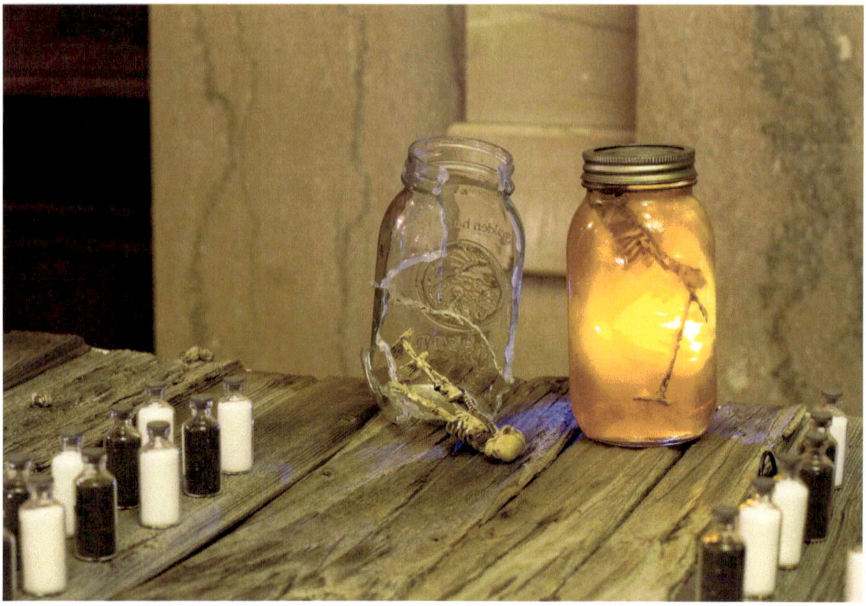

FIGURE 3.3. H. Peter Steeves. Detail of *The Human Genome Projection*. 2008. Photo courtesy of John Sisson Photography, www.sissonphotography.com.

the object itself can seem superfluous (hence, the number of works of conceptual art that exist as mere instructions on how to create something rather than presentations of the actual thing). Actually doing something or making something physical is not the ultimate goal of most conceptual art; it is, rather, having an intellectual realization itself that becomes an aesthetic experience.[4]

Since most conceptual art is deeply dependent on a text or a background story to explain it, many questions are raised about how the meaning of conceptual art is founded. Twentieth-century aestheticians often claimed that the author's intent is not important to the meaning of a traditional work of art. Once the painting or sculpture or installation, etc., exists, it is a communal object and thus finds its meaning in the varied experiences of the community, their interpretations, and the intersubjective meanings they bring to the experience. We cannot, that is, know what *Waiting for Godot really* means by asking Beckett, and we cannot learn what the *Old Guitarist* all in blue *really* means by asking Picasso. The author, it is said, has no privileged position from which to declare some objective, true, complete, full, real meaning. All of this seems fair. We are not always fully aware of our own intentions, and even when we are, those intentions change in the process of making the art, such that asking the artist what something means should garner a changing answer as the artist her-

or himself changes (and as the context changes around the artist). Meaning in art, as with meaning in all things, is a communal project that founds objectivity on intersubjectivity. The author's intent is of no more importance necessarily than any other "fact" we might bring to the discussion.

But with conceptual art such a claim is controversial. Unless the artist explains that the couple of centimeters of brass you are looking at are only the tip of the kilometer-long rod buried in the ground, unless Rauschenberg tells us that it is a drawing by Willem de Kooning that he has erased and is now calling his own work of art,[5] unless, that is, we know the author's intent and story, we don't really get the full picture and thus the full aesthetic experience. At a point in history when the art object itself was becoming less fetishized and thus less important, the artist him- or herself was interestingly becoming more important.

Some critics find this to be something potentially troubling about conceptual art: focused on the artists more than on the art, conceptual art can easily slide toward narcissism if one is not careful; and conceptual art thus leads to a "cult of personality" such that a work becomes important only because some particular person is behind it and has declared it important (e.g., if Rauschenberg sends a telegram and claims it is a portrait, the gallery is happy to display it; if Rauschenberg's dentist did the same, no one would probably care). This is certainly not necessarily the case, but it is one way in which conceptual art is thought to be interestingly distinct and harder to pull off well.

In performance art the challenges are somewhat different—at least at first glance. Performance art is often associated with conceptual art because it is trying to convey an idea in its fleeting moment before us. The idea may be a notion such as "Home" or a feeling such as "Hope," but it is a concept all the same. In many ways, the performance seems to be "about something," which means "about something other than the performance." One can always say the same of Cézanne's apples on the canvas, of course, but there is also just the sense that they are apples. The performance artist typically makes a statement, expounds on an idea, portrays a feeling, or exhibits a concept in a manner that is more direct than "traditional" art. And while we might think that we have not really missed much if we don't get to see the actual postcard, the actual brass rod, or the actual erased drawing (because it was the idea behind each of these things that was the real aesthetic work), this is not the case for most performance art. If one didn't get to see Rachel Rosenthal on stage in 1984 surrounded by a veritable Noah's ark of thirty-five different species of animals in her piece *The Others*, then one indeed missed out on a key element of the aesthetic experience. Perhaps it is the case that the title and the back story and the ideas and concepts are key to making *The Others* work, but seeing the performance itself seems necessary to the aesthetic experience in a way that seeing the Rauschenberg postcard is not necessary. This would mean that the performance artist has a special duty and an

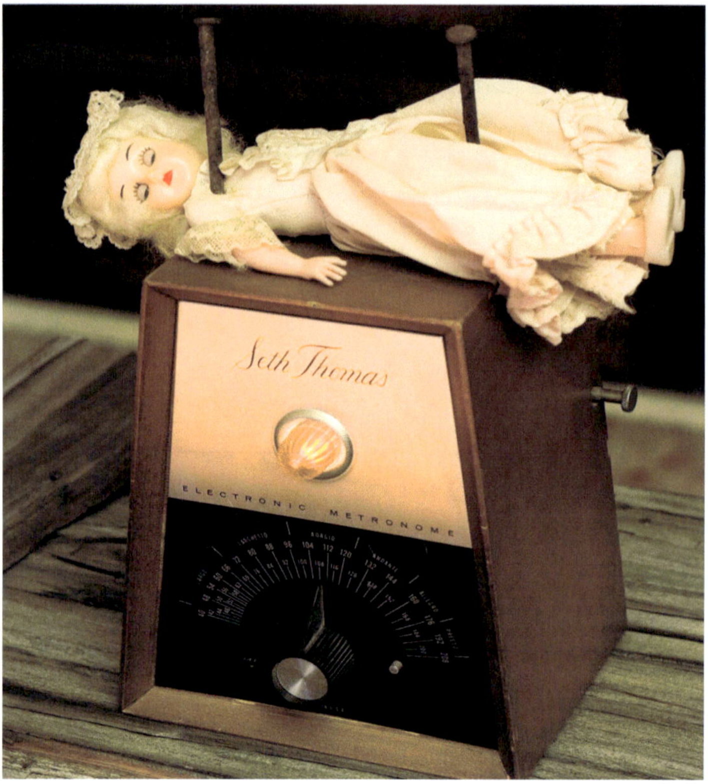

FIGURE 3.4. H. Peter Steeves. Detail of *The Human Genome Projection*. 2008. Photo courtesy of John Sisson Photography, www.sissonphotography.com.

extra challenge. It is not only the concept in his or her art that is important, but also the execution of it.

Phenomenologically, however, performance is always necessary for art. This is because the aesthetic object is never exhausted by our experience of it. The same could be said to be true of any object, but for aesthetic objects it is even more the case (*see figure 3.4*).

For objects in general, the reason we have a sense of things being "outside" of us has little to do with spatiality and the limits of our bodies. It is not the case that we have a sense of an externality to objects because they are "beyond" our flesh. We are not *inside* our flesh, peeking out at the world like voyeurs. Instead, we are *in* the world, and our consciousness is in the world, spreading out and into everything around us. The "outsideness" of objects is, rather, a manifestation of the way in which they always necessarily exceed our conscious grasp. Since the being of an object is found in all of the ways in which it can possibly appear, and since those ways are innumerably infinite (because there are infinitely many ways in which we can experience something), we can never fully know—never possess or constrain or own or overcome—an object. There will always be some profile that is hidden, some way in which it could be experienced that we have not yet enacted and fulfilled. The object races away from us even as we come to know it better. It is never exhausted, used up, known, and done with. If I experience an apple, there is always another vantage point from which I could see it, another profile it has to offer, another context in which it can appear with new meaning. I might study the apple from Here and There, sniff it, bite into it, or toss it back and forth from hand to hand. But even with a lifetime spent getting to know the apple there will always be more left to uncover, another experience I could have had but didn't. The apple is never exhausted by my being conscious of it: it is outside of and beyond me, even if it finds its being in the infinite number of ways it can be given to consciousness.

All of this is true for every object of consciousness, but for aesthetic objects there is something additional going on. The aesthetic object finds part of its being in *the performative expression* of the viewer.[6] What Cézanne's painted apples can mean is more than what they make present. To see this we must first accept a less-than-obvious truth: art does not represent.

To say that art is not representational is to say that art does not replace, echo, or shadow something real, as Plato might have feared. Abstract and conceptual art are typically understood to be nonrepresentational, but the truth is that no art represents something other than what it is. A painting of an apple is not a *sign* of an apple. It does not denote or refer to an apple. Rather, it *is* an apple. A picture or image of something is one way that that thing can be present to consciousness. If I look at an apple directly, taste an apple, remember an apple, imagine an apple, see a photograph of an apple, view a painting of an apple, or even think the word "apple," the object of consciousness in each case is exactly the same: an apple. Each way of presencing merely carries with it its own complex manifold of presence and absence. Language conjures up real things. To say the word "apple" makes an apple present. But a word is a fairly absent way for a thing to be present. A painting of an apple, too, has a great deal of absence to it, but so does a physical encounter with an apple. When I merely look at an apple, I presence the absence of the backside of it, of its sweetness or sourness, of its smell, etc. All of these aspects of the apple are experienced when I look at the apple, but they are experienced through apperception rather than perception, through our ability to experience directly their absence as something positively present. Consequently, when I see a painting of an apple it is an apple that is present to my consciousness (i.e., the object of consciousness is not "an image of an apple"), and I can thus taste, smell, and feel the apple in such an experience, though in very limited ways. A good painting makes these experiences less absent than a bad painting. This is why, perhaps, Cézanne once destroyed a painting he was working on because he felt the viewer couldn't taste the apples enough.[7] Presence and absence—in a complex manifold—are the ways in which things appear, the way in which they have their being.

If art is never about representation, then we must ask ourselves specifically: what is it about an aesthetic object that is so special? All works of art require performance. This is most easily seen in a play or a piece of music, of course, but it is true for all aesthetic objects. When a poet reads a poem aloud, he or she performs the work for us. And even when one reads a poem silently, there is never true silence: the words sound in the reader's mind, ringing and echoing as words always do. A painting, too, is performed. There is both the performance of its original construction and the performance of the audience that sees it. Jackson Pollock became famous for making the narrative of the construction of the painting central to the meaning of the painting, with drips of paint taking the viewer by the hand and walking him or her, Hansel-and-Gretel-bread-crumb-style, backward through the path that Pollock himself had taken through the forest of the canvas. We see the performance that created a Pollock painting quite easily, and as our eyes try to trace that path, we repeat the performance a second time (though like all repetitions, it is never exactly the same). This is an obvious case of performance, but the same is true for all painting. When we look at a Cézanne still life, there is a performance that necessarily created the work, but the artist doesn't wish us merely to repeat or reconstruct that narrative. Rather, Cézanne lets the viewer perform the painting her- or himself, uncovering a new story in the process. The performance begins thus: the viewer stands a certain distance from the canvas and is instantly thrown in space into the spatiality of the painting.[8] If, for instance, the painting is several feet away on a museum wall, but the painting is a painting of a table set with apples and oranges, the viewer instantly enters the spatiality (i.e., the world) of the painting and sees the table from Cézanne's perspective rather than his or her own. For example, if Cézanne painted the table as being about six feet away from him, and if the finished canvas is now on a museum wall ten feet away from the viewer, the viewer does not experience the table as being sixteen feet away. Instead, the viewer sees the table as six feet away, instantly collapsing the (apparent) distance between him- or herself and the wall.[9] This is what it means to *inhabit* the painting. This is what it means to have our consciousness always already "out" in the world. We think from a place inside the canvas because our consciousness is in the work of art. Once we begin to perform the painting from within, our eyes move around the canvas, focusing here and there. This takes time, and as time unfolds a performance takes shape. We move from left to right, or we dart back and forth, or we scan up and down, or we focus for a long time on one apple while ignoring the apple nearby, etc. What makes Cézanne one of the greatest artists of all time is his understanding of how such performances unfold and his ability to orchestrate an experience for the viewer that is rich, informative, beautiful, and rewarding. By painting the table and its contents from different perspectives, Cézanne makes it such that while our eyes move across the canvas it seems as if we are physically moving around the table. As in the Gorky drawing of a table in chapter 2, we walk around inside a Cézanne painting all while "standing still" in front of it, seeing this apple from the far right, this ginger pot from above and to the left, this orange from behind, etc. In the amazing *Madame Cézanne in a Yellow Chair* (1893–1895), if we move into the painting and then let our eyes scan from top to bottom, we can even see Madame Cézanne stand up from her seat to greet us! It is this movement within an animated canvas that, as we have seen, also made it possible for Gorky to meet his mother, to rush toward her over and over, in *The Artist and His Mother*. Performance is thus key to painting itself, and whether the body is thrown and the eye scans a soup can, a starry night sky, a man wearing a derby with an apple obscuring his face, or a series of melting clocks, it is always the case that we perform the work of art. Cézanne just knows this, makes use of it, and creates masterpieces like no other.

An aesthetic object is not exhausted by our experience of it, it does not represent something other than what it is, and it must be performed. What remains to be said is how the performance of an aesthetic object is particularly a performative *expression*. "Expression," here, is not meant to suggest that aesthetics is merely about the affective or emotive. Middle English from the late fifteenth century brought us the term from the Latin "expressio," which meant "a pressing or squeezing out." Thus, rather than suggesting, for instance, that an expression of a feeling is a *sign* of a feeling or something that points to the feeling, we must take an expression of a feeling to be an actual manifestation of a feeling, the bursting-forth not of something that is hidden or internal, but an acknowledgment of a feeling's being out in the world, because we are always already there. Further, the affective is not seen as dualistically related to rationality or reason, but is, instead, part of logos itself. When we press reason, the affective is found to be contained within and throughout. An expression is therefore an acknowledgment and a centering of attention on the way in which reason emotes, and a performative expression is one in which we enact, embody, feel, and think.

In Cézanne's *The Black Clock* (1869–1871), the clock, shell, lemon, tablecloth, etc., are in the world as I take them up. They are beyond me and not exhausted by my experience of them. I will never know them completely even if I might at some point know them well enough to make claims about them. Also, the painting does not represent a clock. I do not experience it as a mere image of a clock, but rather it is the black clock that is the object of my consciousness. Further, I must perform the painting, allowing the painting to move me in space and time even as my body and my gaze unfold a narrative of looking. Finally, I am asked to pay attention to what is *expressed* in the performance of the painting—i.e., what it means to feel, think, and be conscious of death, temporality, sexuality, and all the rest that is experienced with the world of the painting and thus necessarily in my world. All of this expression comes to bear on me and my worldview—I *feel* it shaping me and moving me—and I am changed. A good work of art does this in a major and meaningful way, but all works of art operate in the same manner. Just as a good conversation with someone can change my life, so can a good work of art. All conversations work in basically the same way. What marks a good conversation as apart from all of the others is the manner in which it unfolds and what is said within that conversation. And so it is with art as well. A finger painting fixed with magnets to a refrigerator door and the *Mona Lisa* in the Louvre call to us to think about the performative expression in each instance. They mean something different and change our world in different ways. At different times of our life they are, one hopes, just the sorts of conversations we need.

THIRD INSTALLATION

You Are Here: The Map Precedes the Territory—Live Satellite Feed from Iraq, 2008 (Chicago)

Description: A large sprawling installation with a table made from 120-year-old barn wood as its foundation sits inside a darkened room. The central table holds the majority of items with which the public is asked to interact. A satellite dish affixed to a 9' pole with a blinking strobe light is attached with cables to a wooden crate sitting on the table. Inside the crate there is a black-and-white monitor. The viewer is told that it is possible to see a live video feed from Iraq, scanning the desert across 360-degrees every 300 seconds. When one puts one's head into the crate, one can see the images of the video feed and even hear fighter jets pass over from time to time as well as people yelling in Arabic in the distance. In reality, the images are a recorded loop, and the desert is just outside Las Vegas. If the viewer waits long enough, the outline of the Las Vegas Strip comes into frame, the loud and abrupt sound of a slot machine paying off is heard, and the film flashes the words "YOU ARE NOT HERE BUT YOU ARE HERE" in bright white before resetting. What the people in the distance are yelling in Arabic are such things as: "This is not what you think it is. You are here but you are also there. You do not know where you are. The structures that support There and Here are the same," etc. There are two World War II battlefield telephones on the table. Both are connected to hidden tape players also set on a loop. The visitor is encouraged to pick up the phones and hear a conversation. The first conversation is in Arabic and concerns the nature of simulation, Jean Baudrillard, capitalism, and what constitutes our view of reality and how this makes political occupation possible. The other conversation is an edited version of President George W. Bush's "mission accomplished" speech in which he appears to be talking to himself. Also on the table are several other items, including books (the most important of which is an antique book on the military use of maps that also contains English translations of all of the Arabic spoken in the recorded pieces in the installation). Near the central table are free-standing side tables and barn doors resting to the sides of the table like ramps. Plastic army figures, many of which are burned and melted, are mounting an invasion of the table up the barn door ramps. A reel-to-reel tape recorder is at floor level where the army figures begin; some of the figures are on the reels, spinning. The tape that is playing—at a volume so low that one has to sit down on the floor and put one's ear to the speaker—is a recording of a soldier talking about posttraumatic stress disorder. Nearby, a restored, animated, seventy-year-old wooden mannequin in the form of a young boy is wearing a Soviet-issued gas mask, waving his arms when motion sensors indicate someone has come near. In one hand he holds a royal straight flush poker hand made of cards from the U. S. government-issued Iraq War deck. A 16-mm movie projector from the 1940s lights the mannequin from across the room, showing old war footage across the boy's face and body. A small table to the side of the projector houses a rotating laser that is pointed at a target saying "There." The rotating laser sweeps across a forty-five-degree arc, coming to focus on the "There" target in the center. The laser and target are encased in glass, and the internal walls inside are angled mirrors such that the laser light bounces infinitely from side to side as it moves, hitting the "There" target while also necessarily hitting all of the other targets inside the box as well. Beside the laser is a wooden table with a blue spotlight focusing on a miniature antique globe. The globe, dressed up like a pincushion with recently recovered one-inch flechette darts dropped from U.S. helicopters during the Vietnam War to kill Viet Cong hiding in the jungle, glows in the light.

Materials used: U. S. government Iraq War playing cards, 120-year-old barn wood and nails, child's Soviet Army GP-5 gas mask and canvas pouch, 1940s restored Silhouettes animated store mannequin, 16-mm movie reel and metal case, 1943 16-mm Moviegraph projector E-743, wooden rods, black wooden card table, unfinished pine card table, lasers, mirrors, motors, aluminum foil, plywood, toy globe, six-inch metal black fan propeller, six-volt motors, vintage desk globe, fishing line, G. I. Joe weapons, shell casings, antique hemp rope, blue LED light, strobe lights, satellite dish, enamel paint, World War II U. S. military phones, rusted tray table, U.S. Army dress greens 39R military uniform worn by a soldier

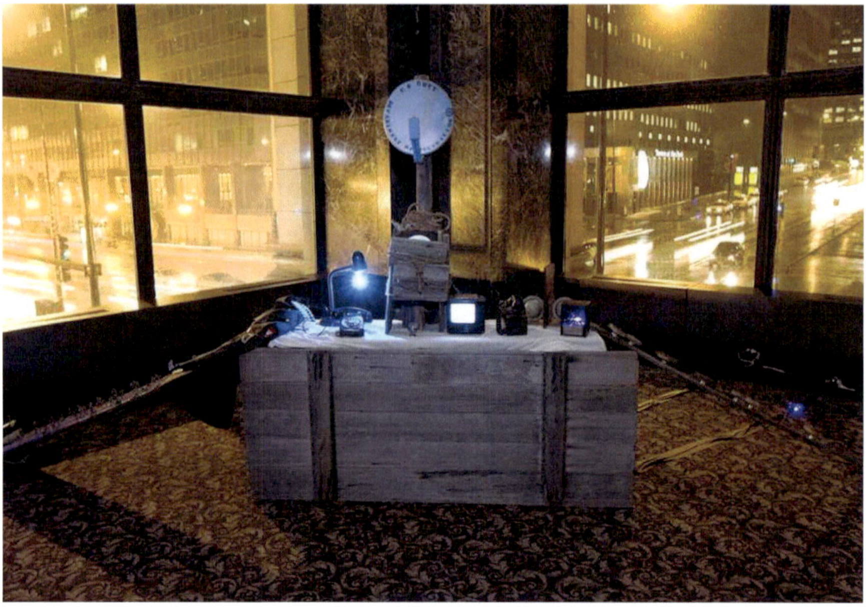

FIGURE 3.5. H. Peter Steeves. Detail of *The Map Precedes the Territory: Live Satellite Feed from Iraq*. 2008. Photograph by Monika Lozinska.

who was injured in a mine explosion, reel-to-reel recording of a Vietnam vet discussing his psychological case history, vintage plastic green army men, "Map Interpretation with Military Applications" (1943 first edition book), black-and-white portable television, antique magnifying lens, vintage reel-to-reel tape recorder, MP3 player, recently recovered one-inch flechette darts dropped from U.S. helicopters during the Vietnam war to kill Viet Cong hiding in the jungle, CD player, blue and black lights, 1940s child's intercom telephone play set, DVD player, twelve-volt motors, antique globe bookends, two U.S. Army ammunition boxes (7.62 small cal. and 50 cal.), shell casings, coaxial cable, crystal globe on brass stand, Russian Navy barometer.

Concepts themselves are tricky things. The history of philosophy is in many ways the history of our struggle to understand concepts. Plato, of course, considered concepts to be so important that he argued that they have more reality than our own physical world. "Tree," that is, is far more real than any tree we have ever seen. And so are "Freedom," "Beauty," "Love," and all other universals. For this reason, in part, Plato banished artists from his proposed utopia. A painting of a tree is a shadow of a physical tree, a shadow of a shadow, and thus even further removed from the true reality, the true Form, the true concept. Kant considered the search

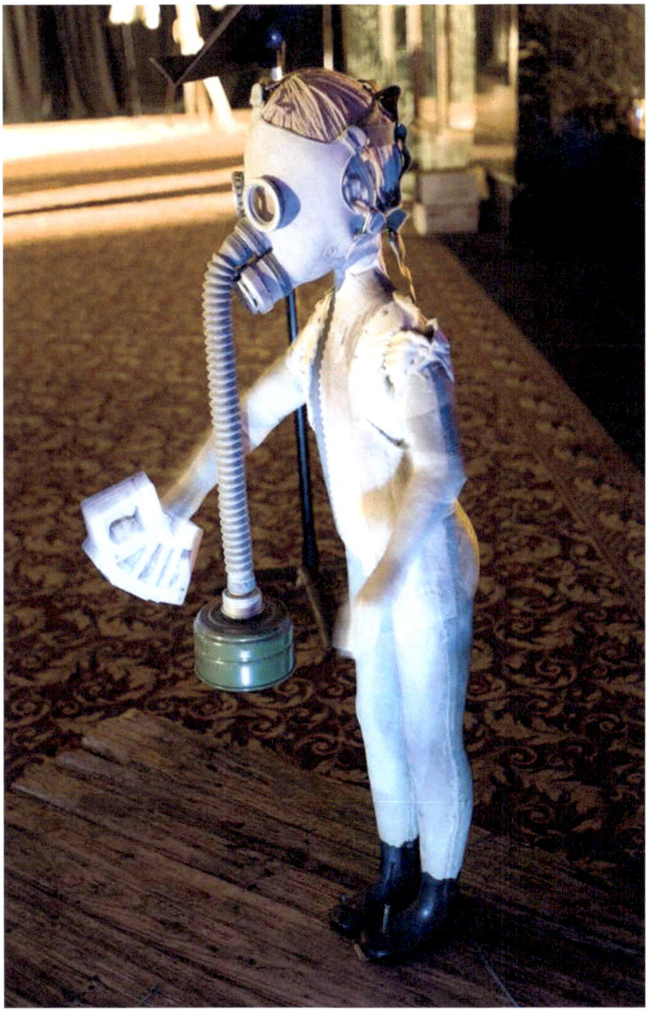

FIGURE 3.6. H. Peter Steeves. Detail of *The Map Precedes the Territory: Live Satellite Feed from Iraq*. 2008. Photograph by Monika Lozinska.

for a priori concepts—concepts that we have in our minds before we experience anything in the world, concepts that thus did not arise from experience and abstraction but are built into conscious thought as the transcendental possibility of thought itself—to be the foundation of all philosophy. In the twentieth century, Deleuze and Derrida also came to focus on concepts. Deleuze defines philosophy as "the activity of creating concepts."[10] And Derrida argues that our concepts are not universal and not a reflection of a reality that is "out there" in some objective scientific sense, but rather all of our concepts are constructs that carve up a malleable world.[11] The world can be carved up, that is, in an infinite number of ways. Concepts, and the language that embodies them, are used to keep the chaos at bay, but they do not reflect anything universally true or necessary in the old, metaphysical senses of such terms.

In English we get the word "concept" from the Latin "conceptus" which is from the past participle of "concipere." "Concipere" means "to conceive" (literally, "to take with"—also related to the Old French "concevoir"). "Conceiving" thus indicates a mental apprehending and a pregnancy, but also a "taking." As a result, a concept is a "taking with." It means we apprehend the world anew, give birth to a new world by becoming pregnant with a new worldview. We take things together that we did not take together before. Multiple trees are now seen as part of "Tree," for instance. The concept does this work for us.

It is important to note, however, that a concept has a violent force to it. It is a *taking*, not a receiving or a giving. It reaches out and grabs the world and forces it to give something up. Chaos is ordered; anarchy is held at bay. Things are now conceptually organized and structured. It is, perhaps, wise to remember that concepts have this power behind them and are, in some sense, always a conservative project—always trying to organize and classify and maintain a precise order, always conserving even when they seem radical and outlandish.

The worries of Plato and the hopes of Kant were metaphysical in nature, based on the belief that our experience of the world is separate from the world itself—indeed, even a distortion of the world that keeps us from knowing things, and the truth, as they really are. The goal of philosophy, according to metaphysics, is to remedy that problem. Philosophy is consequently thought to be unrelated to art and, in a concrete sense, separate from and opposed to daily life. It is this tradition of philosophy that we must overcome. And conceptual art, properly understood, helps us in this task, even as such a reimagined understanding of philosophy strives to help art in return. If art is not about representation, and if all art is performative expression, then the concepts employed are powerful indeed, but perhaps there can be a celebration of the chaos as that which makes an appropriate order appear. It will be a celebration that takes place even while we discuss the values inherent in our conceptualizations and the values that we should promote. This is not to say that art needs to be subservient to politics or ethics. This is not a prescription for propaganda. Rather, it is to realize that the very act of conceptualizing, and the very act of making art, is always already soaked through with moral decision-making. Even seeing, as we saw in chapter 1, has an ethic to it.

Conceptual art, then, is not different from any other type of art in an ontological way. Something is lost if we do not see Duchamp's urinal, do not get to stare at Rauschenberg's erasure, and do not walk through some lesser artist's installations. Simply to read or hear about these things is to be in the presence of them—and to be able to perform the concepts they are bringing to the fore—but it is to presence them in an absent way. All concepts, when not fleshed out fully, when not lived and explored and performed, are ethereal and ghostly, absently intended even while they are directly before us.

And if the artist's intention seems more important in conceptual art than other forms of art, this is just a reminder that conceptual art should be showing us that the opposite is always true. To think we understand an erasure if we know the famous sketch that has been erased is to think, falsely, that our only access to that sketch is outside what is given, outside in some narrative that the author or a commentator might tell us to let us in on the secret. This simply is not the case. First, because what is erased is still there on the page, the traces of its absence still reverberating and present for us to see. To be attuned to that absence, even to project our own erased pencil strokes, is the performance that rewards us. And second, because what is told to us directly by the artist is always just as suspect—and just as trustworthy—as what we can see for ourselves, even in conceptual art. Who is to say, really, that the most important point of Rauschenberg's erasure is what, specifically, has been erased? The background description and the statement of the author's intention are interesting, but they are not the work of art in full. Something is missing if we search them out singly and think we have found the world.

The world, too, figures in the "Earth art" of David Wood, a philosopher and artist who understands well the play of presence and absence—and understands the sense in which "world" always means "Earth." Wood's *Spiral Resonance Field*, for instance, is an on-site installation consisting of a double spiral of white poles decorated with solar lights and prismatic laserdiscs that begins in a central crater in New Mexico and then spirals outward. Without seeing it from above at some distance, one might not be thought to have the full sense of being in the whirlpool. But "full sense," here can be misleading, because one of the possible experiences of a vortex is to be inside of it, right on top of it, unable to see anything but the center; and such an experience is a full and legitimate experience of a vortex.[12] Similarly, Wood's *Chronopod* time-capsule art project literally buries the art beneath the earth. In November 2000, Wood created the *Apology*-themed chronopod, which he buried in the coastal dunes of Australia. The pod contained a variety of items, including a newspaper indicating that the U.S. presidential election was still undecided, with no one yet knowing whether Al Gore or George W. Bush would ascend to the post. Wood explains that the point of the time capsule was, in part, to attempt to apologize to aboriginal Australians for the original white colonists making a declaration of "Terra Nullius" (i.e., stating that the land was uninhabited). To one who knows about the capsule, its present-absence resounds in his or her consciousness every time he or she walks on the land above it. And even for those who have no idea that the capsule is buried beneath, the point is that the ideas of which it is a concrete manifestation—ideas that have to do with regret, apologies, roots, burial, forgetting, and pregnant land full of promise that has been betrayed—should, in fact, be in our minds at all times when walking on aboriginal earth, which means when walking on the Earth in general.

Furthermore, should I encounter a few centimeters of a brass rod sticking out of the ground while walking through a forest, even if I do not know that there is a full kilometer more buried straight below me, I need to be intrigued and amazed and overcome by the beauty of it all in the same way that I need to learn to see and feel the endless rhizomes connecting the forest life, the arterial roots of trees branching out for miles around me as they search for water and comingle their damp fingery tendrils, the web of life and nonlife that is always underfoot supporting me and lifting me up and asking to be seen in all of its unseen glory when all that might be *visible* is just the tip of it all. Metaphysics, and the scientific worldview in which the world is reduced to data and only that which can be presently present, presently measured, presently controlled, and fully known can appear, blinds us. But to miss the hidden

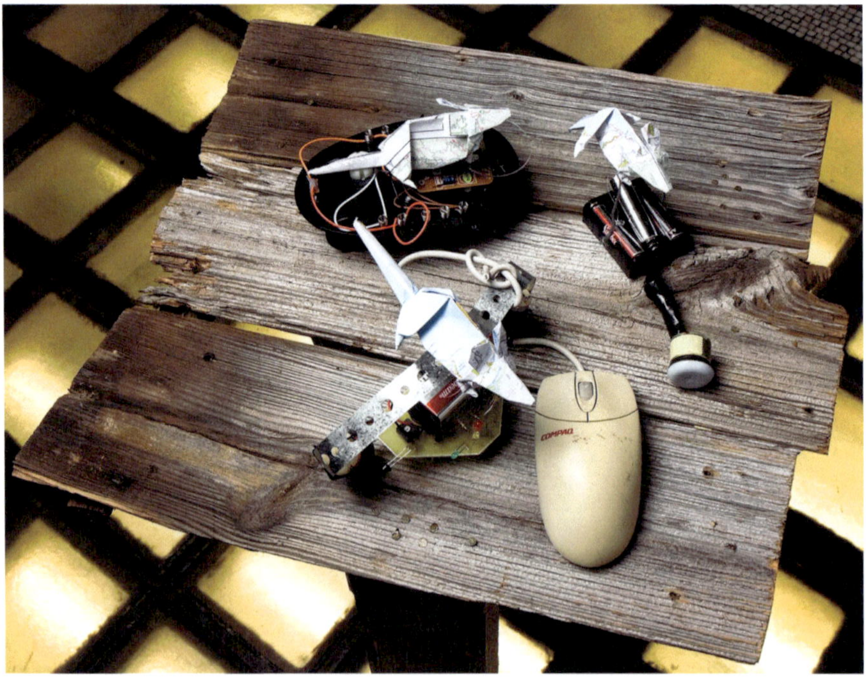

FIGURE 3.7. H. Peter Steeves. Detail of *The Lab Is Dystopia*. 2008. Photo courtesy of John Sisson Photography, www.sissonphotography.com.

kilometer that is always there in all art and in the world around us would be to miss the aesthetic altogether. To miss all of this would be to miss the point. To miss all of this would be to miss the art, to miss our cue to be on stage and perform our world, to miss being alive.

FOURTH INSTALLATION

You Are Here: The Lab Is Dystopia, 2008 (Chicago)

Description: Using old bricks and 2 foot x 4 foot boards from a dismantled nineteenth-century barn, a maze is constructed on the floor of a room. The maze spans 625 square feet, inside of which the viewer encounters a variety of robots. Nearly all of the robots look like mice or have map-origami mice on top of them (i.e., pages of maps that have been folded into origami mice and affixed on top of the robot base). The public, always outside the maze, plays the role of the scientist, either torturing or rescuing the animals inside by using various remote controls and other devices to change the environment and alter the behavior of the robots. There are two remote controls that move

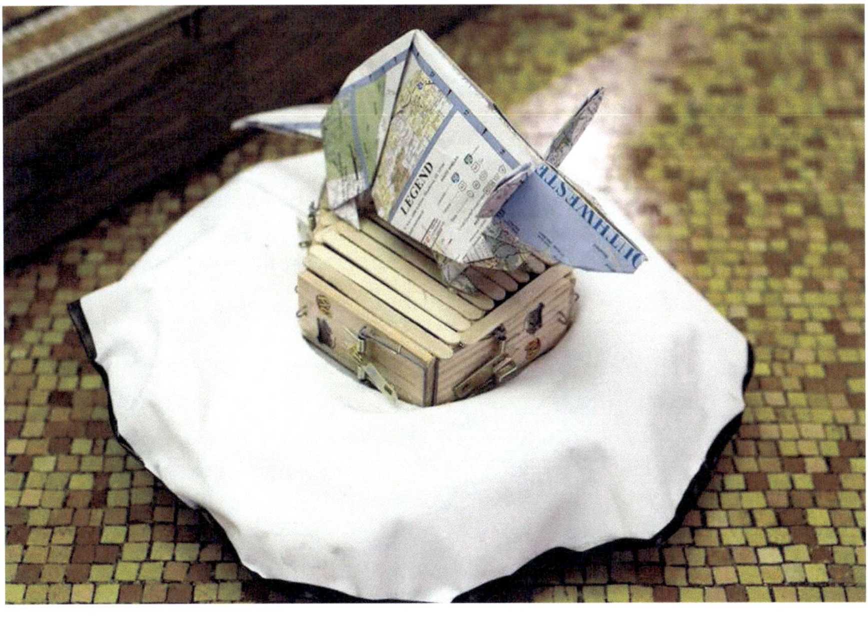

FIGURE 3.8. H. Peter Steeves. Detail of *The Lab Is Dystopia*. 2008. Photo courtesy of John Sisson Photography, www.sissonphotography.com.

the humanoid robotic scientist (standing approximately twenty inches tall and dressed in a white lab coat), and the operator is left to choose whether to help or hinder the mice in their project of being forced to map the scientist's (i.e., the viewer's) maze. Some of the robots feel their way around the edges of the maze, methodically mapping it out as they try to escape; others move randomly. Some respond to sound, light, and/or the proximity of a physical barrier. Viewers are encouraged to shout at the robots to find the ones that respond to sound, to shine the antique flashlights provided to see which ones respond to light, etc. Some mice have been in the maze far too long and scurry, spin, and pace without reason. There is also a cat robot in the maze, programmed to follow the robotic scientist until he encounters a mouse robot, at which point the cat robot autonomously attempts to destroy the mouse robot with his jaws and paws. The maze is completely enclosed. It has no start, no center, no finish, and no exit.

Materials used: Tiffany lamp pieces, bricks from a demolished school, 120-year-old barn wood, antique hemp rope, antique maps, parts from several Roomba I-robots, various motors and gears, batteries, infrared sensors, photocells, heat sensors, sound sensors, nineteenth-century stained glass panels, tongue depressors, motion detectors, various computer mice, refurbished Robosapien redesigned and outfitted in a white lab coat, vintage cloth fabric, antique flashlights, robotic killer cat (designed by the artist), various salvaged and original small robots and mechanical parts, mousetraps.

If the world is ever-malleable, then the concepts we choose to promote and live carry with them ethical and social-political import at every step because they do not exist on their own but rather are our organization of the world, our re-ordering of the chaos even as we celebrate it, our choices against a backdrop of rules that limit us and make choice possible. With such living comes responsibility. To organize the world this way instead of that—to make art about X instead of Y, to celebrate A instead of B, to call this into further absence and bring that into greater presence—is thus a decision that is at once aesthetic, ontological, political, and ethical. In the end it is surely the case not only that the activity of thinking is itself a sort of conceptual art, as thinking organizes and remakes the world, but that the artist her- or himself helps us think, elucidating concepts, introducing new concepts, exploring the nature of concepts, and demonstrating how our minds and the world with which they are engaged are a living aesthetic experience. That we live this life and this art together is a necessary implication of such truth—a realization of a responsibility, and if we do it right, a joy, that has no start, no center, no finish, and no exit.

SECTION 2

Moving Pictures and Memory

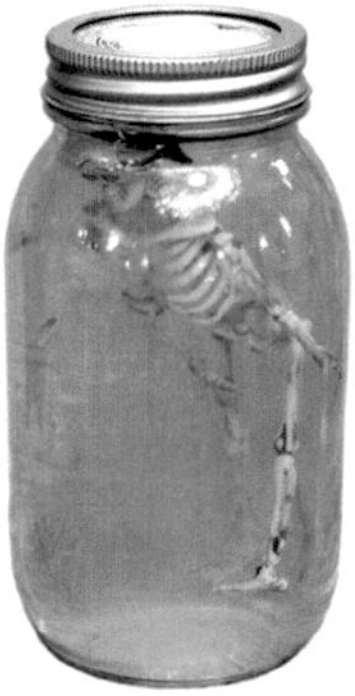

CHAPTER 4

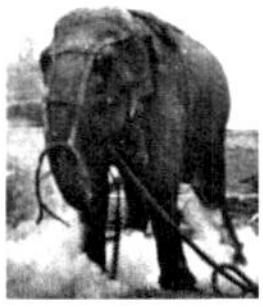

The Doubling of Death in the Films of Michael Haneke

> I've been accused of "raping" the audience, and I admit to that freely. All movies assault the viewer in one way or another. I'm trying to rape the viewer into independence.
>
> —Michael Haneke

Michael Haneke's film *Caché* (2005) plods along slowly. The mood is tense and the tone is somber, but very little actually happens. Until, without warning, everything changes one hour and twenty-seven minutes into the movie, when French television personality Georges Laurent (played by Daniel Auteuil) arrives at the apartment of an Algerian man, Majid (played by Maurice Bénichou), whose parents used to work for Georges's parents when both men were little boys. Majid tells Georges that he wants him to be present for something, at which point the man pulls out a straight razor and slashes his own neck, immediately collapsing on the floor. The blood splatters across the door and wall. Georges stands immobilized, the camera still and unmoving for more than a full minute. And then life goes on.

One of the hallmarks of Haneke's films is a shocking and always unexpected violence, even when we have come to know the filmmaker well. It is the sort of violence that hangs with us long after we watch the film, precisely because it appears so "real." Yet, what is the difference between artistic violence and "real" violence? Does the audience's assumption that the death they see in films is fake give them license to enjoy that violence? Or is something much more complex at work, something that makes Haneke's films particularly interesting and particularly disturbing?

Of course, the human actors in these films are not actually killed. Haneke is European, moody, and avant-garde, but he still hasn't made a true snuff film—at least not yet. The question of what constitutes *real* violence and *real* death is something that must concern us, but there is, in fact, one obvious way in which there are elements of so-called real death on-screen, particularly in terms of the nonhuman actors.

We often read during the credits of movies made in the United States that "no animals were harmed during the making of this film"; in a Haneke film, however, we never receive this assurance because the animals who die—pigs, fish, chickens, and so on—are real and their deaths are real. Haneke's exotic fish, for instance, truly suffocate—these fish whose aquarium is smashed by a family destroying every object in their home in the film *The Seventh Continent* (1989). The fish's death, like the death of the inanimate objects destroyed in the film as well as the deaths of the human characters, is shot calmly and without melodrama. Haneke has claimed that the aquarium-smashing scene was filmed several times, and the fish each time were scooped up in order to "use them again" with only a few of them dying—probably "from shock"—in the end.[1] But this is rather hard to believe. Even in *Benny's Video* (1992), where Benny, a young teenage boy, watches the graphic slaughter of a pig over and over on videotape, there is a sense that death has become removed from us through technology: the stoic eye of Haneke's camera—languid, calm, and unrushed to judgment or to the next scene—appears to be without moral bias (*see figure 4.1*).

This is, of course, not the case. Morality is never something that is added on to bare experience, but instead is always already there, suffusing the world and our experience of the world at every step. As we will see in chapter 7, the presence of the animal, and the ethics of our relations with animals, are there in the food that we eat every day, too, even when that food is not "real" meat but is, instead, an artistic rendering of an animal such as a veggie burger. Is there violence, too, in the artistic death of the animal? Given the complexities of the way in which Haneke manipulates this question in his films, it is, perhaps, best to start thinking about the way in which we conceptualize artistic violence and death in general with the death of animals specifically in cinema.

Do we feel differently about nonhuman animal deaths, cinematic or otherwise, compared to the deaths of humans? Though some viewers are undoubtedly vegetarians, many in the films' audience eat the sorts of animals Haneke has killed; and, like it or not, we all participate in the institutions of modern life that make possible the killing and torturing of animals every day. Perhaps what bothers us is that, strictly speaking, we know that the death of animals is unnecessary. This is true both in day-to-day life (for none of us truly needs to eat meat to live), and it is true in cinema (for no animal truly needs to die just to entertain us).

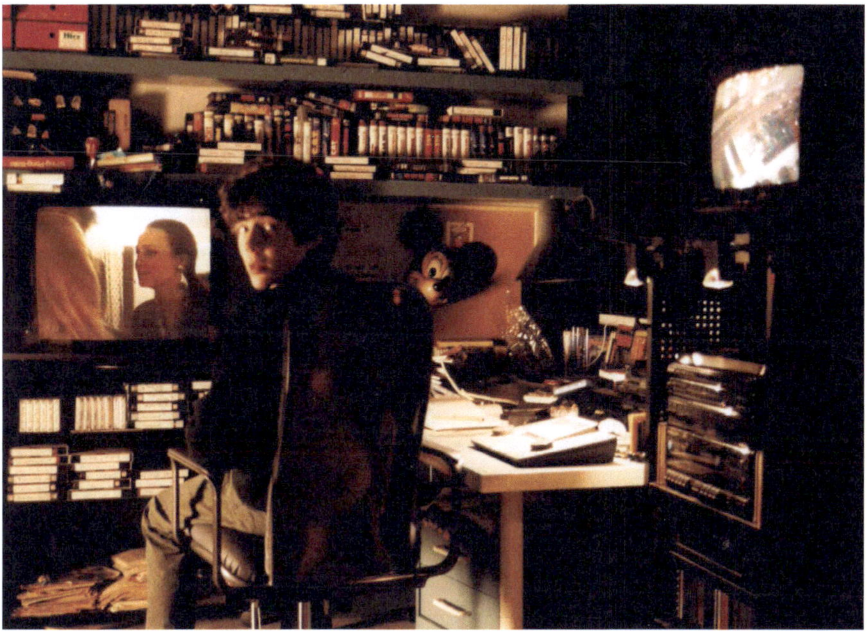

FIGURE 4.1. Still from the film *Benny's Video.* 1992. Dir. Michael Haneke. Courtesy of WEGA-Filmproduktionsges.m.b.H.

But perhaps it is true in different ways. In *Benny's Video*, the pig dies, presumably, to become dinner. For many viewers, such a death is probably more understandable and thus more acceptable than the deaths of other animals on film that take place for no apparent reason other than aesthetics (as is the case, apparently, with the fish in *The Seventh Continent*). Haneke once observed in an interview that audience members objected strongly to the killing of the fish, presumably because people could not see the reason for such "unnecessary" suffering onscreen. These are, after all, beautiful and expensive fish meant for decoration or pleasure; it is in *living* that they are useful to us—as opposed to the pig who is more useful as a consumable object and not as a pet.

Perhaps we do not wish to think of any animal suffering; perhaps we do not wish to think of ourselves measuring animals merely by their use-value. But Haneke's camera forces such thinking, lingering on the suffering of each being to whom violence is being done. The unmoving camera, as always, does not flinch or cut away from the desperately squealing pig (*Benny's Video*), the headless rooster flapping helplessly in his death throes (*Caché*), the laboring gills of the fish as they slowly suffocate on the living room floor (*The Seventh Continent*), silent horses with their throats slit (*The Time of the Wolf* [2004]), or the bird impaled by scissors on a desk (*The White Ribbon* [2009]). There is a reason we flinch a bit when a man finally manages to snatch up a pigeon in *Amour* (2012); it's surprising, in fact, that instead of smothering it, as we expect, he actually caresses it. The apparent reasons these animals die are different, and their deaths mean something different for each film, but do we not think that their suffering is the same? And do we not admit that the end result is necessarily the same as well?

Does art have a license to kill—especially when the killing fulfills merely aesthetic ends? In terms of humans, there are no truly "*bad* guys" in Haneke's films; and those who die are often main characters. It is not as if these humans are being killed off in the name of justice. Such cinematic human deaths are also, in the simplest sense of the word, *unnecessary*. Those who are killed are killed seemingly without reason, and those who do the killing offer no answers.

Of course, Haneke cannot legally kill human actors on-screen—it is doubtful anyone would sign up for such a role. Therefore their deaths, however realistic, are fake. But is there actually a distinction between the real death of a character and the fake death of an actor? If Haneke could find some human willing to die on-screen, how would our experience of seeing the film be different? Phenomenologically, this is a complicated question. A real actor would die, but the character would also be dead—the same kind of dead—in either case; and assuming that the audience does not know one way or the other, the movie-going experience would remain the same. If, however, it were announced beforehand that the actor actually died while making the film, we would have a completely different experience, and would probably be unable to separate the death of the actor from the death of the character. Interestingly, we would be "taken out" of the experience, moving from an act of direct perception to one of imagination such that the imagination would require us to imagine reality.

When Hamlet stabs Polonius in act 3, scene 4 of Shakespeare's *Hamlet*, we do not pull out a cellphone and dial 911. Such a deranged and panicked theater-goer would not be having an experience of *the play Hamlet*. However, if that theater-goer does not care at all—does not feel a jump, a start, a momentary wish to do something and a lingering feeling of trepidation and doom after the stabbing—then the play has not been doing its job as art. Having the right balance of emotional investment and sense of the fictional means that we can take the action to be real, where "real" indicates something other than what could be settled by an appeal to a correspondence theory of truth. We are trying to get at another aspect of *expression*, then—something deeper than what we uncovered in the previous chapter when we found that the emotional relation we have to art is embodied in a performance and is inseparable from our rational engagement with it.

Suppose Haneke filmed and then asked us to watch a human dying. Would we find here the first doubling of death? In the story, on paper, and on-screen, that character ceases once and for all to exist, and so, too, does the actor. They die together, though separately. In the case of nonhuman animals, however, it is far more complicated. The fish, the chicken, and the pig play themselves—they are both acting and not acting. They most likely have no conscious, trained, or intentional role in the film, and so their deaths are as characters, unintentional actors, as well as real animals simultaneously. In the context of the films themselves, all of the deaths are final, regardless of whether an actor leaves the soundstage that day intact or not. The actor's life is not at stake *except in the case of animals.* Which is, perhaps, why viewers object more to the deaths of the animals. Their deaths appear to extend out from the film into real life, and for what reason? Juxtaposed with the deaths of the fictional characters with which they share the screen, how do such deaths talk to each other? What do they say to the audience?

In an act of imagination, human death would be different. If we were to see, say, Juliette Binoche actually die on-screen in *Caché* we would no longer think, "Oh, that character is dead." We would also think, "Oh, Juliette Binoche is dead." This realization would take the viewer away from the movie and into the implications of the apparent real death—the death of the actress looming larger than the death of a make-believe character.[2] But how do we consider the death of the rooster in that same movie? Do we mourn at all, and if we do, what are we mourning? How far from the film this animal death takes us is typically a function of whether or not we wonder if what we are watching is real or somehow staged. But there is a deeper sense in which the animal's nonbeing is at stake. When an animal is slaughtered on-screen, it is, in some sense, merely the character that is killed, for animals are thought not to possess a real identity in the world.

Think, for instance, of Lassie, a dog that exists as a character but also in life as a real dog—or a set of real dogs—who "play" Lassie on-screen. We might identify far more with the death of such a beloved animal if Haneke were to have her shot in one of his films, but we might not really think of the actual dog who would die if Lassie were actually to die on-screen. Lassie per se would still be a dog available to us in the movies (as an aesthetic creation), and it would be a character we would mourn. We might be outraged that an actual animal, as with Haneke's animals in general, was killed for the sake of a film, but consider how different our reaction would be to this death compared to the death of Juliette Binoche on- and off-screen. Lassie does not exist off-screen—"Lassie" is many dogs over many years, each nameless and replaceable—but Binoche supposedly does exist off-screen. Binoche, while being many women in many films, is, we think, one woman in *reality* (whatever that means), and it is that identity that would spark a different kind of outrage than that which is aroused by an anonymous animal's death. In *Funny Games* (1997), for instance, two young men terrorize and murder a family over the course of an evening. The family dog, though, is the first death of the film. Knowing Haneke, one wonders if that dog is really still alive (whatever the word "really" really means). But we somehow rest easy thinking that Susanne Lothar and Ulrich Mühe (or Naomi Watts and Tim Roth from the 2007 American remake that Haneke directed) are still around.

Those of us who take issue with the realness of animal deaths question their necessity on- and off-screen, but we do not necessarily question the necessity of cinematic human deaths, at least not in the same way. Whether or not we think the human characters *had* to die, we all understand on some level the fact that they need to die for the film to be as it is—the film that Haneke intended to make. We may not like it, we may think it is stupid, we may be upset that the films are so violent and people may be watching them and getting frightening ideas, but we do not question the fundamental necessity of the characters' deaths to achieve the filmmaker's goal—in other words, we allow him the authority to do as he wishes with the characters, whether we like or enjoy the narrative or not, because it seems *merely* a question of aesthetics and not morality. The director has creative freedom. But we *do* question the animal deaths and we do debate their necessity in the creation of Haneke's "art": why can't he just use special effects, as most films do, to simulate the violence? What is to be gained with this murderous waste?

Heidegger, of course, maintains that nonhuman animals cannot die. Animals, he explains, merely perish.[3] As poor-in-world, animals and animal-being are distanced from *Dasein*, that particular manner of human being that supposedly marks us, individualizes us, and situates us in the world as something unique. For Heidegger, the mineness of my own being is inescapable. No one can die for me—my death is radically mine—and thus no one can live for me either. But animals, creatures who supposedly are not world-forming and are separated from logos by a chasm that cannot be crossed, have no individual deaths, no death at all, really, of which to speak. Animal actors will never find their deaths singled out, let alone doubled by art.

It is perhaps not an accident, historical or otherwise, that one of the very first films ever made was of the death of an animal. In 1903, Thomas Edison, showing off both his filmmaking advancements and his mastery over electricity, famously electrocuted an elephant named Topsy, filming the slaughter to play the short movie for audiences across the country (*see figure 4.2*). The one-minute film, *Electrocuting an Elephant* (1903), was meant to help persuade the public of the dangers of Nikola Tesla's AC electricity, the type of electricity competing with Edison's own proposed DC plan for the nation. Throughout the late 1800s all across New Jersey, Edison had electrocuted countless dogs and cats—hundreds of animals, in fact—using AC electricity, hoping to sabotage the Westinghouse Company which stood as AC's most outspoken proponent and Edison's biggest competitor. In the short film showcasing Topsy-the-elephant's death, we see—in long shot for the most part, though there are moments of excruciating close-up—the animal *actually*

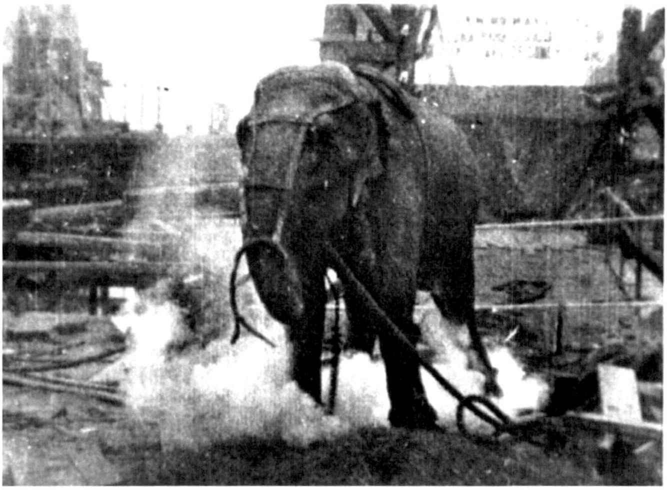

FIGURE 4.2. Still from the film *Electrocuting an Elephant*. 1903. Dir. Thomas Edison.

being executed. Haneke, in many respects, lets his camera work in such a documentarian fashion. One must wonder about the politics here as well.

Indeed, what precisely marks animal death as special on film is the animal's assumed inability to die. From Descartes on, animals have been taken to be machines, and so what better way to present animality to us than through the technological gauze of the camera? As Akira Lippit has argued, the disclaimer that "'No animal was harmed in the making of this film' serves as a form of erasure that brings the death of the animal back into the ethical folds of the human world. But the disclaimer—a disavowal of animal death—never resolves the crisis, only defers it."[4] It is filmmaking itself that provides anima, animation, animality to that which was a lifeless picture and mere static representation. The still camera supposedly makes of things dead objects; the filmmaker's camera puts them into action, allows them movement, and *animates*. Is the animal thus reanimated on film or animated truly for the first time by film? If an image points toward the way in which anything can be made to die, to be still, and not merely to perish, we might say that there is a necessary "animalation" that takes place in cinema. Haneke's work is thus ontologically as well as ethically disturbing, doubling the stakes even as it doubles the possibility of death.

What, then, of the death of humans—what of the same sort of confusion and unresolved questions about life and what moves us, what *animalates* us? Before it is possible to respond to the question of a violent human death, we must first ask about Haneke's relationship to human violence in general.

For the film *Code Unknown* (2000), Juliette Binoche was asked to slap a child.[5] Haneke demanded that the slap be real for fear that it otherwise might look fake and thus pull the viewer out of the fictional moment on film. The nonfictional, that is, is put in service of the fictional. Binoche—the actress, not the character (whatever that means)—recalls not only how difficult it was for her to enact this real violence on a real child, but how impossible it was for Haneke to watch the scene being filmed. "It was very hard to slap the little boy," explains Binoche. "Michael didn't want to involve himself too closely. He told me, 'It's O.K.' But I could see in the little boy's eyes that it was a kind of humiliation. I asked [the boy] to slap me first, but he wouldn't."[6]

We might be tempted to say that this is a special case because it involves violence being enacted on an innocent child. There is something in most of us that recoils when a child is the subject of violence. And yet, this is very telling. If we avert our eyes and condemn acts of violence against innocent children, are we secretly admitting that acts of violence against adults are in general more acceptable because adults are inherently less innocent? This would seem to commit us to the belief that some acts of violence are not as bad as others because the person to whom the violence is directed is guilty of at least something.

If it is not a question of innocence, then perhaps it is a question of power. Perhaps, that is, we think of the child as powerless and vulnerable. And thus violence directed at children—and, for that matter, animals—would be doubly bad because they cannot fight back. Haneke seems to be arguing for this when he tells us:

> You can show all the shortcomings of a society through its children, because they are always on the bottom rung. So are animals. They are those who can't defend themselves. They are predestined victims. . . . Once I bawled out a lady in a train. She was with her child, who was a bit stressed, and she took him out of the compartment and hit him, because she didn't dare to do it inside. And even though I had no right to do so, I went and bawled her out, because that is something I just cannot stand.[7]

There are four things to note in passing here. First is the identification of children and animals. If the boundary between humans and other animals is to be questioned, perhaps this is the spot to begin picking at Haneke: children and animals, he wants to argue, have much in common. Second, there is the notion that the whole of society can be judged by the way it treats its lowest members. Such an ethic, or at least a descriptive claim that is on the way toward an ethic, is not new. We find it in Buddhism, Christianity, and dozens of other cultural moral schemas. But perhaps there is something telling about the assumption of a hierarchy at the very start. Third, we would be wise to note that Haneke is most upset by violence against children and animals because these individuals cannot fight back. That is, they cannot meet violence with more violence, as if somehow violence is not quite as bad if the victim is capable of being violent in return. We are tempted to think that what might be offending Haneke is not the immorality of violence, but a *disrespect* of violence itself. In other words, if the child or the pig or the fish could fight back—could bring more violence to the table—then it would not be so bad. But they are too weak. The morally bad part becomes, in effect, the *stopping* of the cycle of violence. And this should trouble us. An eye for an eye for an eye for an eye et cetera thus becomes less bad than simply poking out a child's eye and having it stop there. We might be wise to keep in mind, then, that there could be an underlying promotion of violence in finding violence against animals and children overly abhorrent. Fourth, and finally, Haneke's choice to conclude his remarks with a reference to a real incident from his own real life involving a real woman and a real act of violence against a real child is interesting. He slips from an analysis of what he is doing on film to a recounting of what he once did in life, as if the latter should help explain the former, always and again standing in service to it. He offers up what amounts to an apology for having Juliette Binoche slap a child on film by evening out the cosmic scale of justice and taking to task a real woman who slapped her real child off camera. Here, Haneke is careful to tell us that he did not enact violence against the woman—other than the vocal and emotional violence of yelling at her. Indeed, perhaps it is important that it is a "lady" and not a "gentleman" in Haneke's story. Perhaps he means to say that women, too, are like children and animals.

We tread lightly inside the mind of Michael Haneke, wanting to avoid a purely psychoanalytic reading of his work. But we cannot help but note how many times he has said in interviews that his mother was more like an angel than a human, how often he proclaims his undying love for his mother, how emotionally he speaks of his mother's overwhelming physical and otherworldly beauty. Haneke's father is not to be found here—as was the case in the young Haneke's real life as well. "I grew up with three women," the filmmaker explains. "My grandmother, my mother, and my aunt. It was *great*. . . . I had a very spoiled childhood. I didn't have to fight with a man. . . . I was never beaten."[8] The real threat of violence is, for Haneke, the threat of the possible appearance of the male. When Haneke thinks of something other than animal, child, or woman, he thinks of death and violence. Indeed, so great is this fear of possible impending disruption and violence that Haneke—both the man and the man-who-is-filmmaker—will happily make a preemptive strike against the potentially violent male, thus becoming the abuser himself, thus starting the cycle of violence himself, *thus becoming the violent male*. Consider: one of the few men in Haneke's early life was his uncle, someone Haneke describes as a "huge man." "There was a moment with my uncle," the filmmaker confesses, "[when] I thought he was going to hit me, so I pushed him [first] . . . and he fell over."[9]

After leaving the safety of his female-populated home, Haneke went off to the university in Vienna. He enrolled to study theater, but after one semester he switched to philosophy. He kept up with the philosophy major for a time, but ultimately found it unsatisfying. Men, potentially violent men, are, as usual, all around in philosophy. As Haneke recalls it, "[I] met a distinguished Hegelian. . . . I thought he would explain the world to me, but I [came to understand] it's not the case."[10] Before real damage could be done, Haneke intellectually pushed Hegel and the Hegelian over. And turned to filmmaking.

There is a quality to the deaths portrayed in Haneke's films that is uncanny. Most of the deaths are unexplained and unexpected. Even in the case of *The Seventh Continent,* which is based on a true story (whatever that means), the deaths, more clearly foreshadowed than in much of Haneke's other work, still retain a sense of mystery: Why do the members of this family commit a sort of group suicide? Why does the man cut his throat in *Caché*? Why does Benny kill the girl in *Benny's Video*? Why are most of the children in *The White Ribbon* (2009) apparently homicidal? Typically there is absolutely no explanation attempted; but even when the characters explain their actions, or the intent of actions may be inferred, no matter how skillfully the explanation is stitched together by the audience, the deaths are still closed to us—perhaps because we are still necessarily alive.

These are not horror films in the normal sense of the term. These are not horror films unless we see all of life as already horrific. If we try to ask why the violent people are acting the way they are acting, we will never get an answer out of Haneke. And this is, perhaps, because to ask such a question is to imply that we don't already have the answer. That is, if we ask, "How could those boys in *Funny Games* sadistically torture that family and kill the dog and the family members off one by one?" we are saying that we are not like that, that we cannot imagine how someone could do that because that sort of action is so completely alien to who we are. But this, argues Haneke, is a bit of bad faith. The truth to which he is pointing is that we are all capable of such things. We each think that we follow truth and beauty in service of peace, but this blinds us to the violence we enact in the course of such pursuits. Haneke explains: "In the name of a beautiful idea you can become a murderer. . . . There is no crime I couldn't have committed. . . . It's so easy to say 'Oh no I would never do that,' but that's dishonest. We are capable of everything. . . . It's so easy to be 'human' when you come from a privileged background. . . . The only reason that I couldn't have been a Nazi is that I can't stand crowds."[11]

Perhaps. But like the characters in Haneke's films who survive, we are left with the consequences and attempts at explanations of violence which, coming before and after the acts themselves, still do not reveal what goes on in that space in between. The camera is there, unmoving, giving us the details. We hear and see death, we watch it happen, but still in the most vital sense *we are not there.* We are, and can only be, viewers. Even Benny cannot know what it is like to die, no matter how many times he watches his video of a pig dying, no matter if he kills his girlfriend, experiences that dying firsthand, and repeatedly watches her death on video as well. He will, indeed, get to "see what it is like," but he will never *know* what it is like until he himself dies. And, to be sure, he (and we) will not know what death is like even at that point, for death is never an experience, never something that takes place for the subject, never something that we can pass through, reflect on, and then can say, "So, that was death." Our own death is an impossible possibility. It is nothing and yet the ground of everything. Death is only experienced as the death of the Other.

We observe Benny as he does many things—goes to school, watches videos, opens and eats a container of yogurt, makes pizza with his friend, shoots a girl and watches her die—but we don't come any closer to the actual knowledge of *why* he does any of these things. The same holds true for the family members in *The Seventh Continent*—we see, in exquisitely minute detail, how they manipulate and manage the objects around them. We know what they eat, where they work, what they wear, how they draw, how they speak to one another—but we still do not know *why they die,* even as we watch how they do it, even as we hear the husband's voice explain, calmly and rationally, the "reasons" behind their deaths. All we know is that one moment there is a whole family there. Then they poison their daughter. And she is dead. Soon, the parents kill themselves as well. And they are dead. And for us, life goes on.

The audience can see and respond, can feel and think, but cannot die with the characters on-screen. And that blank space between the actor and the observer is where the experience of death happens. It is a space we cannot access, and it is the place wherein our responses to Haneke's deaths are manufactured—our fear, or disgust, or confusion, or apathy, or rage, or anger, or sadness. All of our responses to death off-screen as well.

The suicide in *Caché* is one of Haneke's most elliptical deaths. We simply don't have enough information about the character even to begin to grasp why he does what he does. Is his life, as his son asserts, miserable because of what Daniel Auteuil's character did to him so many years ago? Since it is the case that we cannot understand, we are thus asked to stand with the indirect murderer who cannot take responsibility for his actions, who can only see from inside a position of privilege. Watching this man cut his throat—watching him live one moment and in the next, suddenly and without warning, *not* live—is most like watching the pig or the chicken or the fish; there is a heavy sense of distance, an unknowableness that accompanies all death, but these in particular. We do not know what pigs, chicken, and fish think when they die. Because we do not have enough knowledge, our feelings remain abstract to varying degrees. It is terrible to watch a girl suffer as she is shot repeatedly, as it is terrible to watch a family's despair as they take their lives one by one, but is it terrible because we know death itself is terrible or because we can't imagine if it truly is or isn't?

Haneke's films revolve visually around objects—we get varied close-ups of ordinary items (cereal bowls, yogurt cups, coffeepots, and so on) where the object is the focus, and the manipulator (the hand pouring the coffee, the arm delivering the cereal to the off-screen mouth) is on the periphery, visual only in part while the inanimate object enjoys center stage. The camera, as always, does not move, does not get distracted by voices off-screen, does not turn to give us visual cues from the actors: we stay, as we do in any Haneke shot, squarely focused in front of us. Haneke's camera is not an animate camera, it is not a camera that moves to help us or distract us. If a woman is ironing on-screen then we will watch her iron, and that action is made just as important as the more subtle, emotional action taking place within the person performing the action. This kind of emphasis on the object seems to point to the idea that what we know comes first from what we *do*—we become interested, as Haneke himself says, in people and in actions through the objects that invite or submit to manipulation. And if we are not doing the things we see—if we are not pouring the coffee, eating the cereal, or shooting the gun—then how can we make a connection? We have driven cars, we have gone shopping, we have ironed, but not one of us has died. Haneke thus gets us into the visual habit of supplying the emotional content of a scene by projecting ourselves doing the mundane tasks required by life—we imagine ourselves as the double of the characters—and then he hits us with death and asks the viewer: now, can you imagine *this?*

All we can say is: no. We cannot imagine death as anything more than a specter, the ghost of death, the possible impossibility and yet necessity of our own eventual nonbeing. And this is, perhaps, why we turn to art. In chapter 6 we will consider the possibility that our current cultural way of trying to think about death and think what it is to mourn is by means of the zombie. If anything, Haneke is zombifying the mundane—or perhaps saying that there is no need for the supernatural in a world in which the natural is already so terrifying and terrifyingly pointed toward nonbeing. Aesthetics does a far better job of helping us confront this than does metaphysics.

Consider what happens when we go from a family eating a lavish supper to a family engaged in the destruction of their home and of themselves. We see them flushing their life savings down the toilet, and we learn that Haneke actually used real money to film this scene: real money is being used up and flushed away (*see figure 4.3*). All in the name of art; all in the name of making a point?

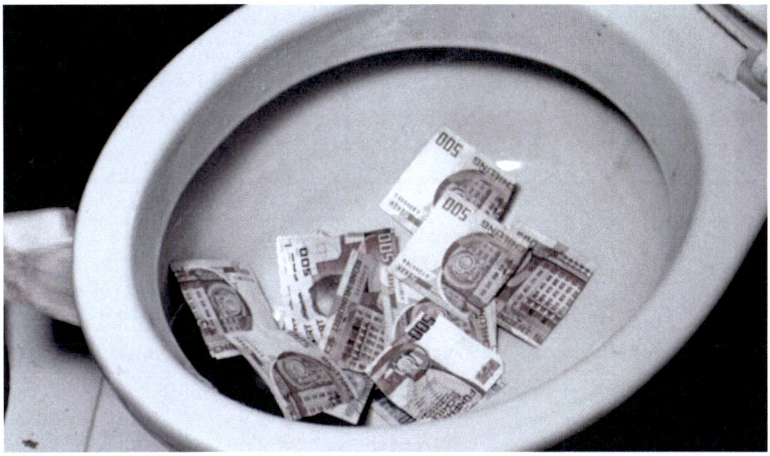

FIGURE 4.3. Still from the film *The Seventh Continent*. 1989. Dir. Michael Haneke. Courtesy of WEGA-Filmproduktionsges.m.b.H.

And yet isn't this always the nature of art? We watch the family destroy everything around them in unimaginable acts of violence, and we say that we feel lost in this movie. But *where* do we get lost and what happens when we realize we are lost—when we realize that we have been left behind in the narrative but are still somehow involved, participating by watching? We have passed by the safety of the last scene we understand—opening a bottle of wine, or answering a telephone—and are plunged into the horror and alienation of a scene we cannot understand, a scene that is presented with a clarity and detachment identical to those preceding it, but the content of which goes from ordinary to extraordinary yet still presenced as ordinary. The irony, of course, is that death *is* ordinary, and it is happening while we iron, or brush our teeth, or draw a picture, or make a film. After all, if you eat a chicken sandwich, you taste death.

But why, then, do we feel differently about a man slashing his throat than we do about a family going through a carwash? And if death is beyond us, if we cannot connect to it or grasp it the way we can the handle of a cup,[12] then can we truly grasp the image of a wife talking to her husband, or a woman making pancakes, or a man simply sitting in a chair? What makes us think that the rest of life, the little things, the things that precede death, are truly any more understandable?

What Haneke ultimately does is make real life irreal. Violent deaths saturate his films, making us question our knowledge of every scene we thought was simple. As the films move along and we absorb their unusual rhythm—the long, stable shots; the amplified sound; the emphasis on absolutely "authentic" gestures, expressions, and language—we have a growing sense of unease as *the simple* seems to move away from us even as we get closer to it. We are not used to such deliberation in film or in real life. We don't consider the breakfast bowl all that carefully in our lives, but by having it pushed in our faces on film, it gains new importance. And in that elevation, that refined and unmoving final focus, it is pulled *away* from us and from what we know. These films are not meant to make us identify with them even as they make life so readily identifiable—they are filled with ordinary things that become, somehow, transformed. They fetishize life itself. Perhaps this is the source of the terrible feeling we get: that beneath the facts and the stark realities, there is something that is, indeed, hidden—and we can never touch it, never know it, never grasp its significance. But Haneke does not reduce death, or life, to meaninglessness or to meaningless violence. He simply implies that the meaning is necessarily unknown.

Plato's artistic account of the death of Socrates gives us a final epitaph.

Prepared to die, to take the poison and become a martyr for Athens, Socrates is philosophizing about the meaning of it all. Like Haneke, Plato (the creative artist) is giving us something in-between a documentary and a work of fiction as he writes *The Phaedo*. The *real* Socrates (whatever that means) *really* drank the hemlock (whatever that means). And the Socrates we meet in Plato's dialogues is thus something of a double. Historical *and* a work of art; philosophical *and* dramatic; man *and* character. Plato's camera stays still and stable, never pointing away from the commonplace that is so fantastical. Socrates announces: "[T]he one aim of those who practice philosophy in the proper manner is to practice for dying and death."[13] Later, taking account of his final mundane obligations before death, Socrates turns to Crito and tells him, "I owe a cock to Asclepius; don't forget to pay the debt." The death of Socrates and the death of the cock soon both take place—off-screen.[14]

CHAPTER 5

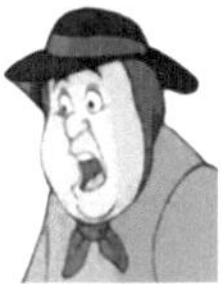

Yep, Gaston's Gay

Disney and the Beauty of a Beastly Love

Once upon a time in a land not far away a young prince lived in a shining castle.

Although he appeared to have everything his heart desired, the prince was unfulfilled. Then, one winter's night a woman came to the castle and offered him "her flower" in return for his agreeing to marry her, take her in, and protect her from the bitter cold. Uninterested and even somewhat repulsed by her feminine form, the prince sneered at "the gift" and turned the woman away. But she warned him not to reject society's norms. And when he dismissed her again, the woman left, and in her place appeared all of the townspeople, angry and judgmental. The prince tried to explain himself, but it was too late, for everyone had seen that there was no lust for women in his heart. And as punishment they indicted him, labeling him a hideous beast—an abomination to nature—and agreed to shun him and all who would call him friend. Ashamed of his monstrous urges, the Beast concealed his desires as he concealed himself in his castle at the margins of society, looking from afar, longing for a magic cure: to see himself transformed to mirror society's ideal. Sexual union with a woman, though, was the only thing so enchanted—it alone had the power to make him into a real man up until his twenty-first year. If he could learn to love a woman and earn her love in return by the time he entered adulthood, the curse would be lifted and he could rejoin society. If not, he would be doomed to be seen as a beast for all time. As the years passed he fell into despair and lost all hope. For who could ever learn to love a beast?[1]

Little towns full of little people can be notoriously judgmental and conservative. It is no surprise, really, that Belle—the heroine of Walt Disney's *Beauty and the Beast* (dir. Gary Trousdale and Kirk Wise, 1991)—fears suffocating in her poor, provincial French village. Like Gaston, her hyper-masculine suitor, she is different. And the last time someone was different in these parts, the townspeople cursed him, labeled him a beast, and forced him into exile. They would undoubtedly do the same to the next neighbor to come out. What options, then, are left for survival?

With all of the theory that we have accumulated so far now at our disposal, I would like to engage in a focused investigation—what Continental philosophers sometimes call a "close reading"—of a single text, arguing that Disney's animated version of *Beauty and the Beast* is, in the end, a story about neither. Instead, we will find that the true focus of the film's narrative is Gaston, with both Beauty and the Beast serving as tragic foils, reflections of Gaston in a twisted magic mirror. Seen anew, the film is at heart a tale of the persecution of those who identify—or are identified by society—as gay. It is about the "curse of heterosexuality" and the struggle to come to terms with sexual preference in a world in which "socially acceptable," "normal," and "morally good" are thought to be interchangeable. Inevitably, the main characters, each at different stages of awareness and acceptance of their own sexuality, find that throughout it all there is only one constant—the immoral and violent treatment by society of those labeled "different." And though the movie ends in marriage for Beauty and the Beast, it ends in death for Gaston; the trappings of the classic conceptions of comedic and tragic narrative conclusions are thus both present. As this is Gaston's story, though, the drama is without doubt, and in a strikingly non-Disney way, a tragedy.

A BEAST IS A BEAST OF CURSE OF CURSE

On the surface, as the opening narration tells us, the prince has been turned into a beast, cursed for his shallow aesthetic, for having shunned an ugly woman who wished to exchange a rose for a night's shelter in the castle. In thinking through the curse, too much attention can easily be paid to the woman's haggard appearance, too little to the symbol of the rose. By which, exactly, was the prince turned off? "Literally," the prince rejected the idea of being with a woman, rejected taking her flower. "Metaphorically," this plays out in terms of the prince rejecting a foundational norm of society. The question, then, is how best to interpret this norm.

Part of the answer can be had here by realizing that there is no such thing as a literal reading of a text. "Literal," when read through the lens of metaphysics, implies that there is some real, true, singular, unchanging, and secure definition of a word. As we have seen, words do not function in this way; they do not denote. Words come to meaning by making the things themselves present in a way that is particular to language and the way in which absence functions by means of language. And words accomplish this mostly by means of referencing each other. "Flower" makes a flower present, then, but it does so precisely by calling up everything that the word "flower" has ever made present—that is, all of the possible meanings in the past, present, and (somewhat more absently) even potential meanings in the future. The whole horizon of everything that "flower" could mean is instantly there when we encounter the word "flower." There is no *literal* meaning because there is no one profile, no one appearing, that is more truly what "flower" means than another. We apperceive all of these copresent meanings along with the word, and this is, precisely, what constitutes the meaning of the word. All of this is, in essence, the way in which the hermeneutical circle starts spinning.

What "literal" usually means is that aspect of a word made present most commonly through historical sedimentation—which is in turn tied to those with the power to make that one aspect of the word appear, and appear as "normal," appear as "the literal meaning." The "literal" meaning of a word comes to seem like the only true meaning by means of forgetting this historical sedimentation that allowed the "literal" meaning to appear in the first place. In doing hermeneutics, we uncover the way in which that "literal" meaning was created, hearing, once again, the echoes of those past utterances, meanings, and metaphors. In chapter 9 we will explore how this leads to "quotational discourse" and the sense in which everything we say is a mimicry of what has already been said, yet is new and original in its own way.

How, then, can we understand the meaning of a text if *everything* is metaphor? As we have repeatedly seen in past chapters, objective truth is still possible for a phenomenologist, but with the understanding that it is based on (inter)subjectivity. And so a text can have true meaning, but only by means of understanding that it is metaphor (i.e., the apperception of various meanings) that makes such truth possible in language. Indeed, we might even wish to reclaim the word "literal" here and argue that what we should mean by "literal" is just such a metaphorical reading. With objective truth in general, we make the intersubjective rounds and try to come to the *eidos*, the essence, of a thing such that our subjective understanding does justice (the best it can) to all of these perspectives. For the literal meaning of a text, we do two parallel things: first, we investigate the hermeneutics of the text, looking at what and how the word has meaning in relation to other texts, other words, and to history and the possibilities of the future, trying to take them all into consideration when asking ourselves what the word means here and now; and second, we give special attention to ways of reading a text that "open it up," that elucidate the text in a way that creates a semblance of cohesion, though we know that such cohesion is always an illusion, always precarious, always up for grabs, because this is an historical, subjective, infinite process. With *Beauty and the Beast*, we consequently have to think about how the words and the movie as a whole are related to the history of fairy tales, literature, films, and all other sorts of narratives. And we have to ask if the reading we are giving coheres and allows a gestalt of the whole to emerge that "hangs together" in an elucidating way.

Someone might want to say, for instance, that the prince is cursed because his soul is chipped, but he must ultimately come to accept his broken soul so that it may be redeemed. The evidence for this could be that there is a character who lives in the castle with the prince who is named "Chip" and who plays a role in progressing the narrative by being the one who gets Belle to return to the castle and usher in the prince/Beast's salvation. Perhaps "chip" means "crack" (like in a magic mirror) which means "broken" (like the door that Chip helps chop down to save Belle) which means "bad" (like eating forbidden fruit from the tree of knowledge) which refers to original sin and the prince's true, fallen nature.

It's not that any of this is *wrong*, but that it is uninteresting. It is unconvincing because it doesn't cohere very well, doesn't bring the story to greater meaning, doesn't bring into relief parts of the story that were flat and distant before, doesn't open itself up to the full history of the past meanings of these words, doesn't expose those parts of the text that seem to work against itself yet might be exactly what help hold the text together, and generally doesn't make sense (i.e., make the whole text sensible to logos in a meaningful way). When we ask about what a word means, what a text means, and even what a work of art means, we thus have to get past the idea, left over from the history of metaphysics, that there is a "literal" meaning that is "right" and a "metaphorical" meaning that is "wrong"—until, at least, we are willing to see the meaning of "literal" and "right" in a more phenomenological way, letting ourselves be open to readings that are "untraditional" but still having the highest standards of evaluation concerning the sense-making of those readings.

Given all of this, what might we say, then, about the meaning of the norm that has been rejected by the prince? For purposes of the story, the norm is turned into, "Don't judge a book by its cover" rather than, "Men should love only women," but the particular choice of metaphor is telling here, for there is—in both norms—an unspoken but widely accepted truth that this is what one is supposed to say even if one knows it is not completely true on some level. That is, it is interesting that what "stands in" for the prince's breaking of heterosexual norms is his breaking of a parallel norm concerning beauty, not, for instance, a norm concerning murder. When townsfolk say, "Do not commit murder," they say it with sincerity and with a more-or-less earnest commitment to its prescriptive truth. When they say, "Don't judge a book by its cover," they utter the words with somewhat less sincerity. They (which is to say, *we*) say such things knowing that it is a norm we are expected to uphold in word more than deed, for the truth of the matter is that sometimes judging a book by its cover makes a good deal of sense. Everyone knows this, even if few speak it out loud. This is how induction works, after all, and how we might rightly come to worry that most red berries are poisonous. Phenomenologically, it is troubling, even, to suggest that a book and its cover can be separated, as if some sort of mind/body dualism were at work in things such that we should "see past external appearance" to some sort of truth that transcends the material realm. Believing that "ugliness" is indicative of an immoral character—or that beauty equates to goodness, for that matter—makes little sense. As does reducing someone to his or her physical materiality. But completely separating the meaning of a book from the meaning of its cover is also nonsensical since the book is given to us as a material thing in the world.

The movie, of course, is complicit in the ruse—fully aware that the standard the prince has violated is questionable and arbitrary, and his punishment unjust. This, in fact, is the point of the narrative, and it suggests that the true point of view of the film's creators is that the *curse* is immoral, not the Beast's behavior. This is hinted at, for instance, in the postmodern play on the meaning of Belle's name. As the townspeople point out in song, it's no wonder that her name means "beauty"—Belle's looks have no parallel. How strange, then, that the prince is originally turned into a beast for caring too much about beauty—for loving only beauty—yet the Beast is turned back into a prince once he "literally" falls in love with Beauty. If we followed the narrative naively—i.e., thinking that this is Beauty and the Beast's story and that the Beast needs merely to learn not to judge a book by its cover—this would make no sense. Why, then, would the curse finally be broken? In the end, wouldn't the prince/Beast still supposedly be favoring and loving *Beauty*?

Indeed, to make it clear that the movie knows very well that the curse is unjust and arbitrary, that there is more going on here than meets the eye, the enchantress—in all of her judgmental meddling—tells the prince a lie. "Beauty is found within," she tells him before turning him into a beast. It is a claim that will turn out to be false on multiple levels. Beauty (literally, *Belle*) comes from without, from outside the castle and outside the Beast's circle of friends. Not only does she come from the outside, but she is the most outwardly beautiful woman in town—something we are told repeatedly. What lesson could the prince be presumed to have learned, then, falling for her in the end? It's not as if he has learned to love a "hag" or even someone just a tiny bit outside the Hollywood definition of "beautiful woman." And yet, the curse is broken in the end. Consequently, we are forced to reconsider the true nature of the rule the Beast had violated all those years ago: clearly, it was not about caring too much for beauty, because he is still doing just this at the conclusion of the movie. Rather, it makes more sense to say that he has relented, given in to the heterosexual norms of society, finally seeking love with a woman. And for this, he is rewarded and no longer seen as a beast.

Against such a reading, it has been suggested that Disney's story actually reinforces and champions heterosexual norms, and is thus not gay-friendly, precisely because the Beast is cursed until he loves a woman. The pronouns in the enchantress's spell supposedly make it clear: "if the Beast could learn to love another and earn *her* love in return. . . . "[2] The enchantress does not leave open the possibility that love with a *him* could break the spell for the Beast. What such a reading misses, however, is that while it is true that heterosexual love is being forced on the Beast, heterosexual love is being *forced* on the Beast. The dénouement is, after all, a coupling that is mandated—one that results from a *curse*. Read appropriately, the narrative thus does not indict the Beast; it indicts society, calling on the audience to identify in part with the Beast.

Indeed, this is an extremely complex narrative and identification because the audience must come to realize that if the Beast succeeds in his quest to rejoin society—to be human again—he will be forced to do so at the expense of his true nature. Success for the Beast means a tragic end—for himself, for Gaston, and for us all. It means that the Beast has given in to society's demands to hide what he is. Once, as a young prince, he was brave enough to come out and state his true feelings. The price was years of isolation and rejection. In the end, he will have his curse lifted, but the Beast we are given is not a hero. We pity him, but we cannot admire him. He will not stand up and demand to be taken for what he is; he longs only to find a way to regain society's trust and acceptance by bending to its demands. He will not fight for the right to walk proudly through the village, his rainbow fur-flag freely flying; he wishes only to obscure what he is, hide his desires, and thus be accepted. And so, if he is successful, it will be a shallow peace, one gained at the cost of truth and love and any hope for a meaningful happily-ever-after.

We see the young prince, pre-curse, in artistic representation only (in stained glass and in a painting hanging in the west wing of the castle that is torn in the first few moments of the film). He exists as a child and a nonbeast only as aesthetic imagination and re-presentation. Static, he is without agency or true body. We know nothing of his past, of his parents, of his boyhood. His being is thus reduced to the choice he made to reject women: and even this choice is represented passively, told in still images and related to us through the voice of a narrator. Later in the film, piecing together the puzzle, we learn that the prince was eleven years old, just approaching puberty, when the enchantress showed up on his doorstep.[3] It is at this time of becoming and the traditional awakening of desire that the boy chooses incorrectly. Clearly, the enchantress, and by extension society, sees the prince's rejection of heterosexuality as a choice, but there is an indication that the prince is not really choosing—that we, the audience, should realize that these things are determined early on.[4]

What glimpses we have of the pre-curse prince provide us with a picture of a somewhat effeminate boy. The prince's face is beautiful, with full, pouting lips.[5] His eyebrows are thin and perfectly plucked. His hair—even before becoming a beast—is long and flowing. He does not want for conditioner. He looks more like Fabio than the traditional Disney hero: this is no butch Prince Charming. In the first two stained-glass panels we are shown, the prince is depicted first with a sword and then a scepter, two phallic images filling his little noble hands. In the larger stained glass we see the prince in the center. To the left is the moon and a night scene of the village with a man and a woman. To the right is the sun and a day scene with another man and woman. The prince is caught between; neither day nor night engulfs him. Below him is the furrowed field. He hovers above, neither urban nor rural. A knight's horse is to his left, a dog to his right—the prince stands between animality and humanity as well as masculinity and femininity, day and night, here and there. He is displaced, alone, different from the very start.

After a decade of being punished for his difference, though, he now wants to be accepted—not for what he is, but for what he can pretend to be. The Beast knows what Belle means for him, not a true love but a ticket back into mainstream society. This is no romantic. "Of course! . . . I'm not a fool" the Beast roars at his staff when they ask if he's considered the possibility that "this girl" could lift the curse for them all. And so he sets his sites on heading back into the closet and marrying. He determines to act macho, saving Belle from vicious wolves; but not too macho, because a woman also wants a sensitive man who likes feeding birds and playing in the snow. He rejects his past sense of flamboyant style: when getting ready for his first "date" with Belle, his staff makes him up with highly teased curly fur and cute little bows in his hair. He quickly rejects the look: he is committed to pretending to be something new, and so he and his hair are made to appear straight. After a night of dining and dancing and acting like he has true feelings for the girl, the staff is impressed at the Beast's ability to pretend. "I knew you had it in you!" says Cogsworth the clock/butler (who earlier had joked that the Beast should admit to Belle that his true gift to her would be a set of "promises [he didn't] intend to keep"). More cautious, more conniving—this is the new Beast.

The new Beast no longer stomps around the castle, resentful and angry at Belle for what he must do. This is a Beast who conceals, who now hopes the young girl won't go into the special forbidden room where he keeps a portrait of himself, a rose, and a lovely hand mirror. This is a Beast who now gets angry when his staff does a big production number (he lives, after all, in a castle where everyone sings and dances and loves show tunes). This is a Beast who is broken, who admits defeat, who hides his fairy tail beneath a gentleman's cape. But try as he might, his true nature is there for anyone who still wishes to see it.[6] Even at the moment of his transformation into *Man*, the Beast does not step easily into the role. In a classic-Disney reversal, it is not a sleeping Beauty who needs the kiss of her prince to end the story. Rather, the defeated prince, fresh from wrestling in sweaty combat with Gaston, is awakened, saved by the kiss of Beauty's tear, ready to embark on a life of lies.

BEAUTY IS PROOF, PROOF BEAUTY

But of course one must wonder why Beauty agrees to this. Once she discovers the Beast's penchant for show tunes, flowers, and fur, why does she agree to play along, to take up the traditional "masculine" role, reviving him with her tears and declaration of love? To see the answer, one must accept a rather startling fact about Belle's character. Belle is not really a very nice person. She is a selfish, scheming, shallow manipulator—worse, by far, than Gaston, whose outward egotism is merely an act.

From the start, Belle holds her neighbors in contempt. They are little people with little dreams, she proclaims, and she wants "so much more than they've got planned." Belle is certain that she is better than everyone around her, that she deserves more out of life than these simple folk. As she walks through town in the film's opening scene, she sings her disparagements: the baker has his "same old bread and rolls to sell"; the quiet village is full of "little people" to whom she feels no connection and for whom she has no respect; she deserves much more than the "provincial life" with which everyone else seems content. The truth is that from the start, Belle appears to be more of a snob than a heroine. She is not satisfied merely to wish for something new, she wants something *more* than everyone else. She is not prepared merely to see herself as different, she feels she is *better* than everyone else.

At first it appears that Belle's shallow character will only admit caring for her father—that this Beauty is only kin deep—but even this is a ruse. Belle doesn't work and she has no plans to marry. Consequently, she needs her father to get by, at least for now. And so when he (and the possibility of his invention's prize money, which he promises will be the start of a new life for them both) is at risk, she takes off to rescue him.

It would undoubtedly be going too far to maintain that Belle is *surely* a lesbian. There are hints that this might be the case, but in the end the narrative is less than conclusive. We know that Belle is uninterested in the men in town, especially Gaston, the most handsome man around. She mocks his proposal of marriage ("'Madame Gaston!' Can't you just see it? 'Madame Gaston!' His little wife. No

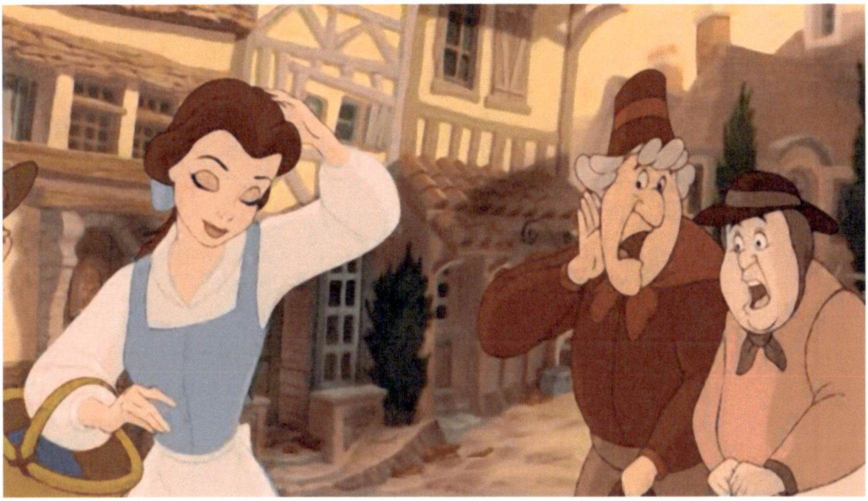

FIGURE 5.1. Scene from the film *Beauty and the Beast.* 1991. Dirs. Gary Trousdale and Kirk Wise.

sir, not me. I guarantee it."), and in the process mocks the institution of marriage itself—which, granted, could do with a bit of mockery. True, Belle is something of a tomboy, though she still dresses rather "girlie." Most interesting, though, are the comments the townsfolk make about Belle being . . . different. The townspeople have an eye for these things, and they will not accept any deviation from their established moral norms. They once ran the prince out of town—out of humanity, even—and they now have their eye on Belle: "Look there she goes that girl is strange, no question. . . . Never part of any crowd. . . . No denying she's a funny girl that Belle. . . . Look there she goes that girl is so peculiar. . . . What a puzzle to the rest of us is Belle. . . . [B]ehind that fair façade, I'm afraid she's rather odd. Very different from the rest of us—she's nothing like the rest of us—Yes, different from the rest of us is Belle. . . . A most peculiar mademoiselle. It's a pity and a sin, she doesn't quite fit in. . . . She really is a funny girl that Belle."[7] (*See figure 5.1.*)

Not only do the townspeople note that Belle is different, but they raise the possibility that her difference constitutes a sin. This religious condemnation will be echoed later in the "The Mob Song" when the town residents set off to kill the Beast for his sexual sins, singing, "Grab your sword, grab your bow, praise the Lord and here we go!" That the town may be home to a moral majority further suggests that the problem the locals have with the Beast's and Belle's lifestyles is not just that they are different, but that they are taken to be sinfully different.

The most straightforward and naive reading of Belle's difference is not that she is a lesbian but rather that she is a feminist trapped in a backward town, surrounded by male chauvinists, dreaming of a new freedom. Most commentators do not see Belle's difference as a sexual orientation difference, but rather as a difference based on her strong sense of independence and rejection of stereotypical female roles. There is good reason to question this reading, though.

Belle is far from a feminist. Her dream, after all, is to be a princess.[8] She is looking for someone to take care of her, spoil her, and give her the finer things in life. True, Belle rejects the role of the traditional housewife: she doesn't want to clean up after, cook for, and tend to a husband. Domestic work is not on her agenda—ask not for whom this Belle toils!—but her rejection of domesticity and its associated labor is not in the name of independence and equality. Rather, Belle is the one who wants to be pampered, to have a husband rich enough to have a staff to work for her. If anything, Belle is rebelling against her class identity, not her gender identity. After all, she longs to live off her father's prize money, and she reads stories about princes falling in love with girls such as herself. The idea that she is a feminist simply does not cohere.

All of this comes together when Beauty finally meets the Beast. But if it is true that Belle is selfish, why does she agree to take her father's place in the Beast's dungeon, thinking she will be locked up forever? Belle is, indeed, making a trade, but she is not really planning on trading her own freedom for her father's. Her scheme is to trade her father's protection and potential prize money for the Beast's royalty and riches.

Seeing that this is so is key to unpacking the meaning of the narrative, so let us take a moment to make a case for such a reading. Before Belle will agree to switch places with her father, she asks the Beast to step into the light. When he does, his outward form is exposed. He is towering and muscular, frightening and furry. Belle recoils a bit, but it is an act—as is much of what follows. In fact, when Belle first asks the Beast to show himself, she does so with an arched eyebrow and in a sly voice. At this moment, we see in Belle's demure demeanor a flash of recognition and insight. What she is realizing is the nature of the story in which she now finds herself a player. She instantly knows that this is not a true Beast, but an enchanted prince. She knows that the prince is rich and powerful, and has servants ready to attend to her every need. She knows that she can get everything she wants out of life if she simply plays along, moves the narrative forward, and helps break the curse. And we know that Belle knows all of this because the filmmakers go out of their way to show us that Belle's favorite book is—somewhat postmodernly—*Beauty and the Beast.*

In the opening scene of the film, Belle stops insulting all of the townspeople for a moment to drop into a bookstore and charm its owner into giving her a copy of her favorite book for free.[9] It is a book she's read twice before, we are told, and while she speaks to the shopkeeper, wanders around town, and sits down near the central fountain to read it again, she points out what her favorite parts are. "Daring sword fights, magic spells, a prince in disguise," she sighs. All of these elements will play out in Belle's real life, making it easy for her to recognize the narrative in which she later becomes involved. That is, when Belle meets the Beast, she knows very well that she is finally going to have her shot at being a princess. Belle has been studying that book. "Here's where she meets Prince Charming," she sings early on while leafing through its pages by the fountain, "but she won't discover that it's him 'til chapter three." No such surprises, then, for Belle in "real life." Perhaps the prince does not get turned back into his human form until the third act of the movie, but Belle is obviously well aware of who he is at the start. To make it all the more clear, we are even shown a page in Belle's book with a picture from the story she is reading. As Belle sings about the prince yet undiscovered, she points to a plate in the book depicting a castle in the background, a furry beastlike prince walking on all fours to the left, and a young girl on the bottom right, with dark hair and a blue dress, suspiciously looking very much like Belle. We know, then, that Belle is aware of the story and her potential place in it. When she later finds these events unfolding in her own life, when she asks the Beast to step into the light, she does so with a cocked eyebrow and a coy voice that suggests she has just become aware of what's really going on around her. When the Beast shows himself, confirming Belle's suspicion, she at once knows how the story will end if she plays it correctly, and so she takes up the part of the reluctant Beauty and agrees to trade places with her father in the Beast's dungeon, knowing that this will set in motion the narrative that will eventually make her a princess.

The postmodern turn, something we will investigate more in section 4, is made possible, of course, because of the sort of hermeneutics and phenomenology we have been discussing. If every word means all past meanings/uses of the word, and every story comes to meaning because it is part of a nexus in which other stories give it meaning, then the self-referentiality that is the hallmark of postmodernity is a necessary part of language, story, metaphor, art, and being. The modernist hides this in an act of cowardice; the postmodernist exposes this and embraces this in an act of truth-telling. The team behind *Beauty and the Beast* is anything but cowardly.

But if Belle knows she is a character in the story "Beauty and the Beast," why does she run off soon after agreeing to stay (at which point she is attacked by wolves), and why does her internal monologue—voiced in song while playing outside in the snow—suggest that she is discovering something new about the Beast and perhaps making the decision to stay with him and "fall in love" with him much later in the film? Such points would seem to argue against the reading that Belle is knowingly playing a part in a story she is sure will reward her eventually.

It is quite possible that all of Belle's hesitations are an act, that all of these rejections and proclamations are fiction, that by running away and feigning an initial lack of interest in the Beast, Belle is consciously playing the role in the narrative that she is expected to play: the initially *reluctant* Beauty. However, it often appears that there is indeed something more going on, something there that wasn't there before. Belle seems truly to have second thoughts early in the film and a realization of her commitment to the Beast much later.

Such initial hesitations make sense if we see Belle as a lesbian who is somewhat conflicted about her choice to take up a union with a man in exchange for seeing her material wishes come true. If she follows through with such a deal, she will bargain away her sexuality as the price for her wealth and power. Even so, and though there are these moments of hesitation, Belle seems ready to go through with it. What finally seals the deal, then, is when Belle realizes that she need not make such a huge sacrifice. This is the turning point in the relationship, the moment after which Belle is sweet to the Beast and prepared to "love" him to the end. It occurs when the two are playing outside. Belle's sudden realization is given voice in the song "Something There." And what she suddenly realizes is the true nature of the curse: she realizes that the Beast is gay. That is, she has read the story before in her book, but she never saw its meaning or understood the nuances of the characters' motivations (perhaps in the same way that many of us have seen the Disney movie *Beauty and the Beast* before but never saw its meaning or understood the nuances of the characters' motivations until the queer reading in which we are currently engaged in this chapter).

The scene in question takes place outside in the snow where the Beast frolics with the little birds and plays with his huge snowballs. This is a Beast with his guard down. He is not adopting his hyper-macho pose: he allows himself to smile and laugh, being kind and sweet and "dear." His body is no longer twisted to some hyper-masculine ideal: it fails him as he falls down in the snow. His massive hyper-male demeanor is dropped as well: he doesn't seek to attack nature, but to be part of it; not to kill wolves to prove his manhood, but to let dozens of birds perch peacefully on his body in communion. The Beast is, for a moment, not trying to be an idealized version of the excessively heterosexual man he thinks he needs to be to win over Belle and break the curse. And Belle takes this moment to put all the pieces together, to see what is truly going on—to see that the Beast has been pretending all along. As she comes to the realization, she wonders how she could have missed it for so long: "And so I'm sure! I wonder why I didn't see it there before." The hints were dropped, the show tunes were sung, the truth—and the Beast—were out there from the start. Ducking behind a tree to collect her thoughts and compose herself, Belle is struck by the irony of it all. Will she, as a lesbian, marry a gay man? With a new look of determination, she sings how it is "new and a bit alarming—who'd have ever thought that this could be?" (The castle staff agrees: "It's so *peculiar*!") But Belle knows that this is the answer to all of her problems: "True . . . he's no Prince Charming, but there's something in him that I simply didn't see." The Beast is gay, and thus Belle need not sacrifice as much as she had thought. She can have her prince without having to *have* him, too. And in the end, the curse will be broken, the scheming Beauty will get what she wants without resorting to sleeping with a man, and the Beast will succeed in his desired transformation, losing his fur and gaining a beard in the process.

LEFOU I'M AFRAID I'VE BEEN THINKING

But there are complications. There is Gaston. And if he has his way, there will be no broken curse and no false union.

The character of Gaston is a new addition to the story of Beauty and the Beast—a Disney addition. We should, then, pay special attention to his presence in the film. He is no minor character; in fact, this is Gaston's story at heart. And as such, it is a tragic recounting of a man forced deep into the closet, an intolerant society that keeps him there, and a final misguided burst of repressed emotion exploding scattershot in the end, dooming the hero to wrong action and death.

Yes, Gaston is the hero, or at least on the way toward being the hero. And for the narrative to fall together he must be seen as such, though he acts without courage at the final moment of choice and crisis. But before condemning Gaston we need to understand him, for he has been generally misunderstood, taken to be the epitome of selfishness and egotism rather than oppression and despair.[10]

Like the Beast, Gaston is gay. Unlike the Beast, Gaston has seen how society deals with those who are labeled as such; consequently, he is determined to avoid the cursed fate. To ensure he will not be marginalized and dehumanized, Gaston adopts an outward appearance of extreme hetero-masculinity, hence his macho behavior and souped-up XY physique. Early test sketches by the animators had Gaston drawn with a powdery white wig and somewhat openly gay affectations—a far cry from the character that made it to the screen. Indeed, supervising Gaston-animator "Andreas Deja [initially] drew a Gaston who was far more foppish than he later became,"[11] but this would not do because the whole point of Gaston's character, his self-made false identity, is the tragic need to hide his true nature in the name of self-preservation in an intolerant society. Consequently, it is interesting to think of the test drawings as if they were the embodiment of a real person at some early stage in his life. In his early years Gaston discovers that such a dandy demeanor is dangerous, and so he works out, encasing himself in a costume of male muscles, remaking himself in the image of idealized macho manhood, trading in his sway for a swagger. This, then, is the Gaston we meet in the film. It is a ruse that fools all of the townspeople, but one need only look past the fair façade, and the real Gaston—trapped and lonely and desperately frightened of being exposed—comes into full relief. Indeed, a close investigation shows the not-so-hidden truth just there beneath the chiseled surface.

Consider. Every girl in town wants to be with Gaston—the three blonde Bimbettes throw themselves at him at every turn. Why, then, does he insist on pursuing Belle, who turns him down repeatedly and publicly? *Because she can be counted on to turn him down repeatedly and publicly.* Belle is the only female around who has made it clear that she wants nothing to do with Gaston (ostensibly—we know, though no one else seems to know for sure—because she is a lesbian); consequently, she is *safe* to pursue. Gaston knows that by making plans to woo and marry Belle he will never actually have to go through with anything. Furthermore, by making the pursuit public he can ensure that his heterosexual cover is maintained. Everyone will think that Belle is the strange one for rejecting the manly and desirable Gaston. To secure the success of the ruse, Gaston even prepares a public wedding and, when he has Belle alone for the impromptu proposal, lays on the macho act to the extreme, thus *guaranteeing* that she will say no. Stressing how she will have to cook and clean and care for their many children, Gaston privately says everything he knows that Belle hates to hear, thus setting the stage for his own rebuffing. When the rejection comes it is public and brutal. It gives the townspeople something funny and shocking on which they can focus their collective attention. This, too, is part of Gaston's plan. He later (publicly) complains about being "rejected, publicly humiliated," but the truth of the matter is that Gaston's overly inflated ego is itself a mechanism to throw the public off the track of a deeper truth. Gaston carefully cultivates his enlarged ego and then orchestrates its public puncturing at every turn as a sort of circus for the masses: give them something to talk about so they will not need to look more closely and find something "worse" to talk about on their own. As a result, Gaston marches around town and pursues the one girl he knows he needn't worry about catching.

The Beast and Gaston thus have much in common—large, muscular, hairy bodies; hangers-on willing to attend to their every need; desires to marry Belle to prove (falsely) their heterosexuality.[12] The parallels are clear in nearly every scene: just as the Beast is surrounded in his castle lair by Lumiere (the enchanted candlestick/butler) and other subservient staff lackeys, so Gaston is surrounded in the tavern by Lefou and other subservient village lackeys. These two back-to-back scenes (the Beast imprisoning Belle in his castle and Gaston plotting in the tavern) are visually alike as well—both end with a camera shot pulling out through a window and into the snow falling on the cold, judgmental, surrounding world.

Consider further. In the tavern scene Lefou is consoling Gaston after Belle's public rejection of his marriage proposal. This, we know, is an act on Gaston's part. He is just where he wants to be—in a men's club getting his wounds licked. Gaston's relationship with Lefou is especially intriguing. Throughout this scene, as throughout the movie, Lefou plays two roles: he is both a partner/sidekick/secret-lover to Gaston and an embodiment of Gaston's phallus.

These two roles are not mutually exclusive, nor are they without literary precedent. The court jester has long been seen as the animated id of the court, the personification of the king's sexual desire run free, the embodiment of the royal penis. The classic painted red clown's nose undoubtedly has some of its origin here. Lefou, as the protagonist's phallus, allows Gaston an outlet for his repressed sexual urges. Note the way Gaston continuously pulls on Lefou and strokes him and holds him and beats him. It is a violent relationship only on the surface. When Gaston visits Belle's house to hatch his plan with the asylum director, he leaves Lefou in the snow to keep guard. Later, we see Lefou frozen and cut off from Gaston, his bulbous head and even more bulbous nose turned blue—as Gaston is bound to be, waiting for (or even being with) Belle. At other times, Lefou assumes the role of partner, caring for Gaston, cheering him up, loving him and lovingly heckling him, playing the part of the paramour hidden within the context of sidekick. These two aspects of Lefou are not at odds with one another: in a kind of phenomenological categoriality, the phallus can be the object of love, and the lover can be the objectified phallus. In the tavern scene, both manifestations of Lefou are evident—as is Gaston's willingness to let his guard down when surrounded by potentially like-minded men.

As we approach a psychoanalytic reading of the text in general and this scene specifically, it is helpful to remember that Husserl and Freud were contemporaries, their birth and death dates off by only a couple of years. And there is something in the water, or perhaps the beer, in Germany at this time that is causing a generation of scholars to question their Cartesian inheritance. Descartes's famous declaration of "I think therefore I am" comes at the end of a line of argument that concludes that the only thing one can be sure of is one's own thoughts, that one's ability to think necessarily implies one's existence, that what one truly is is that ongoing collection of thoughts (mind, that is, and not body), and that the clarity and continuity of that flowing stream of consciousness is what establishes one's identity across time. Freud rejects the idea of a self that is both unified and utterly transparent to itself, arguing instead for a fractured self, each aspect of which has different and often conflicting drives; one does not always understand or even know of one's overall motivations. Husserl's rejection of Cartesian conceptions of mind and selfhood are generally in the same neighborhood as, though certainly not identical to, Freud's. One can clearly see a similar set of worries concerning the legacy of modernity motivating both thinkers.

There is a reason that Heidegger, Derrida, and so many others who came in the next generation of Continental thought wrestled with both Freud and Husserl's work, seeing their projects working in tandem. If we are to do a proper phenomenology of *Beauty and the Beast*, then, we must consider the depiction of Gaston as a self that is complicated, multidimensional, and at best struggling to be self-aware, a self that is potentially splintered, always performative and intersubjectively defined. And we must consider the way in which the art form of the animated movie takes this up. Seen anew, the tavern scene thus gives us a glimpse into the heart of Gaston—a man who proves to be not an egotistical antagonist but a misunderstood and soon to be tragically misdirected hero.

In the tavern the village men are drinking while Gaston sits moping in his beastly throne-like chair. "That girl has tangled with the wrong man," he declares in a moment of transparent truth. Lefou as lover is distressed to see his partner feeling down and so decides to cheer him up; Lefou as phallus is running around happy and wild (he didn't want to be with Belle anyway) and so celebrates. Anticipation is in the air: everyone is about to launch into a fabulous Broadway-style production number with Lefou taking the lead. As the song begins, the first thing the mischievous Lefou does is run to one of the men at the bar and take his belt off, causing the man's pants to fall down and his heart-print underwear to be exposed. Lefou takes the belt over to Gaston and straps it on, tourniquet-like, ringing the base of Gaston's neck. Gaston is getting excited; his juices are starting to flow. "No one's slick as Gaston," sings Lefou. "No one's neck's as incredibly thick as Gaston's." Gaston's neck and head enlarge from the rush of blood, and with some straining, he bursts the belt. Lefou keeps up the party, trying further to convince Gaston that he is not alone and that he is cared for. Hopping on top of the heads of the men seated before him, Lefou assures Gaston that they all "play for the same team."[13] As if to prove the point, the men stand up and begin grabbing Gaston's phallus, literally swinging Lefou through the air, back and forth in rhythmic unison. Lefou, highly excited now, takes a beer and—perhaps prematurely—shoots the liquid, foamy head and all, onto Gaston's face, at which point Gaston finally gets into the song in earnest, lunges at Lefou, and begins beating him. Our hero ends up in an orgiastic pile of men, happily wrestling with them and biting the random body part thrust toward his mouth. His boast that "every last inch of [him is] covered with hair" undoubtedly makes everyone wonder just how many hairy inches of Gaston there are (*see figure 5.2*). Lefou then proclaims, and Gaston confirms, that "no one spits like Gaston," though it appears that Lefou swallows (as he is then seen literally swallowing what Gaston spits). Gaston juggles and plays with some of the "eggs" he finds in the tavern, claims that he's eaten many of them since he was a boy and enjoys them even more today, and then remarks that—in case anyone was still wondering about those inches—he is, today, "roughly the size of a barge." Feeling more at ease in his surroundings now, Gaston reclines sideways in his

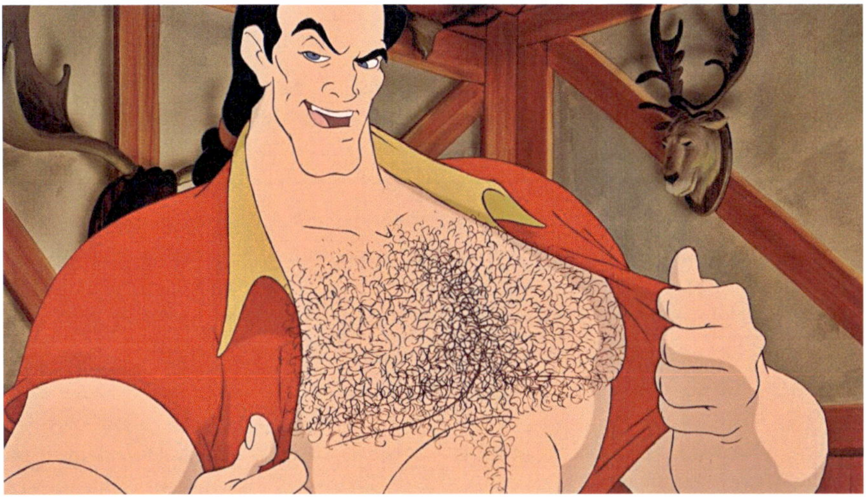

FIGURE 5.2. Scene from the film *Beauty and the Beast.* 1991. Dirs. Gary Trousdale and Kirk Wise.

chair, lets his legs dangle over the arm, points his right foot up in the air in a balletic, graceful arch, and proclaims his pride in his interior decorating skills. At this point Belle's father, Maurice, arrives—an unwelcome guest to the party. He is worried that he has seen a real life homosexual ("a monster!"), and hopes to find support among the men to go hunt it down and save his daughter from such an influence. Maurice's attitude, though, is currently unwelcome, and so he is mocked and tossed outside. But the party is nonetheless interrupted by the old man's rambling intolerances; the mood is apparently and unfortunately broken. In his hate and discrimination, Maurice at least manages inadvertently to give Gaston a new idea for putting on a public spectacle in which Belle can once again burst Gaston's ego while reinforcing his heterosexuality to the outside town at large. Gaston bends down to talk it over with Lefou, whose head, of course, is poking out between Gaston's legs. The two get up, embrace, and dance all around the tavern (Gaston, naturally, leads). Everyone cheers and laughs, Gaston is happy once again, and all pretenses are—for one final fleeting moment—dropped as Gaston and Lefou walk arm in arm between adoring lines of friends in a mock wedding/commitment ceremony. The oppressive mores of the outside world are, if only for that instant, put on hold inside the tavern. And as we see Lefou hook his arm onto Gaston's, the two singing about marriage and walking down the makeshift aisle, the camera pulls back to reveal that the rice everyone seems to be throwing is really the snow falling outside.[14] Snow falling on the cold, judgmental, surrounding world outside.

MOUNTING THE BEAST

It's not easy being Gaston. Yet, who is to blame when one is in the closet? The intolerance of society at large is certainly the main evil, but is there any culpability on the part of those who live the lie, those—like Gaston and the new Beast—who accept the evil and by accepting it in some form perpetuate it? Or is such denial merely a *necessary* evil for survival's sake? Classically put, in ethical terms this is a question of active versus passive duties—perhaps a question of moral heroism as well. To participate actively in hateful discrimination is indefensible. For many, it is less clear that morality also demands one harm one's self in the name of changing the system as a whole for others.[15] This is not an easy dilemma. Gaston's is not an easy dilemma.

The truth of the matter is that the distinction between active and passive duty is a construct in many cases, thus making the moral language dubious and the moral debate muddled. We all have our sins—of omission and commission and many points in between. Active and passive are, in fact, categories that only do work in a nonphenomenologically based ethic, one that reduces morality to a set of abstract rules that are not tied to real questions of communal flourishing.[16] To their credit, the Disney filmmakers do not avoid wading into these waters, doing the best that they can to think it through artistically. Gaston is neither the pure hero in a corrupt world nor the weak villain unwilling to fight for what is right. He is conflicted. He is a victim, surely, but also a victimizer. Gaston is morally troubled and morally troubling. And when he meets his downfall, we are angry with him for having chosen poorly, but we feel for him as well.

It all begins to fall apart when Gaston sees the Beast for the first time. There is an attraction there, to be sure. The film has already set up the meaning of the mirror. Gaston looks into mirrors throughout the movie and feigns love for what he sees. This, too, is part of the public circus of his performed identity. But now, toward the end of the film, Gaston encounters a new mirror: the Beast's magic mirror. And when Gaston looks into it, it shows him the Beast: so of course he will love what he sees; this is his only established relationship with mirrors. But more troubling is the fact that the eerie reflection is itself a depiction of one possible version of Gaston. The Beast is Gaston out of the closet, and at first Gaston hates the Beast for his courage and his openness: even if the price is being labeled a monster, at least the Beast is being true to himself. When Gaston realizes moments later that the Beast is not so courageous, that he is hoping to use Belle to break his curse and take up a life of lies in much the same way that Gaston has been using Belle for similar ends, Gaston is instantly disgusted. It is a self-hatred more than anything, the inability to look into the mirror and accept what he sees there looking back. But of course, the magic mirror is a one-way mirror. The Beast does not look back; Gaston-as-Beast does not have eyes to see. His humanity, his sight, his agency have been stripped away. This, then, will be Gaston's fate if he lets on as to his true nature, becoming what he sees in the mirror. And so his disgust turns to rage. Gaston knows now that Belle is going to take part in the Beast's ruse. "If I didn't know better I'd think you had feelings for this monster," he tells Belle in anger. "He's not the monster, Gaston. You are," replies Belle. And this is the first moment of choice, the crossroads for Gaston. Belle, his one hope for continuing the farce of his public sexual identity, has called Gaston's orientation into question in front of the whole village. Belle has finally figured it out. And now she has brought the issue to a head, publicly announcing the truth that Gaston had worked so hard to obscure. *He* might be monstrous. At this moment he is free to deny the accusation or embrace it, to take the lies even further or to correct Belle and suggest that he is indeed gay but there is nothing hideous at all about it. Overcome with emotion, Gaston cannot sort out his attraction to the Beast, his hatred of himself, and his overall fear and sadness and panic. And so he chooses. And he chooses poorly.

Gaston grabs the mirror from Belle and, in response to her accusation, shouts that she is crazy. He waves the mirror around at the villagers. Their own possible-selves are reflected back at them in the form of the monster they created as such and have themselves become. They turn from the mirror, and themselves, in fear. To divert attention from Belle's indictment, Gaston unleashes his fury at the Beast—really, we must remember, at himself—pulling out the most disgusting and immoral clichés about homosexuals he can muster. "The Beast will make off with your children," yells Gaston. A woman concurs, adding that gays (monsters) have enormous (sexual) urges, that they are insatiable, that complacent villagers will eventually sacrifice their children to these "monstrous appetites." All gays are oversexed child molesters, the crowd is claiming in a whirlwind of emotional fury. And Gaston nods in silent affirmation. "Praise the Lord!" sing the townspeople. "We don't like what we don't understand, in fact it scares us, and this monster is mysterious at least." The villagers take up arms and torches, no longer content to marginalize the Beast. They want him dead. And in a tragic bit of irony, they are "counting on Gaston to lead the way."

As Gaston prepares for the battle and incites his neighbors to murder, his language becomes strangely sexually charged. It is a side effect of his own rampant emotions, his combination of lust and disgust for the Beast. The crowd sings for Gaston to "mount [his] horse." And Gaston counters with a line about "screw[ing] courage to the sticking place"—a literate reference for this supposedly dumb he-man, and an interesting choice of words for the current circumstances. "It's one exciting ride," shouts Gaston, moments after proclaiming his desire to mount the Beast as well—or at least to mount his head on a wall. Whipped into a combination sexual- and fear-frenzy, the villagers follow Gaston to the castle and prepare to do battle, to fight for the purity of the heterosexual straight and narrow life. In a pun or perhaps a Freudian slip, Gaston invites the men fighting at his side to "take whatever *booty* [they] can find" once inside the castle. "But the Beast," he says with a mad mixture of sex and violence on his mind, "is mine."

The village men approach the castle with a humongous pole, a giant erect log they plan to use to ram down the doors of the Beast's secret place. It will be the townspeople's combined massive (hetero?-)phallus versus whatever the Beast can pull out in his defense. But the Beast is depressed. His plan to use Belle and break the curse is not working, and he is tired of living beyond the fray. As the townspeople beat down the doors with their pole, violating the Beast in a most intimate way, a hopeless Beast can only say, "Let them come." Indeed, the climax is near.

Once inside, though, the villagers are confronted with their own homophobia and are quickly (and comically) defeated by their own intolerances. The castle staff, in a bit of guerrilla warfare, separates the villagers and deals with them alone and in small groups. Each staff member uses his or her own talents to construct the attack: Mrs. Potts leads a team of cups who pour hot water on the intruders; Lumiere the candlestick burns his oppressors; the knives in the kitchen stand on guard, ready for slicing and chopping. Instead of retreating and pretending to be something they are not, the castle staffers for once embrace their identities—it is a refreshing thing to see. Ingeniously, the enchanted royal defenders use the villager's homophobia against them at every turn, all while the song "Be Our Guest" is reprised, suggesting that it is a service for which the villagers should one day thank them. One man is forced into the animate armoire and emerges dressed in women's clothes and makeup. The thought of cross-dressing sends him running away in panic.[17] One particularly nasty villager turns the feather-duster/French-maid upside down and begins plucking out her feathers in an apparent hetero rape metaphor. Lumiere saddles up behind the rapist, blows himself (puffing air into his candlestick thumb), and sends a shot of flames up the attacker's rear end. Indeed, several of the village men are attacked "from behind," getting their bottoms burned or kicked or poked. In perhaps the most meaningful of such scenes, Cogsworth slides down the banister toward an invader below, his scissors held out at crotch level, the sharpened point glistening as it heads toward the man's backside. The camera even takes up the scissors-phallus's point of view during the scene, meaning that *we* take up the phallus's point of view, since perspective is always a package deal—to see from someone's perspective is to understand the world anew. The meaning of this moment is further enhanced due to the fact that Cogsworth was the only member of the castle staff previously uncomfortable with the master's way of life. Out of all the castle inhabitants, Cogsworth feared the Beast the most. He was uptight about any possible gay overtures, even embarrassingly and nervously chastising Maurice when the old man first stumbled into the castle, opened up Cogsworth's glass pants/door, and fiddled with his long, swinging pendulum. That Cogsworth is now open to a little fiddling, a little anal poking, is an important moment in the film, though he still has reservations about Lumiere kissing him in the end. (Lest it be thought that Cogsworth is the only hetero staff member, Lumiere, clearly, chases after the sexy French maid as well. But there is something about Lumiere that assures us he happily can be "lit at both ends.") Unfortunately for Cogsworth, the recipient of his scissors attack is Lefou, who is startled but unsurprisingly unscathed. We see Lefou back in full force in the next scene, threatening the kitchen staff before finally running off out of fear of too many knives doing the stabbing. And with Lefou's defeat, the staff has achieved victory, the village men are in retreat, and the attack is over.

But while the attacking mob has been getting its comeuppance, Gaston has been alone, hunting the Beast. It is a hunt layered with multiple meanings. Though Gaston has been shown throughout the film using only a gun, he has failed to bring it along for this pursuit. He carries, instead, a bow and arrow. The switch, we know, is important. The arrow's shaft is more phallic, more indicative of Gaston's desire to penetrate the Beast's body even as he destroys him. The bow and arrow are, after all, the symbol of Cupid and the possibility of love. We presence the absence of such love here in this scene, and also see Gaston's anger, frustration, and desire to do violence as one way in which love can, sadly, be experienced. Throughout the battle, Gaston will refuse to reach for a gun, choosing instead his arrows, a dagger, a large phallic club he fashions from stone torn from the castle. In each case, Gaston seeks to pierce the Beast's body or to pummel it with a stone-hard shaft. The feelings he has for the Beast are muddled, but they are passionate and require close physical contact.

The Beast sees the arrow coming but does nothing to prevent Gaston from taking the shot. The arrow finds its target. The two wrestle around on the roof of the castle, and the Beast is ready to let Gaston have his way with him until he sees Belle down below. She has returned to be by her prince-in-hiding's side, and with the renewal of the possibility of the curse being broken the Beast comes alive and finally begins to fight back.

Now in Gaston's taunting and mockery there is the hint of true self-loathing, the self-hatred and despair that resides at the core of this conflict. "Were you in love with her, Beast?," he shouts into the shadows. Of course the answer is no. Neither was Gaston while he was pursuing Belle. Voicing the question, Gaston condemns the Beast for his ruse, and thus condemns himself. "Did you honestly think she'd want you when she had someone like me?," he continues. The "you" here is the Beast, but in reality it is the mirror version of Gaston, the Gaston who is out and openly gay. The "me" here is the Gaston we have come to know on screen, the man living in a hetero shell, a camouflage of flesh and macho mannerisms that at once both mock and decry straight stereotypes. (Note that Gaston does not say: did you think she'd want you "when she had me," but rather "when she had *someone like* me"—had, that is, what Gaston can pretend to be.) The question is not really a question at all, then, but a declaration: surely Belle could never love an openly gay man; more generally: surely love cannot come to an openly gay man; more to the point: surely Gaston cannot be loved but can at best only hope to live a fake life with a fake wife and an empty heart. Gaston's mockery of the Beast is thus his final statement of sorrow and self-abhorrence. He must kill this Beast-self, and in so doing kill the possibility of his own exposure and, inevitably, his own possible fulfillment.

Gaston is winning, but the battle soon turns. Fighting back, the Beast grips Gaston by the neck—that same neck that burst the belt in the tavern and so secretly impressed the local men—and by this throbbing neck he dangles the defeated Gaston over the edge of the roof and the open ravine below. Gaston is done. His face is a mix of confusion and sorrow, fear and repugnance. He has lost. He is lost—vulnerable and despondent. It is the most exposed Gaston has ever been. "Don't hurt me," he cries with only the Beast able to hear. "I'll do anything. *Anything*." And with this offer, an offer that is at its heart an admission, the Beast recognizes who Gaston is and what he is hiding. But more than this, the Beast knows, too, that he *is* Gaston, one possible version of Gaston, a monster about to become Gaston if all goes as planned with Belle. The Beast's face changes. His rage melts, his eyes turn sad and understanding. He places Gaston back on the roof, releases him, and utters his final request so that only Gaston can hear it. It is something other than a demand. It is said in a soft yet firm whisper. It is a solicitation as much as an imperative, spoken in hope that Gaston will heed its advice and rescue both himself and the Beast as well. It is, in the end, a simple yet impossible prescription in a world of mobs and despair and a Belle drawing near. "Get out," whispers the Beast to a shocked Gaston. Get out, be truly strong. Come out, be newly reborn. Stay out, and save us both.

But Gaston will not come out. And neither will the Beast. Leaving Gaston on the lower roof, the Beast begins to climb to where Belle is waiting for him, placing his hand in hers when he reaches her position. If Gaston does not come to rescue him, he will soon be forced to carry through with his plan to marry this girl. But the Beast asks and hopes for too much. Gaston attacks from behind, producing the embarrassingly small dagger he has been hiding all along, plunging it into the Beast's furry body. The wounded Beast turns, causing his attacker to lose his footing. We do not see him die—for this is Disney, after all, and not Haneke—but we watch Gaston fall into the ravine, never to return again. His scream echoes until it is still; his body gets smaller until it is covered in mist. For fear, for societal demands, for lack of character, for self-loathing, Gaston was not able to rise. The Beast, too, will shortly disappear, with Belle's false love proving the only source for survival—resurrection in a different yet familiar form. With

Gaston gone, the Beast is cleared to take his place. The Beast is dead; long live the prince. Gaston is dead; long live Gaston.

TALE AS OLD AS TIME

Perhaps it is a mob song as old as rhyme. But that doesn't make it any easier to hear—even less so given the terrible truth that its age hides, the truth that violent intolerance has been part of our cultural fabric for so long. True, the world has changed since the early 1990s. And we might wish to pat ourselves on the back when gay marriage is considered constitutional decades later and "tolerance" seems to be on the rise. But tolerance was never really an appropriate goal. Putting up with someone can't lead to true love. And just as racism in the United States didn't end with the election of Barack Obama, so, too, is homophobia not a thing of the past. *Beauty and the Beast* is a brave film, art that delights and inspires even as it holds its magic mirror up to us and confronts us with what we are, how we have constructed our village, what we have allowed to continue around us—perhaps passively, perhaps actively, and most likely in some manner that encompasses a little of all the above.

The narrative is clear: we are all in this together. In a little town where the freedom to choose one's partner is forbidden, no one will be happy, no one will find fulfillment. Intolerance for some inevitably results in such a deep moral social crisis that *all* are doomed—and thus fulfilling heterosexual relationships are not to be found here as well; consequently they are painted as absent, silly, meaningless, and unsatisfying in the film. Where, after all, we must wonder, is Belle's mother? Where are the prince's parents? Where is *Mr.* Potts (was it a bad case of spout envy)? The Bimbettes who offer Gaston the possibility of socially acceptable love are shallow airheads. Lumiere, when he goes after a woman, gives a perverted laugh and tackles the task as if it were a sport. And the village businessman who should be concentrating on his customer's needs is seen leering, instead, at her breasts—to which the woman cagily responds: "Bonjour. How is your *wife*?!" To say that one kind of love is beastly is to condemn all love, to slander love itself. For when "love" is spoken, it appears in its full horizon, every other appearance and way of manifestation apperceived as co-present. It is not, then, that gay relationships will have failed or that straight relationships will have failed. It is that all relationships have failed and are doomed to continue to fail in a context of exclusion for some.

Gaston is on the way toward being the hero, especially when we realize that his persecution of the Beast is merely symbolic of his self-persecution, that his death is thus a form of suicide, that his harassing of Belle is, in the end, a byproduct of the society she perpetuates and does nothing to change. But like a real hero, Gaston has real weaknesses. By painting him as "literally" evil (as a mere naïve reading of the movie would suggest) but at heart oppressed and longing for love and acceptance (as our reading has suggested), we get a Gaston that is conflicted, a fully drawn character who, in the final moment, does not die for his sins or for our sins but for the possibility that we might wake up, realize what we have done, shake off our intolerances, and not only sin no more but have "sin" no more.

And thus the ending is open. The film itself concludes not with the traditional declaration of resolved conflict, but with a question—*literally* two questions, really.

Mrs. Potts's son, Chip, has been transformed from the teacup that he used to be back into a human again, and he watches as the also newly humanized Beast-prince dances with Belle in an apparent marriage celebration—a celebration to which the hypocritical townspeople seem to have shown up. The prince and Belle spin around as the music plays, the beautiful animation catching each character's reflection in the polished dance floor, reminding us of the truth exposed in magic and not-so-magic mirrors all around us if we are only open to them.

"Are they going to live happily ever after?," Chip first asks. It is not enough to conclude with a pat declaration of eternal happiness in this Disney story, for the Beast has chosen to live a life of lies—and so has Belle and so has the town—pretending to be what he is not in order to gain his social acceptance and humanity. It is, in fact, the second coming of Gaston. And so, Chip rightly has to wonder: *is* this a happy ending, will these two really be happy together once the party is over? His mother reassures him that it will all be all right, but Chip is wiser. He has been told throughout the movie that he is too young to understand certain things, but Chip has learned. And so he thinks for a moment, ponders the implications of this sad ending for himself and for us all, and asks his mother a final question.

"Do I still have to sleep in the cupboard?"

Perhaps this story has been about Chip all along because this moment is so important. It is a light scene on the surface, but a troubling query at heart. Chip is unsure of his identity, how society sees him, what is expected of him, who he is and what he may be or be thought to be. If the supposedly happy ending is one in which the Beast goes into the closet and dresses like a prince, will Chip have to go into his cupboard at some point as well? The film thus ends with Chip's final question up in the air and unanswered, with the possibility of closets and cupboards and mobs regathering at a moment's notice when anyone dares step out. It ends, tragically yet honestly, with the possibility of an unhappily-ever-after unless new action is taken, for no one, it turned out, could be brought to love—truly love—a beast. Though the beast was made and unmade by us all.

But once upon a time there was a man named Gaston. He could have loved a beast, could have loved himself, could have shown us all about a love bereft of any absences, adjectives, restrictions, or curses. He could have been a fully realized hero. And this is his story.

CHAPTER 6 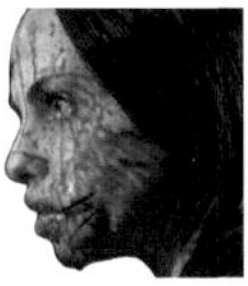

And Say the Zombie Responded?

Or, How I Learned to Stop Living and Unlove the Undead

In February 2011 Serene Branson, a TV reporter for CBS News who was covering the Grammy Awards in Los Angeles, suffered an on-air breakdown. Over the course of ten seconds on live TV, Branson began slurring her speech and, ultimately, spouting gibberish: "Well a very very heavay ah heavy de bertation tonight, we had a very deris-derison. By lets go heah teris tazin loash tiblet hav le pet."[1] The Internet video went viral. Some jokingly claimed Branson had become a real-life zombie on the air. Others worried that she had had a stroke. Either way, it appeared that her brain was suddenly not functioning in the way that a normal human brain functions—she was no longer one of *us*.

Branson's incoherence turned out to be caused by a migraine that mimics the symptoms of a stroke. She recovered quickly and was sent home. But the next day when asked to describe what had happened, her response was still terrifying. At first, she explained, it was not clear to her that something was wrong. She thought she was making sense. All she meant to say was: "Here at the Grammys, Lady Antebellum swept the awards." When she realized that something had gone wrong, she was still unable to summon up the words to communicate her own inner thoughts. She was making sounds, and was compelled to continue, but the sounds were noncommunicative.[2] Even the words "very very" and "tonight we had" were not words that she was *meaning* to say.

It is true that one of the most interesting and confounding characteristics of zombies is their relationship to language and desire—and what this means for consciousness. But before we can confront such complicated issues, we need to meet the zombie head on, thinking through exactly what it means for those of us who are living to have the dead still with us.

Freud tells us that it is pathological to love the dead. Libido is often mistakenly characterized as exclusively sexual energy, but Freud is clear that it merely indicates one's life force or life energy in general—the instinctual drive of the id that propels us all forward. When we love, we invest libido in the object of our affection. And this is the problem with loving the dead. Libido must always be "attached." Once one can no longer attach the libido to an external subject or object, the only way one can continue to love the dead is to re-attach that flailing libido to oneself, taking oneself to be the now-missing Other, mistakenly converting a part of the Self into a puppet version of the Other. It is not only metaphysically wrong, it is a form of narcissism that will inevitably lead to psychological imbalance. The only healthy thing to do once someone dies is to stop loving him or her.

The problem is that the dead are always still present—and thus seemingly ready to accept our love. Phenomenologically, we experience people long after they are dead. It is something Freud never addressed, but when we actually look at our experience, the dead are always present: they are presenced, precisely, *as absent*. In this way, it still seems possible to love them.

What is at work here is what Husserl called "the play of presence of absence." When we investigate the underlying structures of consciousness, we discover that mind is always directed at something, and that something is always a whole. This is an important point that most American and British epistemologists are still not keen on accepting. For them, it seems as if only one side of an object is visible at any given time, and thus the true object of consciousness is at best merely a surface of an object from a single vantage point. As you look before you as you read this book, you see the page as it sits between two covers. It seems that at the moment you can only see the book from one angle right now, and thus the object of your consciousness must be the-front-of-this-particular-page-in-the-book. However, phenomenology calls on us actually to look at our experience rather than reason abstractly about it. And when you look at your experience of the book, you find that you are experiencing—you are *conscious of*—a whole object and not some façade, some two-dimensional surface. In fact, if you truly thought that you were seeing just the front of the things all around you now, if you thought that you were living in some sort of elaborately constructed movie set, there would be good reason to worry about you and your brain.

Instead, it is the case that we actually do experience whole things around us; but how does this happen if all we ever physically see with our eyes are profiles and surfaces? The answer is to be had in understanding how consciousness itself is structured. As we have seen in previous chapters, we are capable of experiencing something that is, in some sense, absent. But the point to stress and repeat here is that this experience is not a lack, a nonexperience, a negation. Instead, it is an actual, full experience: a presence of that which is absent. You are thus experiencing the book as a whole object right now. You can see the current page as present, but you are simultaneously experiencing all of the rest of the book as presently-absent, as there-too, as apperceived rather than directly perceived. The back cover is being experienced right now—it is immediately taken as that which could be fully present if you just turned the book over and took a look. And it is thus that presence and absence are always at work in consciousness.

It is a small step to say that the dead are thus still present for us. This is meant to be taken in a literal way, though not in the sense that there are literal ghosts. It is true that Derrida's notion of "the specter" and "the trace" come out of this phenomenological tradition. The claim that there is no such thing as a complete erasure, that there are always traces in a text both of what has been negated and what is necessarily working to undermine the text as it simultaneously allows the text to come to meaning—these are claims that are indebted to Husserlian phenomenology and the realization that we truly do experience things that are absent. But with our dead loved ones, the point is literal in a different way.

If we undertake a phenomenology of death, we discover that it is never the case that when someone we know and love dies, we then cease to experience that person. The death of the Other is, for us, not an erasure, a lack of experience, a nonexperience. How easy mourning would be if this were the case. How easy it would be if one simply had less experience of the Other after the Other's death. But instead, the dead continue to be present in our life, but present as missing, here and not-here, present as lost. Just as we can actively experience the absence of the back of the book when we look at the book from the front, just as our tongue searches out the missing tooth once it is pulled as if it were still there because it feels as if it still sits in the gum, just as the phantom limb can ache and itch and drive us mad with its present absence, so we directly experience the dead Other—the Other in the mode of being absent in our life. Every dead Other is thus necessarily an apparition of what was. We are, all of us, touched by the death of Others, by the present-absence of those we love. It is the mortal human condition to lose those we love, to be forced into mourning. To be alive is to experience such loss, and thus to be alive is to be haunted.

This could thus very easily become a phenomenology of ghosts, and though there are some good ghost movies, and possibly even some good ghosts out there, our topic is slightly different. The ghost in Western culture is indicative of our realization that something is gone when we lose our loved ones, and something that is completely different and alien is now with us in their place. But zombies suggest that there is something that is *not* gone—there is a presence that is still with us that is not so different from what used to be with us, something, however, that in its presence is horrifying simply because the realization that the dead are still with us is horrifying. And since that presence is of a consciousness that is always incarnate—as all consciousness always is—when we imagine ourselves stalked by zombies in the movies and in other forms of art, we are trying to deal with the reality of mourning.

Freud's admonition not to love the dead is thus not so easily heeded, because the dead are not completely gone when they die. Our libido is not so easily unattached and reeled in so that we can freely invest it elsewhere. There, as an object of consciousness, remains the person we loved, seemingly ready to act as a repository of our libido. But the dead, of course, cannot love us back. And thus we are met with horror. This is why we have some ghost stories with friendly and happy ghosts, but zombies are never friendly or happy. Zombies are a more authentic way of thinking through our relationship with the dead. They are still here, but they can never return our love. As such, can we truly ever really love *them*? The zombie embodies the terror of unrequited love and the realization that all love is headed this way eventually.

In many zombie films we thus encounter a moment at which someone comes across a loved one who is now a zombie. In George A. Romero's *Night of the Living Dead* (1968)—the movie that started it all—Harry and Helen's daughter, Karen, eventually becomes a zombie, eats her father's flesh, and kills the mother who is unwilling to kill her zombified daughter because she still loves the dead. And in the first episode of the AMC television series *The Walking Dead* ("Days Gone Bye," dir. Frank Darbont, original airdate October 31, 2010), sheriff's deputy Rick Grimes encounters a father and son who have survived the zombie apocalypse but are now faced with watching the woman who was once wife and mother to them walk the streets as a zombie. Toward the end of the episode, the father tells his son to stay downstairs while he takes to the second floor of the home to shoot zombies from a window. He kills two zombies with a sense of seriousness but no remorse. When he next has his wife in the sights of his rifle, he cannot bring himself to pull the trigger, setting the gun down, crying uncontrollably.[3]

The Freudian warning is, however, put most succinctly in the sequel to *Night of the Living Dead*. Here, in *Dawn of the Dead* (1978), a scientist explains to a television audience: "We must not be lulled by the concept that they are our family members or our friends. They are not. They will not respond to such emotion. They must be destroyed on sight!"[4] In other words, the dead are still with us, but we must not continue to treat them in the same way. We must, though they are still a part of our lives, move on to placing our libido—our love—elsewhere.

The thought of this is horrific. It feels like we are killing our loved ones by killing our love for them. It is like watching them die a second time. And so, the zombie is a literal recreation of this very philosophical point. The dead must die twice.

All of this phenomenology is what makes zombification possible on film. But of course there are ways in which the structures and cultural manifestations of what it means to be a zombie play out in similar ways in real life as well.

From 1978 to 1991, famed serial killer Jeffrey Dahmer murdered seventeen boys and men, mostly in his Milwaukee apartment. "I carried it too far, that's for sure," Dahmer told police in explaining his frustrated search for a totally compliant, zombie-type sex slave who would always be there for him.[5] To be sure, Dahmer said that he merely wanted to love his victims and to receive their love in return. By drilling holes in their heads in an attempt to turn them into zombies, he meant to "keep them from leaving," to keep them present and compliant with his will. It was, in every important way, a desire for the zombie that operates in the same manner as what we have been investigating on film.

If Freud was incorrect that the problem with loving the dead is that they are no longer present, we can at least admit that although the dead are still with us, they are not present in a way that allows any attached libido to manifest itself in a manner that leads to its flourishing. That is, the pathology of loving the dead is not merely that the dead cannot accept true libidinal investment, but that when we attempt to maintain that relationship we always end up substituting an apparently more-present person to stand in for the Other—namely, ourselves. In our minds, the puppet accepts our love. But since the puppet's strings are pulled by us, the puppet is truly but a reflection of our own will. To love the zombie puppet is to love one's self, and in this way there is always the risk of narcissism at work in our encounters with the dead.

C. S. Lewis, in the book he wrote under a pseudonym about an experience of a crisis of faith he had while mourning his wife, struggles with this exact worry. Lewis writes:

> Already, less than a month after her death, I can feel the slow, insidious beginning of a process that will make the H. I think of into a more and more imaginary woman. . . . The reality is no longer there to check me, to pull me up short, as the real H. so often did, so unexpectedly, by being so thoroughly herself and not me. . . . The image has the . . . disadvantage that it will do whatever you want. . . . It is a puppet of which you hold the strings. . . . [T]he fatal obedience of the image, its insipid dependence on me, is bound to increase. . . . As if I wanted to [be] in love with my memory of her. . . . It would be a sort of incest. . . . I want H., not something that is like her.[6]

This was, in many respects, Dahmer's transgression as well. Dahmer loved the zombie puppet more than the person precisely because the zombie is controllable, precisely because it was a form of self-love. Perhaps "evil" is an empty concept, but if there are actions that are evil, narcissism and the selfishness that goes along with it are most likely at their roots.

In the Voodoo religion of Haiti, zombies are said to be walking dead corpses who are typically controlled by an evil sorcerer, the strings once again pulled by someone with a living desire to control the dead. In the 1930s, Harlem Renaissance anthropologist and novelist Zora Neale Hurston documented a case of a woman in Haiti who had died in 1907 and, three decades later (according to family members and neighbors), returned to life. This work became the inspiration for Wade Davis's research as an ethnobotanist in the 1980s. Davis went to Haiti to search for a pharmacological explanation of why people would seem to be dead and then return to life to do the bidding of others. His work was the source for the 1988 Wes Craven movie, *The Serpent and the Rainbow*. In Haiti, the west African religion of Vodun came to mix with Catholicism, eventually resulting in the amalgam that is Voodoo—a religion practiced today by more than half of the nine million residents of Haiti. In Vodun, a "zombi astral" is said to be the part of the soul of a human being that is captured and controlled by a *bokor*, a wizard or sorcerer. The human, without a soul, is dead. And the *bokor*, having control over the soul of the deceased, thus becomes the ultimate puppet master, able to send the zombie body out to do his or her bidding.

We risk a subtle form of racism and exoticism by summarizing and portraying a religion so strange to mainstream American experience thus. But to be sure, one needn't look beyond the Christian religion for traces of belief in reanimation and resurrection. By definition, one could argue that Jesus became a zombie on the third day after His crucifixion. To those who believe that such a statement borders on the sacrilegious, this is, in fact, one of the risks of Christianity—and precisely one of the risks against which Christians are specifically warned. That is, one of the lessons of liberation theology and the post-theism movement of the 1960s and '70s was that the theistic notion of God had become an idol in Christianity. Christians were treating the metaphysical, supernatural, and paranormal conception of God as a thing to be worshipped, when this completely misses the point of Jesus's teachings. Christianity is a social-political-ethical system more than a metaphysics or a cosmology; and Jesus, at every opportunity, lectures on how we should pursue justice in the world, not wait for a reward in Heaven and not wait for Him magically to create justice for us. When Jesus feeds the masses with a single loaf of bread, we miss the point of the story if we think, "Wow! Jesus had awesome magical baking powers!" Instead, the point is that we must feed those who are hungry around us even if it seems we don't have enough for ourselves—even if it seems impossible. When Jesus tells us to prepare for Heaven, we miss the point if we think we must place all of our hope in some supernatural afterlife in which we will float up into the clouds and live forever in a perfect Disneyland.[7] Instead, He tells us, "The Kingdom of Heaven is spread upon the Earth though men do not see it." In other words, this world and this life are already our Heaven if we only start acting in such a way as to make it a Heaven. And when Jesus dies and is resurrected, we miss the point of the story if we begin worshipping zombie-Jesus (which, to be frank, is what the majority of Christians do today: there is a reason Mel Gibson's *The Passion of the Christ* [2004] plays like a horror movie). Instead, the lesson is that, as the Greek tells us, Jesus can still *appear* to people even after He is, physically, gone. Thus we get words such as "emphanerosen"—meaning "manifested"—to describe the coming-to-faith experience that people have before and after Jesus's resurrection. When Peter, for instance, has the realization that Jesus's teachings are good and true, we are given the words, "Jesus manifested to Peter." This is the same language we get when, after death, Jesus manifested himself to the 500, to Thomas, to his disciples, etc. That is to say, "manifestation" and "appearance" indicate the strength of the message and not a physical sight. To think otherwise is to run the risk of focusing merely on the fact that Jesus died and came back—on the metaphysics and the magic—rather than on what it all means.

We have gone on this extended detour into Christian scripture because it is making the same point we have been investigating concerning zombies. The presence of our lost loved ones, the present absence of the Other, is real. Zombies are a way of working this out in popular culture. And if we try to love that Other in the mode of presently-absent, we risk loving an image rather than a person. We risk horror. Similarly, for Christians there is a real presence of the divine, an actual presence that must be taken seriously. But if we worship the resurrected flesh and the sketchy metaphysics that support it, we commit idolatry. Jesus warns us against this, but many Christians fail to listen. In zombie terms, if we take the zombie to be our loved one, we are soon going to face horror and die ourselves. That zombie that is walking around is not what our loved one was really fully about. And in Christian terms, if we take the resurrected Jesus to be Christ, if we think that this is what Christianity is fully all about, we miss the point, we wallow in the depths of the sacrilegious, and we will face horror and die ourselves.

Of course, there are zombie moments in culture that are somewhere between Jeffrey Dahmer and Jesus Christ. If the threat of the zombie is the threat of idolatry and narcissism, then we must *always* be worried about how we treat our dead. Vladimir Lenin demanded that his body be destroyed after his death precisely so that it could never be kept as an idol, as a false object of love, thus replacing the living revolution that demanded the Russian people's full libidinal attention. But we are a species of zombie lovers, never wanting to take the harder path. Consequently, early in the 1920s influential members of the Russian cosmism movement argued the need to have cryogenic equipment on hand at all times in case of Lenin's death. Their plan was to preserve the leader and his brain for a full-body resurrection at some unknown future date. Though Lenin gave clear orders that nothing of the sort was to be done—because to have the body still there after death would truly jeopardize the Soviet state—doctors were secretly told instead to prepare to mummify Lenin's body should the leader pass. And it was thus that in January 1924, just three days after his death (the same amount of time it took Jesus), Lenin returned to greet the people of Moscow in his vacuum-sealed glass crypt.

The "real" zombie is thus related to the cult of personality. The real zombie is there to stand in for those we have lost, beckoning us to commit those sins of ego, those sins of idolatry, that doom us. No wonder most zombies in the movies move so slowly. They don't need to chase us down. We are drawn to them. And worse yet, we know that each of us will someday become one of them. Whether we are bitten and infected now or simply die from natural causes later, if the dead walk the Earth, this is our shared fate. Every single person will someday become a zombie—each of us haunting the world with the echo of our selfhood, driving those who loved us and whom we have left behind to the horror of that very same realization.

Over the last ten years, "zombie walks" have been growing in popularity. In large cities, college towns, and all over, really, people dress up as zombies, meet at a mall or on some street, and then proceed to walk, stalk, and moan their way around. They wear the clothes of everyday people—the sorts of clothing that people would wear in different walks of life while they are engaged in different sorts of human activities—and they paint their faces like zombies and smear themselves with blood.

The point is that this is less an act of fantasy than it is everyone acting out his or her necessary and ultimate fate. And it is interesting to think about this phenomenon not as an alternative Halloween, but as an inverse Halloween. That is, zombie walks don't always occur in October. They take place throughout the year. But more than this, if we think of Halloween as a time to put on a costume and become something radically other, then the zombie walk is quite the opposite. One of the reasons that zombies are frightening in the movies is precisely because they do not wear scary costumes. They wear the clothing of everyday people because they *are* everyday people. They are plumbers and businessmen and professors and dancers and shoppers and cabdrivers and theoretical physicists and all the rest. Of course, when we realize this—when we see that the zombie walk is something that we can both dress up for and not dress up for at the same time—we also realize that our everyday clothes are already costumes. When we go throughout our day in our so-called *real lives*, we are playing parts and adopting roles. This is what it means to be a person: we are constantly performing our identity. And clothing is one way of costuming for that performance. When I teach classes at my university, for instance, I wear a jacket and tie. It means something to my students to see me in a jacket and tie. It provides context to the words that I speak and helps establish such moments in my fractured identity: I am an academic. It would be strange, for instance, if each evening after teaching, I were to take a shower and prepare to get ready for sleep, putting on a suit and tie again before crawling into bed. One of the things we realize about ourselves from the inverse-Halloween presentation of the zombie is that it is possible to inhabit our clothes—and by extension, our roles—in a zombified manner. There is very little that separates us from the zombie. To become this monster we needn't grow hair everywhere like a werewolf; we needn't sprout fangs and do the other magical things that a vampire does; we don't grow or shrink or change species or mutate as some monsters do. Zombies are special because to become one all we have to do is die (which we will do someday) and then stay around (which we will do someday for those who love us). Or be dead in some way already (a state with which we are all, no doubt, familiar).

When we take images from popular culture and turn them into zombie versions of the same, we thus expose something about the culture that was dead, and frightening, to begin with. There are, thus, zombie Barbies, zombie Hello Kitty, and even images of a zombie Mona Lisa. And during zombie walks, participants sometimes choose to dress up first as a character from popular culture and then turn that character into a zombie. *Star Wars* characters are quite popular (with zombie storm troopers and Ewoks being the costumes of choice), as well as zombified corporate mascots (one hasn't really lived—or died—until one has been terrified by a zombie Ronald McDonald stalking the streets).

The point, of course, is that as cultural commodities, these icons are also always already pointing toward horror. This is one of the reasons that George Romero's zombie movies are so fascinating. Before his death in 2017, Romero would regularly come out with another zombie movie that tackled the state of Western culture, drawing attention to how the line between humans and zombies in the film, and in reality, is a fine one. This is, arguably, most successfully accomplished in Romero's *Dawn of the Dead*, in which the four main characters of the film hole up in a shopping mall after the zombie apocalypse.[8]

In *Dawn of the Dead* it is difficult to tell the difference between the zombies walking the mall and the regular shoppers (*see figure 6.1*). Both move with a dull and steady determination. Both seem directed toward a goal of consumption that seems grotesque, yet they cannot control it and cannot see how grotesque it obviously is. The mall thus becomes the equivalent of a cemetery for the living, a place where dead capital goes to keep mall-walking. As Stephen, one of the

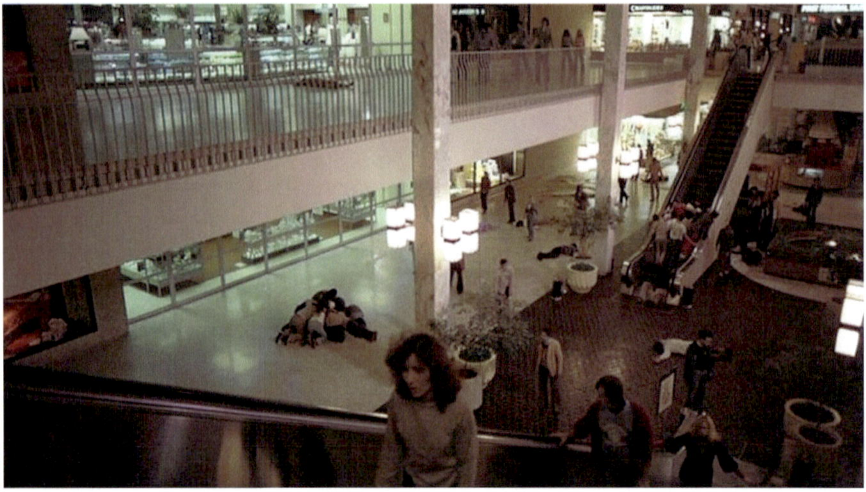

FIGURE 6.1. Scene from the film *Dawn of the Dead*. 1978. Dir. George A. Romero.

main characters of the movie, puts it (after coming back from a post-zombie-apocalypse exuberant shopping trip, seemingly happy that this has all happened because they now have the mall to themselves): "You should see all the great stuff we got, Franny. All kinds of stuff. This place is terrific. It really is. It's perfect. All kinds of things. We've really got it made here, Franny."

Later, discussing why so many zombies would turn up at the mall and try, day after day, to break in, three of the main characters in the film listen to the zombies pounding on the shopping mall's glass doors:

> Francine: They're still here.
>
> Stephen: They're after us. They know we're still in here.
>
> Peter: They're after the *place*. They don't know why, they just remember. Remember that they want to be in here.
>
> Francine: What the hell are they?
>
> Peter: They're us; that's all.

The film *Sean of the Dead* (dir. Edgar Wright, 2004) is a funny movie, but in some ways it is also a disappointment in that its main point is merely that it is difficult to tell the zombies from the regular humans because all of the people in Sean's town are already zombified by modern life.[9] The problem here is that this has always been one of the main messages in the Romero films.[10] One cannot satirize what is already satire in this manner. It is akin to trying to do a satire of *The Bachelor* or *The Jerry Springer Show*. These things are already satires—and as they continue on in our culture, they even, to a certain extent, become satires of themselves. As we will see in chapter 9, postmodernity's challenge lies, in part, in finding a way to engage in postirony.

Let us say, then, that part of the evil of the zombie is what they—and by proxy, *we*—wish to consume. Before we get to the question of consuming brains, it makes sense to see this critique of capitalism play itself out in one other manner as well.

In the fourth—and most ethically and politically complex—of Romero's six zombie movies, *Land of the Dead* (2005), the tables have been turned completely and, morally speaking, we end up on the side of the zombies. As with all good zombies, the movement is slow. At first, when the film begins, we are ready to fear the zombies and take joy in their being killed in new and creative ways—the hallmark of any good zombie movie. But little by little, it becomes clear in *Land of the Dead* that the humans are the evil creatures. Slowly, we come to identify with the zombies and are forced to confront the question of who deserves to continue existing in the end.

The movie starts out with a scene that slyly sets up the twist to come. Some humans have gone out to the zombie-infested suburbs. They crouch in the foliage near a gas station, spying on the zombies with binoculars. When two zombies accidentally step on the air hose, causing a bell to ring in the gas station, a zombie attendant comes out as if to provide service to a car. The humans remark:

> First Speaker: They're trying to be us.
>
> Second Speaker: No. They used to be us. They're learning how to be us again.
>
> First: No way. . . . There's a big difference between us and them. They're dead. It's like they're pretending to be alive.
>
> Second: Isn't that what we're doing? Pretending to be alive?

We, too, are just going through the motions, to be sure. But to admit this is not fundamentally different than our realization that we are the mall-walkers in the earlier film. What makes *Land of the Dead* stand out is that the particular motions through which we are going are so debased and so lacking in any moral foundation, it becomes increasingly difficult to root for the human survivors.

The humans we see watching the zombies through binoculars at the gas station are not afraid of these zombies. They are not even really hiding from them. Instead, the humans have purposefully come to where the zombies are in order to kill them, to raid the local stores for food and supplies, and to take the spoils back to a walled-in city inside a protective zone that is zombie-free. *Land of the Dead* thus works on the level of a sort of allegory for empire and colonialism. The heroes leave their home, pillage the natural resources of the foreign land, kill the locals (whom they deem subhuman), and return once again with the booty. Like all colonial rulers, those with the power far away are actually dependent on maintaining the oppression of their subjects, and this necessarily involves dehumanizing them. Back in the human city, we thus are not surprised to find zombies chained up so that humans can pay to have their picture taken with them, and zombies kept in fighting arenas to have sporting spectacles on which the humans can place bets.

Meanwhile, each time the humans go out to steal the resources of the zombies, they always go at night so that they can shoot fireworks in the sky to distract the zombies (who always look up in shock and awe), thus making them easier to kill. All of this seems to be working well until one of the zombies starts to become aware of what is going on. This is the African American gas-station attendant, who is unnamed in the film but referred to as "Big Daddy" in print because this is what the name-patch sewn on his uniform says. He is defined, that is, by the job he had serving others. But still, the revolution begins. And it begins with a visceral reaction to the violence that always accompanies the human raids, especially as that violence leads to the dismembering and beheading of zombies.

Big Daddy sees a fellow zombie lose a head, and, without even understanding why, he starts to mourn. This is the beginning of the raising of his consciousness. After he learns to mourn and see death for what it is, he starts using tools, starts developing language, and starts organizing the other zombies in something resembling an uprising as they march across the riverbed and lay siege to the walled-in city. It is as if what it means to possess logos is to have the ability to mourn, and Big Daddy is on the way toward a revolutionary logos. When the zombies arrive, the viewer who has been paying attention is glad they are there, rooting for them to take down their oppressors.

Here, the movie ends with a reference to how it began. Riley, one of the humans who was a raider we met in the first scene but is now turned rebel, speeds away from the city and stops to look at Big Daddy through his binoculars. Their eyes meet once again across the distance. And this time, Riley orders his second-in-command not to fire. "All they want is somewhere to go," he says. "Same as us." It is a postcolonial zombie apocalypse that looks more like a beginning than an end. It looks strangely like a chance for hope.

There remain two foundational questions we must consider in our investigation of the nature of zombies, two philosophical questions of the mouth: the question of cannibalism and the question of language. Why do the zombies wish to eat humans, and why can they only moan and mutter as they stumble along? These final inquiries are related, and they provide key pieces of the puzzle if we are to understand fully what the zombie phenomenon is all about.

Part of the horror of the zombie is that he or she might hunt and eat you. And this is a true threat: to be consumed by our love of the Other. Within the various fictional and artistic worlds inhabited by zombies, there is little agreement as to *why* zombies crave human flesh. It is nearly part of the definition of "zombie," however, that they are constantly hungry and have a craving for only one food type.

In some sense, zombies are *merely* ravenous. The only real personality trait all zombies have is that they are always hungry and always desire human flesh. Nothing else will satiate them—and, indeed, not even human flesh will really satiate them, because they act as though no matter how much flesh they eat, they are always starving. We can read this in two ways. We might simply think of this as yet another instance of zombies being an incarnation of our own mad desire for consumption. Like the zombies mindlessly shopping in the mall—mindlessly *consuming*—perhaps this hunger is another cultural marker for our own excesses, our own desires to go on consuming and consuming with no end in sight. Yet we can also see something tragic in this compulsion. The zombies do not seem to have a choice about their desire to eat humans. And actually eating humans doesn't stop the desire. Like the gluttons in the third circle of Dante's version of hell, those who are punished are unaware of each other's presence, forced to live in a mass of flesh that is lubricated with mud caused from the continual rain that falls. The life of sensual pleasure and appetite has reduced the sinners to a world in which they cannot recognize anything other than their own desires. Narcissism and gluttony are thus related. And in this way there is tragedy at work in such insatiable desire both in hell and in a hell-on-Earth. Dante also tells us that Cerberus, the three-headed dog, is the guard of the third circle of hell, and in a nod to this, the *Resident Evil* films and videogames always include zombie dogs, also named Cerberus. In the 2010 film in this series (*Resident Evil: Afterlife*, dir. Paul W. S. Anderson), in fact, one of the zombie dogs opens his mouth and it expands into multiple mouths with multiple rows of teeth.[11] All the better to eat and keep eating.

Given the relationship between zombies and gluttony, it is thus not surprising to see zombies' unending appetite as a theme that occurs repeatedly in zombie films. In the French zombie film, *The Horde* (dir. Benjamin Rocher and Yannick Dahan, 2009), the relationship between tragedy and desire is spoken out loud. As zombies press against the glass doors of an apartment complex, moaning and wailing to get in (in an apparent homage to Romero's mall-based *Dawn of the Dead*), one character watches and listens to the moans, remarking: "It's like some sort of cry for help." "No," another character argues. "They're starving to death."[12] Of course, like all zombies, they are already dead. So the starvation at work is one that is not really related to survival in any way. As is the case with the living, desire is thus always pointing at something other than its own satiation. Desire is its own end.

Zombies, even when they are cut in half and have no stomach, want to eat. This is, in fact, a major point of Romero's third zombie movie, *Day of the Dead* (1985). Here, most of the film takes place underground in a secret army facility where a small group of soldiers and scientists live. The soldiers round up zombies, keep them in a pen, and make them available to the team of scientists who are studying them. The scientists are divided, however, as to whether or not they should be concentrating on curing the zombie virus or simply finding a way of domesticating the zombies and learning to live with them. Dr. Logan, who argues for domestication, treats the zombies as animals, vivisecting them in his lab. "See, it wants me," explains the doctor. "It wants food. But it has no stomach. It can take no nourishment from what it ingests. It's working on instinct, a deep, dark, primordial instinct."[13]

To be sure, the notion of *instinct* plays a central role here. Experimenting on a different patient, Dr. Logan cuts the zombie's brain away, layer by layer. Left with only the brain stem and the bits of tissue typically associated with the reptilian brain, the zombie still moves and reaches out and tries to eat. The implication is that the zombie has been turned into an animal—something like a crocodile, in fact, that works on instinct to hunt fresh meat.

But why do zombies crave *human* flesh? In a seventh-season episode of *The X-Files* written and directed by David Duchovny, Duchovny's character, Fox Mulder, argues that zombies have a hunger for human flesh because they are acting out all of the desires that were impossible while they were alive.[14] The forbidden is fair game only after death, and so zombies enact the greatest of taboos. The desire points at nothing greater than its own enactment.

It seems unquestionable that cannibalism is a marker for the complete breakdown of society, but as always, the real question is how we define our terms to live with ourselves. The Last Supper is not taken to be a zombie banquet, and Christian transubstantiation is not taken to be an act of cannibalism but rather an act of communion. Similarly, when newborn babies drink their mother's milk, literally eat part of the mother's body, this, too, is not defined as cannibalism. And when humans who are not vegetarians eat pork and beef and chicken and the like, they do not think of themselves as cannibals, because such creatures are not us: *we* are thought not to be animal.

To return to *Dawn of the Dead*, as Dr. Rausch puts it:

> Normally, the first question is, "Are these cannibals?" No, they are not. Cannibalism in the truest sense of the word implies an interspecies [sic] activity. These creatures prey on humans. They do not prey on each other, that's the difference. They attack and they feed only on warm flesh. . . . These creatures are nothing but pure, motorized instinct."[15]

One of the things to which this points is, of course, how we humans are basically just sacks of meat. And it is interesting to note the extensive implications of this sort of realization. In *The Walking Dead* television series, for instance, the human survivors initially include a white Southern racist and an African-American man. When the two begin fighting, Deputy Rick Grimes steps in and announces: "Things are different now. There is no black or white. Only white meat and dark meat. Us and them."[16] The assumption is that race goes away after the zombies start chasing us. Race is seen as a quality of flesh that is unimportant to anyone other than humans, and we are thus being chastised for caring so much about something so invisible to other creatures. We humans are caught up on race, that is, because we do not see the body for what it truly is: merely a lump of meat. This is a point that is also driven home in the complete lack of attention to the Asian-American identity of the character Glenn, whose racial background is never really brought up in *The Walking Dead*—not even when he falls in love with and marries a white Southern woman. Post–zombie apocalypse America is apparently postracial America as well. Glenn, in fact, was a fan favorite on the show until his shocking death was revealed in the season 7 premiere, "The Day Will Come When You Won't Be." In this episode, Negan—a human with a psychotic penchant for violence meted out with a barbed-wire-wrapped baseball bat—murders Glenn, and it is clear that the divisions that are drawn among humans are no longer ones that have anything to do with race. Instead, there is "us" and "them," where someone who is an "us" is defined as one you can trust due to your history with that individual person, completely disassociated from race. Of course, race is still functioning in this discourse because race is always more than skin color. In the distinction between white meat and dark meat, there is still division. But what the show seems to be getting at is that even if there are physical differences—even if the category of race initially is founded on some empirical quality—we must abandon the political category of "race" in a postapocalyptic world, realizing that there are always differences among us. The differences on which we choose to focus and reify into something of import become relative. The categories of "black" and "white" and "Asian" have no basis in nature, but rather serve a political and ethical function.

The same, though, can be said of species. To separate a pig from a human is possible because there are differences. But difference is everywhere. It's all a question of what one wishes to do with some difference once it is noted. Having the category distinction between black and white makes it possible to own slaves. Having the category distinction between human and pig keeps eating pork from being an act of cannibalism. The moral question thus does not begin with the question of how to act, but rather how to think, conceptualize, and perceive the world before actions even become possible. If the assumed evil of zombies is partly found in the object of their hunger, then isn't this our secret evil as well? We crave flesh—perhaps not our own species' (as fictional as that category might be), but we do, indeed, want to eat the living. And in this way, the zombie's desire for human flesh is an ethical marker for our own failing, for our own desire to eat meat.

Once again, we are working out our fears and our guilt by means of the zombie. We humans are creatures capable of some degree of choice, capable of taking part in the shaping of our worldview and thus what appears to us as good and right. That so many of us continue to torture animals and eat their flesh is a not-so-secret horror that haunts us as a culture.

Let us make no mistake: this is all about the flesh. It is always about the flesh with zombies and with humans. What it means to say that a zombie is dead is, itself, an interesting philosophical question. If one is animate, responding to external stimuli, and capable of behavior, what more could we want to qualify as a living thing? It seems that zombies are considered dead only because they were once alive and stopped being alive for a time—and, perhaps, they do not metabolize. Something has reanimated their flesh. They are brainless, and this indicates for most that they are consciousness-less as well.

This would certainly be the position of Descartes, who argued that without a mind, a creature is a mere machine. For much of his life, Descartes searched for where the mind might reside inside the human body. He claimed that the mind, that thing that truly is the Self, is "lodged in the body as a pilot in a vessel,"[17] but he could never quite figure out how the two things fused so that the one could control the other. For a time, he considered the possibility that the mind lives inside the pineal gland, but this is a rather dark moment in the history of philosophy given that such a claim is, to put it lightly, incredibly stupid. Perhaps the only good thing that ever came out of Descartes's delusion was the 1959 movie by Ed Wood entitled *Plan 9 from Outer Space*—and the word "good" here is being used rather loosely—in which Cartesian aliens reanimate human corpses and turn them into zombies by stimulating their pineal glands.

Descartes was concerned that it was impossible to experience the consciousness of another person and thus there was no guarantee that there really were other sites of consciousness beyond his own. Historically, analytic philosophers call this "the problem of other minds." More recently, the problem has been restated and renamed "the philosophical zombie problem" such that one worries about creatures that could exist who would act like human beings in every way but would not have the internal conscious life of a human—they would, for instance, do something or experience something but not be conscious that they are doing or experiencing that thing.

All of this is only a worry, however, if one takes the mind to be something separate from the body. And one of the lessons of zombies is that this simply is not the case. Zombies are more in line with French philosophy that came three centuries after Descartes. Consciousness, argues Merleau-Ponty, is in the flesh, it is of the body: to be incarnate is to be conscious.[18] As phenomenology teaches us, there can be no Other, no possibility of other consciousness, without flesh. The body of the Other is the site of consciousness; the mind lives in the flesh. Far from being a question of brain waves, consciousness is always spread throughout the body, and thus without the body there can be no possibility of mind—no possibility, that is, of the true presence of the Self or the Other.[19] Think of the way in which it is your *body* that knows how to ride a bicycle. Think of the pianist's or the guitarist's *hands* that know where to move across the piano and the guitar. Think of the manner in which you inhabit space and your self has heft, of the way in which you constitute yourself as immediately in the world and not really as "looking out at it from inside"—as if the body is merely a vessel, a prison, and not the site of consciousness itself.[20] As we saw in chapter 3, we are not stuck behind our eyes, glimpsing the world as voyeurs.

Zombies, as consciousness incarnate, thus represent another important realization for humans: though our culture is fully Cartesian and embraces the notion of the body as mere object (forcing us to disembody ourselves and think of our own consciousness as something that is apart from the flesh), the truth is that what it means to be minded is to be enfleshed.[21]

If zombies are conscious in a fundamental way, then, why is it that they lack the ability to communicate? Why do they moan and groan, at best asking only for brains, and, more typically, saying nothing at all?

If we recall the reporter at the Grammys, we note that the horror was in thinking that something bad had happened to this woman—something bad had happened to her brain—but we also note that what is truly frightening about the incident is the way in which she continued to talk to us as if she were still communicating, as if she were still saying something. Part of the horror is, in fact, that something has happened to *us*. Perhaps *we* no longer understand. Perhaps *we* are unable to communicate. Beings with whom we are unable to communicate will always be a source of anxiety, regardless of where we place the blame. This is because language is a way of making things present in their absence. It is, as well, to call a world into being. Together, we share the language and we share the world. When the first part of this breaks down, so goes the latter.

What is holding zombies back from communicating with us? They have ears that can hear, and they have tongues that can articulate—or at least some of them still have attached ears and tongues. If they are not talking to us, is it because they are unable to do so, or is it, even more frighteningly, because they choose not to? If a zombie spoke, would we be able to understand him? Would we share a world? Have we really even tried to talk to the zombie—talked in such a way that our talking is not an inquisition, but rather the start of a real conversation; talked in such a way that we are poised to hear a response rather than mere sound?

If the zombie is truly that which resists—the remainder that cannot be dialectized—then we must see the zombie's rejection of logos as a political move. To argue against the Enlightenment is, as Adorno realized, always a project of "dissolvent rationality."[22] The totalizing force of Kantian rationality turns even its critique into another moment of support. The zombie, however, hints at the way "out" (even if we acknowledge that "inside" and "outside" are also part of the Enlightenment's dualistic worldview). The zombie does not argue against rationality—the trap that Kant set that gets continually re-baited by any and all discourse that follows. Instead, the zombie opts out, seeing logos for what it is: at best, an eighteenth-century parlor game; at worst, a means of oppression so insidious that it not only drives empire, colonialism, and capitalism, thus contributing to the true suffering (and consumption) of people all over the world, but the means of the very destruction of that world as well. To speak of "the zombie apocalypse" is a rhetorical trick meant to blind us to the apocalypse that is already unfurled all around us today. To speak at all is to take up the language, and thus live in the world, of the oppressor. Language speaks on behalf of capital. Every sentence sells—not just the latest Apple product or fast-food slab of death-on-a-bun, but the whole world. Language, as a manifestation of instrumental reason (which is the only reason left in town), tells us that we will be okay, we are doing okay, we should ride this thing out, we just need more of the same if there is ever any inkling of a problem. But zombie muttering is a resistance. Zombie moaning is revolutionary. Zombie silence is flourishing. The zombie has met the Enlightenment head-on and has eaten its face off.

When the Grammy reporter lost control of her words, there are those who feared that the only explanation was that zombiehood had set in. There is precedent for this in the culture. When the mouth no longer communicates, we struggle to put it to use—we struggle to understand how we can still be human. And there is no finer artistic investigation of this fear than the Canadian independent film *Pontypool* (dir. Bruce McDonald, 2009), the tagline of which is, "Shut up or die."

Pontypool is the most cerebral zombie movie one might imagine. Some refer to it as a zombie movie without zombies, or the zombie movie that Noam Chomsky could have written. It is all this, but it is much more. The film is based on Anthony Burgess's book, *Pontypool Changes Everything,* and the action takes place almost entirely inside a radio station located in the basement of a church in the small town of Pontypool, Ontario. Filmed on location, and directed with patient and subtle brilliance by Bruce McDonald, the movie came to be after

Burgess adapted his book to create a screenplay that unfolded in the style of Orson Welles's *War of the Worlds*. And the movie is, in many ways, a radio play—fittingly more about words than about visuals.

At the start of the film, controversial shock-jock disc jockey Grant Mazzy has emerged from a scandal and has relocated from the big city to Pontypool's small-town and small-market radio station. He is reduced to reading information about lost pets and setting up segments from field reporter Ken Loney (who pretends to be giving his traffic reports from a helicopter when he is actually just driving around town in his Dodge Dart). Grant has two female assistants, Sydney Briar (his producer) and Laurel-Ann Drummond (his technician). The radio broadcast day begins more or less like any other, but soon Ken is reporting that there are mobs of people gathering and rioting in the streets. They are repeating nonsense words and phrases, and no one is able to understand what is going on. Ken takes refuge in a nearby home and encounters a teenage boy who seems to be mimicking the sounds of his baby brother. Grant sends the report out live over the air, and the sound of the boy making repetitive baby noises is chilling (*see figure 6.2*). Soon after, it seems that Ken himself is starting to experience a breakdown:

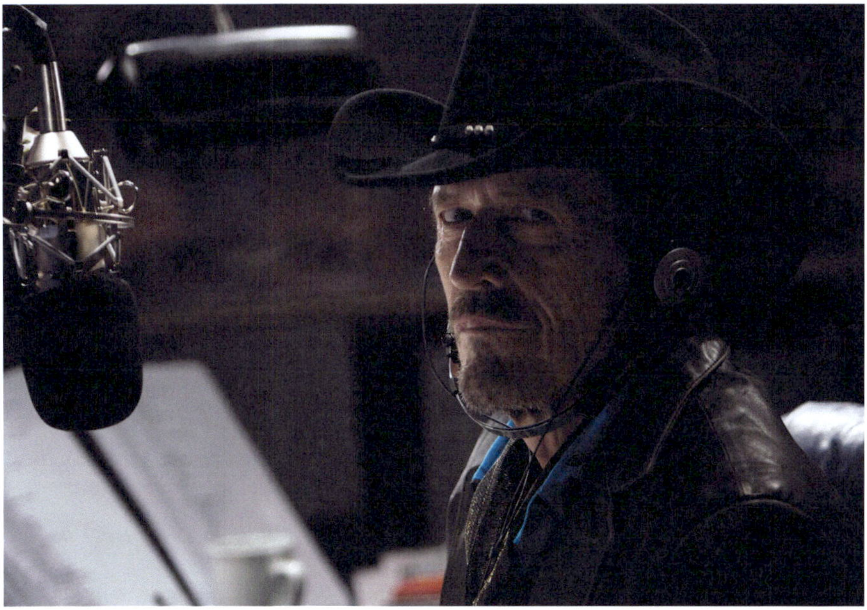

FIGURE 6.2. Scene from the film *Pontypool*. 2009. Dir. Bruce McDonald; Stephen McHattie as Grant Mazzy.

Grant: What's going on Ken?

Ken: This is going to sound weird. I can't stop thinking: do you have a sample?

Grant: I'm sorry. A sample? A sample of what?

Ken: Just simple. I think a simple kind of sample. Uh. Uh. This is what I was saying. I need to. . . . I can't stop thinking. Sample. Some sample. Oh. Sample of, sample of what I'm trying to say. Do you, do you?

Grant: Just try to stay calm, Ken.

Ken: A sample of what I'm trying to say. Uh. Grant?

Grant: Ken? Ken?

Ken: I'm just going to try to to try to uh. . . .

Grant: Can you think?

Ken: I can I can I can't. . . .

Doctor (to Grant, in the studio): Stick to simple questions. Simple.

Ken: Simple questions. Simple. Sample. Simple.

Later, in the church basement, Laurel-Ann starts to show symptoms as well, repeating words and sliding into nonsense before eventually trying to attack her friends and eat them (*see figure 6.3*). Her talking sounds like language. It has the cadence of language. But it means nothing.

When Grant and Sydney are joined by a local doctor, he explains that the problem is a virus. But it is a virus that is being spread by language. Certain words in the English language have become "infected," and when they enter a person's consciousness, their meaning breaks down. The victim begins repeating the word in hopes of making it come to meaning once again. But soon, all language has lost its meaning. As the insanity sets in, it is marked by one simple desire: the desire to communicate. With this desire incapable of being fulfilled, the drive finds a new outlet, a new way to manifest itself. The victim searches out someone who is not infected and, unable to communicate and thus share a world, tries to consume the mouth and tongue of that person. Literally.

As the movie comes to a close, the radio station receives a message in French telling them to stop broadcasting and not to translate the message into English. French, it seems, is still a safe language. Unfortunately, Grant is doing a translation on air as he is receiving the message, and thus becomes even more culpable in the spread of the virus. Eventually, with the entire town pressing against the outside of the church and the military threatening to bomb all of Pontypool, Sydney becomes infected. Terms of endearment—words such as

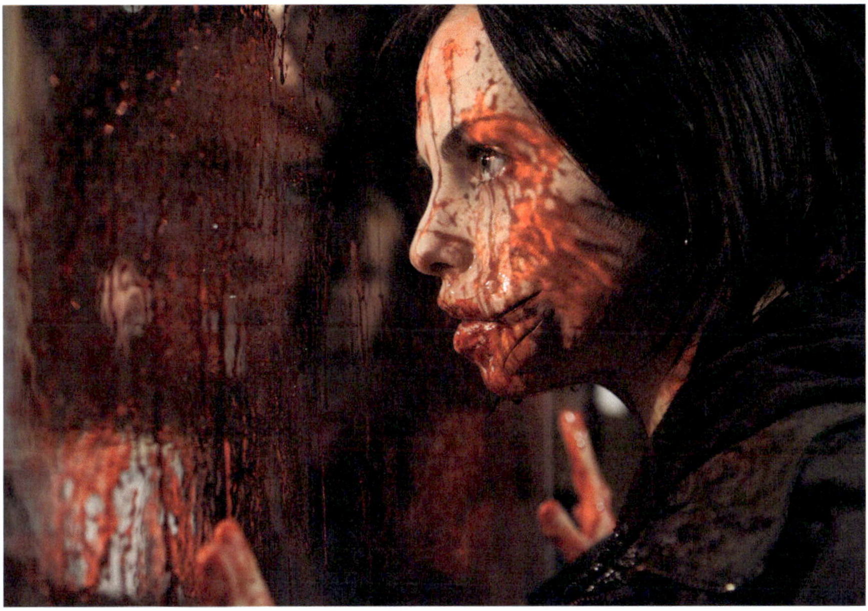

FIGURE 6.3. Still from the film *Pontypool*. 2009. Dir. Bruce McDonald; Georgina Reilly as Laurel-Ann Drummond.

"honey" or "sweetheart"—have turned out to be the most dangerous, but Sydney has stumbled on the word "kill" and cannot stop herself from repeating it. Grant, in a flash of brilliance, manages to cure Sydney by confusing her, telling her that "kiss" means "kill" and that other words do not refer to the things she had earlier believed. They try to broadcast this over the airwaves—"swimming is tomorrow, fidelity is monologue, ceiling is rhinoceros"—but a countdown begins outside the church (in French) and the movie ends when the military reaches zero, Grant and Sydney kiss, and, we presume, the bombs destroy everything.

As we have seen repeatedly, one of the conceits of modernity was that language functioned through denotation. Words were thought to have meaning because they denote things in the world—reaching out and pointing at them, anchoring themselves like signs or labels. But postmodernity, with its critique of all metanarrative and the naïve belief that texts have borders and the world is separate from our understanding of it, put an end to this. In Derridean terms, words refer, but they merely refer to each other. They hang above the world without ever reaching down to point, supported by faith and the force of our collective and mutual will. They carve out a world rather than describe one. In phenomenological terms, words do not point but are one way of making things present (though present in a very absent way). Communication thus becomes more of an ethical project than an ontological or metaphysical one. How we speak carries with it a responsibility for the Other. Even the word "response" and the word "ability" are hidden in "responsibility" (in much the same way that "typo" is hidden in the middle of "Pontypool"), for what it means to be responsible for someone is to have the ability to respond, and to do so with care. What is right or wrong can no longer be settled by an appeal to a correspondence theory of truth based on a belief about there being an objective world outside. And so, the weight of language is a heavy burden on our souls. The demands by which communication maintains community are great. And zombies are the breakdown of all of this. They press against the outside of our most sacred institutions, and we have nothing left to say.

What it means for someone to be dead is never to be able to respond. The dead are, to be sure, still with us. But there will *never* be a response. We write to the dead, talk to them, cry out for them. And they do not answer back. This is Levinas's definition of "death," in fact: a nonresponse, a silence. The zombie is thus a marker both of our cultural fear about settling into the age of postmodernity bereft of the comforts of modernism, and the fear of silence, the fear of the death of the Other. If the zombie moans a bit it is not because he is struggling for language, not because he is some animal on the way toward language, but because he has passed it by—and in so doing, passed us by, passed along, passed away.

Our future lies in that direction. All around us are the markers of where we are heading. One might ask, "How can someone speak and not know what they are saying?" But this is, perhaps, the rule and not the exception to most of our everyday speech. In concrete terms, one need only think of people who say the words "like" or "um" several times per sentence without any awareness that this is what they are saying. Similar to the hand that plays the piano, it is the *tongue* that speaks the words. The illusion of the controllable self—the Cartesian mind—must be abandoned. And like the zombies of *Pontypool*, most of what we say is repetitive and all of what we say is mimicry. You say hello; I say hello. You say you love me; I say I love you, too. Language is the magician's trick: he is able to pull a rabbit out of a hat only because he stuffed the rabbit in there in the first place before the trick ever started.[23] And we respond to a question in a way that is recognizable and understandable because the possible responses to the question preexisted within that question before the conversation ever started. The zombie has merely accepted this and moved on.

Zombies, it might thus be argued, are animated and perhaps even conscious, but they do not seem self-aware. They do not seem aware of the fact that they are aware. They are not thinking in the same way that humans are. Perhaps. But I would, if pressed, even go so far as to champion zombie-like consciousness. Not merely a consciousness of the flesh, but a consciousness where it is the body that is consciously acting without the need for anything like second-order awareness.

I am well aware that I act like this on a regular basis. Frequently, for instance, I will be driving and come to realize that I have no memory of the last several minutes of steering the car. I obviously have kept the car centered, stopped at red lights, and attended to my surroundings and the laws that govern them, but I did not do so consciously. Usually this is when I am caught up in some deep thought about something that ultimately has me worried or sad. In the shower, I sometimes find myself ready to get out, reaching to turn off the water, and then pausing to ask myself if I washed my hair or even soaped up my body. I have no memory of having done any of it, but it is usually the case that the shampoo has been applied and rinsed, and the scrubbing clean has taken place, all without any conscious attention—again, all of this happening most often when I find myself preoccupied with something troubling. If you ask me, I think that I would sometimes gladly give up the worry and the sadness and all the rest, and happily just be a washing, driving, living zombie.

I don't conclude this lightly. I am, for better or worse, an academic, someone who has to some degree or another decided to live a life of the mind. But when I stop to consider it seriously, I often think that self-reflexive consciousness is just the sort of quality that will end up killing off our species in the end—even if *species* is a specious concept.

Natural selection chooses the qualities for any sort of organism that will allow that organism to survive. It must be noted, in fact, that natural selection does this "choosing" mindlessly, without a plan or a design, without any real "choice" in the usual sense of the word. It creates random mutations, stumbles around, and sees if the mutations create more viable beings. If the mutations allow the organism to survive, they are passed on. If the mutations harm survival, they begin to disappear from the population. A short period ago—something on the order of eight million years—natural selection stumbled on "self-reflexive consciousness" and gave it a try with humans. But it turns out that creatures with this quality come to think of themselves as selves—as monadic, solipsistic, selfish beings that are above all other creatures. Slowly, and recently more rapidly, they begin to destroy the very preconditions of their own existence. They wipe out the ecosystem, kill off the environment, and hurry toward their destruction. It will not be long, I think, until nature allows this to take place.

But this will not be the end of life on Earth. Other wonderful and wonderfully non-self-conscious life will flourish and go on about its business. We have another six billion years or so until the sun turns into a red giant and engulfs the Earth, eventually turning into a zombie version of its once-brilliant and blinding yellow self. During that interim time, there will be plenty of new life that will find its way. Perhaps something very much like zombies will, indeed, replace us.

Because the experiment of our type of consciousness will have run its course and proven not to be conducive to survival. Natural selection will select us out. And out of the ashes of our corpses, out of the failed experiment of our rotting organic matter, new beings will arise the natures of which we cannot even imagine.

All of the world is a graveyard. The living soil is itself flesh: dead and reborn, dead and reborn. Look around you even now—the future is wholly already here. The future echoes of those who will take our place are with us, calling without language to us, hungry and impatient to wait for us to turn into their food, into their bodies. They are the zombies-to-come, the promise and the horror of what we are on the way toward. They tempt you to love them. They disarm you with their familiarity. They are hunting you. They hold us accountable for each act of narcissism, for each immoral meal of flesh we have enjoyed, for each failure to communicate with those who need us, for each act of loving the dead, each failure to realize that we are loving only ourselves. Left on their own, they turn you into what they already are, replicating themselves.

And here, now, you and I are already one of them.

SECTION 3

Other Animal Others

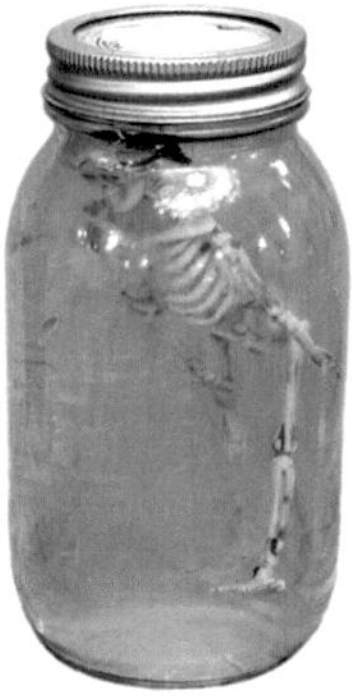

CHAPTER 7 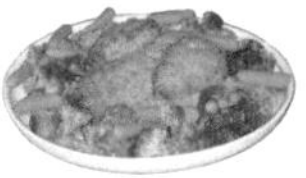

The Man Who Mistook His Meal for a Hot Dog

When I was seven years old my father left us. For my mother it was the end of the world. For me and my brother, less so. He left on March 15 of that year, and by September—the month of my birthday—it was clear he was not coming back. My grandfather—who smoked Tiparillo cigars, hated most of the people around him, and who I saw smile only three times in my life—took the opportunity to take me, my brother, and my mother along with my grandmother on their yearly vacation two hours south to Cincinnati. Cincinnati was The Big City. At the time it was also the home of The Big Red Machine, and so we saw a Cincinnati Reds baseball game (in which they lost to St. Louis) and went to eat at a *nice* restaurant that Saturday night. It was exhilarating. I smiled, perhaps, for the first time in six months.

Pop ordered for me that night and made a big deal of it. Before I could ask for my standard cheeseburger, he told the waiter that I would have a filet mignon, medium rare, with a baked potato. I said nothing. As I waited at the table, it seemed as if hours passed. I had no idea what my plate would hold, what to expect when the waiter finally returned, and so I filled the minutes in fear, assuming it would be something terrible—probably with tentacles or maybe tasting vaguely of dirt—and I would have to eat it (this *filet mignon*) and pretend that everything was okay so as not to ruin this perfect trip.

When the steak finally arrived, I had never seen such a thing of beauty.

The piece of meat looked like it had been sculpted from pure-cream butter, and it floated—wrapped in bacon, *wrapped in bacon!*—on a life-raft of thick toast, bobbing in a sea of juices that smelled like . . . heroism. I began to salivate. Pop leaned over to me and whispered into my ear: "You're the man of the house now. It all rests on your shoulders."

In college, I became a vegetarian. And a few years after that I had my first fake filet mignon. It was homemade, though based on a soy-based product called Stakelets sold by Worthington. It was incredibly delicious, wrapped up in soy bacon with a cup of beef-flavored vegan juice on the side. And all I could think about was Pop—long-gone, dying, just as he had predicted, right before he could enjoy his retirement. Pop, who would look at me with disgust, surely thinking I have become a fake man.

Vegetarian Filet Mignon

1 box (4 patties) Stakelets, thawed

1/2 cup grated Parmesan cheese

1/4 cup Italian seasoned bread crumbs

1 teaspoon garlic powder

1 teaspoon onion powder

1 teaspoon dried oregano

1 teaspoon dried parsley

1/4 teaspoon black pepper (or to taste)

1 1/2 tablespoons of A.1. Sauce

1 teaspoon vegetarian Worcestershire sauce

2 eggs, slightly beaten

4 vegetarian bacon strips

1 onion (sliced vertically)

1 cup sliced mushrooms

1/4 cup red wine

1/4 cup vegetarian beef-flavored broth

2 slices bread, cut thickly

In a food processor, coarsely grind the Stakelets. In a large bowl, thoroughly mix the Stakelets, Parmesan cheese, bread crumbs, garlic powder, onion powder, oregano, parsley, and black pepper. Add the A.1. Sauce, Worcestershire sauce, and eggs. Mix until all of the ingredients are moist. Divide the mixture and make two round, thick patties. Cook

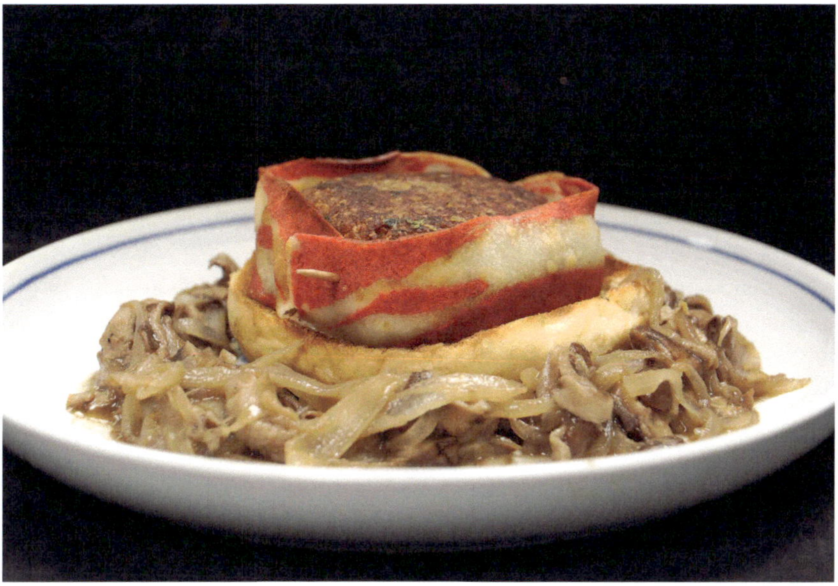

FIGURE 7.1. Vegetarian filet mignon. Photo courtesy of Marinés Fornerino.

for about 3 minutes in the microwave until they achieve a semisolid consistency. (Do not cook completely!) Lightly brown the bacon strips in a frying pan with oil, making sure that the strips are still flexible. Wrap each filet mignon patty with 2 bacon strips and secure them with 2 toothpicks. On low to medium heat, brown the patties in the same frying pan until fully cooked (about 20 minutes). In a separate pan, fry the onions and mushrooms, then add the red wine and beef broth and let the mixture cook until it starts to boil. Salt and pepper to taste. Toast the bread in the oven. To serve, place the filet mignons on the toast and cover with the onion and mushroom sauce.

Recipe by Marinés Fornerino. (*See figure 7.1.*)

It seems to me today that being a fake man is not such a bad thing, especially when the contemporary model for a man is built on misogyny, patriarchy, and oppression. But although all of this is, in fact, directly related to the topic at hand as we consider food as an aesthetic object, we need to begin somewhat more pointedly.

Animal representation routinely takes place in politics, ethics, and art. Someone, or something, stands in for the nonhuman animal, and the animal is re-presented to our consciousness—presented anew but altered, much like a memory. Politically and ethically, without truly knowing the Other such representation is impossible. We cannot make re-present what has never been present to us in the first place. This is, perhaps, the major theoretical failure of American representative democracy, and often the failure of animal rights arguments as well. We cannot represent and thus make re-present what we do not know in the first place, what has never been present for us. But our democratic ideals and much of our ethics are based on this.

Phenomenologically speaking, when I order for us at dinner, for instance, I am attempting to make present you, your will, and your perspective on our common Good. If I say "We will have coffee with dessert" then I am making a claim in first person plural that represents you by attempting to re-present your will, to make it present in its absence. As we have seen, this would be an instance of what Husserl called *apperception*: a making co-present, *there too* but not there, that which is present in its absence. This can misfire. It misfires when I do not reflect your will accurately. It necessarily misfires if I do not first know your will. It also misfires if I do not have your proxy to speak for you and make your will present. The first question we should ask when considering giving voice to other beings, then, is whether or not this giving voice is always good or even possible. As with C. S. Lewis's worries concerning the presence of his dead wife in his consciousness, we do not want the giving of voices to become a ventriloquism act; we do not want to fail in our attempt to apperceive the common Good and speak for others on their behalf when our re-presentations of them are, from the get-go, so often out of whack.

All of this is important, but it is helpful if we come at this point tangentially by way of investigating the manner in which animals, and especially animal flesh, is made present in the medium of soy and other fake meat products for vegetarians. It is, perhaps, no new claim to say that meat represents various things in our culture, that it is tied to misogyny, violence, colonialism, racism, and all sorts of nasty things. It is no accident that my grandfather associated my first steak with my manhood—and a manhood, at that, which seemed based on denying my own mother full subjectivity. But let us begin with a simpler question, one that might even be somewhat more novel: is it in principle immoral to eat fake meat?

Most people would likely say that the obvious answer to such a question is no, assuming that the reason for one's vegetarianism is either the utilitarian worry about the pain and suffering of animals or the deontological worry about respecting an animal life as an end in itself. If no animal is actually harmed to make a vegetarian meat substitute, then no animal's life is actually disrupted or disrespected. One is merely eating soybeans or mushrooms or whatever sort of vegetable or grain from which the vegetarian food is created. These things may be dressed up to look like meat, but they are just vegetables and grains.

One initial response, however, might be that there is, indeed, something special about the fact that the food is dressed up to look like meat, and that the potential immorality of the act lies not in the eating of a veggie burger, for instance, but in the desire to eat the regular burger that the veggie burger is made to represent. It is a desire that is still present in the veggie burger. The craving is for animal flesh. As an enactment of that desire, then, eating the veggie burger would be troublesome. In fact, the more accurate the representation—the more the vegetarian substitute looks, tastes, and smells like meat—the greater the success of the product. Is there not something bad about the desire itself, apart from whether or not any animal is affected?

Consider, for example, a parallel substitution. Child molestation both harms and disrespects the children involved. But imagine we were to develop a child molestation video game to sublimate those desires—an explicit video game in which the goal is to seduce, abduct, and rape little children.

In the world of anime, it sometimes seems as if we are already at this point. And indeed, a few years ago British authorities discovered a corner of a popular virtual world that seems to have been created specifically for the rape of virtual children. Second Life, an Internet site with, at the time of the police investigation, over nine million users in Great Britain, asks people to sign up, create an avatar, interact with other humans by means of their avatars, and help to build a virtual world together. One part of the world that was apparently built back in 2007 lies behind a secret wall in a shopping mall. Here, there was a hidden playground filled with elementary school children who were ready to have sex with the users. Lawyers for the individuals who created and frequented the area within this virtual world maintained that no laws were broken. The British government agreed, but still tried to find a way to prosecute.

The argument often came down to the reality standing behind what appeared to be reality. Not only was it the case, so went the claim, that no real child was being harmed since this was all online in a virtual world, but furthermore the players who had adopted the child avatars were all actually adults pretending to be children in the game. There was a double-layer of fakeness to the molestations, claimed the owners of Second Life: an adult pretending to be a cartoon child, and a cartoon child pretending to be a real child. Two layers of fakeness supposedly separated the virtual world from the real world: so where was the harm?

To make our thought experiment even more complicated, though, let's imagine that our videogame is extremely graphic, and that it's not a virtual world but an actual game in which the goal is simply to rape fictional children. In fact, the more lifelike it is, the better. Let's imagine that programmers are getting more and more skilled at simulating the real thing, and as a result it is getting more and more difficult to tell the difference between an actual molestation and a virtual one. The thrills, the sensations, the physical and emotional rewards are all there for the molester. Yet no particular children are being harmed by the game, no lives are being disrespected, and no sadness is being generated. On the contrary, there are a lot of people who might actually be very happy about the existence of such a game. It would allow the silencing of the harmful desire, or at least the redirection of it in such a way that it would no longer harm *real* children. There might even be less child molestation in the world with such a realistic virtual outlet. And yet, something seems extremely *questionable* about the morality of all this.

I take it that the HBO television series, *Westworld*, in which humans visit an amusement park populated by extremely lifelike human automatons, most typically to enact fantasies of rape and other forms of violence against those automatons, is trying to get at this question, too. If the simulation—whether that simulation is one of rape, violence, or even consciousness itself—is hard to distinguish from the reality, don't we have to treat the simulation and the reality with the same ethical regard?

How is fake meat any different? The closer it gets to being like the real thing, the more *successful* it is. There might be fewer animals being harmed because the fake meat is so tasty. But is this, then, the only thing that matters? Don't we have to treat the simulation and the reality the same ethically if we are treating them the same aesthetically and metaphysically?

I am a fan of fake meat. I would eat it every day if I could. And I have only begun in the last few years to ask these questions of myself, troubling as they are. I enjoy a fake turkey for Thanksgiving, for instance, and I wish that I did not have the desire at all. My palate is even too demanding to embrace mass-produced Tofurkey. I want to have something that approximates the turkey experience even better. I like it with stuffing and gravy and cranberry sauce. But how far do we want to take the simulation? How far would *I* be willing to take it?

Imagine that Morningstar Farms were to come out with a new "turkey dinner experience." The turkey, sculpted entirely from soy but tasting completely like the real thing, would come complete with internal tubes filled with red-tinted corn syrup to simulate blood. Synthetic feathers would cover the body of the tofu-bird, and Disney Imagineers would add audio-animatronics so that you could power up the fake turkey and have it run around your back yard. Part of the preparation of the meal, then, would involve catching the fake bird, chopping its head off, watching the body writhe in simulated death spasms, draining the fake blood, de-feathering the carcass, removing the gummi-organs inside, stuffing it, and roasting it up. Just how far does the simulation have to go before we judge it to have the moral content of the original?

In the movie *The Matrix* (1999, Dir. Lana and Lilly Wachowski), Joe Pantoliano's character, Cypher, agrees to sell out his friends and be re-inserted into the fake world of simulation in part because he is tired of living in the real world where life is hard and food tastes disgusting. He agrees to the traitorous act while eating a virtual steak, proclaiming that he doesn't care that it is not real, he loves how it *seems* to taste! The fake-meat eater is the villain of the story. Am I the villain in real life as well?

But Cypher was a puppet. He was being manipulated by the AI's inside the Matrix. His virtual body was literally a puppet of his own mind; his will was dancing on the strings of the Agents that sought to use him.

There is something uncanny about puppets—traditional puppets—especially when they are literally in the hands of excellent artists. We see in them the movements of a human; we see ourselves in them. But the relationship is actually much more complicated than that. The origin of puppets is hard to trace. There are records from 2,500 years ago of puppets being used in India to entertain and tell stories. Dolls on sticks were, perhaps, the original puppets, but it wasn't long before the jointed puppet became popular. Javanese shadow puppets—one particular kind of jointed puppet—are, to my eyes, the eeriest. Shadow puppets, we know, were popular more than two millennia ago in China during the Han dynasty, but in many ways they reached their pinnacle in Indonesia. No one knows exactly when they were introduced into the islands. There are records of theatre productions of *Wayang kulit* (which means "shadow skin" in Javanese) telling stories from the Hindu Ramayana more than a thousand years ago, though it is suspected that the puppets were being produced long before that time. These shadow puppets, of course, were being made to look like humans—or at least a stylized vision of humans. The joints represented our joints. The limbs bent in the right places, at least two-dimensionally. One might think of it as an imitation or an attempt to mimic. History, of course, is always much more complicated. And so is ontology—especially when informed by phenomenology.

I think, for instance, of the Javanese dance Puspawarna. The name means "many kinds of flowers," with the music being performed by a Javanese gamelan with the intention of creating a state of various *rasas* or moods in the audience, with each flower representing a different *rasa*. Traditionally, the eight *rasas* are love, laughter, fury, compassion, disgust, terror, heroism, and amazement. Although the puppets are ancient, the music was composed in the late 1880s. And the dance is only decades old. The sound of the Puspawarna was actually included on the golden album attached to the Voyager 1 space probe launched in 1977 and meant to act as a greeting from the planet Earth to aliens who might encounter the probe someday in the future. Carl Sagan even said it was one of his favorite tracks on the album. We always imagine aliens as strange versions of ourselves—maybe with a different skin color or pointed ears, but always like some bad imitation of an Earth human. And of course the imitation—the stand-in—is what we're interested in. It is what the history of metaphysics thinks an aesthetic object always is: a stand-in for reality. But little by little we are beginning to know better.

Indeed, the most fascinating thing about the Javanese Puspawarna dance is that it *seems* to be ancient, but it's just a few decades old. And more than this, the dance was created with the Javanese shadow puppets in mind. That is, the dancer is in many respects meant to be moving her body like a shadow puppet, mimicking the mimicry of something attempting to mimic a human. Like a shadow of a shadow, the human dancer's arms bend at strange angles, her body is stiff even while it is flowing, her face is stoic and expressionless—puppet-like. This Javanese dance is an attempt to make the dancer look like a puppet—which was trying to look like a dancer in the first place. And this is but the opening step in a highly choreographed hermeneutical circle dance.

Such a Baudrillardean point is nothing new. We are used to hearing that the Gulf War never took place, that the map preceded the territory, and that the ontological distinction between original and copy is, itself, a fiction. It is a postmodern world we inhabit. But the real point is that once we have moved past the idea that there was some sort of original, pure, true origin that then got copied into a fake—once we reject the foundation of metaphysics—only then is the true task suddenly at hand. Only then do we truly do the work of ethics and politics.

Am I a puppet controlled by appetites, controlled by my past, controlled by unseen forces that keep me desiring meat even if I refuse to eat it? Ethically speaking, nothing could be more dangerous than setting up the question in this way, immediately making me potentially unaccountable for my own actions, immediately seeing the main question to be one of *origins*. It is true that I spend time and energy trying to get fake meat to taste more like the real thing. Taking a store-bought vegetarian product and finding a way to make it even more like the real thing is, I think, one of the finest aesthetic skills imaginable. But the question is not really one of the ethics of mimicry. Perhaps the mimicry question is throwing us off.

Vegetarian Cornish Hens

1 10.6 oz box (4 patties) Quorn Chik'n Patties

1 tablespoon vegetarian chicken-flavored powdered broth

1 teaspoon poultry seasoning

1/2 teaspoon garlic powder

1/2 cup grated Parmesan cheese

1/4 cup Italian seasoned bread crumbs

2 eggs, slightly beaten

1 box Stovetop (pork flavor [which is vegetarian]) or other stuffing mix

Prepare the stuffing according to the directions on the package and let it cool. In the meantime, coarsely grind the Quorn patties in a food processor. In a large bowl, thoroughly combine the Quorn mixture, chicken-flavored broth, poultry seasoning, garlic powder, Parmesan cheese, and bread crumbs. Add the eggs and mix well. In a microwave/oven-safe dish, mound the stuffing into the shape of a dome. Press down (using hands) until the stuffing feels slightly compact. Distribute the chicken mixture evenly over the stuffing, reserving enough to shape into two drumsticks. Shape and place the drumsticks, arranged to look like wings. Microwave uncovered for 6 minutes on high power. Place in a preheated 350-degree oven for 15 minutes or until golden brown. If necessary, cover the bottom of the chicken to avoid premature browning.

Recipe by Marinés Fornerino. (*See figure 7.2.*)

Truth be told, I am not so much a vegetarian as I am a fake-meat-atarian. I'm not really pro-vegetables; I'm just anti-meat. And vegetarian staples dressed up to look, taste, smell, and feel like something they are not raise a particularly

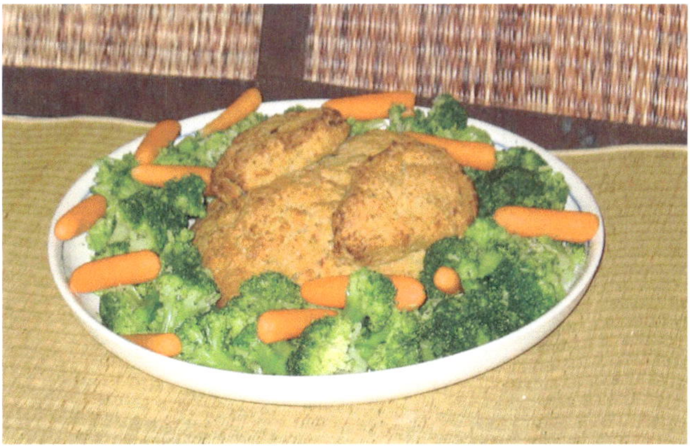

FIGURE 7.2. Vegetarian Cornish hen. Photo courtesy of Marinés Fornerino.

difficult issue in my own life as well as in the study of food. There are not many examples of food items that are necessarily meant to represent other food items—apart from marzipan. Mashed potatoes are not typically served in the shape of mushrooms. Carrots are seldom processed to pass for asparagus. The fact that we take soybeans and make them look like meat is a particular and unique thing in the food world. One could argue, in fact, that the only real food equivalent is animal flesh itself. That is, apart from steaks, ribs, and the like, we often go to great lengths to make meat on our plates look nothing like the animal that it truly was. The relationship between meatloaf and a cow, for instance, is very hard to see. A chicken McNugget looks nothing like a chicken. A fish stick looks nothing like a fish. And a hot dog looks nothing like . . . well . . . whatever a hot dog is made out of. Interesting, then, that we intentionally make our meat not resemble the animal, but make our tofu resemble meat. Fake meat products have even more in common with real meat than we might imagine, as both apparently participate in artistic representation more than most other foods, intentionally offered up to be something that they are not.[1]

So meatloaf never looks like a cow—and it doesn't even really look like Eddie, Meatloaf's character in *The Rocky Horror Picture Show* (1975, dir. Jim Sharman), who eventually gets eaten by the rest of the cast. Since we've stumbled onto the appetizing aesthetic question of cannibalism here, we might as well admit that it is important, too, that Soylent Green not look like people. I take it to be *the* lesson of the movie *Soylent Green* (1973, dir. Richard Fleischer) that cannibalism metaphorically stands in for the complete loss of a society's soul, the final nail in the coffin of our collective future. And in the movie, humans have so devastated the natural world—destroying all of the plants, animals, and ecosystems across the face of the earth—that there are no Others with whom to share a community, no life beyond human life to help construct our own sense of self. Without the alterity—an alterity that we discover, of course, is not truly so *other*—we implode and destroy ourselves. But to hide the fact, human meat is turned into green rectangles—something that looks more like processed vegetable matter than flesh. The movie is thus not merely about the way a world with only human-animal life is actually a world without humanity, it's also about the ethics of eating meat, whether human or nonhuman, and the way in which we always need to fool the public to gag meat down by means of an aesthetic sleight-of-hand that turns it into something more pleasing than flesh. To paraphrase Paul McCartney loosely: in a world in which Soylent Green factories and slaughterhouses had glass walls, everyone would be a vegetarian.

Charlton Heston inhabits a horrible future, but it's not so different from ours, of course. There are some people who think we are on the road to cannibalism simply because of our environmental policies. Still, this dystopic destiny is at odds with the more "peaceful" future painted by other popular forms of science fiction. In *The Jetsons*, Jane would push a button and food would magically materialize from behind the wall. I never imagined that there was a slaughterhouse hidden back there. I always imagined that our greatest god ever—Technology—was somehow making this happen.

In *Star Trek* this is all more explicit. Vulcans, we are told, are vegetarians in the *Star Trek* universe. It is illogical to slaughter another creature for food, and in one episode of the original series ("All Our Yesterdays" [dir. Marvin Chomsly, 1969]), Spock starts regressing, reenacting the barbaric history of his species. When he gets to the point where he tastes animal flesh and likes it, he suddenly realizes what's happening to him. Above all else, the illogic of such violence toward other creatures tips him off to the fact that he is no longer who he thinks himself to be: he has become immoral in every way if he has come to be a meat-eater.

It's nice, then, that the most rational beings in the *Star Trek* universe are all vegetarians, but so, at least to some extent, are most humans in that universe. This is because of a piece of technology called "the replicator." Replicators can shape atoms in specific patterns to recreate matter of any kind. If one stores the pattern for a cup of coffee—or for a steak or a chicken breast or a meatloaf—in the computer's memory banks, the replicator can then assemble the necessary atoms to create an exact duplicate of that food item. This would be the ultimate in fake meat, because such technology could create an atomically identical copy of the real thing, yet no animals would be involved *at all*. Most people would still be eating "meat," but none of it would be "real." It has to be admitted that this does seem better than what we are doing today, but is there still not something wrong with an entire culture that fashions atoms into animal parts to satiate its desire for dead flesh?

We are getting close to this future right now.

In 2013, for instance, a 3D printer made a pizza (*see figures 7.3 and 7.4, page 153*). Such printers typically contain water, oil, and a large number of powders made from proteins and micronutrients. Mixed together in the right way and extruded in dots by micropipettes, this particular printer could, in about twelve minutes, create and then bake a pizza. Appropriately, the company that has made this replicator has been funded by NASA with an eye toward putting hungry human settlers on the barren planet Mars. A spokesman for a competing company recently said that with as few as thirty-nine different bioengineered powders, he felt confident that he could create a printer that could replicate almost *any* food item you could imagine.

This printed meat would still be plant-based fake meat, though. The 3D printer is just like a really smart Worthington Farms factory in miniature, making vegetarian meals one by one. If it's actual replicated meat we're imagining, then this is becoming a reality, too. A few years before the printed pizza, scientists were able to grow a healthy colony of muscle tissues in a test tube: in vitro meat. Granted, most of what has been accomplished so far has been created using

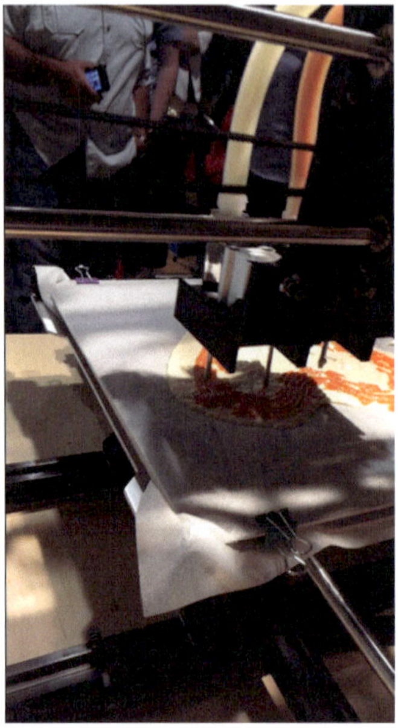

FIGURE 7.3. BeeHex's 3D printed pizza. Photos courtesy of BeeHex, Inc. 3D Printing (www.beehex.com).

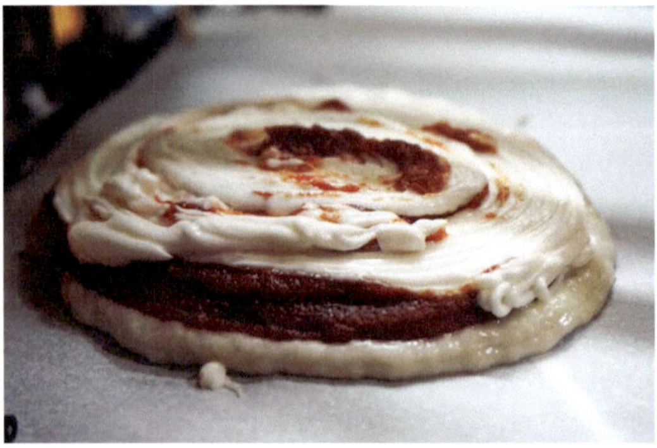

FIGURE 7.4. BeeHex's 3D printed pizza. Photos courtesy of BeeHex, Inc. 3D Printing (www.beehex.com).

home-grown muscle cells from a mouse and frog, but one imagines that thick slabs of mouse muscle are likely to taste a little like chicken. If actual chicken is more to our taste, then we need only note the success of a group in Australia that was able to grow enough cloned poultry muscle cells to process them into a small patty of *actual* chicken steak. And they believe they'll go to market with the chicken sometime around the year this book is to be released.

The company is rushing to get a prize from PETA, in fact, which has an outstanding one-million-dollar award to give to the first person or company to come up with an economically viable way to grow "good-tasting" meat in a lab for mass consumption. The thinking is that just like with the *Star Trek* replicator, there will have to be one animal who might suffer at the very start—one model who will provide the blueprint for all future meat of that type, one martyr for the cause—but then the suffering will end.

Indeed. It will end. And we will all still be a society of meat-eaters.

Thus far there are only questions. So let us imagine one last thought experiment. Let us assume that you are vegetarian, and one fine summer evening you are invited over to a cookout at a friend's house. Everyone in attendance is a vegetarian, and happy to be eating veggie hot dogs. It's like a real American BBQ with baseball, apple pie, and Chevrolets all around. The charcoal grill makes the veggie dogs plump and warm, and you are enjoying the company and the taste. Then, toward the end of the evening, the host announces that he has, all along, secretly been playing a rather horrible game with everyone. It's something he calls "hot dog roulette," in which, hidden among all of the veggie dogs there was one real hot dog served to someone at some point in the evening. For many vegetarians, this would be traumatic. And we need to think this through—to think about why we might have thoroughly enjoyed the taste of the hot dogs that were passed out, commended them for their closeness to the real thing, and then felt outraged when that simulation was so good that we could not tell the difference between having eaten the fake and having eaten the real meat. How would we feel in relation to our desire? How would we come to grips with our complicity? Many vegetarians have, perhaps, mistakenly eaten animal flesh of some sort before, but this is more easily confessed and forgiven for most because they feel less responsibility if the transgression was born of ignorance. How would this be different if the transgression were born both of ignorance *and* a real desire for the real thing? Although we live in a post-Baudrillardian world of simulacra where the real and the simulation have collapsed into one, there is still a major difference between the real hot dog and the veggie dog for most of us. The question is, how might we deal with the ethics of our actions and our desires in a situation such as this?

Let us at least say this. There are two essential concerns here, and phenomenology as well as a phenomenologically based aesthetics such as the one that we have been developing in the previous chapters can help us think them through. First, we must be clear about the relationship between the fake and the real; and second, we must find a way of describing the ethics of intentions and actions that does not rely on Kant or Mill, but instead gets at what lies beneath and ties together intentions and actions, ethics and aesthetics.

It seems that the fake and the real cannot be defined in terms of each other but only in terms of something else outside of the system that they comprise. We cannot say that the dichotomous real/fake system is comprised of merely A and ~A. If we list all of the qualities of A, it is not the case that the second item—the fake—is just a negation of those qualities. In fact, each thing in such a pair has separate and distinct qualities. And so it would seem that to tell which is the real and which is the fake, we would have to compare those qualities with some sort of standard or ideal that stands outside of the system. This thinking is as old as the Greeks, but, as we have seen repeatedly from the very first chapter, we must try to avoid all forms of Platonism. This is also not a dialectic relationship. The fake and the real do not comprise the first two stages of some greater moment that is yet to come but will somehow synthesize them into something better and more rational. The more general problem is that to use the language of "the real" and "the fake" is already to adopt a metaphysics of correspondence where one thing corresponds truly and another falsely. And this, in turn, is based on the belief that there is something outside of experience, and that truth is established when belief lines up with this external reality. It is, in short, everything that phenomenology rejects.

In Husserlian terms we might say that the notion of "the fake" is founded on the faulty principle that there is only one way for a thing to appear truly. It is to say, for instance, that of the following shapes (*see figure 7.5*), each representing the way in which a rectangular table might be seen from some specific angle, only one is a *true* rectangle: the rest are distorted by perspective into parallelograms and trapezoids—into *fake* rectangles.

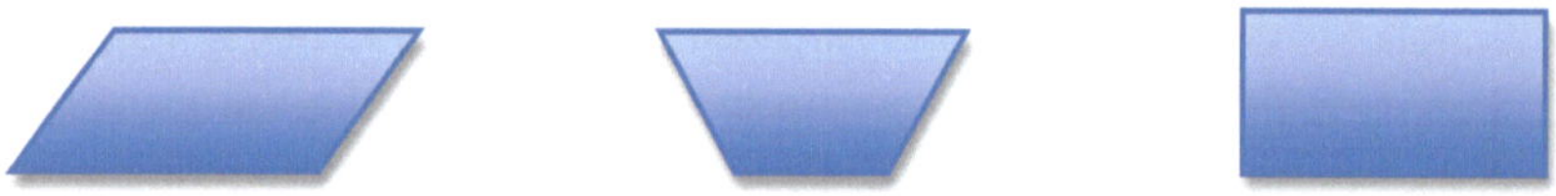

FIGURE 7.5. Rectangles.

One of Husserl's most important insights is that this is not the case. These are all rectangles. They are just rectangles appearing from different vantage points. Each is precisely what we expect a rectangle to look like from some specific angle. This is what a rectangle is: all of the ways in which it can appear. A rectangle *should* look sort of squished and slanty when seen from an angle precisely in order to appear rectangular. As we have seen, perspective is not a distortion; and subjectivity is not something to get around in our search for the truth. To think otherwise is to think that consciousness is in the business of providing us with a passing parade of fakes our whole life, as if we were trapped in some horrible cave looking at shadows and puppets.

To make matters clearer, we might invoke the Husserlian metaphor of an horizon. Whenever I think of this image, I have to admit that I change it up a bit in my head from Husserl's original use of it. The horizon is infinite and spread out before us, argues Husserl, and here he is leading us in a helpful direction. But an horizon has a flatness to it. I always picture the horizon of an object as something closer to a parabolic curved line, or a Gaussian distribution asymptotically stretching off to infinity at the sides. That is, let's say that we have different experiences of things that all look very similar and tend to cluster together more or less, and so we mark our experiences with a little X somewhere on the horizon line (*see figure 7.6*).

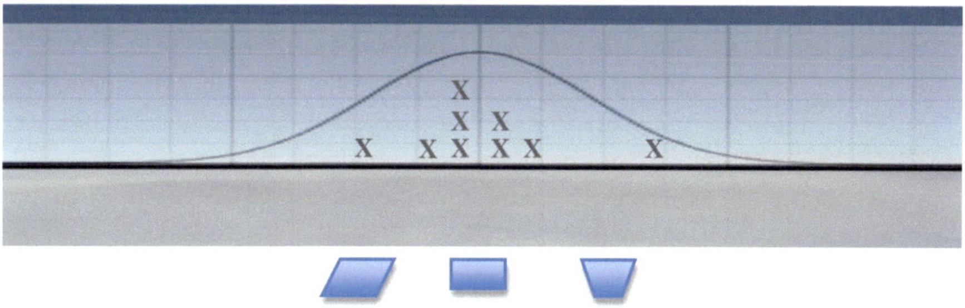

FIGURE 7.6. The Horizon.

Usually, rectangles look something close to the geometric presentation of a rectangle, with just a bit of slant to them. Under the right conditions, though, a rectangle can look curved or circular (for instance if you're looking at a rectangle through a thick piece of glass or underwater). These experiences are rarer, but they are just as valid. So we mark them off to the side a bit. Little by little, as we flesh out the possible ways in which the rectangle can appear, we see that this is an infinite task, but it is still the case that some more common and core experiences seem to pile up. I have only included nine possible mappings of experiences in figure 7.6, but one can see that the data set is leading somewhere. There is a sort of distribution to it, where certain presencings clump together and others are at the periphery. This bell-curve shape is what I tend to picture when I think of an Husserlian horizon.

As we have seen throughout this work, like any other object, the rectangular table appears within an horizon of explicit and implicit appearings. The horizon is infinite and stretches forever, because there is always some new angle and some new context from which to see the table. No matter how we experience it now, there are other possible experiences we could still be having—all presently absent, all apperceived. The object can never be exhausted. And yet, it *is* something specific. Our experiences are grouped together Here and not There, and a noetic act of identity synthesis pulls the experiences together so that we realize they all have the same intentional object: the rectangular table. On the fringe of the horizon, the rectangular table will appear as more curved or jagged or maybe even as a straight flat line. But that is precisely what it means to be a rectangular table when seen under such conditions, and these are not *fake* rectangles or bad appearings of the table.

In the *Cartesian Meditations* Husserl uses the figure of the horizon to explain apperception, the way in which all of the infinite ways of appearing are given along with every experience of a thing that we have. This explains what it's like to see a table from one side and then another, but still have the object of consciousness be the table itself, the table as a whole. But more than just angles and perspective, the horizon can get "fleshed out" by having experiences of the object in a different context, being used in a new way, appearing in fiction, and so on. A table with wings that flies away in a children's fable is not a fake table. It's just one way in which a table can appear, this time in the mode of fiction, which we must not think is the same thing as "fake" or "unreal."

Now, all of this is not to say that there is no such thing as an invalid judgment about the identity of an object. Sometimes we make mistakes. It's closing time in a store and one rushes toward a sales attendant with a purchase only to find out at the last moment that—in the bad lighting and from a distance—one made a mistake and took a mannequin for a real person. What we have learned in such a case is that, under the right conditions, a mannequin can appear as a person. And it is most likely the case that a person can appear as a mannequin as well. There is something like an overlap in the horizons of the two things, though they are two distinct things. In such an instance, we have learned something about the Being of mannequins and the Being of persons.

And so, what of fake meat? Is a veggie dog something that is separate from a hot dog, or is it merely one way in which a hot dog can appear? We can no longer simply say that a veggie dog is a *fake* hot dog. But if we move beyond the discourse of "the fake and the real," can we still make distinctions in a meaningful way? Because sometimes it is definitely the fake thing that we crave and other times it is not the fake thing that we want.

Let us not say that the immorality of a situation is primarily in the desire, in the acting on the desire, or in the consequences of that action. Rather, it is the phenomenological act of taking up another's bad as such as one's own good such that flourishing is not the goal. Life is always already suffused with the ethical because Goods appear to us just as anything else appears to us. To be more precise, ethics is tied to phenomenological categoriality. In the same way that buttered bread is more than just "bread + butter"—in the same way that we can directly experience the being-together of the bread and the butter and the way in which this being-together "permeates" the whole experience, the way in which the buttered bread is presenced—so, too, do we experience the values that are inherent in objects, actions, and states of affairs. If you feed me when I am hungry, the experience is more than you + me + food. I can experience the ethical import of it all, the way in which you are taking up my good as such as your own, the way in which it is an expression of compassion or love. But what if you feed me a vegetarian hot dog? Is this a special sort of love—for me and for the animal that otherwise might have been eaten?

We can, perhaps, tie everything together in this way. What is it we desire when we desire fake meat? The *memory* of having enjoyed meat in the past? What the taste *represents* to us? It is not clear that what we really desire is *meat*—dead animal flesh—itself. I may love fake meat, and I may still salivate when I smell "real" meat, but I would most likely feel sick if I tried to eat the latter. Intentions can be important, but ethics is more than this. If I intend to paint a picture of a lake, then the object of consciousness is the lake, not a picture of the lake. The lake can be meant in many ways because there are many ways in which a thing can be present. Vegetarian meat is, perhaps, a form of art in this way: I intend to create an aesthetic presencing of something else. I shape it, color it, dress it up and try to get it "right." I can't drown in the painting of the lake although it is the lake that is present, but do I get my hands bloody with a veggie dog? Let us at least say that the answer is: not *necessarily*. It is not necessarily a meat hot dog that is made presently absent by a veggie dog. The horizons of separate things can overlap as we are pulled away, running off in two different directions. And the ethics with which the two things are suffused can be quite different as well, for this is, after all, the real question: not whether or not the veggie dog is bad because it metaphysically *resembles* something that is bad, but is it possible for the ethics of the desire for the veggie dog to be so different from the ethics of desire for the meat hot dog that the comparison of the two foods is actually utterly unimportant when it comes time to analyze the moral categoriality at work.

We are not absolved of our wrong-doing by the complexity of appearance: it still all rests on our shoulders. But it is here in this clearing where we can get down to the work of ethics and politics. It is a conclusion for this chapter that leaves things open and up in the air a bit; but it is, at least, to point in a direction toward which we can begin moving in hopes of addressing such an issue. And it is, I hope, a *true* conclusion rather than a *fake* one, though aren't all conclusions truly fake because

CHAPTER 8

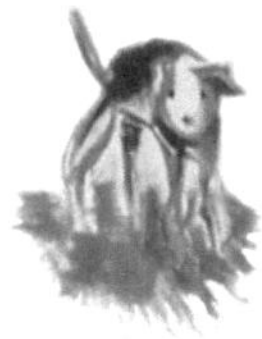

Rachel Rosenthal Was an Animal

AUTHOR: After the false conclusion that is not really false, we start anew. We start at the beginning. We start with the first. The animal is first philosophy, first performer, first image, first sound, first love, first being. This first part is to be read aloud.

ROSENTHAL: (*Stands*) "Communicate! Communicate! My deep preference is always to chuck it all and go live with the animals in the bosom of the Earth. I keep putting it off in order to perform pieces that bring the Earth into conscious focus"[1] (Rosenthal 1997: 196).

AUTHOR: We're grateful for deep lack of freedom. Procrastination in a myopic world. (*Crumples up the paper in his hand, looks with shame to see who is watching, throws it into the PIT which is decorated as a grave, takes a new piece of paper and starts writing.*)

ROSENTHAL: (*Laughing at first as she stands even taller. Then startled, frightened.*)

> "I am a primate.
> Timid. I hide in the branches, in caves, behind rocks.
> I'm naked. I can't defend myself. I am scared.
> Many of my people die of a crunched skull—the leopards. . . ."[2]

(*She reaches down into the PIT and retrieves the skull—a hollowed head of cabbage—from earlier scene. She holds it aloft in one hand.*)

> "To be or. . . ."[3]

KAFKA: (*Rising*) "A parable: Leopards break into the temple and drink the sacrificial vessels dry; this is repeated over and over again; finally it can be calculated in advance and becomes a part of the ceremony."[4]

(*Cue leopards*)

In the fall of 1980 Rachel Rosenthal began performing with a rat. Tatti Wattles—in *Bonsoir, Dr. Schön!* (1980), riding on Rosenthal's head, tangled in her still-present hair—took to the stage as if he had been born for it. He was soon a star. Rosenthal, for her part, and as always, put on a show. At one point, she detonated little fireworks, spun, yelled, and screamed: "I am a vampire!" And in the panic of the performance, Tatti left his nest of hair, slid down Rosenthal's face—claws marking and tearing her cheek, blood streaking to her neck—and settled on her shoulder. His work quick and true, the rat made of Rosenthal a bloody beautiful human-rodent hybrid, *eine schöne Fledermaus*, transforming her before the audience and giving her wings.

ROSENTHAL: "Tatti had a good sense of timing. . . . [He] had a great stage presence. . . . He loved being in the limelight and never hid or presented his backside. All the photos show him, handsome, looking directly into the camera. In performance, he always knew where his light was."[5] (*She tosses the cabbage back into the PIT.*)

In later versions of the production, Rosenthal would construct a miniature bat costume for Tatti and swing him through the air. They were vampires together in those years.

When Nicholas Ridout recalls how he once saw a mouse cautiously and apparently improvisationally make an entrance from downstage left in a London theater's production of Harold Pinter's *The Caretaker,* he uses it as an opportunity to think through how worries about animal exploitation in the theater point to the real exploitation of the human actor on stage. "The theatre is all about humans coming face [to face] with other humans and either liking it or not liking it," explains Ridout. "The animal clearly has no place in such communication. . . . It should not be there because it does not know what to do there, is not capable of performing theatrically by engaging a human audience in experimental thinking about the conditions of their own humanity. . . . "[6] The rodent, for Ridout, is a sign. Though he struggles to "let the animal be" and not "commit the act of violence of putting it on stage as a sign," its exploitation is, inevitably, but a symbol for the human actor's exploitation on stage.[7] Forced to speak the playwright's words, forced to contort her body according to the director's desire, forced to make her work invisible so the paying audience sees only the "play" (i.e., fun, joy, recreation, amusement) rather than the labor, the human actor is exploited, and the animal points to this in its own miserable presence on stage.

This, then, is one of the fascinating and transcendent aspects of Rosenthal's work: she would have none of it.

Not that Rosenthal was not worried about human exploitation in the arts. She fought, time and again, for sweeping political and cultural changes such that artists could be "truly sustained by an economic structure that regards art-making as integral and indispensable to the health of the people"; and she gained national notoriety as an activist for human artists as well as nonhuman animals, having appeared before a 1991 House subcommittee to deliver for Congressional record her denouncement of the NEA's decency clause.[8] One knows of Rosenthal's raging against the economic indecency of having to suffer financially to make art in a capitalist society in the first place, but one imagines her less inclined to see the artist as *especially* exploited. The stage, for Rosenthal, was not *teleologically* a product, though it is a place of production. Art, even located as it is—as all things necessarily are—in the political and economic contexts of its production, is revolutionary and potentially transformative. Not in a naïve sense of creating paradise ex nihilo, but in a postmodern sense of exposing the aesthetic artifice, admitting to its role in the production of that artifice, and envisioning something other. Still, one wouldn't wish to put words in Rosenthal's mouth.

ROSENTHAL: (*Suspicious; mutters inaudibly*) Instead, let us say that for Rosenthal the animal surely has a central place in communication, and a central and indispensable method for getting an audience to think experimentally about its humanity—and its animality. Aesthetically, this is accomplished with grace and beauty. Ethically (as if there is a difference), it is accomplished with questions of justice at the forefront.

AUTHOR: Ontologically—let us abandon all false distinctions at once!—it is accomplished with the realization that animal Others are not signs, not there-for-us, not truly Other even in their being named as such. There is no justification for our most trusted distinctions.

ROSENTHAL: "There is no justification for our persecution of the Others. We do it because we are stronger. This democracy, like every other human society, is erected on the fascist oppression of other sentient beings, because they are *other* and we have might."[9]

AUTHOR: The ethic of "might makes right" is always functioning and always in need of questioning. After Foucault, too long in the pit, we know that Reason is Power, and even those who demand equal consideration of animals are already complicit, already merely hoping to gain the authority and command and strength, as it were, to make the audience see that animals matter. Language, even, can be a whip. We must admit it. And then we must do better.

ROSENTHAL: "'[I]f might makes right,' then we have done away with morality altogether and, as a species, are morally bankrupt."[10] (*She jumps into the PIT.*)

"Might makes right" is not a *bad* ethic; it is the abandonment of morality itself, a forsaking of the debate on what constitutes justice in the first place. And all art, therefore, that employs an animal as a symbol of exploitation is always already exploitative. This is something Rosenthal comes back to over and again in her work. So many others do not.

Think of Robert Rauschenberg's *Monogram* (1955–59), a stuffed dead angora goat with a tire around his waist, standing on hinged and painted wood that has been decorated with a tennis ball, paint, collage, and newspaper. The debate that raged—and perhaps still rages—was, "What does the goat *mean*?" Some saw a postmodern Pan; some saw an organic digester of human trash. Robert Hughes insisted that the work was an homage to "male homosexual love in modern culture, . . . an image of anal sex. . . ." That horny goat head bursting through the opening of the constricting black tire? "The satyr in the sphincter," demanded Hughes. Rauschenberg, characteristically, wanted the art to be about nothing other than itself. Dismissing Hughes's analysis, Rauschenberg claimed: "A stuffed goat is special in the way that a stuffed goat is special."[11] Steve Baker sees this as a quintessential postmodern animal appearance in art: the animal that is not a sign or a symbol, but merely a thing. "Humans," he writes, "have typically wanted [animals] . . . to be meaningful, and want[ed] to control and be consoled by those meanings. Postmodernism mistrusts this comfortably centered self's desire. . . . [T]he postmodern animal is there in the gallery not *as a meaning* or a symbol but in all its pressing thingness."[12] And yet if we follow Baker and his Heideggerian desire to "let the animal be"—poor-in-world as the animal is—are we not forcing the animal's identity, are we not constructing for it an unbending role, the role of a *thing*? Is this not exactly what a postmodern mistrust of identity should help us avoid? An animal's "thingness" is not pressing; "thingness" is something that is pressed upon the animal.

Let us say that Shakespeare's Bottom is a modern ass. He is, typically, read as a symbol of buffoonery, stupidity, and crude animal body—symbols and signs we hope to control, meanings we think are stable and exhaustibly definable. Mufasa in Disney's *The Lion King* (dir. Rob Minkoff and Roger Allers,1994) and the tigers in the Ringling Brothers Circus are also typically read with a modern lens: the animal before us means something in its animality; it stands for something; it is an allegory or a code; it is there for us (which exhausts its being) and means something for us (which exhausts its meaning). What passes for postmodern animals in art, though, are seldom truly postmodern. Rauschenberg's reading of his own piece, and Baker's reading of that reading, are modernist denials that there is a context that comes attached to all production. In further reifying the animal—and note importantly here, a *dead* animal, killed and stuffed and put on display—so that it is claimed to be merely a thing, all possible further meanings and all possible subjectivity are immediately denied. This is, in fact, the epitome rather than the transcendence of modernity's error: a stable identity is suddenly set for the animal in the art: "*What does it mean? It means itself, and that's all. And that's exactly what it means."* The truly postmodern animal is neither paraded on stage as a naïve symbol in some human fable, nor placed before us as if it could possibly mean nothing, as if the artist is somehow beyond or outside the web of culture, language, symbol, etc., that makes the appearance of art possible. Modernism perhaps begins by ignoring its own immersion in context, but it is a modernist mind that still thinks it can identify that context, rise above it so that it is no longer immersed in context, and show us the bird's-eye view of the things-in-themselves. Postmodernity is, in part, marked by the awareness of the context and of one's own complicity in perpetuating the very structures that gave rise to it. What folly to think that a dead, stuffed goat does not necessarily mean myriad things, not the least of which is that the animal is there for us to kill and manipulate and consume. Ralph Ortiz decapitating live chickens on stage and Peter Brook burning a live butterfly before an audience do not raise questions about what is real, what is the symbol, what is the animal, what is the nature of power, what is performance, and so on.[13] They are the worst final throes of modernism: a modernism that actively and knowingly denies its own modernity; not a questioning of the animal and a nullification of the animal's meaning, but, in fact, a tacit assumption of the worst sorts of clichés about animals.

Rosenthal and her nonhuman performing partners were always and utterly different. Tatti Wattles was not a trained rat doing tricks. Tatti Wattles was not put on stage as a sign for human disgust or fear. Tatti Wattles was not presented as meaning *nothing*, as a thing, as "a rat." Instead, Tatti Wattles was acknowledged as animal, as human, as vermin, as rodent, as friend, as lover, as a ham, as feared, as fearful, as brave, as creative, as Rachel, as Tatti, as performer.

In her landmark show *The Others* (1984), forty-two nonhuman animals shared the stage and the playbill with Rosenthal. Goats, snakes, rabbits, squirrels, monkeys, turkeys, macaws, dogs, cats, rats. . . . Each animal had a printed bio; each animal was presented and named during the show; each animal appeared not as a symbol for its kind nor as a blank slate on which Rosenthal and her audience could write, but as equals, as performers, as co-constitutors of this art and this world. The call was for animal rights—the call clear and loud, as Rosenthal attacked the way we control, torture, and murder animals with our language, our hearts, and our hands. But any possibility of a cartoonish sentimental plea was eradicated by the co-constitution of the performance by Rosenthal and the nonhuman actors. This was not Noah's stage: Rosenthal was not parading the animals before us as captor and savior. This was not a modernist's stage: Zato the dog did not mean Domestication or Obedience when he took his turn in the spotlight (and yet, of course, he brought such meanings with him to his performance, twisting them in new ways, yet twisting them not as something he represents but as something we are called on to question in our re-presentation of him). The stage was neither the prelude to the abattoir nor the tabula rasa of heaven, but rather Here, Earth, Community. It was not, that is to say, Ridout's stage, a placeless place that "rigorously excludes nature . . . [and] stays where it is, in the city. [A 'place' where] no natural light comes in, . . . [where] there is culture raised to the power of two, as temporary floors and walls simulate the rooms of our own homes and other built spaces. . . . Bringing an animal in here is courting disaster."[14]

AUTHOR: When her stage lowers and rises, when Rosenthal ascends and descends dais and mechanical orchestra pit, surrounded by human and animal life, . . . (*ROSENTHAL springs out of the PIT and climbs to sit on the highest PLATFORM*) . . . when the artifice of the stage is made apparent and the traditions of theater are acknowledged, not denied, not transcended, we know that she is telling the truth: the stage is real and is never separate from the Earth. Even at the end, in the cliché of the blackout.

(BLACKOUT followed after several seconds by a TIGHT SPOT on the PIT that grows wider to encompass whole CAST.)

ROSENTHAL: "To be enlightened, we have need of darkness. They, the Others, can never be enlightened, for they have never fallen from grace."[15]

This is the real world. What else could it be? The tear cried on stage is a real tear. What else could it be? After their performance the dogs and cats from the local shelter that had been on Rosenthal's stage were put up for adoption. Audience members went home with new family members, *Others* made otherwise. Was the adoption process after the blackout still part of the performance?[16] Did Rachel the artist perform the matchmaking or did dogs and cats find human homes only off the stage? Is this activism? Is it art? Our false distinctions have us chasing our tails to the grave.

We think that animals can't be smart enough to act. All performance must be a cruel trick. We think that the light of reason does not shine in small cabbages. We tell a story about our own Fall, a story that so often exists only to set up the narrative of our rise to dominance. But this is not true Grace, a truly infinite love, mercy, accommodation, and decency.

Rosenthal's body moves with the grace of a dancer in liquid light; her animal voice sings to human, animal, and Goddess. She acts like the Book of Acts (a book she will have none of, of course).

DESCARTES: (*From offstage*) "The community of believers was of one heart and mind, and no one claimed that any of his possessions was his own, but they had everything in common. . . . There was no needy person among them, for those who owned property or houses would sell them, bring the proceeds of the sale . . . and they were distributed to each according to need" (Acts 4: 32–37).

Could Tatti act?

The assumption is not merely that animals are too unenlightened to understand narrative and the realm of the aesthetic, but that having no access to truth they are therefore incapable of lying. And acting, so goes the ill-formed thought, is a lie.

Composer and performance artist Laurie Anderson recalls hiring a dog wrangler to bring some angry-acting canines to her loft so that she could film the dogs for an accompaniment to a song she was recording. The trainer promised, "'They're vicious! Really vicious!' But he could only get them into attack mode for a few seconds at a time before they began to smile those happy dog smiles they've all got. That's what I love about dogs," concludes Anderson, "they're such lousy actors."[17]

Rosenthal performs with animals who share a life with her. She has friends bring animals from their homes as well. Everyone knows everyone else. No wranglers or trainers, no paid strangers are hired. No money is exchanged for tricks that are taught and reproduced. And Rosenthal's scripts allow for a sort of freedom that is unprecedented on the stage. It is a freedom that, rather than let the animal be and rather than force the animal to be something else, allows the humans and animals to become something together.

Shakespeare came close but never quite hit his mark. In *The Two Gentleman of Verona*, Crab the dog often gets the most laughs. On the pages of the script Crab is said to be disobedient and unwilling to take orders; he is not even housebroken. As a matter of necessity, goes the common wisdom, Shakespeare is thought to have written the character in that way, such that while the dog "playing" Crab in each production of the play simply goes about his own doggy life, indifferent to the narrative around him, his supposed inability to act will not hinder the production and break the narrative flow. Animals make lousy actors, so write a play in which they needn't lie, needn't act, needn't be something they are not. Michael Dobson goes so far as to say that "Shakespeare finds in Crab's sheer dogginess a superb comic indifference to the claims of the story into which he is dragged, making him the perfect straight man (or straight dog?) to Lance's unavailing emotional claims on him. So far from being a mere function of the plot, Crab is more likely to make the people around him look as though they are the ones doing mere tricks. . . . Crab embodies a giddy Shakespearean freedom."[18] If, however, we do not look to the author's intention for the meaning of the role (for the author, after all, has—like the rest of us—but one interpretation of that role, and occupies no privileged spot from which to apprehend and announce the true meaning of a work), if instead we merely look at the production itself, are we not forced to say that most dogs who play Crab on stage are in fact *performing* wonderfully, playing the role exactly as it is written, taking the author's direction ("be uncompanionable and unhygienic") seriously and then adding their own creative interpretation to that direction?

DESCARTES: (*From offstage*) Animals have no creativity. They are without mind. They do not belong on stage. Thinking a dog is performing well when it is directed to "Be unhygienic" is like thinking a rock is performing well if its part in the play calls for it to "Stay." Also, this is a terrible philosophy book, and a miserable chapter. It's not even a proper chapter, not even written in proper philosophical prose.

ROSENTHAL: (*To the audience*) "I used to hate a lot. . . . René Descartes, the guy who said that the whole Universe was a mechanism. That animals were machines. That you could vivisect them because their screams were just the sounds of gears and springs. Boy did I loathe him!"[19] (*Rosenthal begins growling like an angry dog then smiles that happy smile she's got.*)

Jannis Kounellis's *Horses* (1969) was an installation of a dozen live horses in an empty wing of the Galleria L'Attico in Rome. Tied facing the walls, the horses ate and defecated, as horses will do, over the days of the installation, apparently not missing the fact that the walls were bare and there was nothing for them to see while in the museum. "Were *we* missing the art as well?" seemed to be one of the questions being asked. "Or, like the horses, were we actually incapable of seeing art if the presence of the horses was itself the art?"

In 1974, Joseph Beuys spent a week in the René Block Gallery in New York City in a chain-link enclosure partitioning his space from the main gallery. Here, he interacted with a live coyote named Little John in a performance entitled *Coyote: I Like America and America Likes Me* (1974). Little John, for his part, would rip apart *The Wall Street Journal* that Beuys brought with him, pull—like a dog with one end of a sock—at the blanket in which Beuys wrapped himself, and be threatened with a stick-beating if he got too ferocious or unpredictable. A pair of brown gloves were continuously thrown at the coyote, which Beuys explains "represent my hands, and the freedom of movement that human beings possess with their hands. . . . Hands are universal. . . . They are not restricted to one specific use like the talons of an eagle or the mole's diggers. So the throwing of the gloves to Little John meant giving him my hands to play with."[20]

The horse and the coyote on stage here are not asked to perform, not expected to perform. And as a result, the ethics, aesthetics, and ontology become questionable. Like a chain-smoking, tuxedo-wearing chimpanzee forced to make faces in front of an audience or else get a shock, so too are the horses and coyotes of such performances disrespected, manipulated, and controlled when they are not thought to be actually part of the show, co-stars, co-authors, co-beings on stage. They are mere props, then. Things, machines, mechanisms in a Cartesian sideshow. Leave it to Rosenthal to put the horse before Descartes, to bring the animal and the human onstage in what is a mutual co-construction of Protean identity and fluid art, in what David Williams might call an "inter-subjective encounter, . . . [a] delirious and deterritorializing provocation."[21]

Of course Tatti Wattles could act. Being is acting.

LINGIS: (*Lowered from the rafters on a crystal chandelier, he wears a turquoise sarong*) "Sage grouse inhabit the vast plains of the northwestern United States and southern Canada. . . . In late February or early March, the cocks gather in traditional ceremonial arenas, on open plains or gentle slopes covered with short grass. . . . They come here from as far as a hundred miles away. The arena is long and narrow; it may be as large as half a mile long and two hundred yards wide. Up to 400 cocks come to perform there. The performances are held each day in the late afternoon. The performers position themselves thirty feet apart, and dance over an area from sixteen to twenty square yards."[22]

ROSENTHAL: (*Stage-whisper*) "I am becoming less and less inclined to think of myself as making 'art.'"[23]

LINGIS: "It is the centre of the arena that is the place of greatest prestige, and eventually the most magnificent performer occupies it. . . . Hens first appear at the arena two or three weeks later. . . . As they stroll through the 400 assembled dancers, they pause near a dancer whose performance impresses them. Over the course of days they gravitate to the master cock, who may thus have 50 to 70 hens watching his performance. . . . Once a hen has chosen her lover, and made love with him, she leaves. . . . The cocks do not acknowledge their paternity, and do not assist her in any way."[24]

ROSENTHAL: "Oh shit."[25]

LINGIS: "They are full-time professional performers. . . . [So too] in the eastern forests of Australia perform the satin bowerbirds . . . [The male] clears a patch of ground of every tiny twig, stem, leaf, and root. . . . He then covers the cleared area with a mat of coarse grasses and twigs . . . [where he also] places a collection of *objets d'art*. He travels far and wide to bring back blue parrot feathers, blue flowers, blue berries, blue beetles, fragments of blue grass, pieces of blue crockery, blue buttons. These decorative objects are laid out in the display area; not one blue object can stray inside the bower. Every day he runs a careful check on his collected objects. If any have lost their color during the night, flowers wilted or berries shriveled, they are discarded on a garbage dump, far from the stage. . . . The performance is scheduled for dawn. . . . At times he seems to pour harmony from his very soul."[26]

DESCARTES: (*From offstage*) Give me a break.

LINGIS: "He imitates the calls of the kookaburra (only the first two bars), the butcher bird, the grating cries of the white cockatoo . . . the crow shrike and the magpie, . . . the peculiar grunt of the native bear is true to nature. Spotted bower birds imitate the cries or calls of eagles, hawks, butcher birds, magpies, . . . domestic cat[s]."[27]

AUTHOR: They perform comedy.

LINGIS: "One spotted bower bird precisely mimicked the sound created by sheep scrambling though a wire fence, . . . the whirring of a cicada when held by a bird, . . . the distressed croak of a frog when caught by a snake."[28]

AUTHOR: Tragedy.

ROSENTHAL: "When we hear a bird we are overjoyed. Song birds, like in the old days, are gone, of course. But other birds still do make croaking sounds."[29]

LINGIS: "A female who comes to watch stands inside the bower. . . . After making love with their chosen top performer, a female leaves. . . . The fathers continue to tend their bowers, embellish them, and vocalize and dance for months after. When the young are raised, the males leave their bowers, and collect in gregarious flocks, until the next theater season."[30]

(A Bach fugue plays and LINGIS is raised into the rafters, humming along, waving goodbye.)

KAFKA: (*Lowering*) "I have completed the construction of my burrow and it seems to be successful. . . . I begin once more to dream my dream of a completely perfect burrow and that somewhat calms me; with closed eyes I behold with delight perfect or almost perfect structural devices for enabling me to slip out and in unobserved. . . . [T]he smaller rooms, each familiar to me: . . . they enclose me more peacefully and warmly than a bird is enclosed in its nest. And all, all still and empty."[31]

All living things—and perhaps nonliving things—perform. Always. We exist in narrative, playing communitarian roles, affirming or denying or strengthening or weakening the relationships that inflate us to being and constitute us. When the leopards broke into the temple and emptied the sacrificial vessels, who is to say that the notion of incorporating the ransacking into the ceremony came later? Who is to say that the leopards have not been playing their part all along and the artist merely acknowledges their performance and draws attention to it: *now* it is part of the ceremony; *now* the leopards appear on cue to wreck the temple;

now everything is—in shambles, destroyed, drunk, and gone—ordered because it is performed, because it is a story. We merely came in late.

As we saw in chapter 6, there is not a moment in life that you and I are not performing. I stand before my students and act out the part of the professor. It is a show. When the lecture is done, the sacrificial vessels dry, the last student gone from the room, I feel the change in me. I drop out of character. My body contorts and shifts, eases and then tightens and repositions. Not to something that is now *truly me* but to another performer and another show: I walk through the hallway and then through the day as a colleague, as a worker, as a man, as a Midwesterner, as a husband, as a worrier, as a failure, as a comedian, as a would-be savior, as a tragic figure, as this and that and the other thing. I practice each part, always standing from the vantage point of yet another character as I rehearse and learn. It is not a lie. It is the necessary structure of being.

And I imitate. The Deleuzean conception of "becoming-animal" rather than "being animal" is supposed to keep us from the trap of the production of identity, but it goes astray. Imitation does not need to assume a fixed identity for the thing being imitated in order to work. Deleuze and Guatarri condemn imitation, identification, allegory, and anthropomorphism. Yet to condemn anthropomorphizing an animal is to think that there is something it definitely means to be human and something it definitely means to be animal and never the two shall meet. A postmodern anthropomorphism is potentially true and good because it realizes the bilateral nature of the projection, the fluidity with which judgments are made and change and are always up for grabs. It is all right to see one's dog as feeling ashamed after he has messed the floor because, in part, we come to have the experience of performing shame ourselves by learning it from the performance of dogs.

Humanity itself is a performance. I sleep like a rock, dream like a dog, wake like a whale. I face the day and go about preparing to perform my humanity: I choose the appropriate costume, hairstyle, and smell before going on stage. I put on a suit and tie, trim my beard, and shower. (When Rosenthal shaved her head bald on stage in *Leave Her in Naxos* [1981] it was not merely an act of identification with the horrors of Auschwitz. It was an act of animality. [The two, of course, are sadly linked.] It was not merely a new beginning for her, a new moment for a heart to grow from the snow and love again, but an act of clearing, of starting over, of going feral.) I perform my humanity all day long. I grunt at other humans, making human noises they anticipate and will understand—different noises from the mooing I do with cows, the whistling I do with birds, the silence in which I sit with rocks. All of this is imitative and echoing. It is performing. And this is what it means to be human.

Animality is performance. Performance is found not merely in the strutting of the bowerbird or the chaos of Crab's trodding the boards in all his lack of hygiene. It is in the raccoon who, long ago, accidentally popped my three-year-old friend Leah's inflatable kiddie pool after spending an hour late at night one summer floating, swimming, and playing with the colorful plastic balls left there from earlier in the day. It is in the mouse, Mr. Jingles, who both frightened and kept my mother company in her apartment when it started to get cold outside and when they were both alive. It is in the lazy self-assurance of iguanas eating rotten mangos in the streets of Venezuela when I lived down there. In the birds who sing at my feeders, the squirrels who plot schemes to get more sunflower seeds for themselves, the rabbits who yearn for pizza crust and turn up their noses at celery tops on my porch. All of these beings are performing, performing their animality and their existence, inhabiting roles and becoming their relationships. It is only performance; and this is what it means to be an animal.

ROSENTHAL: "I remember gathering when I was a child in France. In the woods. Berries, mushrooms, lilies of the valley. . . . It was great. Finding something that isn't guaranteed to be there. What a rush!"[32]

The world is not built for us. And the script is always changing because we are always changing. Recognizing that performance is not something relegated to a stage—or better yet, that the stage is part of the Earth and art is the necessary mode of our existence—Rosenthal would cast and co-author productions with animals without force and without presumption. Knowing that they will be performing at all times, just as she will be, Rosenthal allowed animals to be with her in a way that is unprecedented in performance art. Or any art, for that matter, for all art needs to be performed. We read the poem aloud in our head to the audience of our many selves; we touch the statue with our eyes and feel it build up in the phenomenological play of presence and absence as we circle around it; we scan the painting in staccato stochastic circadian rhythms, focusing here, focusing there, building up the painting temporally and spatially; we even perform philosophy, rehearse academic arguments, and tend to think in the form of a play. You, READER, performer, human, animal; you with this book in your hand: you know what I mean.

Tatti Wattles brings blood to Rosenthal's neck and the moment is ripe with vampirism. Did he mean it? Did he perform it? Did she?

Even when animals were not present on stage, they were always with Rosenthal. Each performance of *Zato* (1990) was improvisational, and each performance told the story of Rosenthal's dog, a blind poodle she rescued and named Zatoichi, an echo of the blind swordsman of the same name in Japanese samurai films. Warrior and wanderer: we are immediately reminded of Homer, too, the blind storyteller of the west, as Rosenthal begins her performance, the oral account of the odyssey of her hero dog.

Deaf, arthritic, epileptic, senile, and incontinent as well as blind, Zato, Rosenthal tells us, "tried to be a dog. . . . He knew he didn't have the knack."[33] *Canis familiaris* like *Homo sapiens* is a performance: bark at the right time, wag the tail in a way that is understood, love and learn and live *like* a dog in order to *be* a dog. It is, as the character's name implies, a familiar and familial performance to be a dog star. Domestication, for humans and for nonhumans, is merely a form of rehearsal, and most dogs are Method actors. Zato tried to be a dog. And even in his failure to be a dog, he helped expand the description of what it means to be a dog: it is a contradiction only to a metaphysic that demands stable, finite identity.

Zato's heart, we learn, was enlarged ("too much loving, perhaps"); he walked in circles and pushed his head against walls as if they would crumble against the force of one sick dog's skull. Zato and Rosenthal performed/lived/existed together: they slept together, woke up together, urinated together. He took away her freedom and, in dying, liberated her: it is a contradiction only to an ethic that demands finite, calculable duty. Rosenthal, the hero who will not euthanize a happy dog no matter how her own suffering grows, is no mere maiden in distress. "Kill me!" she screams. "Not the dog!" But this part Zato could play and write: the warrior who wanders in, saves the girl, liberates with his heart, and dies "easy, simple, and brave."

As the performance unfolds, when Rosenthal speaks of Zato she does more than speak. She shows us the limits of speech, turning—as she must in order to convey truth—to the flesh, to song, and to silence. She turns to Zato. To say that she becomes Zato on stage is to fail to capture the point: she is Rosenthal and she is Zato and she is more. This becoming-animal is not some Disneyfied mockery, and yet it is more than a Deleuzean daydream. Rosenthal is not on all fours barking before us with a pink—or white—panting tongue, as if mockery and mimicry were the same thing. And yet Zato is present in her every move. Zato, in his absence, is of her present flesh, her voice that becomes a sweet dog-howl in song to express love unutterable by humans. These are the limits of language and the blurry boundary of the aesthetic: emotion and torment and indecision personified in cried gibberish after she learns that the dog who demands her constant care and attention is not dying and will likely live another *year*; the horror of the puddle-of-pee repeated—***the puddle!*** the puddle! ***the puddle!*** **THE PUDDLE!**—in every way until any meaning of the word "puddle" is gone and there is only the felt sense of mutual frustration; the growing realization reflected in the growing intensity of her precise pronunciation that she is no more special than Zato, though she alone, she is told, possesses logos and makes art; the silence that hangs at the end marking the death of the warrior, the space between despair and relief, life and death, presence and absence. This space is not an empty space on Rosenthal's stage. Like the space between words, it is responsible for all meaning: without silence there is no communication. And without the animal, no Rosenthal, no performance, no art, no hope for us all.

AUTHOR: We are using words to talk about words. It is a form of narcissism—reflexive, human, blinding us to the Others not in the mirror. And it is a recipe for failure. Like screaming to make a child be quiet, or killing to stop a war.

(ROSENTHAL becomes KOKO the gorilla and climbs down from her platform. DESCARTES enters dressed in modern scientist clothes and plays the role of her TRAINER. The AUTHOR cracks a whip and DESCARTES jumps nervously; it is clear that DESCARTES is being forced into this, that he is being trained as well as training. KOKO jumps into the PIT, discovers the cabbage, and sits on the edge of the PIT, nibbling at the cabbage as she begins to speak.)

KOKO: "Koko wants to tell about the sky, the food, the playing, and the breaking of branches. She wants people to know about the feelings of a fine animal who loves life. Everything is sensuous and important. . . . Hard to remember to say things in small pieces. . . ."[34]

TRAINER: One last time, Koko, this is the good one. To be or not to be, I think therefore I am.

KOKO: (*Chuckling and scratching herself*) "I am my beard's friend, my nipples' friend, my big belly's friend. And I like all these parts tickled, fondled, and hugged. Moments ever new, surprising, nurturing, dependable. I know and trust they'll be there. So I abandon myself and drift, tenderly rocked as I navigate among the branches, feeling the tug of the Mother in my gut. (*She mimes hanging and swinging gently from a branch, her eyes closed, ecstatic. She comes to, sits on the platform, signs correctly.*) To be or not to be, I think therefore I am."[35]

TRAINER: You got it, Koko! Good girl! Smart gorilla!

KOKO: (*Yawns*) "Gorilla sleepy. . . ."[36]

AUTHOR: "We communicate with other human beings through language. Most of our relations with animals are therefore based on attempts to teach them words, for the most part 'commands': 'Sit!,' 'Stay!,' 'Heel!,' 'Whoa!,' 'Giddyup!,' etc. We get impatient and angry when animals don't 'understand,' and we think them bad, stupid, or in need of more training. We seldom consider learning their language."[37]

(The lights dim and everyone finds a place to lie down on stage to take a nap. Jungle sounds play softly in the background. Everyone sleeps. From the back of the theater SOCRATES enters. He makes his way through the audience and toward the stage. He seems ready to give a speech, but no one is awake to hear him, so he is disappointed. He kicks the AUTHOR lightly with his sandaled foot to wake him and quickly looks away.

He does it again with a bit more force, and the AUTHOR speaks, apparently dreaming and still fully asleep.)

AUTHOR: Just a few more pages. I'm almost done.

(SOCRATES, disgruntled, kicks the AUTHOR firmly in the crotch. The AUTHOR, who will now play the role of PHAEDRUS, screams and jumps up. SOCRATES is looking the other way, pretending not to have done anything.)

SOCRATES: Oh, say, Phaedrus. Is that you?

PHAEDRUS: What? I. . . . Oh. It's you. Yeah, I guess. Yes. It's me, Phaedrus. Pray tell me Socrates, whence come you and whither are you going?

SOCRATES: I come from my walk outside the walls of the city zoo, and I am going to the grave, sweet boy, and then to immortality with the Forms; but first to the theater. I'm off to see *Painting Is Hell* by Irosenthal of Gaul. They say she offends the Gods, speaks with animals, and has a head as smooth as the lower cheeks of Venus. I plan to heckle her loudly.

PHAEDRUS: I don't see the point.

SOCRATES: She will.

PHAEDRUS: Sometimes I fear you have no soul, Socrates. By the gods, you are mean.

SOCRATES: You jest, Phaedrus. Now tell me what you thought of Irosenthal's show. Did you find the performance inspired and the paintings inspiring? Recount to me in every detail how the spectacle unfolded and tell me what you made of it so that I can, myself, be better prepared and know when best it will be to dislodge these rotten apples I have hidden beneath my robes and thus make my point heard on her stage.

PHAEDRUS: Nothing would please me less, Socrates, but I have not seen the show. I've been writing lately and have been busy at home.

SOCRATES: I would have believed your every word and left you here to your own misguided reverie had I not seen the playbill from the show there tucked in your pack on the ground. So tell me of the performance and of the evening you had. Start with what you wore, end with what you did at home later that night, and leave nothing out in between.

PHAEDRUS: Ah, you are too snub-nosey for me to practice my art on you. Shall we speak, then, of the nature of the soul and the horses and charioteer that comprise it?

SOCRATES: I love you, Phaedrus, but you really shouldn't take me so literally. Half of this stuff I'm just pulling out of my . . .

PHAEDRUS: Literally or literarily, Socrates? Aren't most distinctions questions of convenience? I think you miss the point. Irosenthal is an artist, and her work is constantly questioning distinctions, rejecting violence, showing as well as saying. I have written a commentary on *Painting Is Hell*. Here, let me share some of it with you.

SOCRATES: "You know, Phaedrus, writing shares a strange feature with painting. The off-springs of painting stand there as if they are alive, but if anyone asks them anything, they remain solemnly silent. The same is true of written words. You'd think they were speaking as if they had some understanding, but if you question anything that has been said because you want to learn more, it continues to signify just that very same thing forever. When it has once been written down, every discourse roams about everywhere, reaching indiscriminately those with understanding no less than those who have no business with it, and it doesn't know to whom it should speak and to whom it should not. And when it is faulted and attacked unfairly, it always needs its father's support; alone, it can neither defend itself nor come to its own support."[38]

PHAEDRUS: Its mother should have taught it not to speak to strangers.

SOCRATES: Hmm?

PHAEDRUS: Or perhaps forcing others to listen and to talk back is really merely putting words in their mouths. But listen: painting is not silent. It is more like a dialogue. The trainer writes words in the air with Koko's hands; he writes in monologue for her. But Irosenthal, when she is becoming-gorilla, has more to say, more truth to reveal without logos than we ever seem able to muster. Irosenthal, alone on stage, dialogues.

SOCRATES: Madness! How I look forward to seeing this for myself. (*His hand disappears as he reaches for the apples beneath his tunic.*) Rotten! Oh! You really have my juices flowing now. Tell me, please dear Phaedrus, about her latest performance; tell me of *Painting Is Hell* and don't make me beg again.

PHAEDRUS: First you should know that she says it is not a performance. She's retired, you know. She smiles and says—while on stage, mind you—that she is not performing. In fact, the audience is told that this is to be a "reality show."

SOCRATES: Like *Survivor: Thrace*?

PHAEDRUS: Stay with me, Socrates. She is making a point about how reality is always already a show. When she tells everyone that this is the story of how she "transitioned" from performer to painter, she is performing. The script is referring to itself—though she also tells us that there is no written script, and I'm inclined to believe her. The stage is essentially barren as Irosenthal explains that she is going to tell us about her becoming-painter journey. Gilah, the painting mentor, is introduced. She will be critiquing the artist's work just as she does in her home studio. For the first time, we, the audience, will witness such a session and thereby purportedly gain insight into Irosenthal's work and her life.

SOCRATES: I see.

PHAEDRUS: A slide comes up on the large screen on stage. An image of one of Irosenthal's paintings—one of dozens that will be projected during the show, nearly all of them a painting of a dog. (*See figure 8.1.*)

SOCRATES: What a waste! Exquisite!

PHAEDRUS: Indeed, they are exquisite. The colors are vibrant and primary, pastel and earthy, sweet and evocative. She begins with an early work—something with "Identity" in the title, I recall. In the center there is a little brown-and-white dog, sketched in only the quickest outline, mere points for eyes and nose, yet wholly there, his tail wagging and his haunches trembling. He is frightened yet bravely facing his performance—that is to say his being, his life. He stands in water—on water—light blue and white. On either side there is earth, soil, land, cave, solidity: brown. These patches of cave-dark-brown have ethereal female

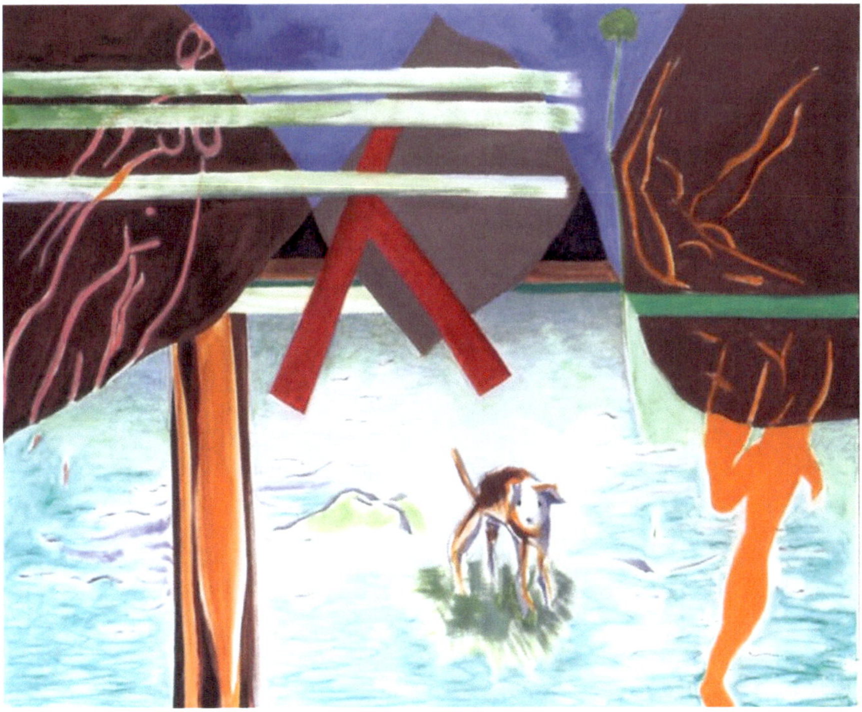

FIGURE 8.1. Rachel Rosenthal. *Identity*. 2004. Oil on canvas, unknown dimensions.

outlines drawn on them, nude women in pink and orange. And will it surprise you, Socrates, to learn that the "costume" Irosenthal uses on stage is a pink blouse, covered with an orange-red shirt, covered with a brown-black vest, with orange pants? She is there, materialized from the first painting she shows us! The pink and orange figures' limbs are elongated and graceful (with feet still planted below), as if prehistoric paintings on the wall. The setting, we know, is primal. In the center, where the patches of curved brown rise up and meet like buttocks, there is a gray diamond—a void, a vulva, the eternal cavity-abyss and emptiness from which all things emerge and come into being. The pup has just been born, the Ur-creature of the universe fallen to the earth. His birth was unexpected and askew (the off-center Y of blood leaking into the world tells us this), but he is strong. There are rocks and wood to offer him a home, streaks of green on the horizon to offer him hope. And the Mother is miraculously full again, new water to break, a little seed growing in her sky-womb: company, soon, for the First Dog. But now, here, alone, small, and strong, he will make us all possible, make who we are possible. It was amazing, Socrates.

SOCRATES: Yes, well. . . .

PHAEDRUS: Gilah critiques the work, speaking only of mechanics, weight, and balance. "You have a blue problem," she says.

(A SLIDE appears, projected on the screen on stage:) "'In those difficult times, Tatti seemed to be my only link to life. . . . I said his name and he clucked back. This scanty dialogue was enough to anchor me when it seemed the ground had shifted dangerously under my feet.'—Rachel Rosenthal."[39]

(SLIDES of stills from various ROSENTHAL productions now begin to show in rapid succession over the course of three or four minutes. They conclude with a SLIDE of ROSENTHAL in Painting Is Hell (2004). *PHAEDRUS watches the SLIDES but SOCRATES seems oblivious.)*

PHAEDRUS: Irosenthal tells us that her only problem now is that she has a carpet of dogs in her studio and it makes it hard to paint. Things are a chaotic mess. "The dogs come into the studio one color and they leave another," she remarks.

SOCRATES: You mean she literally paints her dogs?

PHAEDRUS: Literarily. Now pay attention because this next part you are going to like. A dog comes onto the stage.

SOCRATES: *(Jumping up and down excitedly)* Then it's true! Oh, the folly!

PHAEDRUS: His name is Cagney. He enters with a human named Tad, and the two dance and sing. Cagney is spun on his back on the floor, break dancing, and then is nestled in the arms of Tad while they ballroom dance across the stage.

SOCRATES: I can barely contain this joy, Phaedrus. The hound has a human name? And his passivity and manipulation are taken for true dancing?

PHAEDRUS: That he does and that it is. And it is, further, some of the finest stage dancing I have seen. At any rate, the slides continue to flash on the screen, Gilah continues to no avail to try to engage Irosenthal in discussion about her art, and dogs continue to appear on the stage, each one being named by the artist along with the dog's human companion. As the dogs increase in number—one, two, a dozen, two dozen—the audience is taken over by huge fits of laughter.

SOCRATES: Ah, so the people of Athens are not seduced after all, but see this debacle for what it is.

PHAEDRUS: On the contrary. They laugh not because it is unserious, but because it is the opposite of tragedy. Sasha the dog, for instance, makes his appearance and commands the stage; and the audience is in awe of his beauty.

SOCRATES: This is my point, dear boy. There are relations among things, yes, but there are clear boundaries between what is good and evil, what is true and false, what is this and that. A dog—even a handsome dog named Sasha—is not to be accorded such laurels. He is but a shadow of the true Dog. Just as a single sandal can make many impressions in the mud as a man walks along the banks of a river, and each impression will be similar to yet distinct from the last, so is each individual earthly dog but an impression of the Formal Dog. Now, the common man studies mud; the philosopher ponders sandals. And the artist merely paints muddy toe impressions with mud that . . . uh . . . without sandals . . . and . . . uh . . .

PHAEDRUS: So much obsession with feet, Socrates! This performance was about art as much as it was about animality. When Sasha, for instance, is there on stage, Sasha also suddenly appears in a painting in one of the slides. Gilah tries desperately to entice Irosenthal to attend to the painting. "Look here, it's Sasha," she says. "A painting of Sasha. Let's talk about it." The artist glances up, says "No, no, no. Oh, yes, that is Sasha" and then adds, pointing to the flesh-and-blood dog before her, "But this is Sasha. Let me just explain. . . . " Do you see what she is doing here? She is an artist; she creates these beautiful canvases; she performs for us. And yet she insists that we not make the animal an artistic abstraction, a theme, a bodiless object that is a *mere* symbol—either for something else or for itself. We hear the story of how Sasha was rescued, for instance, and we cannot see Sasha in the painting as a mere thing. Suddenly, art and life are not separate. All of these false dichotomies are crumbling before us as she works her craft. "Sasha is my lover," Irosenthal announces. "The best lover I have ever had." But then, immediately, she tells us that he is not her lover because she is, unfortunately, not into bestiality. Later, she will introduce Lucy, a sweet little human girl wearing a T-shirt that says "The Amazing Duckie," telling everyone that Lucy is a "two-legged dog."

SOCRATES: But . . .

PHAEDRUS: Art and reality, human and animal, painting and flesh, lover and nonlover. What is the nature of art, the human, the painting as opposed to these latter concepts in each pair? What is the nature of the lover? Consider: in this "nonperformance," Irosenthal brings out the friends and animals she loves so dearly, and, so that we can get the point—the point about the "reality" and the performance of it all, the point about the relationship between animality and art—she then begins to insult everyone. Praising, for instance, her friend Anna's kindness, and her dog Annabel's beauty, Irosenthal turns and says, "Don't be fooled! Annabel is a bitch and Anna is a witch!" (Neither of which, of course, is a label Irosenthal actually thinks is bad!) Appearance and truth are the topic here, and the artist is calling everything into question. If this is a reality show, the reality is that everything is performance and everything is art, yet not in the sense that such things are untruthful. Like you, Socrates, Irosenthal wants to question authority and shake things up. She lets her dogs run off leash, we are next told, because the state has no right to dictate such oppression of the flesh. I heard her say that the police are looking for a woman with a big white dog: "We are the Bonnie and Clyde of the park!," she tells the audience. Of course she would choose such a metaphor, alluding to performance—fixing roles to secure identity for a moment—from the artistic past of Hollywood, film, and lore. But she might as well have said that she is being chased by the elders of the city for corrupting the pups of Athens.

SOCRATES: This I don't follow. Why risk so much for an animal? What could they ever give us in return? What could they ever truly appreciate being given from us, appreciate *as such*?

PHAEDRUS: Socrates, all the way back in chapter 4 we learned that you owe a cock to Asclepius, but what do you owe the *cock*? Think carefully about your true final debts.

SOCRATES: Watch your tongue, Peter. Do not deny me a third time.

PHAEDRUS: I owe you a great deal, my friend, but not more than I owe the truth.

(Andrew Lloyd Webber's "John Nineteen: Forty-One" plays softly in the background. The sound is scratchy, as if on an old phonograph. After a minute, the song begins to skip, stuck on the same groove. The music fades, skipping. During this time, DESCARTES has awakened, looked around, and climbed down into the PIT where he cannot be seen, laid to rest. Now the jungle sounds gradually grow louder as the show concludes. ROSENTHAL sits up, stretches, and listens to the continuing dialogue.)

SOCRATES: I think I'd better cover my head. (*He puts on a pair of Mickey Mouse ears and closes his eyes.*)

PHAEDRUS: To speak to dogs, one must know the language of dogs. "'Dog,'" the artist tells us, "is not a dog word." Neither are "Come" or "Sit." Spoken words get closer: "Herewego!" and "Tothecorner!," Irosenthal suggests, are acceptable in certain local canine patois. Nothing is universal, I'm afraid. Nothing ever is. Our own English has already taken much from Dog. We get the word "awesome" from the word a dog pronounces when he yawns, the word "like" from the word he repeats when he licklicklicks his chops. As with all true dialogue, the exchange goes both ways. I have to admit that I especially like the awesome fact that at this part in her performance when she is talking about language, words, and communication, the stage is so crowded with dogs and humans moving around and talking to each other, that it is increasingly hard to hear what Irosenthal is saying. She has to project more than normal, almost shouting to the audience. We feel as if we are in her studio, perhaps—so many friends underfoot—and the act of talking and the act of painting are being compared and explained for us. What a joyous chaos! Oh, and it is then that the siren begins to sound. (*Pause. The jungle sounds stop. Silence. Everyone waits as if a siren is about to go off. After ten to fifteen seconds of silence, the jungle sounds return and PHAEDRUS continues:*) The dogs in the studio always howl when an emergency truck with sirens blaring passes by, and so Irosenthal plans to have a siren go off to interrupt her speech and fill the theater with howls. The sound begins, but with the siren being a mere recording, the context of the stage, and the excitement of the performance, not a single dog howls. Immediately, though, without pause and without time for thought, the humans on stage—followed by the humans in the audience (another dichotomy being taken apart for us here)—all begin to bay and howl in harmony with the siren, the canines staring at the humans in amazement. It is a lovely moment, a deep moment. Humans in the throes of antilinguistic language, singing their nonwords; dogs silent and still, as if puzzled. As the dogs watch in wonder, performing perfectly their silence, we come to see language—ours and theirs and the false dichotomy of ours-and-theirs—in a new light. We are all brought together. And now that Irosenthal has us just where she wants us—the paintings on the screen flying by at too great a speed to make much out (color! dog! color! sky! dog! dog! dog!), the drumming in the background increasing in volume and intensity, the communal howl fresh in our ears—she preaches again her sermon against the leash and has us scream together "I hate leash laws!" before announcing in a guttural shriek of freedom "*Everybody* off leash!" (*ROSENTHAL stands and walks off stage.*) The dogs that were leashed and held and embraced and restrained by the cast members are now let loose; and as she lets slip the dogs of chaos, they wander all around the theater, sniffing the humans, sniffing each other, petting and being petted, creating a kinetic painting and dissolving the final scaffolding of the artifice of the theater and the expectation that we are somehow different, somehow better, somehow Other. I close my eyes now, Socrates, and I am still in the midst of those fine dogs, still able to see her paintings nearly turned into a kinescope flashing so quickly before me, still basking in the freedom she bestowed upon me. I am transformed.

SOCRATES: (*Removes his hat and speaks humbly*) I never. . . . I wonder. . . . How. . . . Do they throw flowers and sweet figs down upon her when she concludes and receives her final tribute onstage?

PHAEDRUS: She merely waves goodbye in the middle of the chaos and leaves, the dogs still roaming, the show still going. If you are not attentive, you might miss that she has stepped aside because everything she has created is still there. As it will be even after she has left the living.

SOCRATES: Then, no conclusion? No critique of what it means? No bows and no acknowledgement of the ending?

PHAEDRUS: Look. (*He points off stage*) It never ends.

(BLACKOUT. Jungle sounds STOP.)

(No CURTAIN CALL.)

(The leopards are left loose in the theater.)

SECTION 4

Laughing Beyond Modernity

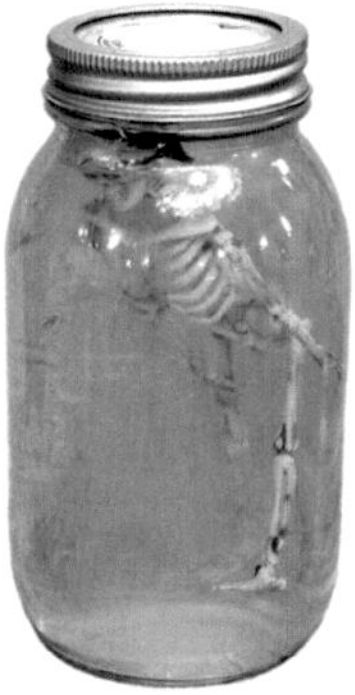

CHAPTER 9 

"It's Just a Bunch of Stuff that Happened"

The Simpsons and the Possibility of Postmodern Comedy

At the center of the finest episodes of *The Simpsons* there is absolutely nothing. ("Ummm . . . creamy nothing center. Aghghghgh. . . .") This should only be disappointing if we were thinking that something should have been there, that we deserve something there. Part of the postmodern condition, of our condition, is such frustration of expectation—not just particular expectations, but the notion of expectation in general with its linear conception of cause and effect, its reliance on there being a stable and coherent self to do the expecting, its overall naïve innocence about how the world operates. *The Simpsons*, hollow as it is, is anything but naïve; and thus it demands a sophisticated conception of humor.

Traditional theories of comedy worked for more traditional times. Immanuel Kant's (very Kantian and thus very unfunny) description of what is funny—"the placing of heterogeneous notions under common genera"—explain why jokes about rabbis, priests, and ministers who hang out together in bars and on golf courses can get laughs. But who tells these sorts of jokes anymore—at least unironically? Thomas Hobbes's insistence that all humor stems from a sudden sense of superiority—that jokes bring pleasure precisely because someone is in pain *and it's not me*—might explain why it's funny to watch the Three Stooges, why it's funny (for some) to tell ethnic jokes, or why it's hilarious to note that Hobbes is dead and you and I aren't. But so much comedy today is about self-deprecation (David Letterman's late-night incarnations, perhaps, started the revolution, Larry David's HBO series *Curb Your Enthusiasm* and Louis C. K. continued it, and most comedians in the first half of the twenty-first century have this as part of their DNA) that Hobbes seems quaintly out of place—like Don Rickles's ghost starring in a *Key & Peele* reboot. Henri Bergson's claim that humor arises from involuntary actions, that we expect to find adaptability and pliability in human beings but when met with a stumbling block—literally or metaphorically—we often still stumble, speaks to the human condition. But in a world where stumbling has become the norm and the possibility of a universal human condition is continually under question, tripping is not as funny as it used to be.

Here, then, is the problem: had this book been published decades ago, a nice chapter could have be written on Kant and *Three's Company* ("Come and Knock on Our Door: Mr. Kant, Mr. Roper, and the Placing of Hetero-Homo-Sexual Notions Under a Common Apartment Roof"), on Hobbes and *Saved By the Bell* ("The Importance of Not Being Screech"), or on Bergson and *The Dick Van Dyke Show* ("On Hassocks, Both Real and Metaphorical"). But who can speak to *The Simpsons*? Though we might laugh at the improbable coupling of Burns and Smithers, or with a sense of superiority when we watch Chief Wiggum, or with surprise at the eternal lack of adaptability in Homer, this sort of laughing does not seem to get at the heart of what is funny about the show. This is not to say, of course, that *The Simpsons* is new. With nearly three decades under its belt, *The Simpsons* is not only the longest-running animated TV series but also the longest-running sitcom and the longest-running scripted, prime-time television series in general. What was new—and arguably still is new—about *The Simpsons* is its relation to modernity. Springfield is located squarely in a newly postmodern world.

Of course, this is "literally" true. Springfield, the hometown of the Simpsons, is not in any particular American state but is, instead, an eclectic geographic mixture of places. Fans noted this early on, and the show has since made a coyly self-aware running joke out of it. The way in which Springfield is (dis)located is telling.

Place, for the modern, is unimportant. Modernity's politics, metaphysics, aesthetics, and ethics rejected the importance of context and situation, the possible importance of being one place instead of another. Universal rights and universal conceptions of Being were the goals, and universal notions of the individual were thus assumed. Beauty is Truth and Truth, Beauty—even in New Jersey. From Hobbes's placeless state of nature to the placeless marketplace of capitalism to the American assumption that U.S. democracy is the finest form of government for everyone in the world, there is thus a long history of thinking that the specifics of place are unimportant to anything that really matters. The project of modernity can even be described in terms of the systematic destruction of place: the golden arches of McDonald's look the same around the globe and a Big Mac tastes the same as well; cosmopolitanism destroys true difference even as it commodifies it; the Liberal state would have us treated as generic, isolated, individual selves with generic, isolationist, and individual rights; and mass communications technologies trick us into thinking that we are near family and friends—and home—even when we are separated by untold miles. One of the myths of modernity, then, is that we can happily live dislocated.

Postmodernity becomes aware of such false assumptions but without resorting to melancholy over similarly false constructions of the "good old days" with their good old places. If the zombies of chapter 4 taught us that there is a danger inherent in nostalgia, then it is the postmodern world of the post–zombie apocalypse that calls to us from Springfield. As an artistic representation, Springfield is both generic and specific at the same time. It is not a particular place of this world, yet it is not placeless. Think of the importance of the town to the show; compare this to the seeming unimportance of "real" locations to other comedies. The New York City of *I Love Lucy*, *The Cosby Show*, *Friends*, or *The Mindy Project* is essentially irrelevant to the identities of the characters and the nature of the action. If it does appear (as in *Friends* in the one in which Ross's new girlfriend lives a long train ride away, or the one in which Jean Claude Van Damme shows up to film a movie in the city), the plot seems contrived and the city is at most a backdrop, not a character in itself. The Mayberry of *The Andy Griffith Show* falls into the melancholy category. The small town seems to have created the good-natured neighbors who populate the show, but the maudlin tone and utter lack of politics of race and sex (even while the show was being produced during the time of the civil rights movement) suggest a whitewashing of true Southern geographic embodiment.

Not so in Springfield. The town may flaunt its inability to be located squarely in one state, but this fluid positioning does not turn it into a placeless everyplace. Springfield is unique and rooted. Its history informs the characters, though that history is always ready for rewriting (see, for instance, Lisa's discovery that the town's pioneer founder and namesake, Jebediah Springfield, was in reality a terrible man, and her refusal in the end to announce this discovery when she realizes that "truth" is always up for grabs and the townspeople are legitimately constructing themselves and their history at every moment ["Lisa the Iconoclast" (11 February 1996)]). Springfield, too, is self-sufficient in a way most towns are not but should be. Though there are moments of disruptive globalism, local products (such as Duff beer) are more prevalent than multinational corporate products (such as Mr. Sparkle). Even the local nuclear power plant is run by a local billionaire, whose mistake in one episode of selling the plant to "the Germans" (who, it turns out, aren't all smiles and sunshine) is quickly righted ("Burns Verkaufen der Kraftwerk" [5 December 1991]).

Critics have suggested that Springfield comes close to the classical polis, but that it unrealistically portrays a modern local community. "[W]hat are authentic movie stars like Rainer Wolfcastle doing living in Springfield? And what about the fact that the world-famous Itchy and Scratchy cartoons are produced in Springfield?"[1] In placing the stars and industries in Springfield, though, an important point is being made. The distinction between local culture and global culture is eroded, but not in the way it is being eroded today in our world. In our "real" world (or at least, let us say, "nonanimated world"), homogenization of culture works in such a way as to destroy what is local. Architecture, food, language, music, humor, and nearly all customs embedded in local communities are giving way to mass-produced artifacts and thinking. Hence those aforementioned ubiquitous golden arches and Big Macs. *The Simpsons*'s twist on this is to make the local culture the dominant culture—to erode the distinction, but from the other end. That is, Krusty Burger restaurants are not only a mockery of McDonald's; they are an inversion of McDonald's. Krusty is a local celebrity, and his local business is presented as if it were the homogenizing, corporate, distantly owned fast-food franchise; as if the local were homogenizing the rest of the world. Itchy and Scratchy are world-renowned cartoon characters enjoyed by kids everywhere, but they are created locally and are produced locally. Duff beer, the local drink of choice, has its corporate offices in Springfield—and the assumption is that everyone, everywhere drinks Duff (except, perhaps, for the backwards residents of country singer Lurleen Lumpkin's hometown, who seem to enjoy Fudd beer at their local "Beer-n-Brawl" tavern ["Colonel Homer" (26 March 1992)] and, of course, Ned Flanders, who once invited Homer to his basement rec room for draft beer from Holland ["Dead Putting Society" (15 November 1990)]). When Duffman needs hip-replacement surgery and a new Duffman must be chosen as a corporate spokesman, the corporation naturally created a reality show, *So You Think You Can Duff?*, hosted by Cat Deeley, but of course the competition was filmed in Springfield, and Homer won ("Waiting for Duffman" [15 March 2015]).[2] What *The Simpsons* realizes is that commercialization is caught up in webs of global production and consumption, and that the world the show presents—and even the show itself—is complicit in this.

Let's be clear about how this is so. At the risk of forcing concepts on the world, we might say that there are three sorts of (television) comedy: traditionalist, modern, and postmodern. Though they tend to be chronologically ordered (roughly: traditionalist television comedies range from the 1950s to the 1960s, modernist comedies from the 1970s to the 1980s, and postmodernists from the 1990s on), there is nothing necessarily chronological about this. Indeed, *Monty Python's Flying Circus* in the 1970s was, perhaps, the first truly postmodern television comedy, *The Cosby Show* of the 1980s was surely traditionalist, and very few twenty-first century programs are truly postmodern. Still, there is something to be said for such quaint linear classification schemes. Regardless, the types can be defined in part by their reaction to their own status in the culture and thus their relation to their production.

All production is somehow complicit in the modern market, including the production that makes television comedies possible. If a show does not acknowledge this, and is even seemingly unaware of it, it would be *traditionalist*. Commercialization never was a theme for *Donna Reed* (though it was undoubtedly so for Donna Reed). If a show realizes this and tries to find a way out, it would be *modernist*. There are multiple modernist tricks toward this end. Some modernist television naïvely attempts to create community by showing local products being consumed as if they were the only products on the shelf. Others cynically exhibit only mass-produced products (thereby accepting their status) and lure us into false community with the characters by naming these as products we all have in common. *Seinfeld*, for instance, chose this latter tactic. Realizing that brand names are everywhere, *Seinfeld* would refer to them explicitly, thus making the viewer think that he or she had something in common with the characters ("I love Junior Mints, too!"). Acknowledging the nature of the commercial culture thus makes the show modernist rather than traditionalist. It could have taken the postmodern turn, though, if it had admitted its own complicity and immersion in this culture.[3]

Modern art thinks that it can escape the culture (and thus its own status as art), look down on it, satirize it, twist it for our amusement. The postmodernist realizes that there is no escaping the culture, no "view from nowhere" or vantage point from which to look down, no possibility of satirical twists since satire always involves an assumption that one can rise above what is being satirized. In terms of consumption, *Seinfeld* was itself a brand name. Community was not being created but was being destroyed in part because of *Seinfeld*. Rather than local jokes appealing to and co-constituting local senses of humor, a mass-produced show about New Yorkers (being filmed, of course, in Los Angeles) was beamed out to the rest of the world, thus helping to homogenize our expectations and tastes. In today's world, the truth is that we do not share much. There is no substantial life in common. We tend to know people, if at all, in one capacity only: you are my coworker or my dry cleaner or my neighbor or my child's schoolteacher—but seldom more than one of these things. When we meet at the water cooler at work, what is there to talk about? All that we have in common is our consumption of mass-produced products—a love of Junior Mints, Bosco, and *Seinfeld* reruns. We think that when we discuss these things, we are sharing a life in common. It is illusion. *Seinfeld*, then, contributed to the illusion by bringing us "together" with the characters, making them part of our "community" (which really just means mass-produced culture), by name-dropping brand names. What it failed to acknowledge is both the fact that this is illusory community and the related fact that *Seinfeld* contributed to this false community in that it is a product itself and thus a topic for our discussion at the water cooler. We do not have real friends in common, so what can we discuss when we are together apart from the life of what friends on TV have in common?

The Simpsons, however, acknowledges what it is and how it is situated in the world. It exposes the artifice that holds it up. It admits its complicity in late capitalism. And it gives us a reason to smile that does not simultaneously demand bad faith, demand that we either ignore the complexities of the world (as the traditionalist would have us do) or imagine that we can rise above those complexities (as the modernist maintains we can). By making local products and local culture in Springfield into the assumed mass culture of the world, *The Simpsons* concedes the relation between the two but forces us to think about that relation in a new way. It does not stand outside of that relation, but twists it from within. It is hard to do such topological maneuvers when one is immersed in the medium being contorted, but it is the only authentic stance to take in a postmodern world.

When all the world is McDonaldized, every burger is a Big Mac. In the postmodern world, McDonald's has not re-placed anything; it is the norm, place is gone, and thus so is the possibility of *the local*. To imagine, in general, a burger is to imagine the globalized product that is a Big Mac. This is how a hamburger is constituted today: conceptually, we think of it as a mass-produced commodity. To imagine a new burger, to conceive of the possibility of a new burger, is to see it in relation to its conceptual place holder. Thus, the new local burger, accurately described, is always on the way toward becoming the global commodity if it is to appear at all. If, artistically, I want to point this out to you—to poke fun at this rather serious political and economic issue—I can only cast my burger in this way. The Krusty Burger burger is thus the truly postmodern burger.

The point is made in a similar way in a 2014 episode of the show in which Marge decides to open up a franchise of Mother Hubbard's Sandwich Cupboard restaurant, only to be run out of business by Cletus opening up a franchise of the same restaurant across the street ("Super Franchise Me" [12 October 2014]), the upshot being a commentary on what happens when far-away corporations try to control the local. But more to the point, consider a "real-life" corporate crossover in the form of the Butterfinger candy bar. The *Simpsons*-Butterfinger alliance has been going strong since the late 1990s, with Bart and other Springfield residents appearing in various commercials both on television and in print. A package of Butterfinger BBs (an incarnation of the candy consisting of little round candy-bar pieces) is decorated, for instance, with a picture of Bart laughing hysterically and Krusty the Klown saying, "I heartily endorse this product and/or promotion." These are the moments in which *The Simpsons* confesses its complicity. There are multiple levels to this text. Most obviously, the presentation is different from other product tie-ins. The image of the character or celebrity is typically what is meant to sell the product. It is enough, then, to have a picture of Will Ferrell playing the cowbell on a T-shirt, or more to the point of the tie-in, images of LeBron James on a Wheaties box, or—think back, now, to just days before the new millennium arrived and you'll undoubtedly remember—Jar-Jar

Binks shilling for Pepsi while a young Britney Spears gyrated in the Pepsi TV commercial, of course, showing us her can. With Butterfinger, Krusty speaks, acknowledging that he is pushing a product, not trying to rise above it. Furthermore, he confesses that this is the norm, that he does so often enough to need a generic pitch statement. The fact that he (and thus the Butterfinger folks) feel comfortable keeping the pitch generic—not changing "this product and/or promotion" for "these Butterfinger BBs"—indicates an assumed cynicism over such commercialism, as if there is no need to go out of the way to point out what the product is since we all know it doesn't really matter to the spokesman, or perhaps to anyone. And the fact that Bart laughs at us on the wrapper for buying into it seals the deal. Bart not only laughs because he is aware of his (and our) complicity. He laughs because he knows what we know: he knows that Krusty is famous on *The Simpsons* for endorsing terrible products, for having a line of dangerous household appliances and children's toys with his likeness, for selling boxes of Krusty-O's cereal with a surprise jagged metal O in each box ("Round Springfield" [30 April 1995]) and a Krusty Home Pregnancy Test that carries the warning "May cause birth defects" ("I Love Lisa" [11 February 1993]). Thus, to buy the Butterfinger endorsed by Krusty (who is, after all, not even interested in knowing what it is he is endorsing) is to buy a shoddy and potentially dangerous product. And we happily do so.

In some sense this postmodern hipness may just be making capitalism easier to swallow. In some sense it may just be the latest marketing ploy meant to attract a seemingly ever-more-jaded public.[4] And perhaps this is inescapably true for any object of art today: it is instantly commodified, arriving and arising as part of the system of exchange. We cannot even accurately say that it is co-opted because this would suggest that it was outside the system at some point before. Still, once self-aware—as only postmodern art is—the question becomes how the work deals with its status as commodity. To *The Simpsons*' credit, important points about late capitalism are often made.

In the show's 300th episode ("Barting Over" [16 February 2003]), when Bart and Lisa discover a videotape of a commercial Bart did as a baby (for a product to cure "baby's bad breath"), Bart is surprised. "I don't remember ever being in a commercial," he says, further claiming that it was clearly an act of exploitation. Then Bart takes out a Butterfinger candy bar, opens it up, and takes a bite in silence.

This might make it "cool" to go out and buy a Butterfinger, but perhaps something deeper is at work. There is more than a cute winking at the camera going on here. By 2003, Bart is indeed no longer appearing in Butterfinger commercials, though the candy continues to sponsor the show. In the original airing of this episode, in fact, a Butterfinger commercial was shown in which an old man is eating the candy bar while a toothless old woman watches in anticipation;

finally, he passes the half-eaten Butterfinger to her, she waits a moment, and he takes out and passes his dentures to her as well. When we consider this text as a whole—when we take the show together with its commercials as we must, and as the show, even, would have us do—we are reminded that there is surely a link between capital and art, between the production of the comedy and the consumption of the sponsor's product. And Bart's cynicism and admission forces us to see the relation and deal with it. The commercial has been defanged—detoothed—and cannot simply sit in the background as a given or as something we do not think about. It appears, instead, *as a commercial.* And the show itself—which is to say, *The Simpsons*—appears *as commercial.* And both can still appear *as art.* The old have usurped the place of the young, the "real" has replaced the "animated," and the artifice that supports all of this is exposed. Yet even the act of exposure is not itself coming from someplace outside of the text, as if the exposure is somehow more real than the show or the commercial, a truth handed down by someone standing above the broadcast and thus from an "objective" standpoint. Instead, everything is placed alongside everything else. And the world changes.

In some ways, the world—which everyone says is getting smaller these days (this is an illusion of technology, a lie of late capitalism)—gets a little bit larger. And more morally complex. Indeed, making local products into global ones does not make local products good and pure for *The Simpsons*. Duff beer, the local brew that is on the way toward globalism, becomes the "evil corporation" that Homer must protest against when he discovers that the company is secretly planning on relocating their locally owned baseball team, the Springfield Isotopes, to Albuquerque ("Hungry, Hungry Homer" [4 March 2001]). Once the local goes global, the local is destroyed—literally, there is no possibility of the local, of the local team. And *The Simpsons* admits to this. Marge's protest against the violence in Itchy and Scratchy cartoons can take place locally because the cartoons are produced locally ("Itchy & Scratchy & Marge" [20 December 1990]). That Marge can picket and Homer can chain himself to a post in a hunger strike at the stadium relies on the enemy being local and accessible. Perhaps in this way, *The Simpsons* opens a space in which "Think globally, act locally" can have new meaning in a postmodern world.

And still *The Simpsons* flaunts its complicity at every turn, making clear that none of us—itself included—is pure enough to cast the first stone at the next anti-WTO rally. Simpsons T-shirts and other merchandise are mocked on the show. Homer makes fun of fly-by-night cartoon characters getting a blimp in the Thanksgiving Day parade as a Bart balloon passes by on the television screen behind him. Bart spawns several catchphrases—"Eat my shorts," "Don't have a cow," etc.—and the show constructs an episode around Bart creating a catchphrase on a TV show ("I didn't do it"), which everyone loves at first but tires of quickly ("Bart Gets Famous" [3 February 1994]). Twenty years later, the opening couch gag to the twenty-sixth season premiere was guest-animated by Academy Award–nominated surrealist Don Hertzfeldt, who chose to show Homer traveling in time: back to his original 1987 self (drawn quite differently then), and then forward to some point in the future where he is now the star of the mutated *The Sampsans*: hideous creatures that only say catchphrases and seem to have no other artistic/commercial purpose or mental content ("Clown in the Dumps" [28 September 2014]).

The traditionalist is unaware (or unwilling to admit) his role in creating culture. The modernist attempts to mock culture by being above it and satirizing it. The postmodernist concedes our collective submersion in the culture and brings this to the fore.

This is what separates catchphrases born of traditional comedy (e.g., "Lucy, you have some 'splaining to do!" or "To the moon, Alice!") from modernist catchphrases (e.g., "Well, isn't that special?" or "Excuuuuuse me!"). The modernist is aware that the catchphrase is a catchphrase—that it has become a commodity, even—and uses it as such, uses it perhaps to suggest how silly past catchphrases were. But in doing so, the modernist is involved in the production of that commodity and in the culture, not truly above or outside of it. The modernist is in fact making money from the catchphrase and is no different, really, from anyone with a more traditional agenda. The postmodernist is different only in the admission of his or her complicity. How can one radically gouge the commercial culture, as *Saturday Night Live* seems to think it is doing with their commercial parodies, and then cut to a commercial? How can one make fun of television on television? How can one mock a catchphrase by using a catchphrase? The postmodernist takes the path of David Letterman, for instance, creating a segment on the show (as he did in the 1980s) in which a new catchphrase will be chosen, making sure to strip it of all potential meaning and reference beyond reference to itself and its status as a commodified catchphrase. This is how we ended up with the contextless, "They pelted us with rocks and garbage" and, "What do you want for nothing, wicker?" on the postmodern *Late Night*. And how we ended up with "I didn't do it" on the similar *The Simpsons*.

To return to the Krusty Burger, in "I Am Spelling as Fast as I Can" (16 February 2003) Krusty introduces a new and "for a limited time only" Ribwich sandwich to which Homer quickly becomes addicted. In classic *Simpsons* form, the sandwich, we learn, is made from insects rather than beef or pork, the rib-like shape being a product of the "meat" having been poured and molded in a factory. The box also carries a warning, with a smiling picture of Krusty not unlike the one on the old "real" Butterfinger wrapper, saying: "Will Cause Early Death." When the Ribwich is discontinued in Springfield, Homer panics and decides to join a group of Rib Heads who travel in a psychedelic bus from town to town, following the introduction of the Ribwich at Krusty Burgers across America (until eventually landing in San Francisco, of course, the final stop on the "tour"). The local is again made into the national (and perhaps global), and the overlapping of counterculture (Grateful Dead music) and commercial culture (fast food) shows that there is, in the end, no distinction—a continuum, perhaps, but no hard lines to be drawn. Yet most importantly, the show's original airing was sponsored by Wendy's, which included a commercial for the "limited-time-only return of Wendy's Monterey Chicken Ranch Sandwich." The commercial, shown during *The Simpsons* episode, focused on a group of men in Ohio (one possible location of Springfield?) reading a letter from their dim-witted friend Jimmy (Homer?), who traveled to California (San Francisco?) and wrote back about the fabulous fast-food sandwich he discovered out there: the Monterey Chicken Ranch Sandwich (The Ribwich?).

Here, then, is where *The Simpsons* succeeds on a level that modernist comedy, e.g., *Saturday Night Live*, typically does not. *SNL*'s commercial parodies are often intelligent and funny—from "It's a floor wax *and* a dessert topping?" to Phil Hartman's yuppie "Colon Blow" character sitting on a mountain of high-fiber cereal—but the commercials tend to be presented as parody, as above the "real" commercials they are mocking. The Ribwich, instead, is more of an admission of our willing complicity to fetishize the commodity and participate in the mass action of consumption that makes the product (sandwich *and* sitcom) possible. At least let us say that when watching the Ribwich episode, the Wendy's commercial we see moments later stands out as having new meaning. And this seldom happens when watching a commercial parody and then a "real" commercial on *SNL*. We can laugh at a "corn chip nail tips" commercial parody on *SNL* (where hip-hop music blares and the "ghetto fabulous" characters feign excitement about being able to eat their newly extended nacho-tasting fingernails), but when we then see, moments later, a "real" commercial—even one in which hip-hop has been co-opted to sell a product or a clearly unhealthy product is being unethically targeted at "urban" populations—there is little force to take it as anything new, to see it in a new light. Wendy's, however, is changed forever.

Like Butterfinger and *The Simpsons*, Budweiser and *SNL* have had a long relationship. But from the early years of John Belushi et al. performing in a giant mouth and tongue as "the taste Buds" (the commercial parody that was, in fact, an actual live commercial and thus not a parody at all but rather an attempt just to do a funny commercial) to the 2002 appearance of a Budweiser bottle on screen after the first song by the evening's musical guest (with the announcement that Budweiser was the official sponsor of the musical guest on *SNL*), *Saturday Night Live* has blurred the boundaries of show and commercial, but not in a postmodern way. In my youth, I can recall thinking that the taste Buds were, at first, another sketch—like the killer bees!—only to be disappointed when it became clear that it all was a commercial. And I recall, in my encroaching middle age, first seeing the Budweiser bottle appear after the musical number and thinking that it must be some setup for a joke—only to be disappointed that it all was still a commercial. There was nothing out of the ordinary here. There was nothing that different from the Baby Boomers' Dinah Shore interrupting her own show to sing "See the USA in your Chevrolet" or having a live commercial performed in the middle of Milton Berle's *Texaco Star Theater* by the backup singers dressed in Texaco uniforms. Had Uncle Miltie been allowed to have an alcohol sponsor, he might have thought up the taste Buds himself.

The Ribwich, however, is neither fiction nor parody. It neither ignores nor stands apart from its culture. It is not a funhouse mirror reflection of the Monterey Chicken Sandwich (or, more obviously, the McDonald's McRib), and it is not purely a comment on and condemnation of our thoughtless willingness to consume. The Wendy's sandwich comments on the Krusty Burger sandwich as much as vice versa, though it is the Krusty Burger sandwich that makes such lines of commentary open, forging new possibilities of bilateral meaning. Thus does *The Simpsons* open up horizons and truths left unexplored by traditional and modernist comedy.

This doesn't mean that there is little reason to laugh at such nonpostmodern comedy. None of this is to say that *Seinfeld* or *Friends* or *The Donna Reed Show* or even *Three's Company* aren't funny. They are (though perhaps in decreasing order, and perhaps in exponentially decreasing order). Defining postmodern comedy is not the same as putting down modernist or traditional comedy. I have been doing quite modernist things throughout this chapter in the name of trying to be a little humorous. Mentioning moments from these sitcoms without explanation (such as an offhand reference to Mr. Sparkle or Mr. Roper) is a way of cheap inclusion: if you get the reference, you laugh; if you laugh, you're part of the "community." You and I most likely do not have much more in common, so I—the struggling philosopher—take what I can get. It would only turn postmodernly funny if I were to admit to you that I am doing this and you were to find this liberating and humorous. Neither, I fear, is likely to happen.

So we cannot rise above the world. This is not to be lamented. Nothing rises.

Language was once thought to rise above it all, or at least to ride on top of it. Language, before postmodernity, was about reflecting the world. Words had meaning because they reached out and denoted things. Propositions had meaning because they reached out and denoted states of affairs. Language magically floated above us, with words mirroring our reality back to us rather than creating it. But nothing really floats. It has been a point with us from the very first chapter, and to which we have returned time and again.

To make the point one last time, but to come at it from a slightly different aesthetic angle, consider the episode of *Star Trek: The Next Generation*—a thoroughly modern show,[5] if not a modern comedy—where Capt. Picard has to learn to crack the code of a strange race of creatures for whom the universal translator won't work ("Darmok" [25 May 1994]). Picard is transported down to a planet with one of the aliens, and they must learn to communicate or be killed by an invisible beast.[6] All the alien will say is things such as, "Sucat, his eyes uncovered" and, "Chaka, when the walls fell." Eventually, Picard comes to realize that the aliens use a *metaphoric language*. Counselor Troi says something like: "It's as if instead of saying 'I love you, isn't this romantic?,' we were instead to say 'Juliet on her balcony,' referencing the feeling evoked by the image and the story." And so the alien speaks only in metaphor, frustratedly yelling at Picard, "Darmok and Jilad at Tanagra!," and Picard has to learn that the Federation-issued universal communicator translates the words—"walls" and "fell" and "and"—but not the meaning, since the meaning of this crazy language is more than the referent of the words. How alien.

The underlying assumption here is that very modern assumption that *our* language is not like this: ours is straightforward and nonmetaphoric. Which is patently false. Words do not reach out and touch objects for their meaning, anchoring themselves like labels stuck to things. Language does not work like the Post-its in Ned Flanders's beach house, labeling the world around us and instructing us as to meaning ("Summer of 4 Ft. 2" [19 May 1996]). Words, instead, are linked in intricate webs of self-reference. They mean each other; they mean what we agree to allow them to mean. And with them, we carve up an ever-malleable world rather than reflect a rigid world. Thus, when I say, "I love you," there is no stable and universal referent for each word—there is, as we saw in our discussion of *Beauty and the Beast*, no literal meaning. No necessary self, no Other, no Platonic relation of love to be instantiated in between. "I love you" has meaning because each word means other words, and because when I speak it I am speaking an echo of every time the phrase has ever been uttered before: it means everything it has always meant because all of these past utterances, meanings, profiles, and experiences are apperceived. "I love you" means "Juliet on her balcony." All language is metaphor, bringing the-things-themselves to presence, but bringing them here in context, within a history, in a performance.

This is important for postmodern comedy in two major ways. It means that satire and irony are no longer possible; and it means that "quotational discourse" is the only legitimate way to express emotion, meaning, and intent.

Irony is an attempt to use language in a particular way. Irony—and its ironic cohorts, sarcasm, cynicism, satire, ridicule, etc.—are often associated with postmodern comedy in general and *The Simpsons* in particular, but this is mistaken.[7] Postmodernity is the age of postirony, an era marked by the realization that as late modernity turned to irony as its main mode of discourse, irony in fact became impossible.

It is akin to Kant's worst nightmare come true. Kant considered lying to be immoral, for instance, because if it were to become universalized—if everyone were to lie all of the time—lying would become impossible. Lying rests on an assumption of truth. I can only get away with lying to you when you expect that my statements in general are true. If everyone were to lie all of the time, then there would no longer be any general expectation of truth. With no expectation of truth, lying becomes impossible. Thus, universalizing lying makes lying impossible. It is logically contradictory and, for Kant, immoral. For Kant—as for Ralph Wiggum, who once claimed, "If mommy's purse didn't belong in the microwave, why did it fit?" ("Mathlete's Feat" [17 May 2015])—logic is everything.

Now imagine instead that everyone meant everything they said ironically, that every utterance dripped with sarcasm. Kant never considered this. He never had cable. Or the Internet. But the problem with universalizing irony is a problem Kant would have recognized. How could one tell the ironic from the unironic statement any longer in a world where irony has become the norm? With the distinction gone, true irony becomes impossible: there is no straight discourse left to rise above in a mocking way, no squares of whom to make fun.

Such Kantian analysis is (as expected) not very funny. *The Simpsons*, luckily, makes the same point and pulls it off humorously. Consider, for instance, the episode in which Homer joins a traveling rock festival as a sideshow performer who gets shot in the stomach with a cannonball ("Homerpalooza" [19 May 1996]). At first, Homer's act is popular, but as the tour wears on, its hip status is in doubt. Two young concert-goers thus have the following exchange:

> First Teenager: Oh, here comes that cannonball guy. He's cool.
>
> Second Teenager: Are you being sarcastic, dude?
>
> First Teenager: I don't even know anymore.

A sophisticated realization about language is in play here. The traditionalist would express dislike by claiming, "I don't like the cannonball guy." Each word would be thought to denote straightforwardly an object or relation. The modernist would adopt a naïve ironic tone and express dislike by claiming "I like the cannonball guy" or "He's cool" in a sarcastic manner. The modernist realizes that simple denotation is insufficient for a full theory of language, that context can convey meaning, that tone can alter the trajectory of the words so that they mean something more than that at which they were first pointed. Jean-Paul Sartre thus famously claimed that language is *elliptical*: it always means more than what it says.[8] While this is an improvement, it is still based on an assumption that one can identify context or tone as simply as one can identify the referent of a word. It is based on the belief that straightforward discourse is itself the base, the norm, the value- and context-free null point from which one can then go off and add context to change meaning. But—as in the assumption that African philosophy must discuss its racial foundation and agenda but "regular" philosophy need not since "whiteness" is an invisible value-free norm, and as in the assumption that Latin American politics must begin with its geographic embodiment and colonial history but "regular" political theory need not address such issues since Europe is the norm that is without cultural bias—so too does the modernist's theory of language assume that "straightforward" discourse is a value-free norm, a linguistic mode with the bland pH level of water such that one can then stray, becoming a mixologist, speaking words in contexts that provide a more acidic or base meaning. The postmodernist rejects the stable, value-free norm in all of its mythical incarnations. The postmodernist realizes that context is everywhere, that it is fluid, and that once irony has become *the* mode of discourse in a culture, irony becomes impossible. Consequently, claims such as "I like him" or "I don't like him" or "Oh, he's cool" have no necessary relation to whether or not I actually like the cannonball guy. We have thus arrived at the era in which Jean Baudrillard's simulacra has been realized: it is not that the territory precedes the map or that the map precedes the territory;[9] instead there is no priority—"the image [here: the word] . . . bears no relation to any reality whatever: it is its own pure simulacrum."[10] We cannot rise above the language; we are implicated in it. When sarcasm is presented as truth there can no longer be any sarcasm. Or truth. *The Simpsons* realizes this and turns our postmodern situation into the self-referential punch line.[11]

In a more metaphorical way, this is the lesson Moe learns when he tries to update his bar with a postmodern theme. Lenny asks Moe what all of the eye images on paintings and video screens represent in the bar, concluding that they must represent eyes. Moe tries to explain the new decorating theme to his oblivious friends: "It's po-mo!," he says. Blank stares. "Post-modern?" Blanker stares. "Okay, weird for the sake of weird" ("Homer the Moe" [9 November 2001]).

There is no way out, no rising above, no escaping language. But there is still a chance to speak "truthfully." Doing so requires quotation marks; when truth is gone, "truth" is all we have left. And *The Simpsons* is masterful in its use of what we might call "quotational discourse."

Umberto Eco explains:

> I think of the postmodern attitude as that of a man who loves a very cultivated woman who knows he cannot say to her, "I love you madly," because he knows that she knows (and that she knows that he knows) that these words have been written by Barbara Cartland. Still, there is a solution. He can say, "As Barbara Cartland would put it, I love you madly." At this point, having avoided false innocence, having said clearly

> that it is no longer possible to speak innocently, he will nevertheless have said what he wanted to say to the woman: that he loves her, but he loves her in an age of lost innocence. . . . [B]oth [the man and the woman] will consciously and with pleasure play the game of irony.[12]

Eco is on to something here, but perhaps with a few caveats. Irony is not just a game; it's the only game in town. It is the inescapable foundational late-modern context of all meaning. Once we realize this—and we realize that our words constantly ring with the echoes of all their past uses, that innocence is not only lost but was never really there to begin with—we need not remain in silence for fear of speaking naïvely. Instead, we must acknowledge our state and our complicity. One way of doing this is to usher in quotational discourse. It is not really that the romance novelists have taken "I love you madly" away from us, making it too cheesy for everyday use. It is that *all* words are simultaneously utterances of other words and other past meanings; and thus to speak at all is to risk sounding trite and clichéd. Even Eco echoes. We cannot rise above this, but our discourse can acknowledge it. Hence, we speak using quotation marks: "As they have said in the romance novels and on soap operas and in Shakespeare and in parked cars and everyplace everywhere throughout time, 'I love you madly.'" All of speech is a form of art.

Sometimes we do this explicitly. When I stub a toe or otherwise hurt myself superficially, I will occasionally respond to a query about my condition in a bad British accent: "It's just a flesh wound." Forced to excuse myself from a room at an inopportune time—during a meal or a conversation, for instance—I have once or twice muttered in a bad Austrian-German accent: "I'll be back." And I pity the fool who dares say to me, "Surely, you must be joking." Because I am seldom joking. And I don't like to be called Shirley.[13]

I know that some people do such things to an annoying degree. I know some people who do such things to an annoying degree. I consciously attempt not to be one of them. It's just not funny after a very short while; one appears to be a maladjusted showoff, aping every cultural moment of the past, never seeming to speak in one's own voice. But the point to remember is that we are all doing this, whether we admit to it or not, all the time. And admitting to it is the only authentic thing left to do. Still, a joke told every five minutes quickly loses its luster.

The Simpsons admits to its involvement in quotational discourse on multiple levels, telling different jokes about the same thing, it seems, every five seconds. At times, the quotations are used to indicate the impossibility of irony. In "Lady Bouvier's Lover" (12 May 1994), when an infomercial is shown offering original animation cels from classic "Itchy and Scratchy" cartoons, the claim is made that even cynical members of Generation X love the collector's items.[14]

There is a quick cut to a twenty-ish TV viewer, the forerunner to the postironic Cannonball-guy commentators, who says in a deadpan voice, "Yeah. 'Groovy.'" He even makes the sign of the quotation marks in the air when he says the word "groovy." At first this seems easy to interpret. The young man uses a purposively nongroovy old-time word such as "groovy" precisely to indicate his disdain; and yet the quotation marks around the word make him doubly distanced from the label, from, in essence, his own opinion. Irony already is the assumed norm; the quotations serve to indicate that he—and we—already know this and thus can never again be ironic. And add to this the fact that there is a rather groovy lava lamp in his room—he will become the hipster just a decade later.[15]

The mixing of quotational discourse and postirony is complex. At other times, *The Simpsons'* use of the former is more straightforwardly Ecoian. In the ultimate postmodern turn, the show often quotes itself (this is another way of understanding the self-references to its own commodification); but it also quotes other art—linguistically, visually, and thematically. As such, it is a commentary not on the American family but on the American family's appearance in television. Indeed, it could not be otherwise, for the meaning of the family today is (in part) the meaning it has through television. On a more basic level, the show, realizing that it is a visual art and that other works of art have come before, will often conjure a scene in terms of scenes that have come before.

In 2002, season thirteen ended with an episode in which Homer is targeted by the mob, and as Fat Tony and his crew drove to the Simpsons' house, the opening credits of *The Sopranos* were recreated with Springfield landmarks rather than Jersey ones ("Poppa's Got a Brand New Badge" [22 May 2002]). Why? How could one authentically make art about a mob hit in 2002 without quoting *The Sopranos* (which itself was often literally quoting *The Godfather*)?

The sixth season cliff-hanger ("Who Shot Mr. Burns?" [21 May 1995]) was, in its entirety, a reference to *Dallas* and the ultimate cliffhanger of "Who shot J. R.?" Why? How can one stage a nonnaïve cliffhanger without admitting that the ultimate cliffhanger has already been done?

In the fourth season's "A Streetcar Named Marge" (1 October 1992), there are at least half a dozen references to classic movies: Maggie attempts escape from the Ayn Rand Daycare Center (!) in the style of *The Great Escape*; Homer, Bart, and Lisa show up at the center to find that the babies have taken over in the style of *The Birds* (complete with pacified babies perched everywhere and a walk-on cameo from an animated Hitchcock); and Homer expresses his initial boredom at Marge's performance by tearing his program into a fan and playing with it in the same way that Joseph Cotton's character does in *Citizen Kane* when he is forced to watch Kane's wife in her own terrible performance. Why, why, why? How can one speak to the desire to escape unjust authority, the creepiness of seeing the small and supposedly powerless suddenly take over, the boredom associated with bad live performance, without quoting these past moments of our collective experience? To have Homer say, "I'm bored"—which means, visually, drawing Homer looking bored—is to say, "I love you madly." To have Homer quote someone else to indicate his boredom—which means, visually, recreating (quoting) a scene from *Citizen Kane*—is to say, "As Barbara Cartland would put it 'I love you madly.'"

As the Comic Book Guy would say, this may be the . . . worst . . . chapter . . . ever. *The Simpsons*, it turns out, is not really hollow. And all that talk up front about needing a new theory of comedy to deal with the show was just, well, talk. We have talked a lot about talking, really. About words and language and self-reference. And though we have taken some time to address the way in which *The Simpsons* is postmodern art, we haven't really touched on why it is so funny. There have been hints here and there as to what makes it all so successfully comedic, but no fully drawn theory of postmodern comedy has emerged. As we will see in the concluding chapter, this is a topic that will be central to the work of Andy Kaufman as well.

Of course, this should only be disappointing if we were thinking that something should have been here, that we deserve something at the end. In uprooting modernity, *The Simpsons* uproots the trappings of modernity, including linearity, narrative flow, and expectation in general. Sometimes the monster at the end of the book has been there all along; sometimes it is the lovable old narrator himself, and the end is thus the means—and always has been.

In an early episode in which Bart gave blood to a dying Mr. Burns only to be met with a thank-you card in place of a reward, Homer responded by writing a nasty letter: "Dear Mr. Burns . . . I'm so *glad* you enjoyed my son's blood. And your *card* was *just great.* In case you can't tell, I'm being sarcastic" ("Blood Feud" [11 July 1991]). After considering having Homer beaten for his insolence, Burns relents and buys the Simpsons an extravagant gift—a gigantic $32,000 sacred Olmec carved statue in the form of a giant god-head. At the end of the episode, the Simpsons sit at home trying to figure out the meaning of it all:

> Homer: Save a guy's life and what do you get? Nothing. Worse than nothing. Just a big scary rock.
>
> Bart: Hey, man, don't bad-mouth the head.
>
> Marge: Homer, it's the thought that counts. The moral of the story is a good deed is its own reward.
>
> Bart: Hey, we got a reward. The head is cool.
>
> Marge: Then . . . I guess the moral is no good deed goes unrewarded.

Homer: Wait a minute. If I hadn't written that nasty letter we wouldn't have gotten anything.

Marge: Well . . . Then I guess the moral is the squeaky wheel gets the grease.

Lisa: Perhaps there is no moral to this story.

Homer: Exactly! It's just a bunch of stuff that happened.

Marge: But it certainly was a memorable few days.

Homer: Amen to that! [Everyone laughs.]

It's not, I suppose, that any one moral doesn't really fit. It's that they all fit. And in fitting, they draw attention to the plasticity of narrative itself and the clichéd manner in which narrative is necessarily understood. As in the films of Michael Haneke, it's just a bunch of stuff that happened: comedy and tragedy being labels we apply to try to make sense of it all.

And so we have the possibility that an episode—or a penultimate chapter of a book—can be content to be aware that it is just a bunch of stuff that happens, headed only where one wants it to head, meaning exactly what it has always meant—itself and, simultaneously, everything else—avowing, especially, that even in questioning the possibility of an ending and a moral, the claim that, "It's just a bunch of stuff that happened" *becomes* the moral and the ending. In our Fallen era, it is thus that we can maintain and display what is most important to us: our lack of innocence. What, after all, is not to like about the fall? We have reclaimed it to be the time of season premieres rather than finales. And so we wear with pride our true achievements: the collection of scarlet letters that comprise our language, our giddy impurity, our proudly mongrel nature and culture, the knowledge that we know what *The Simpsons* knows and *The Simpsons* knows what we know and we all know that we love each other madly ad infinitum. This, then, is how we can maintain our lack of innocence and keep our cool. And it is, in the end, the only way to avoid the cliché, the moral, and the trite conclusion. Amen.

CHAPTER 10

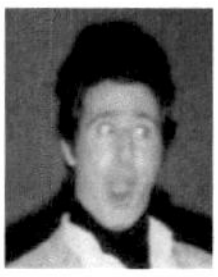

Quantum Andy

We come to the conclusion, though even after we conclude we shall not cease from exploring. And the end of all our exploring will be to arrive where we started and . . . not really know the place at all because Andy Kaufman has moved in. Suddenly, all that we thought we knew about what makes something art and what it means to live a life of art must be reevaluated. And this is good. A good phenomenologist must always be reevaluating, understanding anew, never resting, never content with the status quo. You'll *tenk me veddy much* for this later.

But understanding Andy? The charge is not as simple as, say, laughing at Andy—though perhaps there are times we laughed, in part, because we didn't understand. Understanding *which* Andy? No other performer has ever so completely created and become a set of characters and then admitted to us, through his unwillingness to break character, that there is nothing beyond character. One character may replace another, but neither is more basic, neither indicates the "real" individual.

Andy was the aesthetic embodiment of postmodernity, speaking to us in an age when language had grown weary of denoting and turned, instead, to establishing meaning through social agreement and intricate webs of cross-reference: all reference is ultimately self-reference, and the commitment to a world beyond—a world *outside*—vanishes.[1] This was the vanishing Andy. (*See figure 10.1, page 200.*) Andy Kaufman did not generate the characters Foreign Man and Tony Clifton, standing behind them like a father, an Origin, a Platonic Form. Andy was generated by Tony just as much as vice versa—the one has meaning only in reference to the other, which is to say *himself*.

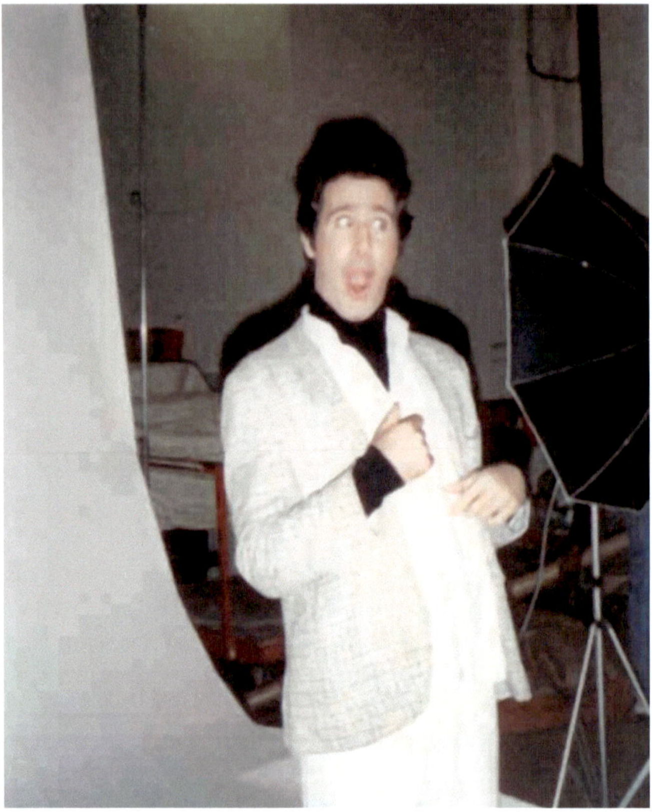

FIGURE 10.1. Andy Kaufman as Foreign Man on the set of ABC's *Buckshot*. March 1980. Photo courtesy of the Kaufman family.

Once, when Steve Martin was guest-hosting *The Tonight Show*, Andy performed as Foreign Man and then sat on the couch to talk to Steve, convincing him, or trying to convince him, that Foreign Man was the real person and the Andy who was sitting on the couch was a character. In the course of the conversation Andy claimed that there were several "real me's" and several characters, including the one being interviewed. Here, ostensibly, was the character referencing himself; here was the beauty of the postmodern circle putting its spin on an ancient liar's paradox. "Steve, I am just a character," he said in the not-too-sub subtext. Our first instinct is to believe; but if this is just a character how would he know this, why would he admit it? Even using the word "character" seems to be taking up a space outside of the fictional: characters don't call themselves characters—*authors* speak of their creations this way. And if this character is not

Andy, then where is Andy? But of course the opposite assertion does not solve the matter. Claiming, "I am not a character," there is no way to know if the claim itself is part of the script, if this is something some character has claimed. The failure is not our failure as an audience or as knowers—it is a failure of epistemology, of identity itself, of space collapsing until there is no outside. Or better yet, it is Andy's way of showing us that the instability of identity is not a failure, it is a given. It is something to celebrate, something at which to laugh. There are no other real Andys, and yet there are. The aporia is the space of laughter. And given that language, that logos, that life itself are only made possible through aporia, then this means that comedy—and not tragedy—is our main mode of being in the world.

Too little time is spent thinking about Andy, and too much of that too little time is spent asking uninteresting questions. "Is Andy funny?" "Was Andy a genius?" Yes, yes. But not because he told good jokes and constructed them beautifully. We worry about whether or not Andy can be called a comedian, but the true question is whether or not we are willing to let our conception of comedy change to accommodate Andy.

So let us begin our conclusion by saying that Andy was a comedian because everything he did was simultaneously comedy and an expansion of what comedy is. Do jokes have to have a punch line or an audience? Does comedy have to be funny? Andy asked and answered such questions as a performer and a writer. We need to look at both of these characters.

There were times when Andy would simply go on stage and eat a meal without saying a word. Once, he led an audience out of a comedy club in a conga line around New York City. On *Saturday Night Live*, Andy wrestled women, impersonated Elvis, and lip-synched one of the lines—only one line—to the "Mighty Mouse" theme song. The Wrestler seemed to hate women, telling them they were only good for "peeling the potatoes, washing the carrots, scrubbing the floors, and raising the babies." Tony Clifton seemed to hate everybody, interrupting his Vegas-style lounge act to berate audience members and tell them how little they meant to him. Andy appeared on Letterman, claiming to be homeless and penniless. He wanted to attempt suicide on stage, but Dave only agreed to let him beg for spare change from the audience. Foreign Man—somehow different from and yet the same as Latka Gravas on *Taxi*—could never tell a joke or do an impression correctly. And at times he spoke a gibberish "language" we assume only he understood (we were sure, at least, that we were not a part of the society establishing its social constructive nature). Andy would commandeer the television shows *Bananaz* and *Fridays*, pretending (?) to fight with the other cast members, breaking character, and ruining the sketches and the show. Then he would pretend to apologize, pretend that the outburst had been part of the script all along. Later he would pretend that the apology itself had been forced and scripted by the angry network bosses and everything before—the fight, the chaos—had been real. Andy's Carnegie Hall show, one of the greatest works of art of the twentieth century, received bad press at first because of the psychotic, long-haired man picketing the box office, screaming that Andy Kaufman was the anti-Christ, warning everyone not to buy tickets. The protester was, of course, Andy. And the show itself was an incredible success by any measure, escalating to the point of giddiness at the end as the Mormon Tabernacle Choir, the Radio City Music Hall Rockettes, and Santa Claus arrived on stage. This, too, was a show without an ending, a show in which Andy invited the audience out for milk and cookies, shipping them off in buses to the rented hall where his family members were busy serving up the treats. And then there were times Andy would simply go on stage at a comedy club, unroll a sleeping bag, and take a nap for his entire fifteen-minute set.

Performance, it is often thought, can be distinguished from real life in part by the presence of the stage. The majority of Andy's performances, though, took place without a stage. Tony Clifton would be booked into Italian restaurants rather than comedy clubs. Andy also maintained a part-time job as a busboy after getting famous, and he would *perform* by clearing away guests' plates as soon as they were delivered by the waitress or by asking someone if he wanted a refill of his water every ten seconds. With his girlfriend, Elayne Boosler, Andy would visit Coney Island, where they would act like lovers having a big fight. How could we have ever known if Andy and Elayne had truly been fighting? Where is the solid ground to anchor a true belief? We know, of course, and in part because of Andy, that there is none. As we saw in our analysis of zombies, I am always wearing a costume, always performing. As we saw in our analysis of animality in art, there is never a moment I am not "in character." But we have reached the pinnacle of discovery now concerning the relationship between being and performing. Andy's performances off the stage brilliantly demonstrate to us that performance is all around us, that we are performing at every moment—in the guise of one character or another—and there is never a moment of rest in which we can find the act and the actor, pin down a true identity, and label this moment a "real" moment if what we mean by "real" is that it is a moment without context, character, and performance. To live is to live a life of art.

True, and true again. But how is this *funny*?

In 1973 Steve Martin invited the whole audience at the university where he was playing to McDonald's. He went up to the counter and ordered six hundred hamburgers, then—as the order was coming up—canceled it and changed the request to one bag of French fries.[2] Martin also had a routine in which he would appear to bomb on stage, telling very bad jokes very poorly, only to rip open his shirt a few minutes later to reveal dynamite taped to his chest. "Somebody better start laughing," he would yell, "or we're all going to die!"

This is pretty funny. And it seems similar to some of Andy's routines, but with important differences. Andy would never have shown the audience the dynamite beneath his shirt—he might have worn it, but he wouldn't have shown it. And Andy would have bought the six hundred hamburgers—even if it meant a financial loss for the evening.

So which is funnier? Both are funny, but Andy is funny in a deeper and more shocking way. The problem with the dynamite and the bag of fries is that they are punch lines; their presence makes the routine more traditional in terms of comedic structure. Martin smartly challenges us to think about the setting and the breadth of a joke's setup. He challenges us to think about the relationships between the performer and his audience and between the world and the combined performer/audience. But in giving us a punch line—a relief, a focal point on which to hang our laughter—he ultimately does not challenge the nature of comedy itself. The Bada-Bing is inventive, the Bada-Boom is hilarious, but the rhythm is as it always has been. Andy was a destroyer of rhythm. He consistently told jokes without a punch line. Or so it seemed.

There was no easy payoff to British Man reading *The Great Gatsby*—at least not in the sense of a traditional punch line. Andy—or, rather, British Man—simply read the book to audiences from time to time—in its entirety, if the mythology is to be believed. Tony Clifton never ripped off his mask and embraced the poor slob, often a plant in the form of Andy's partner, Bob Zmuda, whom he had earlier destroyed and humiliated. And Foreign Man would often literally tell jokes without punch lines, just in case we hadn't caught on to what Andy was doing. Biographer Bill Zehme remembers:

> And then there was the one about the four men on *de aeroplane and it was going to, um, sink* so the men needed to get out and so the first man, from Texas, jumps and, as he does, he says "Remember the Alamo!" And the next man, from France, jumps and says "Vive la France!" So *eet was only a man from England and a man from New York. So de man from England push out the man from New York. And as he push him, he say . . . eehh, something dat was very funny, but I don't remember what eet was. But but eet was very funny. Tenk you veddy much!*[3]

Andy is always suggesting that a joke is worth telling without the punch line. This is not just a case of defeating our expectations—any fool who screws up a delivery can do this. It is laughing at the fact that we had such expectations to begin with. Why did we want to hear a punch line? Why did we think we were going to get one? Why did we think we deserved it, merely for showing up? Like the missing moral at the end of *The Simpsons* episode discussed in the previous chapter, Andy's act was often just a bunch of stuff that happened.

Foreign Man keeps thanking us—it has been turned into a catchphrase by Andy's fans. *Tenk you veddy much!* He does it in part to signal the end of the performance, of the joke. In the absence of a punch line, the verbal bow marks the end and offers us something like relief. It also suggests that we have a reason to be grateful, a reason to be offering this man our praise. *Now is the time you may wish to laugh*, he is telling us—and whether or not we understand, whether or not there is actual laughter and applause, he thanks us.

Ted Cohen has argued that comedy is about confirming our similarities, jokes are about our shared identity. When we laugh together, he writes, it is "the realization of a desperate hope . . . that we are enough like one another to sense one another, to be able to live together."[4] But Andy's comedy is about difference; and the absence of a punch line makes this clear. Andy's comedy is not about getting us to laugh at the same thing he is laughing at; often, he finds our lack of laughter funny. "The comedian's promise," explains Andy, "is that he will go out there and make you laugh *with* him. I've never done that in my life. . . . There are different kinds of laughter."[5]

Even when the audience members got the joke and laughed—learned to laugh in the absence of a traditional punch line—Andy would challenge them, forcing them to consider and reconsider the nature of their laughter. "I don't understand one thing . . . no, seriously. . . . Why is everyone going *boo* when I tell some of the jokes and then when I don't want you to laugh, you're laughing, like right now? I don't understand. . . . [*Andy starts to cry.*] Ladies and gentleman, thank you. I think I . . . it's not working, so . . . I think . . . thank you and I'm sorry and there's other acts and so I really shouldn't have done this."[6]

Thank you, again—it is Andy's gift to us as we try to understand this humor and the way in which it is changing our conception of humor even as we experience it. The thank-yous punctuate the piece, turning the sorrowful exit into triumph. And what have we learned? Comedy has been stripped from the comedian, emancipated from his rhythms and his will, and returned to us. What, after all, is the problem this character has with our laughing? *We are doing it when he doesn't want us to and we are not doing it when he demands it from us.* Suddenly, comedy—modernist, traditional, pre-Andy comedy—takes on a negative light. Now we know: the *structure* of a joke coerces us into laughter. The comedian typically harnesses this rhythm and goes along for the easy ride, cheapening us in the process.

Think of the last time someone told you a terribly unfunny joke in a social situation. Think of your strained smile, the way you rewarded the joke with the gift of your laughter because the situation demanded it, the teller coerced you into it, the punch line held you down and forced you to submit. Such imagery is not too overblown. Laughter is of the body yet also of the intellect (if one goes in for such funny dichotomies) just as sex and love can come together in a coupling; but when forced, both are dead spiritually—something special has been stolen. Think of the last time you were used and discarded by a sitcom, the last time the canned laugh track laughter goaded you into a degrading group chuckle, urging you to participate in something debased. Think of the way the script builds its familiar rhythms such that you know when the joke is coming, you know when to expect a snappy comeback, a droll observation, a catty put-down—you know so well that you don't even have to hear the joke, your body has been taken by the rhythm and laughs in all the right places—it would do so even in silence. This, we imagine, is part of the reason Andy hated *Taxi*: even though it was a great sitcom, it was a sitcom.

One could never coast along on a laugh with Andy. When people laughed at his homeless act on Letterman, Andy would admonish them for being cruel. This surprised us and hurt us, showing the ethic always already at work in the aesthetic—a point we have repeatedly encountered in our investigations of a phenomenological aesthetic. With Andy we were forced to rethink the source of the laughter: Was it our knowledge (suspended in supposed disbelief) that this was just Andy's act? Was it somehow related to the cruel laughter that someone is suffering and it's not me—a theory often cited as the source of all laughter by philosophers such as those we took up in the previous chapter (e.g., Hobbes) who appear never to have told a joke in their life? Andy made people feel uncomfortable about laughing. Of course once you got to know him you came to expect the unexpected—you assumed he was putting you on. But when an old lady seems to have a heart attack on stage with Andy, should we laugh? In retrospect, seeing it turned out not to be "real," it is easy to make the choice; but the emotional turmoil Andy created in the guts of those in his audience was *real* and deep. Suddenly, we realize that laughter is a complex matter tied up with fear and pity and relief and confusion and everything else that is there in a full, meaningful relationship. And it is *ours* to give and share, not the comedian's, not the joke's, to demand.

When we laugh at Foreign Man are we laughing because we think we see Andy behind the curtain? Andy wouldn't want such tawdry laughter from us. Indeed, he lamented the fact that so many people would think the premise of an immigrant who can't tell jokes was funny, "but they would miss the whole *point*, the whole *depth* of where it came from. And where it *came* from—the drama, the sadness—is what makes it funny."[7] (*See figure 10.2, page 206.*)

The *sadness* is what makes it funny? How is this possible? It is only possible when the distinction between comedy and tragedy is eradicated and we are free to react, to laugh—perhaps for the first time—in earnest.

Consider the tradition. For most, the distinction between comedy and tragedy is well defined. Classically, the former provokes laughter and the latter provokes

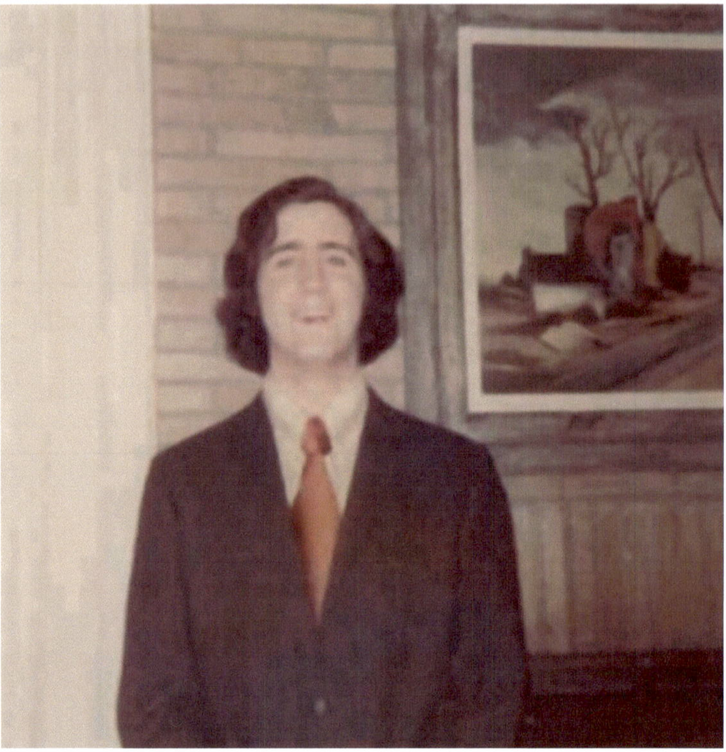

FIGURE 10.2. A young Andy Kaufman, perhaps contemplating the nature of laughter. Photo courtesy of the Kaufman family.

tears. That is, the distinction is based on physical manifestations of a mental state in the audience (comedy/tragedy theory is often built on the back of mind/body dualism). Andy's comedy, however, cannot be defined so easily. He could create comedy from any reaction: fear, anger, sorrow, joy. As he so often said: "I just want real reactions—any reactions—from the gut."[8]

Christopher Fry suggests, along classical lines, that tragedy plunges into despair while comedy is an escape from despair.[9] But Andy's humor did both. We laughed at his declaration of homelessness and poverty on Letterman as much as we laughed at the Rockettes, Santa, and the milk and cookies he had waiting for us after a show.

Susanne Langer considers several ways of distinguishing comedy from tragedy. Perhaps it is point of view, she begins: in tragedy we feel "within the character" but in comedy we are "outside the character." With Andy, of course, we are both. We feel the fear and nervousness of Foreign Man; but we are always necessarily "outside" of Tony Clifton at all times—he exists to torment us, to be Other. More likely, argues Langer, it is the teleological focus of the piece that creates the dichotomy. All of life is headed toward death, but if we focus on the *journey* we have comedy, whereas if we focus on the *destination* we have tragedy. As we are pulled toward the tragic end, we are knocked off the path, stumbling, wobbling to and fro. The story of how we right ourselves again is comedy. Such stories are about meeting and making our Fortune along the way, Langer maintains.[10] Tragedy focuses on Fate, the destination, and has a true ending; comedy focuses on Fortune, the journey, and has no true ending. Except that Andy's comedy destroys these dichotomies once again.

It could be argued that Langer's (and many other authors') definitions are based on distinguishing types of *drama*, not all types of discourse; but it is fair, I think, to apply Langer's work to comedy in general. Jokes, for instance, might be analyzed in terms of their teleology: the *journey* is the setup, the premise, the delivery, the story; the *destination* is the punch line. Although punch lines are thought to be important to the success of a joke, it is, in actuality, the journey that we prize. This is why those tedious mass emailed lists of jokes are never as funny as the jokes we hear told by skilled comedians. It is why sitcoms have more action than resolution,[11] why a great comedian can get a laugh with a look, why we are willing to sit through a long story-joke knowing that the payoff may not be that grand. But here is Andy's twist: it is not just that he is skilled at delivery—at the journey—and thus at comedy. It is that he denies the punch line completely, and, in doing so, denies the possibility that there is a destination. With no punch line there is only journey—or perhaps not even journey, for we aren't really going anywhere—and the comedy/tragedy distinction again crumbles.

Maurice Charney suggests that comedy "is committed to plot in a way that tragedy isn't."[12] Tragedy is character-driven, whereas comedy is story-driven. Problematically, Andy's humor is almost all based on being different characters, yet *something happens*: Tony Clifton pours water on an audience member's head and humiliates him; "Andy" eats a meal on stage; British Man reaches the end of *The Great Gatsby*. There is plot, but the characters are essential to the plot in a deep way, and thus they are essential to the success of the comedy.

True, adds Henri Bergson, all comedy has character, but what distinguishes the tragic character from the comedic character is the depth of his vice. The tragic character's vice is deep—"plunging into his soul"—to the degree that we can scarcely separate in our minds the character from his vice.[13] Such are Hamlet and Lady Macbeth. But so, too, is Tony Clifton.

The point is that Andy's performances do not fit any of these standard definitions of comedy and tragedy. But perhaps more importantly, in his failure to conform, he forces us to reconsider the definitions themselves. Phenomenologically, what we know is this: we are having an experience that gives rise to laughter.[14] The essential paradoxes that are created—Why am I laughing at the vile Tony Clifton? How can eating a meal on stage be funny?—arise when we try to understand this laughter using modernist or traditional terminology. It is, perhaps, analogous to the birth of quantum mechanics in physics. In the quantum world, particles seem to be doing paradoxical things—being in two places at the same time, spinning both up and down, passing information at a speed greater than the speed of light from one paired particle to its partner (Einstein's funny phrase for this was: "spooky action at a distance"). Yet the problem is not that the quantum world is crazy, indeterministic, and paradoxical. The problem is that we are using classical terminology designed for macroscopic objects to describe a nonclassical microscopic world. Andy is, let us say, engaged in quantum comedy, and if we simply go on using the same concepts in our attempt to understand him, we will be forever confused.

When modernists try to capture Andy, they search for a way to explain their experience using old and familiar categories. To some extent Steve Martin does this when he analyzes Andy as an "anticomedian": "[I]t was a classic example of anticomedy. In anticomedy, one of the most difficult things to accomplish is [that] once you state the premise which is funny and they laugh, you have to keep it going. That's what he managed to do. . . . And it was funny all the way through. To me, that was a miracle. He managed to sustain it by being funny internally after the premise was stated."[15] This is smartly put, by a comedian and author who is clearly a talented and thoughtful man. But the problem is that its reliance on modernist concepts does not really capture our experience of Andy. The premise is not necessarily funny in a traditional way when Andy performs. What, really, is funny about Foreign Man speaking gibberish or Andy playing bongos or Tony Clifton berating an audience member? In fact, one of the hallmarks of Andy's humor is that it is *not* funny throughout. Comedy and anticomedy are categories that are questioned by Andy, just as he questioned what it would mean to be internally rather than externally funny. This latter distinction fits traditionalist sketch comedy. A funny premise need not result in a funny sketch (indeed, this is the rock on which countless modernist *Saturday Night Live* sketches have run aground and sunk). But Andy is not doing sketches—there is no inside and outside. How could one separate the premise and the performance of Andy simply eating on stage? It's not as if he did wacky things with the food while eating. In fact, it is just this fact—the fact that he did not do "jokes" with the food, the fact that the piece never led to a spit-take, the fact that there was no punch line—that in part defines Andy's comedy. Andy would sing "100 Bottles of Beer on the Wall" to an audience—the whole way through, of course, until audience members were beyond agitation and anger; and this cannot be separated into an external premise and an internal performance. Our old categories and concepts cannot do justice to such an experience.

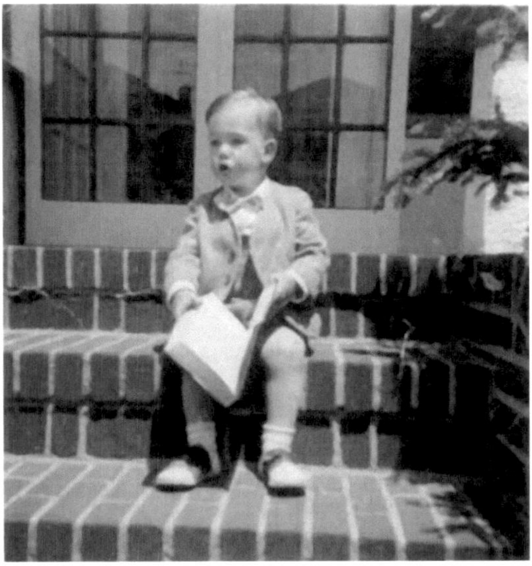

FIGURE 10.3. Andy Kaufman, c. 1951. Photo courtesy of the Kaufman family.

Still, they can add *something* to our understanding. And so, on the way toward pointing the direction to a new understanding of comedy, it is wise to pause at some of the more relevant and adaptable modernist theories. (*See figure 10.3.*)

Think of Freud. The name alone can get a laugh. Instantly, one's mind is flooded with images of naughty bits, the ghostly specter of the dirty old man himself somewhere off in the corner, his smiling, bearded, bespectacled face happily sprouting a fat cigar.

It is undoubtedly the case that a Freudian reading of Andy's work could be interesting. A psychoanalysis of his life and personal relationships with women, of the depths to which he took Tony Clifton to be a separate individual (they had, after all, separate managers, agents, contracts, trailers, eating habits, etc.), of the reasons he had (some undoubtedly sexual and subconscious) for wrestling women in his audience might provide more insight into the man. But we are after greater insight into his comedy. Still, Freud can service us.

According to Sigmund, most jokes, and nearly all tendentious jokes, require three parties: the speaker, the enabler, and the listener. Dirty jokes—what Freud so winkingly called "smut"—are based on this second person being a woman; whereas hostile jokes require the presence of an enemy or at least a disliked party of either sex. In both cases, the humor arises not so much from the joke itself, but from the complex reactions to the performance of the joke. The speaker gets pleasure; the enabler is harmed (ashamed, offended, embarrassed, or even hurt); and the listener laughs while bearing witness to the effect of the joke on the enabler. Specifically, smut is based on a woman's inability to deal with the public exposure of sexual images and thoughts—she resists the dirty language and scenarios due to the ever-present repression of her own sexuality as brought about by society. Freud explains:

> The ideal case of a resistance of this kind on the woman's part occurs if another man is present at the same time—a third person. . . . This third person soon acquires the greatest importance in the development of the smut. . . . Generally speaking, a tendentious joke calls for three people: in addition to the one who makes the joke, there must be a second who is taken as the object of the hostile or sexual aggressiveness, and a third in whom the joke's aim of producing pleasure is fulfilled. . . . [I]t is not the person who makes the joke who laughs at it and who therefore enjoys its pleasurable effect. . . . A person who laughs at smut that he hears is laughing as though he were the spectator of an act of sexual aggression.[16]

The hostile joke is similar in that our repressed tendencies toward violence (rather than sexual aggression) are made manifest in the joke told to a third person such that "[b]y making our enemy small, inferior, despicable or comic, we achieve in a roundabout way the enjoyment of overcoming him—to which the third person, who has made no efforts, bears witness by his laughter. . . . [The joke] bribe[s] the hearer with its yield of pleasure into taking sides with us without any very close investigation."[17]

To laugh at smut is to enjoy sexual harassment; to laugh at a hostile joke is to enjoy, without any concern for justice, another's pain and defeat. Freud's theory, of course, is much more complex than all of this, but the essential three-person relationship is fairly characterized by this short explication; and it is this comedic trinity that we need to consider in terms of Andy's humor.

To my knowledge, Andy never worked blue, so it would be hard to imagine how Freud's analysis of smut might be applicable. Perhaps when he wrestled women, Andy was trying to humiliate them for the benefit of the audience? I think that such an analysis would be stretching things a bit. If anything, The Wrestler was engaged in hostile humor, much like Tony Clifton. Thus it would seem that Freud's analysis of the hostile joke would be the better fit: we laugh when another woman is defeated on the mat; we laugh when Bob Zmuda gets a drink poured on his head; we laugh at Andy defeating his enemy. The modernist would stop here, having pinned down (at least part of) Andy's humor with a set category: Andy is the speaker, the picked-on audience member is the enabler, and we are the listeners happily accepting the bribe of the pleasurable laugh to take Andy's side.

But matters are never so easy.

Often, the audience didn't laugh. When Andy moved The Wrestler to "real" wrestling venues (whatever this means), hardly anyone laughed. Unsuspecting comedy club patrons felt genuinely nervous watching Foreign Man struggle through his set. Millions of viewers of the television show *Fridays* had no idea the next day whether they had witnessed the chaotic collapse of a network TV show or a *very* strange sketch.

Andy explains it—well, more or less explains it—thus: his goal, in every instance, was simply to "deceive" and "embarrass" the audience.[18]

This is a strange admission. It is immediately confusing, in fact, since comedy is typically thought to offer the audience delight and pleasure. Deceit is seldom a major goal of art, even if some consider it to be a means. Of course we recognize that the nature of fiction is not to be telling the truth—at least given a realist, denotative conception of truth. And Plato, as we saw in chapter 3, was no patron of the arts, arguing that a representation of a thing is twice removed from Truth—a shadow of a shadow. But these are poor or at least incomplete attempts at understanding the being of art. Art is surely not deceit. Picasso's faces don't lie. They show us one way in which the face can appear—they fill in part of the absent horizon of the face. We learn something about what it is *to be a face* when we study Picasso's paintings. And comedy, too, has such phenomenological horizons. If I were to tell you the one about the guy who goes into a bar, reaches into his pocket, and takes out a miniature piano and a twelve-inch pianist—if I were a different sort of person, one who told such jokes—I wouldn't expect you to take the story literally. I would be hoping to make you smile at a new way of seeing the world, our language, our attitudes toward sexuality. Freud to the contrary, I would not be out to molest the women within earshot.

But Freud is helpful in understanding Andy's claim that his goal is to deceive and embarrass—especially in terms of embarrassing. Contrary to common sense, however, it is not the hostile joke but the smutty joke that best fits Andy's comedy. If in straightforward Freudian analysis the comedian is the speaker, the embarrassed person is the enabler, and the audience is the listener who laughs, what happens when Andy attempts to embarrass the whole audience? Surprisingly, the audience becomes the enabler—the second "person" in the comedic trinity. So who, then, is person number three, the listener, the one who laughs, the traditional audience? Often, Andy was person one *and* person three. (*See figure 10.4, page 212.*)

This is one way of understanding how Andy's performances could be conceptualized as comedy even if the entire audience experienced only bewilder-

	FREUDIAN ROLE	FREUDIAN COMEDY	ANDY'S COMEDY
PERSON 1	speaker (speaks)	comedian	Andy
PERSON 2	enabler (is embarrassed)	victim/straight-(wo)man	audience
PERSON 3	listener (laughs)	audience	Andy

FIGURE 10.4. How Andy Kaufman fits into the Freudian conception of a joke.

ment or anger. The joke exists, but Andy, in a sense, does not let the audience in on the joke. Comedy is taking place, but it is such a radically new kind of comedy that it will be difficult to recognize it as such. And all of this stems from Andy's continued playing with notions of identity. Just as Tony Clifton was in some sense as real as Andy, and just as Andy was constantly questioning the concept of the stable and fixed identity of the performer in his comedy, so was the identity of the audience being questioned. This is even harder for us to accept because it is *our* role that we are being forced to reconsider when we watch Andy; it is *our* identity *as an audience* that we feel slipping out from beneath our feet. If the public shows up and doesn't play the role of person number three—if the public is in some sense the straight man ("in some sense" here because the public is often not even aware of the joke)—then members of the public must either learn to think of themselves as something other than "audience" or they must come to redefine what it means to be an audience. Andy is asking a lot of us. Like Picasso's face, we are seeing ourselves in a whole new way, coming to realize that we can *be* in new ways. And we further become aware that one of the ways in which comedy can appear—one of its profiles within an infinite horizon—is as frustration.

"Kaufman is capable of inflicting tremendous cruelty on an audience," declared Steve Allen. "Unless you let the audience in on the joke," concurred Carl Reiner, "you are making fools of them, and that's what he's doing with this Tony Clifton."[19] In his defense, and as a partial answer to our query of "Why?" Andy offers the following: "As for not letting people in on the joke, there are times when real life is funnier than deliberate comedy. Therefore I try to create the illusion of a 'real-life' situation or character. However, it must be believed totally; if I were to let people in on the joke, it wouldn't have that effect."[20]

Not letting the audience in on the joke is a way of vanishing the punch line—though only from the perspective of the audience. The punch line is, in a sense, publicly silent; it is heard only back in the dressing room—it belongs only to Andy. This complicates everything, because it is not clear that Andy is not simply telling jokes without punch lines; rather the punch line has moved from where we expected it to be to a place where we may not even hear it or recognize it. Still, as phenomenology shows us, it can be experienced in its absence once we know it is missing.

Andy is concerned with being funny, but if we simply sit back waiting to be hand-fed a punch line, it will never come and we will never know why the whole scenario was comedic. Once we go looking for the payoff, we are changed (and the comedy has changed). Perhaps it no longer even makes sense to call it a punch line. It's like some strange Heisenberg Comedic Uncertainty Principle: the system changes once we start investigating; we can never experience an uninterpreted laugh in Andy's world.

But notice, more importantly, that Andy is challenging the very conception of "real" life—a word we have been putting in quotation marks since the first section of this book. Andy is not merely trying to deceive the audience; he is offering us something even beyond the simulation. He uses the word "illusion," but we should not be so quick to accept it. For Andy, it's not that the show must be "real-looking" like a well-staged play (with authentic costumes, scenery, etc.); it's that what he is doing must *be* the reality for the audience: all distinction must be gone. Here, the juxtaposition of "real life" against "deliberate comedy" is not meant to suggest a true dichotomy, but, ultimately, to question such dichotomies. Consider Baudrillard:

> If we were to take as the finest allegory of simulation the Borges tale where the cartographers of the Empire draw up a map so detailed that it ends up exactly covering the territory . . . then this fable has come full circle for us, and now has nothing but the discrete charm of second-order simulacra. Abstraction today is no longer that of the map, the double, the mirror, or the concept. . . . The territory no longer precedes the map, nor survives it. Henceforth, it is the map that precedes the territory. . . . [I]t is no longer anything but a gigantic simulacrum—not unreal, but a simulacrum, never again exchanging for what is real, but exchanging in itself.[21]

Andy's deception is not meant to play a trick on us, to bring to fruition Plato's worst nightmare in which we are mistaken about what is real. Because Andy gives us no way to distinguish "real life" from the simulacra, we come to realize that there is no real distinction. He is being *honest* with us, and we might find it frightening. "What's real? What's not?" Andy explains. "That's what I do in my act, test how other people deal with reality. . . . The critics try to intellectualize my material. There's no satire involved. . . . My stuff is straight."[22] But of course there is no satire. Satire, as our analysis of *The Simpsons* in the previous chapter has shown us, requires that the satirist take a position outside of the thing he is satirizing, requires him to be able to look down on it, copy it in a distorted way, and (re)present it to us as funny. When there is no outside, when the map precedes the territory, satire becomes impossible—everything is straight.

Analyzing Andy's exchange with Steve Martin about the Foreign Man, we discovered that the claim, "I am not a character," is part of the script—of, at least, *some* script—and thus we can never get at a "real" Andy. What we are realizing now is that this same problem of simulacrum—engaged, as it must be, only in self-reference—calls into question our role as audience as well because it is no longer clear where the performance is, where it begins and ends, and thus how we fit into it all. When we saw Tony Clifton perform at an Italian restaurant or saw The Wrestler berate women (and Southerners) in a coliseum in Memphis or even met Andy at his busboy job or walking down the street, how could we be sure where the performance was? Langer argues that the "phenomenon of laughter in the theater brings into sharp focus the whole question of the distinction between emotion symbolically presented, and emotion directly stimulated. . . . It is different in the theater. . . . A very mild joke in just the right place may score a big laugh. . . . [P]eople are laughing at the play, not at a string of jokes."[23] But Andy doesn't let us know it is theater; he doesn't let us off so easily. This bypasses the cheap laugh, the laugh we get merely for showing up in the right context, on the right night. Hence we realize that there is a false dichotomy at work when we separate the symbolically presented emotion from the experienced emotion. A tear shed for Old Yeller is not any less or any more of a sign of "real emotion" than the tears I shed when my boyhood dog Snowball died—in part because tears are never signs that refer beyond themselves. A laugh enticed to erupt by Foreign Man cannot stand for anything else, anything more real, because Foreign Man lives and has brought us to live in a place where identity is malleable, the map precedes the territory, and all the world may indeed be a stage.

To use another classical conception that is bound to fail in the final analysis, we might think of Andy's "jokes" as practical jokes, for the jokes were often on us and, just as often, we didn't even realize it. Can there be a performance when no one knows about it (apart from the performer)? Yes, but we might not laugh. We will naïvely assume that this is "real life" (which is built on the naïve assumption that there is such a thing as "real life"). We will really think Andy The Wrestler hates women; we will experience real anger. We will really think Andy is a foreigner struggling through a joke; we will experience real embarrassment and discomfort. We will really think Andy is homeless; we will experience real pity. Later, should we find out that this was not real life, we will ask ourselves whether we were having real feelings. It is only when we make the move to understand the nature of the simulacra, the true challenge of Andy's work, that we will realize the distinctions are meaningless: How could they not have been real feelings? How could it fail to be the case that all jokes are practical jokes because all of life is a stage, all of life is a joke? We will discover that comedy is the realest thing around, that to live a life is to live a life of comedic art. And we will laugh.

This takes time. Timing is critical in all comedy, but especially in Andy's. Never content with the cheap laugh, Andy refused to ride the rhythm of comedy that coerces our laughter, yet the temporal structure of his humor is fundamental to its success.

Typically, Andy's performances are funniest in retrospect. It is easy for us to laugh at the *idea* of Andy singing "100 Bottles of Beer on the Wall," reading aloud the entire book *The Great Gatsby*, or sleeping on stage, but imagine being there in the moment. Even knowing that Andy was brilliant, it was hard to laugh in the middle of the performance. We laugh later, upon reflection, which is a challenge to the temporal structure of the comedy: when is it over?

Consider Andy's 1983 PBS television special, *Soundstage: The Andy Kaufman Show.* As the show begins, it begins "already in progress." The audience is nearly literally rolling around in uncontrollable laughter after just hearing a joke we missed. Andy has again done the opposite of what Cohen argues is the mechanism of successful comedy: Andy has excluded us rather than included us. *We* are not a part of *his* audience even if we think we are because we have taken the time to tune in. At the very start, *we* don't fit in. This time Andy hasn't merely denied us the punch line, he's denied us the entire joke. And yet there is the presence of laughter. We learn something about laughter as we eventually find ourselves laughing along with the audience a bit. It is not instant laughter—the kind that is supposed to follow in the beat after the punch line or along with the laugh track. And we are not laughing at the same thing as Andy and his studio audience. This laughter takes time to develop, and its object, perhaps, is comedy (laughter?) itself—not *what* has taken place, but *that* it has taken place. Perhaps Heidegger got this one thing right: we are thrown into a world already up and running. And with Andy, our thrownness is immediately apparent, tossed into a show already in progress.

Following this rather shocking beginning, the show continues. For an hour Andy deconstructs the television variety show, chatting with his announcer (Tony Clifton in Howdy Doody marionette form), fighting with his guest ("real-life" ex-girlfriend Elayne Boosler) when he "thinks the camera is not on," looming above everyone else from his ridiculously high interviewer's desk. The show is fascinating, though there are, truth be told, few immediate laughs. At times it is slow; at times it seems to be suffering from substandard production values. But we watch and play along. Finally, we anticipate that the show is about to loop around again. The comedian we recognize from the start—the one who had the audience roaring with laughter—is introduced by Andy with the claim that he is going to tell the funniest story, the funniest joke, ever. There is a slow buildup, and right when the comedian is about to start the story…the camera cuts to a couple watching the show at home. They remark that this looks like where they came in. By the time the camera goes back to the studio we have missed the joke once again because the audience is—once again—roaring with laughter. This time, the show does not loop. Andy comes out and happily sings a goodbye song. As he waves and smiles, as time passes, we can faintly hear Andy muttering under his breath that he does not respect us for having watched his TV show. We in the audience are idiots, Andy tells us. We are like sheep. We'll watch anything he does. We're morons. When the cute song is over, the credits have run, and Andy "thinks the camera is off," he fully changes personalities and outwardly yells at the studio audience to shut up. He screams at his assistants. He orders a hamburger (as if Andy's vegetarianism were all an act). Then, in a bit of 1980s special effects, Andy as Foreign Man comes on the screen and talks to himself, asking why he has to be so angry, why he must be so mean, why he is harming both of their careers. Foreign Man Andy calms down Angry Andy. The latter exits the screen, crying and hoping for redemption. Foreign Man Andy then turns to the camera and tells us, in his cute and innocent accent, goodbye. And once he is told the cameras are off, Foreign Man Andy suddenly changes personality, screams at his assistants, and orders someone to bring him a hamburger and wrestle. The show "ends."

We watch the PBS logo come on the screen. We pause a moment, wondering if it really is over. But yes, finally, the show is complete (or was it over the moment it started to loop again—"over," we realize, is subjective; it requires, as Husserl realized, the dative case: things are always over *for* someone and necessarily not, perhaps, for someone else). And thus we have a show that "ends" at least four times. We have Andy addressing himself in second person as his various identities meet on screen. We have one of the characters reference the fact that another character is just "an act." We have dialogue nested within dialogue, with each nest claiming it is no longer scripted, no longer part of the show, only to be disproved when one of the characters eventually turns to the camera to say goodbye. We have no place that is truly offstage. And we have Andy mocking and belittling us for having watched. This is the most difficult of all the endings because it seems to hit so close to home. At some point we may have started to get the feeling that we were stupid for watching this—"it's not even funny," we might think. And then Andy comes out and says so. We were sheep, following along with Andy. We would listen to anything he had to say. Andy belittles us, and we eat it up. (*See figure 10.5.*)

All of this may elicit anger or frustration or embarrassment. If it immediately elicits a smile, it is merely the smile of someone who realizes defeat, realizes he has been had; it is seldom a smile that accompanies laughter. All of this will only be funny once we have gained some temporal distance. It will be funny

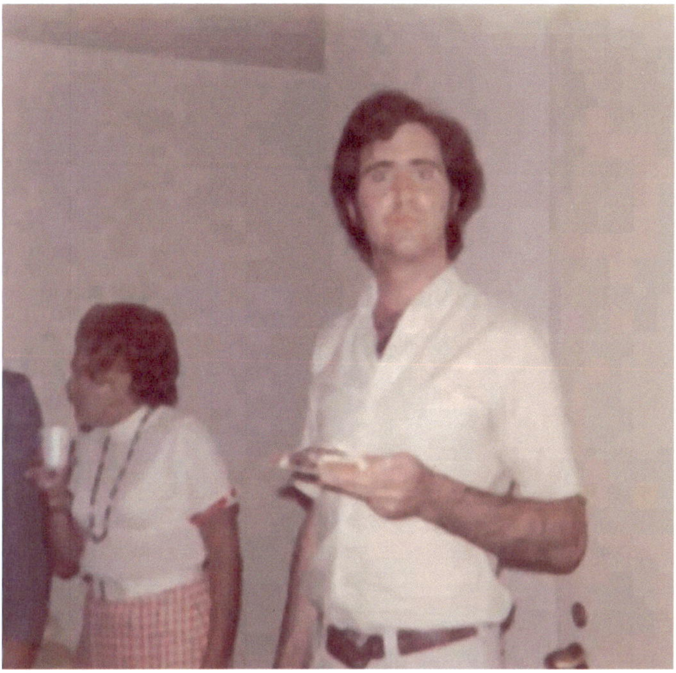

FIGURE 10.5. Andy Kaufman, eating it up with family. Photo courtesy of the Kaufman family.

when we realize our role as audience, the role of simulacra, the way in which our expectations concerning comedy were questioned, and the degree to which Andy's sheep speech was true (we really were idiots all along) and yet at the same time was just a part of the bigger show—a show that may not be over yet.

We haven't really missed the joke in these instances. We are part of the joke; the joke is still going on until we realize this. (*See figure 10.6, page 218.*)

Part of what we laugh at later is our original reaction (which is based on our earlier expectations). And part of what we laugh at is this deconstruction of comedy itself and the way we are liberated by it.

It has long been suggested that comedy is about freedom—the ways we are free and not free. Walter Kerr writes that "this is the basic joke, the one incongruity upon which all other incongruities rest. That a being so entirely free should be so little free is absurd. That a creature capable of transcending himself should at the same time be incapable of controlling himself is hilarious. . . . A bishop should never have to go to the bathroom."[24] But Andy's twist to this is to show us that *we are freed by comedy itself even as comedy (and thus laughter) overcomes us.*

<table>
<tr><th></th><th colspan="2">Traditional Comedy</th><th colspan="2">Andy's Comedy</th></tr>
<tr><td>Chronology</td><td>Where is the joke?</td><td>Analysis</td><td>Where is the joke?</td><td>Analysis</td></tr>
<tr><td>1. We go to performance</td><td></td><td>not part of comedy</td><td rowspan="5">Joke</td><td>the fact that we went (with certain expectations) becomes part of the comedy</td></tr>
<tr><td>2. Comedien: sets up joke</td><td rowspan="2">Joke</td><td></td><td rowspan="2">content here is virtually unimportant</td></tr>
<tr><td>3. Comedian: delivers punchline</td><td></td></tr>
<tr><td>4. We react</td><td></td><td>laughter</td><td>any reaction (anger, frustration, etc.)</td></tr>
<tr><td>5. We leave performance</td><td></td><td>not part of comedy</td><td>not necessarily the end of comedy</td></tr>
<tr><td>6. (Meta-reaction later)</td><td></td><td>(no meta-reaction)</td><td></td><td>laughter</td></tr>
</table>

FIGURE 10.6. Traditional comedy v. Andy Kaufman's comedy.

This is true in all of Andy's comedy, but especially in his "sweeter and innocent" comedy such as the various instantiations of "Uncle Andy's Playhouse." As our expectations of the standard joke are set aside, we are freed to laugh at other things. Children laugh with freedom (Freud recognized and made much of this), and Andy always wanted to perform for children. When we allow our identity as audience to become malleable, we can become a group of children. Andy was often inviting us to do this. (*See figure 10.7.*)

When he would first start to sing "100 Bottles of Beer on the Wall" there would be some laughter. This is standard laughter, the cheap laughter that Andy scorned, a laughter born of shock and surprise and incongruity. As Andy continued, the audience would often boo. In the moment, there is nothing funny about listening to twenty minutes of this song. When it became clear that Andy wouldn't stop, though, the emotions in the audience would shift and blur. Some audience members would grow more impatient, others would tune out completely. But then, typically, Andy would finally stop the song after getting to a low number (say eight or nine bottles left on the wall) and suddenly walk off the stage. After a moment of stunned silence, everyone would cheer for him to return and finish. We, the audience, would once again find ourselves as a coherent whole. We had wanted nothing more than for this torture to end a few moments ago, but now we are surprised to find ourselves engaged by the performance—by this silly song—and we laugh. It is an innocent laughter, a laughter that is only possible once we are freed from traditional comic expectations, yet a

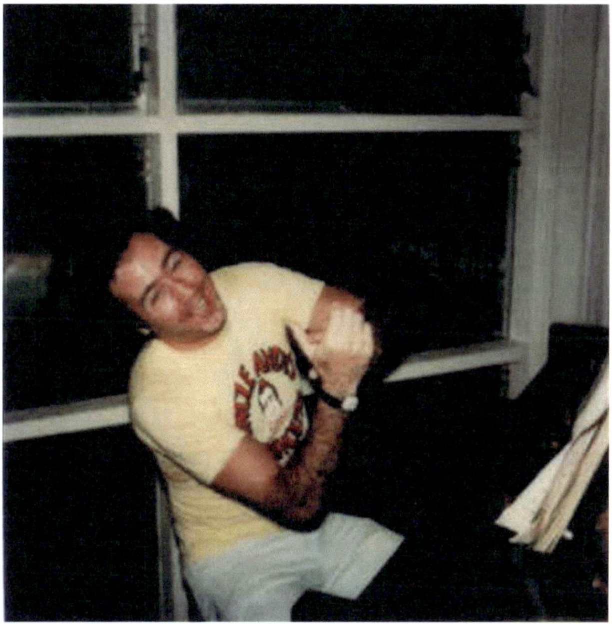

FIGURE 10.7. Andy Kaufman wearing his "Uncle Andy's Funhouse" T-shirt. Photo courtesy of the Kaufman family.

laughter that realizes that we are engaged in the show and engaged by our own laughter and our shifting expectations and desires. And Andy did all of this by manipulating the point at which he ended his act.

When did the Carnegie Hall show begin? When Andy appeared in disguise outside the box office as a mad protester? When Andy took the stage on opening night? When did it end? With the arrival of Santa? With the last sketch? Blocks away where the audience ate milk and cookies? (In fact, at one of these shows the crowd stayed so late that Andy had to rush them back before the rented buses needed to be returned. He announced that the show would *continue* the next morning on the Staten Island ferry. Not knowing if anyone would show up, Andy went to the dock the next day at sunrise and was greeted by a crowd of three hundred, all waiting for the next part of the show. He bought tickets on the ferry for everyone, treated the whole audience to ice cream, and wrestled women on the deck of the boat coming and going from Staten Island.) One laughs along the way, laughs at the fun and the spectacle. But the laughter that Andy cherished was the laughter that came later. And so, long after his last performance, we are still laughing. Freely and appropriately. With a new understanding of comedy as time and space collapse. It's not only unclear when the

Carnegie Hall show began and ended, it's unclear if it essentially took place in the space that is Carnegie Hall.

Andy was a song-and-dance man. And he was a comedian. Some of his comedy survives today on film and video; but some of it is in written form as well. Andy the author is less known than Andy the performer, but there are three important books from Zilch Publishing that collect Andy's novel, poetry, short stories, and plays that are worth our attention. A careful analysis of his written corpus, in fact, shows that his forays into drama were very much in keeping with his comedic performances. Indeed, he demanded that it all be *performed*, even if the pieces were just read aloud. As we move to conclude this investigation of Andy in particular, and our project on phenomenological aesthetics in general, dealing with a work that few are likely to know, will, I hope, help demonstrate how the ideas we have been developing can help make anything come to meaning—and come to (redefine and question) beauty. Andy has already shown us that living is a performance, challenging the boundaries between life and aesthetics, comedy and tragedy. Now, for one last time, we move to challenge a final few traditions and dichotomies by engaging with *God . . . and Other Plays*, a collection of six dramatic works written by Andy over a span of twenty years.[25] (*See figure 10.8.*)

Is *God* a play? It has none of the traditional elements of a play: no stage directions or scene descriptions, no dialogue formatted in terms of a character's name followed by his or her line. The work sits on the page like prose, though at times even this begins to fall apart as some pages have only one sentence while others consist mostly of repeated onomatopoeic letters. It is a play—a "one-man play," as Andy called it—only in the sense that it is written to be performed. As always, Andy was questioning genres and concepts.

God begins with its titular character condemning everyone as sinners. This includes, we assume, the epileptic Tincture Puncture—a protagonist who has the ability to float, is often referred to as "the blessed one," and does not speak until near the conclusion of the play. We are next introduced to King Fluke and Queen Silga of the nearby land of Alegadonia; paradigms of the worst sorts of leaders possible, they are continually fighting, jealously bickering, and leaving their children to be raised by their servants. One day, the throne swallows the Queen, and Tincture Puncture, or Tinc (as he is often called), is summoned to pull the queen out of her chair. While searching for Tinc in order to have him perform this delivery, the royal messenger spies a woman, Gina, who is able to fly because she wears a special pair of bell-bottom jeans. Gina also speaks only at the end of the play; otherwise she merely keeps giggling "hee hee hee" throughout, flying around in her jeans.

Once Tinc performs the royal rescue, the messenger tells the King and Queen about Gina and her flying pants. The royal couple orders the girl to appear before them and to surrender her jeans; but when their request is met only

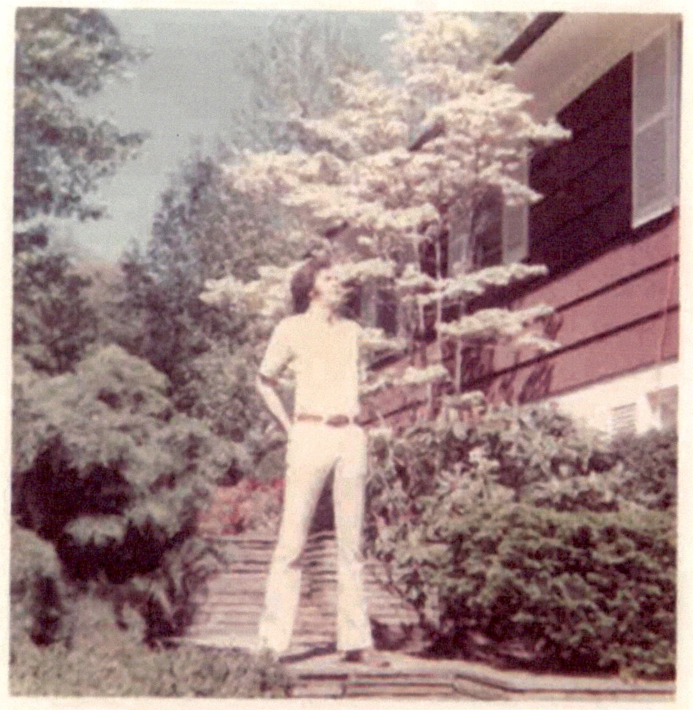

FIGURE 10.8. Andy Kaufman, master of all he surveys. Photo courtesy of the Kaufman family.

with Gina's laughter, the King and Queen order that Gina be executed. In the middle of the execution, a mysterious man arrives at the palace and, through some special power, passes by the guards without detection. He saves Gina, killing nearly everyone in the palace with his machine gun in the process. We find out later that the gunman was Tinc. The five surviving members of the court—including the royal heir—inherit, collectively, two billion dollars.

In a parallel plotline within the play, Larry the truck driver becomes a recording star, eventually reaching an Elvis-like status of fame and fortune. Before long, Larry has so much money that he no longer knows what to do with it, but he determines that with the combined investment of the survivors from the court massacre, they could all purchase and drain the Atlantic Ocean and build a massive amusement park in the sea basin, which Larry christens "Heaven." The park, once constructed, can be entered from any of the adjoining continents, and it is arranged in concentric rings of fun and attractions. At the very center, however, there is nothing, as Larry has not yet found something worthy to be at the core of his "Heaven."

God, meanwhile, is angry at such a sacrilegious display, so He flies down to Earth and begins to destroy it with a flood. As the world fills with water, everyone in the domed and self-contained amusement park, including Tinc and Gina, is oblivious to the ensuing apocalypse. Eventually, Tinc realizes something is wrong and leaves "Heaven" to confront God outside and convince Him to stop the flood. God relents, but finds, for some reason, that He can no longer fly, and is thus trapped on a partially devastated Earth.

Larry offers God a job sitting on a throne in the center of his amusement park. With few other options and no way back up to the real heaven, God accepts and soon finds himself a fixture in Larry's "Heaven." The job is humiliating, as God is forced to put up with obnoxious visitors who bring their babies to sit on His lap and pull on His beard as if He were Santa Claus. In a desperate bid to retain some dignity, God asks Gina for her bell-bottoms so that He can escape and fly back to the real heaven. But Gina refuses. Soon after, Larry takes the center stage to begin another performance, and God—jealous and miserable and in desperate need of worship—tries to out-sing Larry in an attempt to win the support of the people. When it becomes clear that the crowd prefers Larry, God's patience is finally at an end. He sends out lightning bolts, killing everyone around Him, everyone in the park, nearly everyone in the world—finishing with fire what he had earlier started with water.

Sammy, a little boy who began digging on a beach early in the play and eventually reached China, saves Tinc and Gina from God's wrath by offering them refuge in the hole that he dug. When the lightning storm is over, Tinc and Gina emerge from Sammy's hole to find everyone dead and God lamenting, "They deserved it!" But with no one to talk to and with no one to watch over, God dies. And Tinc and Gina fly away together.

There is some question as to whether or not *God* is a comedy. At first glance, there is very little humor in the piece. There are some puns and plays on words, and some of the descriptions of the attractions in "Heaven" are amusing and amazing, but there are no jokes or really any funny situations.

To a certain extent, *God* destroys the comedy/tragedy barrier just as Andy's performances did. To return to another classical conception of the distinction, tragedy, it is often said, ends in death while comedy ends in marriage. *God* ends in both—at least in the sense that all the world is killed yet Tinc and Gina are paired in symbolic union and sent off into the sunset. Langer's contention that tragedies have real endings whereas comedies do not is also called into question by Andy's play, for this work has a clear ending—nearly everyone dies (even God)—yet it is also a beginning (Tinc and Gina fly off into a pristine world to start again). And Charney's claim that "[t]here is no way for the structure of comedy to avoid the prevailing mores, and the end of comedy, which is a much more conservative genre than tragedy, must reflect the ends of society,"[26] falls apart for the reader of *God* as the mores of our society are indeed played out in the extreme (consumerism, the cult of fame, our tendencies toward violence amid our longing for love, etc.), yet no one would call this a play that ends conservatively. God, after all, is humiliated and dies.

God, the play, is not alone. Other works have been labeled comedies that are not *clearly* comedies—Dante's *Divine Comedy*, for instance—and it is illuminating, in fact, to read *God* as a postmodern update on the *Divine Comedy*.

Dante's work is, on one level, about humanity's journey to God. Andy's work is about the death of God, but not about the transcendence of humanity. This would have been the modernist's turn: kill God and replace Him with the human. But Andy does not substitute the one for the other. As usual, all categories are questioned. It is true that Andy allows innocence to survive, yet it is not a naïve but rather a self-aware innocence.

The most obvious resemblance of *God* to *The Divine Comedy* is the journey through "Paradiso," which in Andy's work is turned into the amusement park named "Heaven." Like Paradise, Heaven is marked by concentric circles, each more intricately interesting than the last. In the center, for Dante, there is God. In the center, for Andy, is Larry (who is called an idol, and who achieves godlike status) until, at Larry's invitation, God takes a seat at the center of Heaven as well. The description Andy gives of Heaven mimics that of Dante: each circle is described in detail (what it looks like, what the people are doing, etc.). And just as Dante's style changes when he begins "Paradiso," so Andy's style changes when we reach Act V, the only act of the play with a subtitle: "Heaven." (*See figure 10.9.*) For the first time, Andy fills the whole page with text—straightforward, descriptive prose. The change in style is abrupt and startling, much like Dante's adoption of a new style of writing when he, too, reaches paradise.

The greatest difference, perhaps, between "Paradiso" and "Heaven" is that in Andy's version it is not a human being traveling through heaven on the way to God, but rather it is God working his way through Heaven toward a human being (Larry). After God attempts to destroy the world outside Heaven with another flood, Tinc convinces Him to stop, but God can't get back to His heaven because He can no longer fly. This marks the beginning of the end for God—His downfall, His final act of anger and vengeance. (The opposite, interestingly, is true for Tinc. He begins his journey to speech and fulfillment with the massacre of the King and Queen who are about to kill Gina. That is, Tinc's turn to violence—indeed, extreme and vengeful violence—is his salvation, the point at which he begins truly to prosper. God's turn to violence is the mark of His impending death.) Consequently, God is forced to enter humanity's Heaven, even to pay for a ticket, and work His way toward the center. Stripped of the power of flight, Larry must fly God in a helicopter to the throne. Soon, God gets

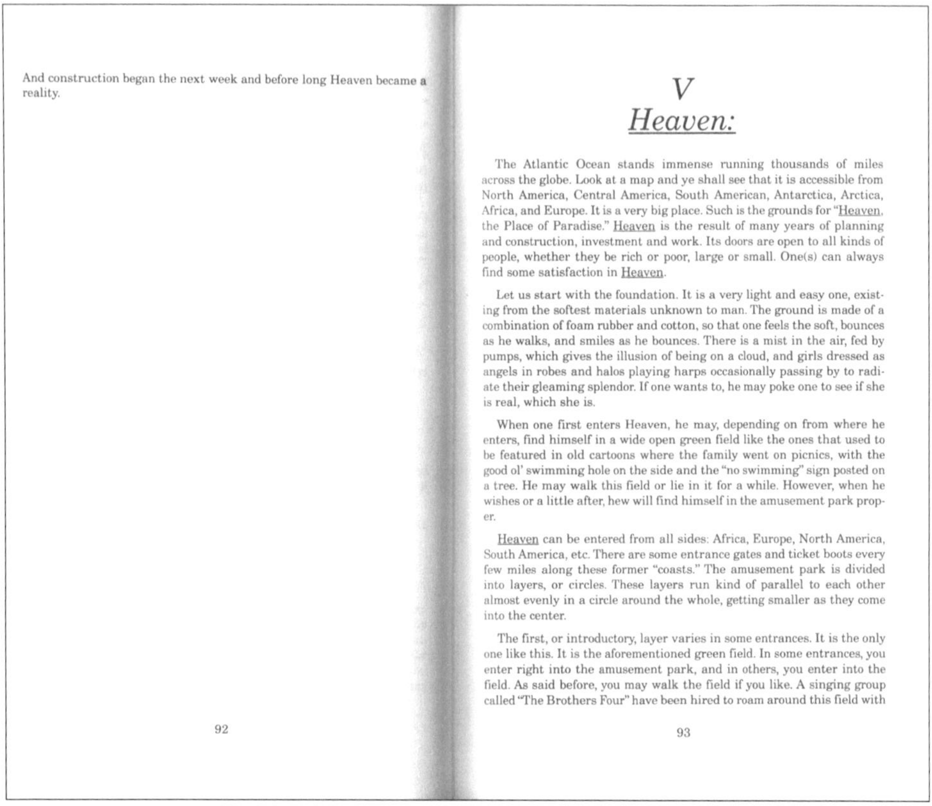

And construction began the next week and before long Heaven became a reality.

92

V

Heaven:

The Atlantic Ocean stands immense running thousands of miles across the globe. Look at a map and ye shall see that it is accessible from North America, Central America, South American, Antarctica, Arctica, Africa, and Europe. It is a very big place. Such is the grounds for "Heaven, the Place of Paradise." Heaven is the result of many years of planning and construction, investment and work. Its doors are open to all kinds of people, whether they be rich or poor, large or small. One(s) can always find some satisfaction in Heaven.

Let us start with the foundation. It is a very light and easy one, existing from the softest materials unknown to man. The ground is made of a combination of foam rubber and cotton, so that one feels the soft, bounces as he walks, and smiles as he bounces. There is a mist in the air, fed by pumps, which gives the illusion of being on a cloud, and girls dressed as angels in robes and halos playing harps occasionally passing by to radiate their gleaming splendor. If one wants to, he may poke one to see if she is real, which she is.

When one first enters Heaven, he may, depending on from where he enters, find himself in a wide open green field like the ones that used to be featured in old cartoons where the family went on picnics, with the good ol' swimming hole on the side and the "no swimming" sign posted on a tree. He may walk this field or lie in it for a while. However, when he wishes or a little after, hew will find himself in the amusement park proper.

Heaven can be entered from all sides: Africa, Europe, North America, South America, etc. There are some entrance gates and ticket boots every few miles along these former "coasts." The amusement park is divided into layers, or circles. These layers run kind of parallel to each other almost evenly in a circle around the whole, getting smaller as they come into the center.

The first, or introductory, layer varies in some entrances. It is the only one like this. It is the aforementioned green field. In some entrances, you enter right into the amusement park, and in others, you enter into the field. As said before, you may walk the field if you like. A singing group called "The Brothers Four" have been hired to roam around this field with

93

FIGURE 10.9. Pages 92–93 of Andy Kaufman's play, *God*.

angry and jealous, destroys the world, and dies. The opposite of Dante holds in Andy's work: finally reaching the center of Heaven ushers in death and demise. And God, we learn, dies because He has no one to whom He can talk, no one to watch over. God owes His life to us—and His death to our absence, His experience of our present-absence.

Andy methodically constructs Tincture Puncture as a Christ figure, but it is helpful if we take Tinc to be closer to Adam than he is to Christ. This is certainly true at the end of the play where Tinc and Gina go off to start up a new world. Earlier, Gina's persona as Eve has been firmly established through her sexuality. She is, most basically, the lure of sex, the promise of carnal transcendence. To get into her pants is, literally, to depart this earthly realm and transcend. But despite the imagery, this is not a temptress Eve. Gina, with all of her girlish giggling and faux coy sexuality, seems innocent. Larry recognizes this when he first sees her, and Tinc recognizes it when he goes to her rescue and massacres those in the palace. Tinc, in fact, as neo-Adam, is somewhat contradictorily ushering in a new age of innocence by means of this mass murder.

In "Paradiso" VII 42, Dante startlingly reveals that the Crucifixion, too, was a strange act of justice. As Robin Kirkpatrick explains: "God took on the form of the Old Adam, and human beings—acting through the Imperial power of Rome as the appointed vessel of justice—were able to repair the Fall by executing the 'Adam' in Christ."[27] This is Dante's vision of the Crucifixion, and it is inversely reflected in Andy's description of the palace massacre in which Tinc (the simple human individual—not of the royal, imperial, divine ruling class) executes those in the court who have lost innocence. Instead of coming to Earth and having humans destroy the humanity in Christ, thus ending the time of Adam, Tinc comes down to Earth and destroys the divinity of humans, thus making himself into the new Adam (and inevitably leaving us without God). The divine part of us is thus the part that is moved to anger, vengeance, condemnation, jealousy, and greed. The King and Queen, after all, wanted Gina's pants. As did God.

The evidence for Tincture Puncture's status as neo-Adam was there, perhaps, from the very beginning. "Tincture" indicates a dyeing substance, a colorant, a trace, or a vestige. Is the "puncture," then, the deflation, the end of what was, the Fall? Is there a hidden pun on dyeing/dying? Tincture Puncture would literally represent a vestige of Man before the Fall, the trace of what was thought to have died: Adam.

This becomes clearer if we investigate the theme of flying/floating. Dante (the character), we remember, struggled in Hell and Purgatory. The latter was an arduous mountain climb, but he rose effortlessly to Paradise. In contrast, once in Paradise—that is, in the amusement park "Heaven"—Andy's God falters and must be helped to the center in a helicopter. In the play *God*, the ability to fly seems to be functioning as a symbol of power: God loses it when he tries to destroy all Creation, but Tinc, the protagonist, has it and Gina has it as well. Gina's ability to fly, however, is different and in some sense artificial. She needs magical bell-bottom pants, whereas the male characters can fly by sheer force of their will. Gina's power, here, is her sex (her power, after all, is in her *pants*). In his jealous desire for Gina's power, the King straps her to a phallic log and threatens rape and death (i.e., threatens to take her pants by force). Throughout the play, those who want Gina's pants always want both her sex and her power. She is pursued by most of the main characters, in fact, with the exception of Tinc. Before he is a star, Larry's attempt to kiss Gina comes close to molestation. The King desperately wants Gina's pants, and the Queen is jealous of them. Even God wants them, which would suggest that He wishes to convert her into a Mary character (the only woman ever "sexually" related to God). But Gina will not allow this, and in her refusal she ushers in God's wrath. Rather than become the mother of humanity's savior, she helps bring about humanity's destruction—while at the same time identifying herself as non-Mary/non-virgin. This is a paradoxical identification, to be sure, for it is precisely Gina's unwillingness to give up her sex that cements her image as non-Mary and therefore *non-virgin*. There is only one time that Gina gives her pants to anyone. This takes place symbolically, at the end of the play, when Tinc has trouble flying. Gina lends him a hand—lends him her power, her sex, her pants—until he can float again. Tinc's need for sex, and Gina's willingness to offer it to him, affirm their identities as a new Adam and Eve at this point in the story, the point at which the protagonists fly off to repopulate the world—something, we know, Tinc could not do by himself. Like Dante's Beatrice, Gina fulfills the role of the main male protagonist's love interest. But unlike Dante, who is ultimately tied to the world and unable to turn from the material and the mundane due to his worship of Beatrice, Tinc escapes the world with the help of Gina's love.[28]

Before paradise, before the garden of Eden, before creation there was the Word. Language, inevitably, has a relationship to power in the Judeo-Christian tradition and in Dante's and Andy's work.

Dante's relationship to language is complex. His style changes at times throughout *The Divine Comedy*, ushering in an awareness that the setting and the meaning of the poem have changed as well. Dante is a self-aware poet. Virgil is his guide—both for the Dante who is a character and needs help navigating the afterlife, and for Dante the poet who is writing *The Divine Comedy* (a dual character-author identity role Andy would no doubt appreciate). It is important to remember that one *reads* Dante: the *Comedy* is not a painting, Charles Singleton reminds us.[29] How do we relate to language through both Dantes, then?

In "The Inferno," Dante realizes that language is *untrustworthy*. The seducer Jason spoke to his victim Hypsiphile with ornate words, and Thais the Whore verbally faked satisfaction with her customers. The examples of tormented souls that bother Dante here are interesting because they are not supposedly simple liars—users of language that does not accurately denote—but rather users of ornate and emotive language. Dante will claim that while Thais was a prostitute, she is not being tormented for her fornicating ways. While it is true, too, that she lied to a customer, telling him that he had indeed supplied her with pleasure "beyond all measure," she is not being punished for such lies per se. Instead, she wallows in a ditch of human filth with the other *flatterers*. Like a thirteenth-century Meg-Ryan-as-"Sally," when Thais met her "Harry," she convincingly faked her pleasure, putting on a show of orgasmic utterances meant to indicate the depths of her pleasure. Language apparently twisted and became mere sound; affective moans stood in for truth. And yet here is the risk: Virgil's (and Dante's) words, too, are ornate and affective; they speak in verse and with emotion; they moan on the page even as they condemn Thais's moaning—in short: they'll have what she's having. To speak to us of the evil of ornate language, Dante uses the most ornate poetic verse. And he sets up the *poet* Virgil as our guide. Must Dante and Virgil themselves thus fear speaking sin? Of course. Yet luckily, Dante assures us that he can tell when something is mere flattery or seduction. He knows the tricks that language plays and thus can always speak the truth. This should ring as highly suspect, but even if we are inclined to trust Dante, things are not so simple.

Language, to say it once again, is merely a way of making the things themselves present, but present in a way that includes a great deal of absence. As we saw in chapter 7, one cannot drown in a picture of a lake or in the word "lake," even if it is a lake—a watery, liquid lake—that is present in both instances. Thais's moaning truly made satisfaction present, truly was indicative of the presence of pleasure. Her sin was not that the moaning failed to refer to actual pleasure. Rather, she is being punished because she conjured up pleasure—a rather hollow way of pleasure being experienced—in an attempt to promote the bad rather than the good of someone else, getting her customer to take something as X when she clearly knew it was not X (i.e., getting her customer farther from the truth by means of flattery). Ethics, we also see again and again, is not a matter of ontology. Ethics is a matter of *ethics*. A lie is wrong in the ethical sense and not the metaphysical sense of the word "wrong." It is wrong because it hurts someone.

This sort of determination is not always easy to make. Context is always important. Especially in Thais's case, we would have to ask about the particular context in which she has been "asked the question." A conversation is an ethical enterprise. It assumes that the people involved wish to use language as a way to get at the truth together. When someone is being tortured there can be no conversation, and so we must also accept the fact that the ethics of lying under torture is completely different—as is the ethics of flattery. Patriarchy is a form of torture for women. If we might rightly say, then, that Thais's position within a patriarchy was, from the start, unfair, then we must question whether it really is a legitimate assessment of her ethical worth and her supposed crime to have her moaning in Hell for all eternity. Thais was originally from ancient Athens, a woman valued merely for her beauty. After Alexander the Great finished his schooling with Aristotle and went off to conquer the world (putting *theoria* into *praxis* by killing tens of thousands of people), Thais joined him on the voyage to Persia. She was later "passed along" to Ptolemy, Alexander's top general who became Pharaoh of Egypt after Alexander's death. Her reputation was that she used her beauty and sexuality to procure her own status and secure her own future, and that she took joy in getting men to believe that she loved them. She was passed along from one powerful man to the next until finally she lost her status and had to find common men to pay her for sex. It is men, though, who are writing this story. Men who fear flattery when the flattery is exposed as such, otherwise reveling in it. Thais, in her physical beauty and by means of her command of beautiful sounds and beautiful words, is said to have used her beauty against men. In Dante-the-author's own command of beauty, in his mastery of words that drip like honey from the page even as he describes the most hideous tortures, does he not seduce us into accepting as just what is clearly unjust? Is there not some deconstructive moment to be found here where the text is working against itself precisely at the moment that it claims to be making its strongest moral arguments?

Andy, let us admit, does not write with the obvious beauty or command of the poet.[30] But in his colloquial style, there are traits he shares with Dante. In "Paradiso" XVIII 91, the souls of the Just appear as words in the sky of heaven. Just as God's Word became flesh, so the flesh of the Just melts away and their souls become words. The religious implications are important, but Dante is also saying something about how truth and justice appear visually: we learn something about them not only by speaking of them, but by seeing them present as spelled out.

Andy, too, fixates on the visual element of language. I have no doubt that what Andy's family and friends say is true: we lose a lot by not hearing and seeing Andy perform his work.[31] But seeing the text of *God* is also enlightening. Pages 12 and 13, for example, are visual blocks of letters that barely form the same words over and over. (*See figure 10.10.*) On page 12, the "hmms" are shaped into wave-like patterns that seem to float up on the page just as their speaker (Tinc) floats. On these facing pages, in fact, Tinc and Gina meet—though they have not really met yet in the play. Their words meet, their language meets, "hmms" and "tee hees" meet, and their style is one. It is the text itself that foreshadows the characters' being together.

Throughout most of the play Tinc merely says "hmm" and Gina giggles. The first time Tinc speaks is obviously important. It happens after he has rescued Gina, who is unconscious and in shock, from the King and Queen's buzz saw. Tinc flies Gina to a saloon, sets her down, and yells out, "I've got a hurt child out here!" (81–85). Once Gina is revived, she too speaks: saying, merely, "Hi." But Tinc cannot immediately answer back; Gina must coax him and teach him. When he finally begins speaking (again) he proves his intelligence by saying pseudointellectual, clichéd smart things (this is, we must never forget, Andy's postironic world). Tinc's speech, nevertheless, is *for* Gina, for the sake of Gina. It is meant to save her, as is the speech he later gives to God that convinces Him to stop the flood. If Gina is Eve then we might think that she has tempted Tinc toward knowledge as made manifest in language. But Gina is passive when Tinc first speaks—indeed, she is unconscious. If knowledge is logos, reason, and the control of language, then Tinc has gained it due to Gina, but not due to temptation. Rather, Gina's *innocence*—a desire to protect Gina's innocent life—is Tinc's motivation to move toward language. And once he possesses logos, he does not display it indiscriminately, for his silence has its secret power as well. It is language that gives new meaning to silence—like the zombies that moaned us toward revolution in chapter 6. Tinc's early silence, in fact, was the equivalent to

Mmmmmmmmmmmmmmmmmmmmmmmmmmmmmmmmmmmm
mmmmmmmmmmmmmmmmmmmmmmmmmmmmmmmmmmmm
mmmmmmmmmmmmmmmmmmmmmmmmmmmmmmmmmmmm
mmmmmmmmmmmmmmmmmmmmmmmmmmmmmmmmmmmm
mmmmmmmmmmmmmmmmmmmmmmmmmmmmmmmmmmmm
mmmmmmmmmmmmmmmmmmmmmmmmmmmmmmmmmmmm
mmmmmmmmmmmmmmmmmmmmmmmmmmmmmmmmmmmm
mmmmmmmmmmmmmmmmmmmmmmmmmmhhhhhhhhhhhhhhhhh
hhhhhhhhhhhhhhhhhhhhhhhhhhhhhhhhhhhhhhhhhhhhhhhhhhhh
hhhhhhhhhhhhhhhhhhhhhhhhhhhhhhhhhhhhhhhhhhhhhhhhhhhh
hhhhhhhhhhhhhhhhhhhhhhhhhhhhhhhhhhhhhhhhhhhhhhhhhhhh
hhhhhhhhhhhhhhhhhhhhhhhhhhhhhhhhhhhhhhhhhhhhhhhhhhhh
hhhhhhhhhhhhhhhhhhhhhhhhhhhhhhhhhhhhhhhhhhhhhhhhhhhh
hhhhhhhhhhhhhhhhhhhhhhhhhhhhhhhhhhhhhhhhhhhhhhhhhhhh
hhhhhhhhhhhhhhhhhhhhhhhhhhhhhhhhhhhhhhhhhhhhhhhhhhhh
hhhhhhhhhhhhhhhhhhhhhhhhhhhhhhhhhhhhhhhhhhhhhhhhhhhh
hhhhhhhhhhhhhhhhhhhhhhhhhhhhhhhhhhhhhhhhhhhhhhhhhhhh
hhhhhhhhhhhhhhhhhhhhhhhhhhhhhhhhhhhhhhhhhhhhhhhhhhhh

hmhmhmhmhmhmhmhmhmhmhmhmhmhmhmhmhmhmhmhmhm
hmhmhmhmhmhmhmhmhmhmhmhmhmhmhmhmhmhmhmhmhm
hmhmhmhmhmhmhmhmhmhmhmhmhmhmhmhmhmhmhmhmhm
hmhmhmhmhmhmhmhmhmhmhmhmhmhmhmhmhmhmhmhmhm
hmhmhmhmhmhmhmhmhmhmhmhmhmhmhmhmhmhmhmhmhm
hmhmhmhmhmhmhmhmhmhmhmhmhmhmhmhmhmhmhmhmhm

hmmmmmmmmmmmmmmmmmmmmmhmmmmmmmmmmmmmmmm
mmmhhmmmhmmmhhmmmhhmmmhhmmmhhmmmhhmmmhhmm
mmmmmmmmmmmmmmmmmmmmmmmmmmmmmmmmmmmmmm
mmhhmmmmmmmmmmmmmmmmmmmmmmmmmmmmmmmmmmm
mmmmmmmmmmmmmmmmmmmmmmmmmmmmmmmmmmmmmm

12

Tee-hee-hee--tee-hee-hee--tee-hee-hee--tee-hee-hee--tee-hee-hee
tee-hee hee--tee-hee-hee--tee-hee-hee--tee-hee-hee--tee-hee-hee--tee-hee-hee
tee-hee hee--tee-hee-hee--tee-hee-hee--tee-hee-hee--tee-hee-hee--tee-hee-hee
tee-hee hee--tee-hee-hee--tee-hee-hee--tee-hee-hee--tee-hee-hee--tee-hee-hee
tee-hee hee--tee-hee-hee--tee-hee-hee--tee-hee-hee--tee-hee-hee--tee-hee-hee
tee-hee hee--tee-hee-hee--tee-hee-hee--tee-hee-hee--tee-hee-hee--tee-hee-hee
tee-hee hee--tee-hee-hee--tee-hee-hee--tee-hee-hee--tee-hee-hee--tee-hee-hee
tee-hee hee--tee-hee-hee--tee-hee-hee--tee-hee-hee--tee-hee-hee--tee-hee-hee
tee-hee hee--tee-hee-hee--tee-hee-hee--tee-hee-hee--tee-hee-hee--tee-hee-hee
tee-hee hee--tee-hee-hee--tee-hee-hee--tee-hee-hee--tee-hee-hee--tee-hee-hee
tee-hee hee--tee-hee-hee--tee-hee-hee--tee-hee-hee--tee-hee-hee--tee-hee-hee
tee-hee hee--tee-hee-hee--tee-hee-hee--tee-hee-hee--tee-hee-hee--tee-hee-hee
tee-hee hee--tee-hee-hee--tee-hee-hee--tee-hee-hee--tee-hee-hee--tee-hee-hee
tee-hee hee--tee-hee-hee--tee-hee-hee--tee-hee-hee--tee-hee-hee--tee-hee-hee
tee-hee hee--tee-hee-hee--tee-hee-hee--tee-hee-hee--tee-hee-hee--tee-hee-hee
tee-hee hee--tee-hee-hee--tee-hee-hee--tee-hee-hee--tee-hee-hee--tee-hee-hee
tee-hee hee--tee-hee-hee--tee-hee-hee--tee-hee-hee--tee-hee-hee--tee-hee-hee
tee-hee hee--tee-hee-hee--tee-hee-hee--tee-hee-hee--tee-hee-hee--tee-hee-hee
tee-hee hee--tee-hee-hee--tee-hee-hee--tee-hee-hee--tee-hee-hee--tee-hee-hee
tee-hee hee--tee-hee-hee--tee-hee-hee--tee-hee-hee--tee-hee-hee--tee-hee-hee
tee-hee hee--tee-hee-hee--tee-hee-hee--tee-hee-hee--tee-hee-hee--tee-hee-hee
tee-hee hee--tee-hee-hee--tee-hee-hee--tee-hee-hee--tee-hee-hee--tee-hee-hee
tee-hee hee--tee-hee-hee--tee-hee-hee--tee-hee-hee--tee-hee-hee--tee-hee-hee
tee-hee hee--tee-hee-hee--tee-hee-hee--tee-hee-hee--tee-hee-hee--tee-hee-hee
tee-hee hee--tee-hee-hee--tee-hee-hee--tee-hee-hee--tee-hee-hee--tee-hee-hee

13

FIGURE 10.10. Pages 12–13 of Andy Kaufman's play, *God*.

Gina's giggling, both reactions to false authority, a rejection of the interrogations of language in general (but especially language in the employ of those who are not innocent). Tinc knows that logos cannot be trusted, that language cannot denote, that all utterance is affect. Unlike Dante, he also knows that he cannot easily separate truth from falsehood. And so he is silent.

This is a risky move for Andy to make. His protagonist is committed to silence, but Andy the comedic playwright must not be silent—he must speak, write, and control language to describe a silence that is a response to language's inability to be controlled. The paradoxical nature of all of this is not overlooked by Andy. Dante, too, realizes his dilemma, but seems to take the easy way out by having Dante-in-hell declare his (and Virgil's) superiority over the flatterers and seducers. Dante-in-hell, Virgil, and therefore Dante-the-writer all claim to be able to control language, recognizing a lie for a lie, recognizing that not *all* ornate language is poetry, and not *all* poetry is deceit—especially

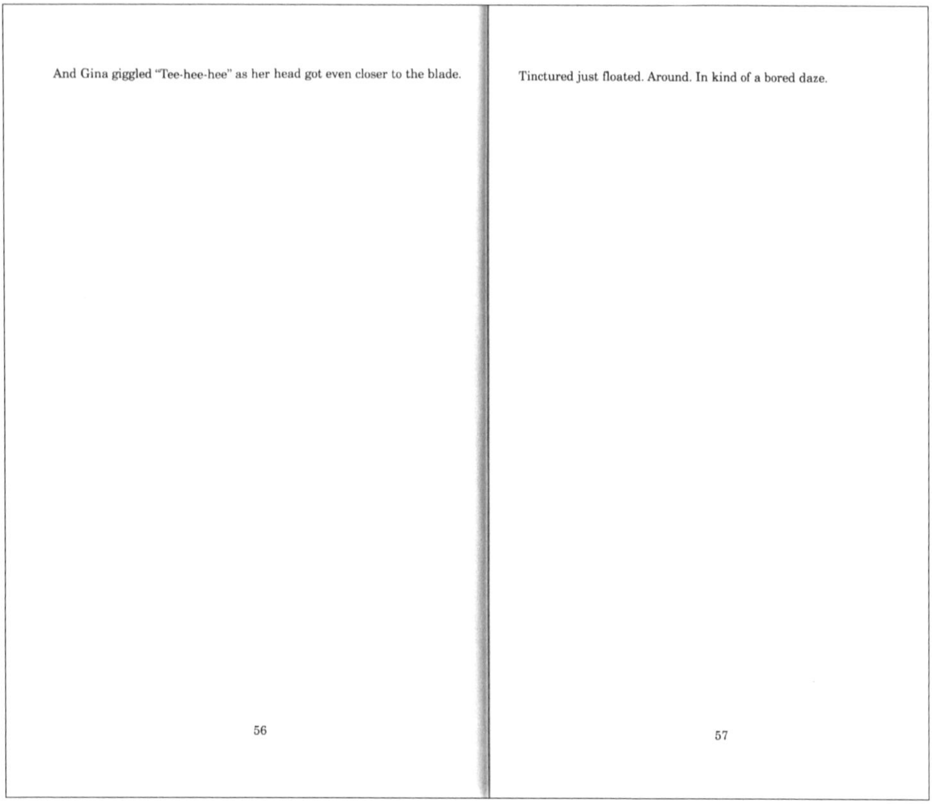
And Gina giggled "Tee-hee-hee" as her head got even closer to the blade.

56

Tinctured just floated. Around. In kind of a bored daze.

57

FIGURE 10.11. Pages 56–57 of Andy Kaufman's play, *God.*

their poetry. But Andy realizes that this is only possible if language in fact does denote, if it can be pinned down, captured, and controlled. It cannot. Language has power behind it; every utterance demands response. Thus Tinc is often silent when interrogated. Language has multiple true meanings. Thus Tinc lets it play itself out in every direction by stepping back and out of the conversation. Language conceals as much as it reveals; and in this Heideggerian manner, language is out of control. Thus Andy lets it be out of control. He does this by letting large sections of the page sit in blank silence, hanging only a sentence or two at the top. (*See figure 10.11.*) He does this by letting words and letters run around free on the page so that they are always one step ahead of our eyes.[32] (*See figure 10.12.*) He does this by letting words spill together when they want to, by letting the aural experience of the words mean more than their dictionary identities (*see figure 10.13*). And he does it by playing with comedy (which is itself so often playing with language). Puns are brought out in the text

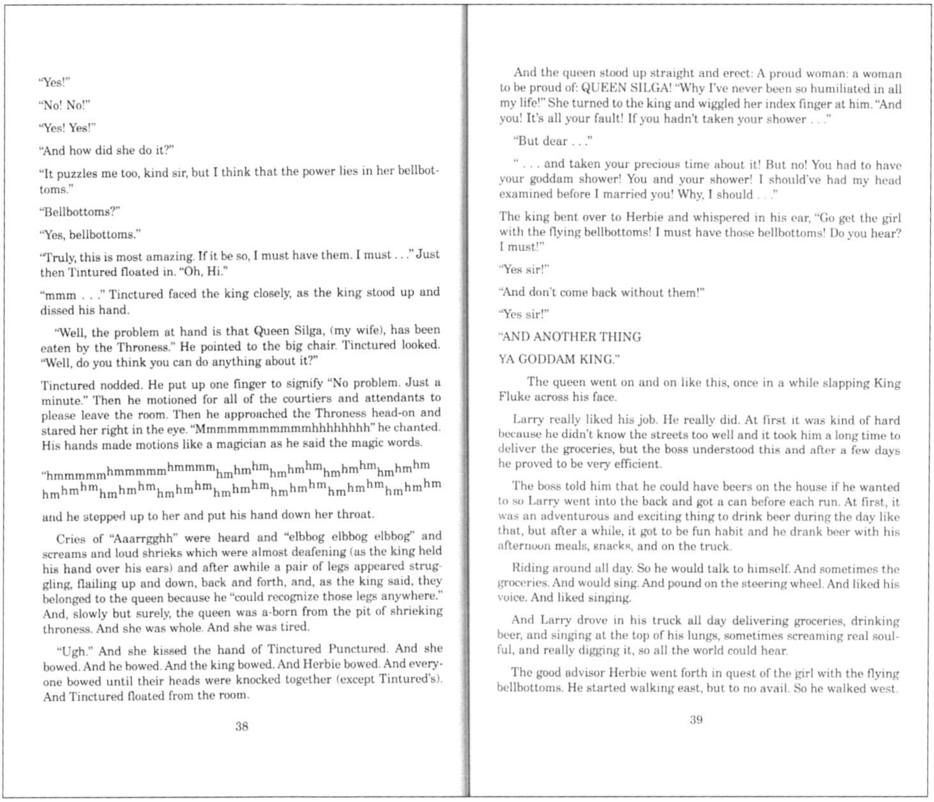

"Yes!"

"No! No!"

"Yes! Yes!"

"And how did she do it?"

"It puzzles me too, kind sir, but I think that the power lies in her bellbottoms."

"Bellbottoms?"

"Yes, bellbottoms."

"Truly, this is most amazing. If it be so, I must have them. I must . . ." Just then Tintured floated in. "Oh, Hi."

"mmm . . ." Tinctured faced the king closely, as the king stood up and dissed his hand.

"Well, the problem at hand is that Queen Silga, (my wife), has been eaten by the Throness." He pointed to the big chair. Tinctured looked. "Well, do you think you can do anything about it?"

Tinctured nodded. He put up one finger to signify "No problem. Just a minute." Then he motioned for all of the courtiers and attendants to please leave the room. Then he approached the Throness head-on and stared her right in the eye. "Mmmmmmmmmmmmhhhhhhhh" he chanted. His hands made motions like a magician as he said the magic words.

"hmmmmmhmmmmmhmmmmhmhmhmhmhmhmhmhmhmhmhmhm
hmhmhmhmhmhmhmhmhmhmhmhmhmhmhmhmhmhmhmhmhm

and he stepped up to her and put his hand down her throat.

Cries of "Aaarrgghh" were heard and "elbbog elbbog elbbog" and screams and loud shrieks which were almost deafening (as the king held his hand over his ears) and after awhile a pair of legs appeared struggling, flailing up and down, back and forth, and, as the king said, they belonged to the queen because he "could recognize those legs anywhere." And, slowly but surely, the queen was a-born from the pit of shrieking throness. And she was whole. And she was tired.

"Ugh." And she kissed the hand of Tinctured Punctured. And she bowed. And he bowed. And the king bowed. And Herbie bowed. And everyone bowed until their heads were knocked together (except Tintured's). And Tinctured floated from the room.

38

And the queen stood up straight and erect: A proud woman: a woman to be proud of: QUEEN SILGA! "Why I've never been so humiliated in all my life!" She turned to the king and wiggled her index finger at him. "And you! It's all your fault! If you hadn't taken your shower . . ."

"But dear . . ."

" . . . and taken your precious time about it! But no! You had to have your goddam shower! You and your shower! I should've had my head examined before I married you! Why, I should . . ."

The king bent over to Herbie and whispered in his ear, "Go get the girl with the flying bellbottoms! I must have those bellbottoms! Do you hear? I must!"

"Yes sir!"

"And don't come back without them!"

"Yes sir!"

"AND ANOTHER THING

YA GODDAM KING."

The queen went on and on like this, once in a while slapping King Fluke across his face.

Larry really liked his job. He really did. At first it was kind of hard because he didn't know the streets too well and it took him a long time to deliver the groceries, but the boss understood this and after a few days he proved to be very efficient.

The boss told him that he could have beers on the house if he wanted to so Larry went into the back and got a can before each run. At first, it was an adventurous and exciting thing to drink beer during the day like that, but after a while, it got to be fun habit and he drank beer with his afternoon meals, snacks, and on the truck.

Riding around all day. So he would talk to himself. And sometimes the groceries. And would sing. And pound on the steering wheel. And liked his voice. And liked singing.

And Larry drove in his truck all day delivering groceries, drinking beer, and singing at the top of his lungs, sometimes screaming real soulful, and really digging it, so all the world could hear.

The good advisor Herbie went forth in quest of the girl with the flying bellbottoms. He started walking east, but to no avail. So he walked west.

39

FIGURE 10.12. Pages 38–39 of Andy Kaufman's play, *God.*

without the fanfare of traditional humor. There is no setup, no waiting for that beat to make space for the laughter afterward. When Andy tells us, for instance, that the children of the royal court were kept in line because the nurse used castor oil, and then follows this immediately with, "Castor Oil was a slob. He spit [sic] at people" (4), we wonder to whom the pronoun is referring until we realize that Castor Oil is a person. But there is no rimshot that follows, no pause to take in our laughter. Andy presents the comedy as if it were normal, ordinary language—*because it is*. Recall that Andy declared, "All my stuff is straight," which is only true because all straight stuff is comedic.[33] *All* language refers to multiple things, every pronoun possibly has a mad referent, every word is a pun, every utterance is a potential punch line. And Andy acknowledges this by refusing to call attention to his humor, by presenting it all as straight. As a result, we know that Andy knows what Dante doesn't appear to know: all words seduce and every speaker is a whore.

"He can't!"

"He can!"

"He can't!"

"He can't, Mommy!"

"mmm . . ."

"Oh yes he can!" She went into the kitchen and came out with some potatoes. "Tinctured. Ya want some potatoes?"

"mmm . . ."

She held the plate in front of him. His hand went out. She took it away. "Say 'I want potatoes'."

"mmm . . ."

" 'I want potatoes'."

"mmm . . ."

"It's amazing!"

"He can't talk!"

"He's DUMB!"

"mmm . . ."

King Fluke took off his pants. He gathered his soap and towel and putemontherack. Wiggled toes. He stepped into the shower.

ssssssssssssssssssssssssssssssssssssssssssssssssssssssssssssssss

"aaaaahh," he smiled.

RELAXTION.

ARREST.

CONCILIATION.

(good)

And he wiggled his toes and stepped out.

Drying off his towel and do the twist.

And King Fluke was putting on his pants.

"A-vé, Ma-rí-hí-ah . . ."

32

And got dressed.

when all of a sudden he heard---

"GOBBLE-GOBBLE-GOBBLE"

and

"AAAAAAAARRRRRRRRRRRRRRGGGGGGGGGGGGGHHHHHH!!!!"

andheranoutjustasfastashislittlelegswouldcarryhim and saw the legs of Queen Silga justakickin as the Throness gobbled her up in one fell swoop.

"GET OUT OF THIS HOUSE AND DON'T COME BACK UNTIL YOU CAN ACT LIKE A GENTLEMEN AND BE PART OF THE FAMILY AND ACT CIVIL WITH YOUR PARENTS!" said Father in a disturbing voice.

"Yeah, ya big stupid dumb," added Susan.

"My boy!" cried Mother. "Where have we failed, Ed?"

Tinctured exited from the house and strolled slowly on a sidewalk.

Felt lonely.

Looked downward. Onto hard pavement.

No one. Else. In the world. Maybe.

And remembering when he had lost his peers after the first epileptic fit.

He kind of stumbled. Downward. Now who was left?

He stopped. Looked up. Smiled. At his Lord. "Well, I guess it's just you and me, old buddie," he thought.

And started to float.

"Get me my advisor!" order the King after witnessing the tragedy. He stood for a moment of silence.

"At your service, sire," saluted the advisor.

"Advisor?"

"Yes, sire."

"Look.---What should I do?"

"Just what has transpired, sire?"

"Why---the Throness has gobbled up the queen in one fell swoop!"

"Oh my!"

33

FIGURE 10.13. Pages 32–33 of Andy Kaufman's play, *God*.

In "Paradiso" XIII–XIV, Dante encounters King Solomon, the paragon of humanity. Solomon's control over language, his mastery of rationality, his triumph of logos are celebrated in *The Divine Comedy* as manifestations of modesty. The King pursued practical wisdom rather than speculative wisdom, seeking only to govern his people well. And for this he has a prime spot in heaven.

King Fluke and Queen Silga are paragons as well, though Andy's vision of humanity is utterly different. The royal couple does not know how to rule. They seem to possess *no* wisdom. The speculative/practical dichotomy—which is essentially a theory/praxis dichotomy—does not exist here. The King and Queen fight over everything (even the sheets on the bed); they are greedy, envious, and without mercy.[34] The Queen is especially envious and covetous of Gina's pants—so much so that she is the one who eventually demands Gina's execution (45).

Dante tells us that envy is a sin of the eyes; and in hell, the envious have their eyes sewn up. As always, in Dante's creatively retributivist conception of justice, the eternal punishment must fit the earthly crime. But for Andy, Hell is in some sense spread upon the Earth. In the end, the Queen cannot watch Gina's execution—she wants to see it, even demands that it be public, but then, in a metaphorical sewing of her eyes, cannot watch. The Queen, we might conclude, is already in Hell, punishing herself as Dante's envious are punished, but how do we know this for sure?

Consider an earlier scene in which the throne swallows the Queen. It might be thought that the Queen is being taken away to Hell but Tinc rescues her. Indeed, the throneness—Andy calls it "throneness" rather than "the throne" not only to play with the way language supposedly indicates gender, but also to indicate that it is the institution of human government itself that is responsible for the descent here—is called a "pit of shrieking" (38). To be sure, the Queen seems to go into the pit, to descend to Hell, and Tinc saves her. But this is not exactly what is happening. When Tinc pulls the Queen out of her throne she is born again. She is being reborn not into the Earth, but into Hell, into the only Hell there is: the one we have made here ourselves. Tinc is not saving her from her descent, but rather delivering her afterward to a twisted world (he delivers her legs-first incidentally—the opposite of a "natural" birth). Following her rescue, any pretense of goodness is gone from the Queen; she is free to lust, covet, and murder. Now Hell has truly come to the world, and Tinc can begin the cleansing. His murder of the Queen (and most of the rest of the royal court) is, in fact, the first step toward creating Heaven.

But like Hell, Heaven will not last. Heaven—the amusement park, that is—is destroyed by God's wrath, leaving Tinc and Gina with neither Heaven nor Hell. In another interesting, comedic twist, though, Andy has Sammy save Tinc and Gina, and here we get an inverse of the Genesis story. Inverse, in that Andy's Genesis story comes at the end of the play; inverse, in that the snake is the hero.

Sammy has dug all the way to China. Along the way, the image of the center becomes important. For Dante, the center of Hell has Satan and the center of Heaven has God. Once Sammy reaches the center of Earth—the center, that is, of Hell—he sees a sign telling him so. Neon letters appear on a yellow ball that burns when Sammy touches it. The letters spell out "CENTER," but Sammy, we are told, thinks they spell out "God." Andy is once again letting language play here, showing us how a literal sign always fails to denote. But more importantly, Sammy has refused to make a distinction between the place Satan should be and the place God should be, between, therefore, Satan and God, Hell and Heaven. Sammy is innocent enough to realize these false dichotomies for what they are—and he keeps on digging.

And then at the moment of God's literal destruction of Heaven (the amusement park) and Hell (Earth), Tinc and Gina turn to Sammy for salvation. Sammy comes out of a hole—like a snake in the ground—invites Tinc and Gina in, and saves them. The imagery is startling: the snake saves Adam and Eve from God.

What kind of a pitiful God is this—a God defeated by the serpent, a God who essentially kills Himself, a God who is jealous of a man named "Larry"? Larry is rising to the level of a deity throughout the play. He is being worshipped; he is accumulating enough money to become nearly all-powerful; he recreates parts of the Earth to his own design; he is an idol. His desire to build Heaven in a drained ocean, to have the Kingdom of Heaven spread upon the Earth, is the dream of creation and salvation, the dream of becoming divine. In Larry's Heaven, God sits on a throne.[35] Like a god, Larry is constructing God according to his image of what a theistic God would be: a Santa Claus, a figurehead, a cash cow, an attraction. It is a deep insight into God's character that He does not destroy Larry immediately or lament the fact that these humans are not trying to be better, more divine, more Godlike. On the contrary, God tries to be more Larry-like. God tries to sing like Larry, move like Larry, and win an audience like Larry's. But He fails.

If this were simply modernist sacrilege, Larry would replace God and the play would end. But this does not happen. God dies. And Larry dies. Nearly everything alive dies—apart from Tinc, Gina, Sammy (and Sammy's Chinese friends)[36]—and no one, nothing, arises to replace God. Or replace Larry. Tinc and Gina simply float off into a new world, presumably to repopulate it and keep innocence alive. It is a world beyond good and evil—beyond God, Larry, the devil, and monarchs. It is neither Paradiso nor Inferno. It is a new Eden, but not a naïve Eden. It is an Eden that has been through Hell (and Heaven) and still offers hope. A truly comedic hope.

At the end of the *Divine Comedy*, Dante realizes the paradox of Christian religious truth captured in "*Vergine Madre, figlia del tuo figlio*" ("Paradiso" XXXIII). Dante ponders—"Virgin Mother, daughter of your son"—and suddenly "realizes in the last canto of his poem the inconceivable truth that a creature may become the creator of its own Creator."[37] And so in Andy's work we realize that we can become the destroyer of our own destroyer; but more importantly we come to terms with the emptiness behind all such concepts, roles, and distinctions. We realize that concepts are ethical and political commitments before they are ontological ones. We realize that living means living a life soaked through with ethics, politics, and aesthetics. Once the mutual destruction has taken place on every level of every old metaphysical binary, we are not left with total annihilation; we are left with the possibility of that comedic hope. It is not a hope that we can transcend or that there is a God who can transcend. It is a hope that is at home in a world in which we realize that nothing transcends, but nothing needs to transcend: true innocence is born of the end of naïve innocence. And so *God* ends innocently, with a self-aware cliché where the heroes ride off into the sunset. And we laugh. Of course, we laugh. Because there they go; and there—but with no need for the grace of an idolatrous theistic God—go we.

And that is the meaning of Andy Kaufman's play *God*. Unless, of course, it doesn't mean anything. Unless, of course, Andy is somewhere laughing, the only one in on the joke, thinking it funny how sheep will read anything.

I miss Andy. Whenever he tried to leave, I always tried to keep him around. I remember in high school dialing that 900 number to vote to keep Andy from being banished from *Saturday Night Live*. We lost. And then, like so many others, when his death was announced I expected to see Andy appear again—expected to see him rise from the grave, daring us to touch his wounds, to believe in him, to laugh with him, be laughed at by him, and wrestle. But here, too, we lost. Andy never rose. How could he? It would have been too much like a punch line.

Physicist David Lindley explains that "[q]uantum mechanics took away absolute determinism, because there's an element of probability in every interaction. . . . [With the] example of food coloring being mixed into a bowl of frosting, there's always some tiny but not quite zero probability that continued random stirring could spontaneously 'unmix' the frosting."[38] There is little solace in the postmodern announcement that identity never coheres and therefore we never really lost "Andy." There is little comfort in the pseudoquantum thinking that it is not impossible that Andy lives, only highly improbable. But there is reason to smile when we know that because we had Andy we learned to see comedy from a new profile in its manifold way of appearing, learned that it can appear differently than we had imagined before, and, in the process, change us all. We smile that phenomenology has not only led us to a new aesthetic, but to the realization that comedy is at the center of the world.

And I'm sure that Andy would have got a kick out of a cake with colored frosting spontaneously changing back to white. Even if the occurrence were highly improbable, he would have smilingly served it to us after a show and asked us to sit with him for hours, waiting for the change, pondering how beautiful, bright, and blinding it can all be.

And we would have eaten it up.

Notes

INTRODUCTION

1. I am. Cézanne rules. That's just an objective fact.

2. The great song, "Tasty Pudding," was released in 1953 by Miles Davis. This is, perhaps, as good a place as any to say that this book will mostly be focusing on *visual* art. This is not in any way because music, for instance, isn't a legitimate art form. On the contrary. I am planning a separate book project on phenomenological aesthetics and music. But it was all too much to handle in one place, so the chapters that follow are, for the most part, all about visual art and do not, other than in passing, deal with literature, poetry, music, tactile art, etc.

CHAPTER 1

1. Franz Kafka, "The Burrow," in *Selected Short Stories of Franz Kafka*, trans. Willa and Edwin Muir (New York: The Modern Library, 1993): 284, 287.

2. Helen Rees Leahy, "Exhibiting Absence in the Museum," in *The Thing About Museums: Objects and Experience, Representation and Contestation,* eds. Sandra Dudley et al. (New York: Routledge, 2012): 256.

3. Jacques Derrida, *Memoirs of the Blind: The Self-Portrait and Other Ruins*, trans. Pascale-Anne Brault and Michael Naas (Chicago: University of Chicago Press, 1993): 39.

4. Ibid.: 36–37.

5. Michelangelo famously said that he saw the forms inside the slabs of marble before he began carving a statue; his job was merely to chip away at the negative spaces and allow what was inside to emerge. This phenomenological description is essentially the same as what I am arguing takes place in drawing and painting. The blank canvas contains the subject. The artist's job is to bring that into presence, to make what is apperceived by the artist capable of being perceived by the world.

6. Both paths are difficult, but let's be honest: there is greater hope for beauty in studying Cézanne than there ever will be in reading Husserl.

7. I am grateful to Matthew Girson for his generosity, for allowing me access to his work, and for letting me rework here some of the text and a few ideas that I first published in a short essay in his 2006 exhibition catalog. Most of the paintings I am discussing here can be seen online (in full color as large files) at matthewgirson.com. The photographs of Girson's work have all been taken by Tom Van Eynde.

8. Girson has even developed a Scotoma font to rival a smudged Times New Roman. In the Scotoma font, each letter seems to be invisibly cut into a 3 x 3 grid with the center square vacant. The result is that we never see the central marks that make up any letter, which makes it difficult, for instance, to tell a "c" from an "e." Reading a text in Scotoma font is consistently frustrating and often headache-inducing. Having to pay so much attention to letters in the font points to how we were previously blind to how easily we normally "read through" and thus never see letters and words, directly experiencing their meaning instead. I will address this phenomenology of reading below.

9. The Migraine Aura Foundation, http://www.migraine-aura.org/EN/Visual_Loss.html. (accessed 30 November 2005).

10. Jacques Lacan, *The Seminar of Jacques Lacan. Book VII—The Ethics of Psychoanalysis 1959–1960*, trans. Dennis Porter, ed. Jacques-Alain Miller (New York: W. W. Norton & Company, 1997): 140.

11. Derrida will make this point again with *différance*—something he acknowledges has a relation to Lacan's anamorphosis.

12. Cf. Carl Gustav Carus, *Nine Letters on Landscape Painting, Written in the Years 1815–1824; with a Letter from Goethe by Way of Introduction*, trans. David Britt. (Los Angeles: Getty Research Institute, 2002): 87. Marx lived from 1818 to 1883, Carus from 1789 to 1869.

13. Cf., e.g., Caspar David Friedrich, *Monaco in Riva al Mare* (1810) and *The Cross on the Baltic* (1815).

14. Heinrich von Kleist quoted in Enzo Carli, *The Landscape in Art.* (New York: William Morrow and Company, 1980): 217. Friedrich lived from 1774 to 1840; Kleist from 1777 to 1811.

15. Cf., e.g., Georgia O'Keeffe, *Sky Above Clouds IV* (1965).

16. Cf., e.g., Margret Dreikausen, *Hurricane* (2000) and *Faltering Storm* (2000).

17. Quoted in Abigail Tucker, "Hard-Wired for Art," *The Smithsonian Magazine* (November 2012): 20.

18. These stories are related in Oliver Sacks, *The Mind's Eye* (New York: Vintage Books, 2011): 214–18.

19. Ibid.: 229.

20. This story is recounted in Ibid.: 206.

21. In Girson's other 2010 series of paintings, *The House Was Quiet and the World Was Calm*, large canvases are filled with thick, dark curtains—curtains hanging on a theater stage, down and closed tightly. One can feel their heft and their closure. Has the audience not yet shown up? Is the show about to start? Is the show long over? Is there no

curtain call or encore because the audience has hated what it's seen? Each silence—and each darkness—is different. All of this taking place in the spaces between the seen and the unseen.

22. My own generation, I believe, will be the last to have experienced libraries. I was in Middle School in the Midwest around 1979–1980 when they officially changed the name of our school library to the I.M.C. (the Instructional Media Center). And just last month, a representative from the DePaul University library came to speak to the philosophy faculty at a department meeting, telling us that "the future is here." It was soon explained that this meant that over the coming months the library would be undergoing a grand renovation, especially on the main floor. The main floor, of course, no longer has a card catalog (R.I.P.). That body was removed and cremated long ago. (For a brilliant eulogy of the card catalog—and a fascinating analysis of how and why so many libraries celebrated their demise in the early 1990s, sometimes by chopping them up or *burning* them—see Nicholson Baker, "Discards," *The New Yorker* [April 4, 1994]: 64–70). Instead, we were told that the main floor of the library would, from now on, no longer have any books whatsoever. None. All of the books on the first floor of the library will soon be moved to upper floors or put in storage to make room for more banks of computers with Internet connections as well as a tech "Genius Bar." One hesitantly wonders where Guillaume Apollinaire is when he is truly needed.

23. David Hume, *An Enquiry Concerning Human Understanding* (Chicago: Open Court Press, 1912): 176.

24. Cf. Alan Gailey and G. B. Adams, "The Bonfire in North Irish Tradition," *Folklore* 88, no. 1 (1977): 3–38.

25. For good measure, Helen Keller's work, too, was tossed in the flaming mix.

26. Goebbels quoted in Judy Bartel, *The Holocaust: A Primary Source History (In Their Own Words)* (New York: Gareth Stevens Publishing, 2005): 17.

27. "Germany: Read No Evil," *Time Magazine* (May 27, 1946).

28. The library and the Internet are fundamentally different institutions and different technology, and thus harbingers of different values. But from a distance one can see that the desire motivating them both is a shared desire—a desire to possess information (rather than come to knowledge)—even as this desire is also caused by these institutions in a self-feeding loop. Furthermore, it is (ironically) necessarily the case that once knowledge is replaced by information, the desire for information is undone by its own coming to be. Once the information is had, it is spent and no longer valued. There is a parallel with the way we have 500 channels of television but nothing to watch, or 15,000 MP3 songs downloaded to the hard drive but nothing we want to hear. One thinks, as well, of Kafka's little burrowing creature. He has managed to accumulate a vast storehouse of food, but now this only serves as a burden since he is forced to worry about invading marauders to the point of paranoia and insanity. As the story unfolds, he considers the possibility of just frantically eating it all in one sitting, thus finally getting "use" out of his food storage (which, of course, would be of no use to him, really, and would, actually, lead to poor health). And even the burrow itself has the same ironic function: a place he has constructed at great cost to feel secure, but now obsesses over by wanting to crouch outside of it (where it is not safe) and watch

its entrance (to think about his safety). Capitalism, modernity, and the Enlightenment are clearly parallel projects.

29. Albert Camus, "Appendix: Hope and the Absurd in the Work of Kafka," *The Myth of Sisyphus: And Other Essays* (New York: Vintage International, 1991): 136.

CHAPTER 2

1. Gorky in a letter to his sister, 9 February 1942, in *Arshile Gorky: The Breakthrough Years*, ed. Michael Auping (New York: Rizzoli, 1995): 82.

2. Ibid., 26 September 1939: 79.

3. Homer, *The Iliad*, Book 1.

4. Gorky in a letter to his sister, 9 February 1942, in *Gorky: The Breakthrough Years*: 82.

5. I take up the theme of Cézanne in depth in the chapter entitled "Cézanne's Out," in *The Things Themselves: Phenomenology and the Return to the Everyday* (Albany: SUNY Press, 2006).

6. Gorky in a letter to his sister, 17 February 1947, in *Gorky: The Breakthrough Years*: 88.

7. Ibid.: 55.

CHAPTER 3

1. I created all of the individual installations discussed here for the 2008 *Site Unseen* installation and conceptual art juried festival hosted annually by the Chicago Cultural Center. Each was a part of my large exhibition entitled *You Are Here* which spanned four halls/theaters in the Center. I am grateful to Dolores Wilber, Julie Laffin, Claire Geall Sutton, Jess Mott, Clark Hayes, and everyone at the Chicago Department of Cultural Affairs for their help in mounting the exhibits and their boundless support. Thanks also to Danielle Meijer, Maryse Meijer, Nileen Clark, Tommy Truong, Brian Proffitt, Mae the Bellydancer, Marci Roesch, Christina Green, Laura Mahler, Pete Parsons, Bill Martin, Matthew Girson, Jesús Pando, Lesandre Ayrey, Jim Brenner, Lynda Garza, Dinah D'Antoni-Niedas, Jorge Niedas, Dilek Huseyinzadegan, Jeremy Bell, Ali Abbas, Felicia Campbell, Salwa Abbas, Aziz Bawany, Adam Bawany, and Robert Maldonado for "performing" the works. Also many thanks to photographers Monika Lozinska-Lee and John W. Sisson, Jr., for their incredible photographs.

2. One thinks also of artists such as Henry Flynt, Yoko Ono, Robert Morris, Dan Graham, Hans Haacke, Douglas Huebler, etc., who were working at this time.

3. For more on Diogenes see my "The Dog on the Fly," in *Plato's Animals: Gadflies, Horses, Swans, and Other Philosophical Beasts*, eds. Jeremy Bell and Michael Naas (Bloomington: Indiana University Press, 2015): 96–111.

4. One is reminded of the bumper sticker that reads: "Think about what it's like to honk if you love conceptual art."

5. In fact, in Rauschenberg's *Erased De Kooning Drawing* (1953) it seems we know

even more about the truth of the being of the work of art when we dig into the story of how Rauschenberg approached De Kooning and demanded that it be a major, excellent drawing that he erased and not just a quick knockoff that De Kooning offered to draw especially for "the stunt."

6. Mikel Dufrenne makes a similar appeal to "expression" in his aesthetics, though what I am suggesting is somewhat different in ways that I hope to make clear. Cf., e.g., Mikel Dufrenne, *Phénoménologie de l' expérience esthétique* (Paris: Presses Universitaires de France, 1953).

7. See my *The Things Themselves: Phenomenology and the Return to the Everyday* (Albany: SUNY Press, 2006): 107.

8. This is true if one sees the painting on a museum wall, in a book, on a computer screen, etc. There is always a diagetic as well as physical space in which the following unfolds.

9. For more on this point, see my *The Things Themselves*: 99.

10. Cf. Gilles Deleuze and Felix Guattari, *What Is Philosophy?*, trans. Graham Burchell and High Tomlinson (New York: Columbia University Press, 1996).

11. This is worked out throughout Derrida's oeuvre, but one might consult, e.g., *Margins of Philosophy*, trans. Alan Bass (Chicago: University of Chicago Press, 1982) and *Of Grammatology*, trans. Gayatri Chakravorty Spivak (Baltimore: Johns Hopkins University Press, 1976).

12. That is, in phenomenological terms, the object of consciousness is still a *spiral* or *vortex* in either case. For the "Chronopod" project, cf. http://www.vanderbilt.edu/chronopod/series.html, accessed December 2012.

CHAPTER 4

1. Cf. Peter Conrad, "Michael Haneke: There's no easy way to say this. . . ," *The Guardian*, 3 November 2012.

2. To be clear, however, it is not *imagination* that is engaged when one is viewing art. Phenomenologically, if this were the case, then the object of consciousness in art would not be the play, movie, painting, etc., per se but instead would be some imaginary, projected object beyond direct perception. Rather, in art there is a fundamental act of perception, but the way perception functions in the sense of the aesthetic needs further explication. This is what is at stake when we say that no one needs to call 911 for Polonius, but one must still feel the horror of the death *as if it were actual*. In the theater, there is a categoriality at work that allows the action to be taken as real and not-real at the same time.

3. See, e.g., Martin Heidegger, *Being and Time*, trans. Edward Robinson and John Macquarrie (Oxford, UK: Blackwell, 1962): 240–41, 246–47.

4. Akira Mizuta Lippit, "The Death of an Animal," *Film Quarterly* 56, no. 1 (Fall 2002): 9–22.

5. Anthony Lane, "Happy Haneke: Michael Haneke and His Movies," *The New Yorker* (5 October 2009): 63.

6. Ibid.

7. Ibid.: 63.

8. Ibid.: 64.

9. Ibid.: 63.

10. Ibid.: 64.

11. Ibid.: 66.

12. I would like to acknowledge and thank Maryse Meijer and Danielle Meijer for their help, consultation, and inspiration in the preparation of this chapter in general; and especially Maryse Meijer for the image of grasping death like the handle of Haneke-filmed-cup.

13. Plato, "Phaedo," *Five Dialogues*, trans. G. M. A. Grube (Indianapolis, IN: Hackett, 1981): 64.

14. We will see this moment of Socrates's debt of the cock come up again in our discussion of Rachel Rosenthal in chapter 8. Interestingly, the implications will be similar, though the scene is closer to comedy than tragedy.

CHAPTER 5

1. The "literal" introduction to Walt Disney's animated film *Beauty and the Beast* (1991) is as follows:

> Once upon a time in far away land, a young prince lived in a shining castle. Although he had everything his heart desired, the prince was spoiled, selfish, and unkind. But then one winter's night an old beggar woman came to the castle and offered him a single rose in return for shelter from the bitter cold. Repulsed by her haggard appearance, the prince sneered at the gift and turned the old woman away. But she warned him not to be deceived by appearances for beauty is found within. And when he dismissed her again, the old woman's ugliness melted away to reveal a beautiful enchantress. The prince tried to apologize but it was too late, for she had seen that there was no love in his heart. And as punishment, she transformed him into a hideous beast and placed a powerful spell on the castle and all who lived there. Ashamed of his monstrous form, the Beast concealed himself inside his castle with a magic mirror as his only window to the outside world. The rose she had offered was truly an enchanted rose which would bloom until his twenty-first year. If he could learn to love another and earn her love in return by the time the last petal fell, then the curse would be broken. If not, he would be doomed to remain a beast for all time. As the years passed he fell into despair and lost all hope. For who could ever learn to love a beast?

2. Interestingly, the curse is gender-specific in the Disney movie (and in the video release of the movie), but gender-neutral in the soundtrack release. On the soundtrack, the narrator's voice-over says that the Beast must love someone and earn "their" love in return, rather than "her" love. While this soundtrack version is grammatically incorrect, it also shifts the meaning of the curse somewhat. The difference here is intriguing: one wonders which came first, the movie voice-track or the soundtrack—and why is there a difference? I will be using the movie version of the curse as the definitive rendering

as this essay is a reading of the *movie*; however, even given the soundtrack change and its lack of a gender-specific pronoun, there is ample evidence, I believe, to support the position for which I am arguing.

3. In the song "Be Our Guest," Lumiere sings that the staff has been enchanted for ten years. We are told that the magic rose will lose its final petal on the prince's twenty-first birthday. Since that day has now come, we can thus assume that the curse took place when the prince was eleven years old (21 − 10 = 11).

4. Which is not to say that choice is the most important thing here. Lady Gaga and LGBT groups have made a lot out of the "born this way" claim and hashtag, arguing that mainstream cultural acceptance of those who identify as other than "straight" are not to blame because they have no choice about being the way that they are. But it seems to me that this misses the point of ethics completely and is, if anything, just another version of the naturalistic fallacy—the same sort of fallacy that those who have oppressed gay people trotted out so readily in the past in which some appeal to what is "natural" ends the moral debate. I have argued elsewhere that there is nothing natural at all—we can't even claim we are born into a set *species,* let alone a gender, sex, or sexual orientation. The real point here, though, is that the ethical-political question should not be tied in any way to matters of biology, science, metaphysics, or ontology. If a man chooses to love a man, for instance, this should be no different, morally, than a man who feels a "natural drive" to love a man.

5. It is important to note at this point that such stereotypes will become important to our analysis of the film, but the film itself employs the stereotypes with a subtle and, indeed, masterful touch. This is no cliché-ridden work of art. If it suggests that gay men like interior design, floristry, and show tunes, it does so with full awareness that the stereotypes are at once both instantly recognizably artistic tropes meant to indicate an other-than-straight orientation and at the same time the sort of stereotypical generalizations that are repressive and are meant to be shaken up and done away with by this critique. Though Disney's *Beauty and the Beast* is a tragedy, it is revolutionary and empowering if read correctly.

6. "True nature" not making an appeal to something true by nature or true because of nature, but simply meaning that this is what he most truly is/wants to be, the way in which he most feels at home in his own identity.

7. This long quote is a set of utterances sung by various villagers in the opening song "Belle."

8. We know that this is so because her favorite book is about a girl becoming a princess. This book is, in the end, *Beauty and the Beast.* We will take up this point in more detail below.

9. Belle is showing her true nature here. The shop is clearly a book *store*, not a library, yet Belle has been borrowing books from the doting, smitten, older owner rather than buying them. And now the poor man gives Belle her favorite book for free, though she clearly has no sexual interest in the store owner. (Neither, of course, does she care for any of the men staring through the store window at her—an important point in the movie because it makes it clear that Belle has many potential male suitors [not just Gaston] and no interest in *any* of them.) The gift of a book by a male suitor in which Belle

has no real interest will become a theme, echoed when the Beast gives Belle the castle library and its contents. In both cases the books are offered as something of a prelude; in both cases the man says (in nearly identical words) "if you like it so much, it's yours"; and in both cases, Belle has no real interest in the suitor but merely wants something from him and isn't afraid to use her charms to get it.

10. For an example of such a thoughtful yet, I would argue, misdirected interpretation of Gaston, see Susan Jeffords, "The Curse of Masculinity: Disney's *Beauty and the Beast*," in *From Mouse to Mermaid: The Politics of Film, Gender, and Culture*, eds. Elizabeth Bell, Lynda Haas, and Laura Sells (Bloomington: Indiana University Press, 1995): 169–70.

11. Christopher Finch, *The Art of Walt Disney* (New York: Harry N. Abrams, 1995): 299.

12. But of course, given the choice, Belle will reject Gaston and go along with the Beast simply because the latter is rich and royal. Gaston is thus doomed to lose the battle and the comparison.

13. In the song "Gaston," Lefou sings: "You can ask any Tom, Dick, or Stanley. And they'll tell you whose team they prefer to be on."

14. As with the human/mannequin confusion we will talk about in chapter 7, taking rice to be snow shows us that the horizons of the two things "overlap," and we thus learn something about the being of rice and the being of snow. Importantly for the aesthetic analysis in play here, we see the ways in which the *emotional* aspect of the experiences come into conflict and speak to each other: the joy of seeing rice being thrown becomes the sadness/coldness of the snow falling, and we thus experience the sadness of the marriage that cannot be transferred back on our what is going on inside the tavern.

15. For many, purposely drowning a child is one thing, watching a child drown in turbulent waters while doing nothing to save him is another, and refusing to pay taxes to increase the number of lifeguards on duty and thereby probably increasing the number of adolescent drownings in a year is still another. Or is it? To provide a detailed answer would take us too far off topic, but I have touched on such matters elsewhere, arguing that active/passive debates in ethics are always misguided and need to be founded by a more communitarian understanding of moral theory in general (Cf., e.g., my *Founding Community: A Phenomenological-Ethical Inquiry.* Phaenomenologica 143 (Dordrecht, the Netherlands: Kluwer, 1998), esp. ch. 4).

16. It would get us too much off track here, but I have discussed the need to found ethics on a phenomenological categoriality elsewhere. See, e.g., *Founding Community.* Though it is only touched on briefly there as well, it is also clear that phenomenological communitarianism requires a commitment to political anarchy, thus making moot the question of whether we blame the closet-makers or the closet-dwellers. It's a problem of having bad institutions that give rise to false dilemmas—and closets in general.

17. This cross-dressing fear mirrors an earlier scene in which we first meet Maurice. An explosion in Maurice's cellar causes a wooden barrel to lodge itself around the old man's waist. When he shakes it off, the barrel splits and ends up looking like a skirt. Maurice quickly, and perhaps a bit too frantically, wiggles his way out of it.

CHAPTER 6

1. <http://www.youtube.com/watch?v=ZJ4shANmIN8>.

2. See, e.g., "TV reporter speaks about speech problem at Grammys," *Shreveport Times* (18 February 2011). http://www.shreveporttimes.com/article/20110219/ENT/110218010/1005/TV-reporter-speaks-about-speech-problem-Grammys.

3. *The Walking Dead*, "Days Gone Bye" (Frank Darabont, dir., 31 October 2010).

4. *Dawn of the Dead* (George A. Romero, dir., 1978).

5. Joan Ullman, "I Carried It Too Far, That's for Sure," *Psychology Today* (May 1, 1992).

6. C. S. Lewis, *A Grief Observed* (San Francisco: HarperSanFrancisco, 1961): 18, 20–22, 65.

7. Or a perfect Las Vegas, if that's more your style.

8. *Dawn of the Dead* (George A. Romero, dir., 1978).

9. The point is made in a much more subtle and successful way by *The Walking Dead*. In the second episode of the television series, "Guts," Glen and Rick decide to attempt to walk to freedom through the zombie hoard by becoming one of them. To accomplish this, they systematically take apart a zombie they have killed and begin using its body. They smear the entrails on their own clothes. They chop pieces of the zombie's flesh and attach those pieces to their own bodies. Covered in the smell of rotting zombie bodies, they thus hope to pass as zombies (a plan that works well until it begins to rain and the blood and gore are washed away). Before they chop up the zombie, they hesitate, unsure as to whether or not it is ethical. Rick takes out the zombie's wallet to announce the name of the man he used to be and pay him respect. Glen, looking at the wallet, announces: "He was an organ donor." (*The Walking Dead*, ep. 2 "Guts," written by Frank Darabont; dir. Michelle MacLaren; original airdate: 7 November 2010).

10. "They are us. They are the extension of us. They are the same animal, simply functioning less perfectly." *Day of the Dead* (George A. Romero, dir., 1985).

11. *Resident Evil: Afterlife* (Paul W. S. Anderson, dir., 2010).

12. *The Horde* (Yannick Dahan and Benjamin Rocher, dir., 2010).

13. Dr. Logan, *Day of the Dead* (George A. Romero, dir., 1985).

14. "Hollywood A. D.," *The X-Files*, original airdate: 30 April 2000, written and directed by David Duchovny.

15. Dr. Millard Rausch, *Dawn of the Dead* (George A. Romero, dir., 1978).

16. Rick Grimes, in regards to the racial strife between Dixon and T-Dog; "Guts," *The Walking Dead*.

17. René Descartes, *Discourse on the Method*, trans. John Veitch (New York: Cosimo Classics, 2008 [1637]: 117.

18. Cf. Maurice Merleau-Ponty, *Phenomenology of Perception,* trans. by Colin Smith (New York: Humanities Press, 1962).

19. Cf., e.g., my "Ichabodies, or The Tail of the Headless Clones," *Conscious Choice* 13, no. 10 (October 2000): 32.

20. This is a point to which science is slowly drawing us as well. As Dick Teresi reports in "The Evolution of Death," (Salon.com, March 18, 2012):

Candace Pert, the discoverer of the opiate receptor in the brain, says that there has been a new paradigm in neuroscience since about 1995. More than three hundred common molecules, chemicals, are found in the brain, the immune system, and bone marrow. In other words, brain chemicals partly responsible for consciousness are being found all over the body. When Pert says, "The body-mind is one," she's speaking not as a Buddhist but as a biochemist, though Buddhism, she says, may have anticipated this discovery. "Consciousness," she adds, "is a property of the entire body."

21. This is something that *Pinocchio* (Norman Ferguson et al., dirs., 1940) and the mummy films starring Brendan Frasier (*The Mummy* [Stephen Sommers, dir., 1999], *The Mummy Returns* [Stephen Sommers, dir. 2001], *The Mummy: Tomb of the Dragon Emperor* [Rob Cohen, dir., 2008]) do not understand. The protagonists seek flesh, they desire the body, but they are already conscious. There is a Cartesian dualism at work that simply is untenable.

22. Cf., Theodor W. Adorno and Max Horkheimer, *Dialectic of Enlightenment,* trans. John Cumming (New York: Continuum, 1993 [1944]): 6.

23. Cf. "Monkey See" in *The Things Themselves: Phenomenology and the Return to the Everyday* (Albany: SUNY Press, 2006) in which I argue that mimicry is the basis of all logos, and since mimicry is an artistic choice, aesthetics is at the heart of all language.

CHAPTER 7

1. Which is not at all to say that food in general is not within the realm of the aesthetic. Things must smell good, have interesting textures, and look beautiful. There is a reason that we are said to "eat with the eyes." But the point here is that long before a chef might think of plating, there is something special—if not in kind then at least in degree—about meat and fake-meat.

CHAPTER 8

1. *Rachel Rosenthal: Art + Performance,* ed. Moira Roth (Baltimore, MD: Johns Hopkins University Press, 1997): 196.

2. "Rachel's Brain," performance transcript in *Rachel's Brain and Other Storms,* ed. Una Chaudhuri (New York: Continuum, 2001): 121.

3. Ibid.: 130.

4. Franz Kafka, *The Collected Aphorisms,* trans. Malcolm Pasley (London: Penguin Books, 1994): 7.

5. Rachel Rosenthal, *Tatti Wattles: A Love Story* (Santa Monica, CA: Smart Art Press, 1996): 50.

6. Nicholas Ridout, "Animal Labour in the Theatrical Economy," *Theatre Research International* 29, 1 (2004): 58.

7. Ibid.: 61.

8. Cf. *Rachel Rosenthal: Art + Performance*: 199.

9. Rachel Rosenthal, "The Others," performance transcript, *Performance Research* 5, no. 2 (2000): 106.

10. Ibid.

11. These quotes come from Steve Baker, *The Postmodern Animal* (London: Reaktion Books, 2000): 80.

12. Ibid.: 82.

13. Michael Kirby, "On Acting and Not-Acting," *The Drama Review* 16, no. 1 (1972): 12–13.

14. Nicholas Ridout, "Animal Labour in the Theatrical Economy," *Theatre Research International* 29, no. 1 (2004): 58–59.

15. Rosenthal, "The Others" performance transcript: 105.

16. The same question will come up again in the final chapter on Andy Kaufman, especially as we think about Andy's Carnegie Hall show and his PBS Soundstage episode. The manipulation of time, narrative flow, progress, and beginnings and endings is part of the postmodern artist's challenge to modernity.

17. In David Williams, "The Right Horse, The Animal Eye—Bartabas and the Théâtre Zingaro," *Performance Research* 5, no. 2 (2000): 35.

18. Michael Dobson, "Renaissance Dogs: The Transformation of the Onstage Canine, 1550–1850," *Performance Research* 5, no. 2 (2000): 118–19.

19. Rachel Rosenthal, "filename: FUTURFAX," performance transcript in *Rachel's Brain and Other Storms,* ed. Una Chaudhuri (New York: Continuum, 2001): 206.

20. Steve Baker, "Sloughing the Human," *Performance Research* 5, no. 2 (2000): 73.

21. Williams, "The Right Horse": 36, 38.

22. Alphonso Lingis, "Quadrille," *Performance Research* 5, no. 2 (2000): 1–10.

23. *Rachel Rosenthal: Art + Performance*: 195.

24. Lingis, "Quadrille": 1–10.

25. Rosenthal, "Pangaean Dreams," performance transcript in *Rachel's Brain*: 183.

26. Lingis, "Quadrille," *Performance Research* 5, no. 2 (2000): 1–10.

27. Ibid.

28. Ibid.

29. *Rachel Rosenthal: Art + Performance*: 198.

30. Lingis, "Quadrille": 1–10.

31. Franz Kafka, "The Burrow," in *Selected Short Stories of Franz Kafka,* trans. Willa and Edwin Muir (New York: The Modern Library, 1993): 271, 291, 294.

32. Rosenthal, "filename: FUTURFAX," performance transcript in *Rachel's Brain*: 206.

33. This quote and the ones that follow are all from the VHS recording of Rachel Rosenthal's "Zato" (1990).

34. Rosenthal, "Rachel's Brain": 129.

35. Rosenthal, "Rachel's Brain": 129–30.

36. Rosenthal, "Rachel's Brain": 130.

37. Rosenthal, *Tatti Wattles*: 28.

38. Plato, *Phaedrus* 275 d–e, in *Plato: The Complete Works*, ed. John M. Cooper, trans. Alexander Nehamas and Paul Woodruff (New York: Hackett, 1997): 552.

39. Rosenthal, *Tatti Wattles*: 40–41.

CHAPTER 9

1. Paul A. Cantor, "The Simpsons: Atomistic Politics and the Nuclear Family," *Political Theory* 27, no. 6 (1999): 744.

2. And Homer is sworn in as Duffman by taking an oath parallel to one that members of the Night's Watch take on *Game of Thrones*: "Night gathers and now my Duff-Watch begins. It shall not end until my death, or my twelve-week option is not picked up. I shall take no wife, hold no lands and father no children, except for the wife and house and kids I'm already stuck with. I shall wear no other beers' crowns. I am the six-pack hidden in daddy's secret cabinet, I put the fest in Oktoberfest, and sell for eight bucks at ballparks. Though I have nothing to offer but my suds, head, and beers, and promotional-cosies, for this night and all nights to come."

3. There were attempts at this, especially in terms of the storyline involving Jerry and George trying to sell a sitcom to NBC based on their lives—on "nothing"—or when Kramer started the Peterman Reality Tour in response to the "real-life" Kramer starting a "real" reality tour based on *Seinfeld* in NYC. But the show as a whole was decidedly modernist with postmodern moments; and even these moments were more parodies of real life than postmodern acknowledgments of the lack of distinction between real life and art.

4. One thinks of the postmodern Sprite soda commercials that order us to obey our thirst and not commercials—to follow our own style and not buy into what commercials tell us to do and be. If the campaign were not so obviously aware of its own complicity and the irony of its consumer command, it would undoubtedly not be as successful.

5. My friend, Steve Ingeman, and I used to joke in graduate school that *ST:TNG* was all about the further adventures of the phallologocentricenterprise, boldly going to spread the Enlightenment across the galaxy. Data, for instance, wanted to be human and the show continually told us that technology was merely a tool and not our salvation, but in countless episodes it was Data who saved the day precisely by *not* being human. And this is not even to begin to scratch the surface of the classical liberal social-political theory that drives nearly every incarnation of *Star Trek*—from the can't-we-all-just-get-along-as-individuals-who-tolerate-each-other racial politics of the original 1960s series to the-Borg-are-trying-to-force-us-into-communitarianism-and-intersubjective-identities mass hysteria of everything after *ST:TNG*. The philosophy of language being discussed in this chapter is one small example of such problems. For more on the early-2000s TV version of *Star Trek*, see my "Liberalism, the Same Old

Frontier" (review of UPN's *Enterprise*), in PopMatters (10 June 2002): http://www.popmatters.com/tv/reviews/e/enterprise2.shtml.

6. An essay, if not a book, needs to be devoted to animals and language in *Star Trek*. The fact that the universal translators work with aliens that are humanoid, but not with alien animals or even Earth animals—the fact that the technology continues the separation of the animal and the nonhuman Other, the fact that in *Star Trek IV* even an alien probe communicates with humpback whales before we galaxy-hopping humans think to do so—needs a good postmodern deconstructing. But this is another project, of course.

7. Cf., e.g., both Paul A. Cantor, "The Simpsons: Atomistic Politics and the Nuclear Family," *Political Theory* 27, no. 6 (1999): 744; and Tom Carson, "The Gospel According to Homer," *Esquire* 132, no. 1 (1999): 32–35.

8. Sartre's point is much deeper and more insightful than this, but the example, I think, is a valid one. See Jean-Paul Sartre, "For Whom Does One Write?" in *"What Is Literature?" and Other Essays* (Cambridge, MA: Harvard University Press, 1988): 70–71.

9. See chapter 10 for a more thorough analysis of this notion of simulacra and Beaudrillard's map/territory question.

10. Jean Baudrillard, *Simulations*, trans. Paul Foss, Paul Patton, and Philip Beitchman (New York: Semiotext(e), 1983): 4.

11. There is yet another nice riff on this same theme to end the episode:

> Homer: So, I realized that being with my family is more important than being cool.
>
> Bart: Dad, what you just said was powerfully uncool.
>
> Homer: You know what the song says: "It's hip to be square."
>
> Lisa: That song is so lame.
>
> Homer: So lame that it's . . . cool?
>
> Bart/Lisa: No.
>
> Marge: Am I cool, kids?
>
> Bart/Lisa: No.
>
> Marge: Good. I'm glad. And that's what makes me cool, not caring, right?
>
> Bart/Lisa: No.
>
> Marge: Well, how the hell do you be cool? I feel like we've tried everything here.
>
> Homer: Wait, Marge. Maybe if you're truly cool you don't need to be told you're cool.
>
> Bart: Well, sure you do.
>
> Lisa: How else would you know?

12. Umberto Eco, Postscript to *The Name of the Rose*, trans. William Weaver (New York: Harcourt Brace Jovanovich, 1994): 67–68.

13. Of course you do not need to be told, but the quotational discourse references are—in order—to *Monty Python and the Holy Grail*, *The Terminator*, Mr. T, and *Airplane!*.

14. In the infomercial, the creator of "Itchy and Scratchy" goes on to say that the animation cels are "absolutely, positively, 100% guaranteed to increase in value," and an announcer quickly adds: "Not a guarantee." At once we have the cynicism of our consumer society and a further indication that words do not refer but rather change their meaning at every moment.

15. This episode offers a wealth of self-aware quotational discourse of the type that will be discussed below. Grandpa Simpson mimics—quotes—both Charlie Chaplin and Jimmy Durante at different points in the narrative, only to have lawyers appear from nowhere, threatening to sue him if he does not cease and desist from further activities of a quotational nature. The "quotation" of Jimmy Durante was meant to indicate Grandpa Simpson's loneliness when Marge's mother spurns him ("Goodnight Mrs. Bouvier, wherever you are"); and his quotation of Chaplin is, perhaps, the more complex as it is actually a triple quotation, referencing the film "Benny and Joon" in which Johnny Depp mimics Chaplin to impress a girl (the same reason Grandpa Simpson is engaging in the activity!). Later, of course, Grandpa Simpson stops Marge's mother's wedding in a quotation of *The Graduate*, pounding on the glass of the church window and screaming "Mrs. Bouvier!" As the closing credits role, a duo fittingly sings over the Simon and Garfunkel song "The Sound of Silence": "Hello Grandpa my old friend. / Your busy day is at an end. / Your exploits have been sad and boring. / They tell a tale that's worth ignoring. . . ."

CHAPTER 10

1. Here, the word "chair" does not have meaning because it indicates—in some metaphysical sense reaches out and touches—some chair in the world. "Chair" has meaning because "legs" and "sit" have meaning; and "sit" has meaning (in part) because "chair" has meaning. This is, of course, all part of the phenomenology of language we have been exploring in nearly every chapter.

2. See Bill Zehme, *Lost in the Funhouse: The Life and Mind of Andy Kaufman* (New York: Delacorte, 1999): 197.

3. Zehme, *Lost in the Funhouse*, 145–46.

4. Ted Cohen, *Jokes: Philosophical Thoughts on Joking Matters* (Chicago: University of Chicago Press, 1999): 29–31.

5. Andy Kaufman, "The Kaufman Chronicles": http://andykaufman.jvlnet.com/kaufchro.htm.

6. Zehme, quoting Andy, *Lost in the Funhouse*, 194.

7. Andy, talking to Steve Martin, as quoted by Zehme, *Lost in the Funhouse*, 199.

8. Ibid.

9. Cf. Christopher Fry, "Comedy," *Vogue Magazine* (January 1951).

10. Susanne K. Langer, "The Great Dramatic Forms: The Comic Rhythm," in *Comedy: Plays, Theory, and Criticism*, ed. Marvin Felhelm (New York: Harcourt, Brace, and World, 1962): 245.

11. *The Simpsons*, which we have seen in the previous chapter is another great icon in postmodern comedy, drives this point home well. In one episode, for instance, the children are shipwrecked on a deserted island and the plot becomes a parody of *Lord of*

the Flies. At the very end, Bart and Lisa and the others are still not rescued. The narrator's voice comes on over the final credits, saying "And so the children survived until they were rescued by . . . oh . . . let's say, Moe." The resolution, the destination, is not really important—it can be thoughtlessly tacked on without any great loss to the comedy.

12. Maurice Charney, *Comedy High and Low: An Introduction to the Experience of Comedy* (New York: Oxford University Press, 1978): 79.

13. Cf. Henri Bergson, *Laughter: An Essay on the Meaning of the Comic*, trans. Cloudesley Bereton & Fred Rothwell (Københaun, Denmark, & Los Angeles: Green Integer, 1999): 19.

14. The experience can also give rise to fear or frustration or pity, etc., yet the experience ends up being one of comedy. More on this below.

15. Steve Martin, quoted in Zehme, *Lost in the Funhouse*": 198.

16. Sigmund Freud, *Jokes and Their Relation to the Unconscious*, trans. James Strachey (New York: W. W. Norton & Co., 1960): 99, 100, 97.

17. Freud, *Jokes and Their Relation to the Unconscious*, 103.

18. Andy explained this to Steve Martin (who was guest-hosting *The Tonight Show*). See Zehme, *Lost in the Funhouse*: 199.

19. The Steve Allen quote is from Dan Jewel and Lorenzo Benet, "Nervous Laughter," in *People Weekly* 52, no. 22 (6 December 1999): 149–52; the Carl Reiner quote is from Zehme, *Lost in the Funhouse*: 296.

20. Andy writing in *Rolling Stone*, quoted by Zehme, *Lost in the Funhouse* 297.

21. Jean Baudrillard, *Simulations*, trans. Paul Foss, Paul Patton, Philip Beitchman (New York: Semiotext(e), 1983): 1–4.

22. Andy Kaufman, "The Kaufman Chronicles": http://andykaufman.jvlnet.com/kaufchro.htm.

23. Langer, "The Great Dramatic Forms": 251–52.

24. Walter Kerr, *Tragedy and Comedy* (New York: DeCapo Paperbacks, 1985): 145.

25. Andy Kaufman, *God . . . and Other Plays* (Wayne, NJ: Zilch Publishing, 2000). Unless otherwise noted, the page numbers that follow in the main text refer to this work.

26. Charney, *Comedy High and Low: An Introduction to the Experience of Comedy*, 90.

27. Robin Kirkpatrick, *Dante: The Divine Comedy* (Cambridge, UK: Cambridge University Press, 2004): 101.

28. See, e.g., Tim Parks, "Hell and Back: A New Translation of Dante's Inferno," *The New Yorker* (January 15, 2001): 85.

29. Cf. Charles Singleton, *Dante's* Comedia: *Elements of Structure* (Baltimore, MD: The Johns Hopkins University Press, 1977): 36.

30. There are many mistakes in the text, and we cannot be sure that he intended them—he has not yet won our trust to misuse the language meaningfully.

31. See the preface and newspaper insert in *God . . . and Other Plays* and Andy's father's comments in the *Rolling Stone* article.

32. Try catching the m's and h's on page 12—they elude the eye's grasp, running forward, just out of reach, madly and freely and happily.

33. Andy Kaufman, "The Kaufman Chronicles": http://andykaufman.jvlnet.com/kaufchro.htm.

34. The latter traits are more divine than human for Andy, but the King and Queen—like all humans—are made in the image of their God.

35. Note that there are already indications of God's demise here, as earlier the throne image has been established as the mouth of Hell when the Queen is swallowed and reborn.

36. The Chinese friends play two roles in the play. First, they allow Andy to play further with language (see all of his attempts to capture the textures of a foreign language in sound [esp. pp. 112–13]). And second, they allow him to deal comedically with the Other. The Chinese men represent otherness for Andy—they are on the other side of the world, speaking another language, and engaging in other practices. At first, such otherness responds with aggression: the men try to kill Sammy. But all it takes is time for everyone to realize that innocence comes in many forms. Sparing the lives of the two Chinese men at the end tells us that there will be diversity in the new world, the new Eden.

37. Kirkpatrick, *Dante's Divine Comedy*, 106.

38. David Lindley, *Where Does the Weirdness Go? Why Quantum Mechanics Is Strange, But Not as Strange as You Think* (New York: Basic Books, 1996): 221, 212.

Index